HUMAN ORIGINS

Methodology and History in Anthropology

Series Editors:
David Parkin, Fellow of All Souls College, University of Oxford
David Gellner, Fellow of All Souls College, University of Oxford

HUMAN ORIGINS

Contributions from Social Anthropology

Edited by
Camilla Power, Morna Finnegan and Hilary Callan

berghahn
NEW YORK • OXFORD
www.berghahnbooks.com

First published in 2017 by

Berghahn Books

www.berghahnbooks.com

© 2017 Camilla Power, Morna Finnegan and Hilary Callan

Library of Congress Cataloging-in-Publication Data

A C.I.P. cataloging record is available from the Library of Congress

British Library Cataloguing in Publication Data

A catalogue record for this book is available from the British Library

Printed on acid-free paper

ISBN 978-1-78533-378-1 (hardback)
ISBN 978-1-78533-426-9 (paperback)
ISBN 978-1-78533-379-8 (ebook)

CONTENTS

ILLUSTRATIONS

Figures

Tables

INTRODUCTION

Camilla Power, Morna Finnegan and Hilary Callan

A rift runs through anthropology. Year on year we explain to our students that anthropology is the overarching study of what it means to be human; and yet our discipline is fragmented. We can, we explain, study humans as biological beings, understanding the anatomical, physiological and life-history differences between ourselves and the other great apes, or the Neanderthals. Or we can study humans within their own communities as cultural beings, analysing the rituals they perform and the stories they tell. What defines us as *Homo sapiens* compared with other hominins appears a tractable scientific area of enquiry. Interpretations of cultural voices, values and meanings feel by contrast negotiable and contested, throwing into question the prospect of scientific objectivity. On each side of this divide data takes different forms and is collected quite differently; theory and hypothesis are applied with hypothetico-deductive method, inductively or not at all; and epistemologies are radically opposed.

As detailed in *Metaphors We Live By* (Lakoff and Johnson 1980), the human body forms a basis of universal shared experiences, structures of cognition and mutual understandings. Yet the body and its reproduction generate a multiplicity of folk models, with highly variable ideas about sex, kinship and shared substance each able to operate with perfect, or at least practical logic in its own cultural setting. Social and cultural anthropologists glory in the contrariness of these folk models to the scientifically accumulated 'facts' of how human bodies work and reproduce. Fundamentally it is 'fictions' which are the business of social anthropologists – fictions about kinship, about gods and spirits, in our rules and games, fictions on our tongues as we speak and in taxonomies as we carve up the world. Given that we are fiction-sharing and game-playing apes, do shared fictions and games matter for the understanding of our origins?

Darwinism, the coherent and unifying theory that powers all investigation of living beings, has itself been named a fiction, the origins myth that fitted the newly emergent world of high Victorian capitalism. As we enter 'a period in which evolutionary theory is being applied to every conceivable domain of enquiry' (Aunger 2000: 1), including economics, moral philosophy, psychology, linguistics, law, medicine and beyond, social anthropology could be respected for holding out, swimming against this powerful tide, maintaining its critical faculties in solidarity with the humanities. Or it could be viewed as insular and idealist, obfuscating and jealously guarding its domain of ideology from unwelcome intrusion (cf Bloch 2000: 202). In *Engaging Anthropology*, Thomas Eriksen (2006: 23) certainly sees social anthropology as having withdrawn from general intellectual discourse, pondering why contemporary anthropologists are so reluctant to present their work to large audiences, lay and academic.

It would seem that social anthropology has lost its voice in debates about human origins. The broad comparative framework inherited from Morgan and Tylor in the nineteenth century has given way to perspectives emphasizing reflexivity and cultural particularism. Yet the opportunities for intervention have never been greater. Evolutionary and physical anthropology, archaeology and palaeogenetics have made major advances in an emerging picture of human origins. A range of new evidence is revealing the place of the human species in the natural world and the material record of our past. Given these developments, it must be time to rethink social anthropology's absenteeism.

This book seeks to take up that challenge by bringing together a group of anthropologists to examine key areas of human origins research that could and should be informed by social anthropology. As we show, the social anthropology that can be brought into play for this purpose naturally includes writings specifically addressed to human origins, but it is not confined to these. As will be seen, questions about origins bring key figures from social anthropology's own history into new focus, while ethnography, originally conducted for entirely different purposes, gains new significance in this context. The book's chapters cover areas including the sexual division of labour and gender egalitarianism (Finnegan); sexual insult and female militancy as a mode of resistance (Shirley Ardener); metaphor as the basic principle of the symbolic (Smith and Hoefler; Knight and Lewis); shared structures of cosmology, ritual and myth (Power, Skaanes, Watts); body techniques in healing and cognition (Low); the evolution of kinship (Joseph); and ethnobiological classification (Ellen). Spanning several decades of debates around disciplinary boundaries and territories, the book begins with Hilary Callan's examination of the interdisciplinary dialogue forty years ago and ends with Wendy James reflecting on connections – or the lack of such – of social anthropology with the recent 'Lucy to language' project.

How could social anthropology and its canon of writings contribute to relevant debates, and change a culture of human origins research which barely addresses social anthropological insights? The recent African origin of modern humans offers a short timeframe for the emergence of symbolic culture. Genetics and archaeology can now fill in significant detail about modern humanity's expansion within Africa and then beyond (Table 0.1).

Yet all too few social anthropologists are well-informed on human origins research and even fewer are prepared to engage across disciplines. Without that engagement from within social anthropology, we risk leaving questions about the social aspect of our species' evolution to those with least ethnographic and theoretical expertise.

Why the Alienation?

The Nineteenth-century Legacy

The sources of alienation between evolutionary and social anthropology stem from the nineteenth century. Lewis Henry Morgan, the founder of kinship studies as the core of social anthropology, was a materialist advocate of Darwin's theory of natural selection, and can justly be considered the pioneer of what would today be called evolutionary anthropology. His realization that different kin terminologies represented differing types of mating or marriage system, and were motored by different degrees of paternity certainty, has found significant support in modern human behavioural ecology (e.g. Hughes 1981; Holden, Sear and Mace 2003). Influenced by Bachofen and his own developing knowledge of Iroquois matriliny, Morgan (1871, 1877) provided the most substantive arguments for the priority of matriliny in earliest human kinship. His project to reconstruct an evolutionary history of marriage and the family was enthusiastically embraced by Engels (1986 [1884]) and Marx.

Thanks to endorsement by the leading communists, 'Morgan's theory was destined to become a casualty of the central conflict of the age' (Knight and Power 2005: 84). With Morgan's evolutionist scheme incorporated into Communist doctrine, writes Marvin Harris 'the struggling science of anthropology crossed the threshold of the

Table 0.1: Timeline showing species dispersals, and major shifts in technology and culture.

Date ka	Species/dispersals/sites	Lithic technology	Subsistence	Culture
10			Farming	
15	*H. sapiens*, America			
40	*H. sapiens*, Europe	Upper Palaeolithic, Eurasia; Later Stone Age, Africa		Rock painting, Europe, Asia
55	*H. sapiens*, Australia			
70	*H. sapiens* out of Africa; classic Neanderthals		Fishing	
73	Blombos			Beads
120	*H. sapiens*, Near East			Ritual burial
164	Pinnacle Point		Shell-fishing	
170				Ubiquitous ochre use, S. Africa?
195	*H. sapiens* (Omo I)			
240				Pigment use, Europe
300	Neanderthal ancestors Qesem, Tabun	Middle Palaeolithic, Mousterian Europe/Near East; Middle Stone Age, Africa	European, Near East campsites	

Date ka	Species/dispersals/sites	Lithic technology	Subsistence	Culture
400	Atapuerca SH			
500	Boxgrove, Kathu Pan	Fauresmith, S. Africa (Acheulean-MSA transitional); Hafted spears	African campsites?	Pigment use, Africa
600		Handaxes in Europe		
700	*H. heidelbergensis* Gesher Benot Ya'aqov	Symmetrical handaxes, Africa	Central place foraging	
900	late *H. erectus*, Africa, Asia; Olorgesailie		Ambush hunting?	
1000	*H. antecessor*, Europe; Woonderwerk		Early fire use	
1600		Early Acheulean handaxes		
1800	*H. erectus* dispersal, Dmanisi		Regular meat-eating	

twentieth century with a clear mandate for its own survival and well-being: expose Morgan's scheme and destroy the method on which it was based' (1969: 249). So on each side of the Atlantic, for arguably political motives, cultural anthropologists Boas, Lowie and Kroeber, and social anthropologists Malinowksi and Radcliffe-Brown targeted evolutionism and with it any taint of evolutionary theory applied to culture and society (Knight and Power 2005: 83–86; Knight 2008). As Alain Testart described it several decades later: 'anti-evolutionist feeling has been intense for most of this century' (1988: 1).

Already from the early to the mid-twentieth century, the two branches of anthropology were deeply split. One consequence was that Darwinians were cut off from specialist knowledge of cross-cultural variability in human kinship systems, and their historic development. All too often, as the century proceeded, those who began to model human evolution in palaeoanthropology and evolutionary psychology were inclined to fill in the gaps of their knowledge with unrecognized aspects of their own cultural backgrounds. In the case of US evolutionary psychology in the 1980s to 1990s this became explicit, its chief sources of data derived from survey studies of college students who might have begun mating but not yet reproducing. Assumptions that western-style monogamy, the nuclear family and paternal residence and inheritance were basic to the human condition were rarely challenged. Since Darwinian theory is inherently gradualist, it readily assumes continuity between nonhuman primate and human life, hence of male dominance and competitive jealousy. In such work, as Callan notes in Chapter 1, 'the cultural embeddedness of the theorizing itself is ignored or played down'.

Even the mid-twentieth-century resurgence of neo-evolutionism in the US with Leslie White and his students brought about a major modification of Morgan's model with 'matrilineal priority' replaced by the 'patrilocal band' as standard for hunter-gatherers (e.g. Service 1962). This model came in for strong critique from social anthropologist fieldworkers like Richard Lee, Colin Turnbull and James Woodburn in the 1966 interdisciplinary 'Man the Hunter' conference (Lee and DeVore 1968), but the default assumptions about patrilocality and male sexual and social control have proved hard to dislodge to this day. Rather than these ethnographers with their understanding of African hunter-gatherer societies and politics rooted in local ecology, it was to Claude Lévi-Strauss and his highly schematic origins model of groups of men exchanging women that many evolutionary anthropologists appealed (e.g. Van den Berghe 1979; Chapais 2008).

Feminist Re-envisioning

Feminist social and cultural anthropology of the 1970s began to revisit the Morgan/Engels matriliny thesis in a critical examination of the sources of women's subordination across cultures (e.g. Rosaldo and Lamphere 1974; Sacks 1975; Leacock 1978). At the same time came a renewal of attention in British social anthropology to the theoretical treatment of gender in ethnography, particularly the treatment of women's experience and how its symbolic weight – and that of 'muted' groups generally, which may or may not include women – can find expression in specific cultural settings (E. Ardener 1975). In 1973, Shirley Ardener published her essay, reprinted here in Chapter 4, on the Cameroonian concepts of *titi ikoli* (Bakweri), *ndong* (Balong) and *anlu* (Kom). This, together with her later essay on gender iconography (1987), offered a subtle account of women's responses to the silencing or denial by dominant cultural forms of their deepest sense of self.

Referring to the inviolability and beauty of both the female genitals and 'women's secrets' (reminiscent of the Mbendjele women's ritual association of *Ngoku*), these concepts denote areas of great cultural sensitivity. Women's alertness to insult or attack, and their swift corporate response to transgressions, can override even kin bonds. Obscene language and gesture are employed to evoke female collectivity and counterpower, rooted in the sexual and procreative body. Pregnant women, Ardener notes, are particularly sensitive to insult through *titi ikoli*. She uses the Cameroonian data to ask whether this emphasizing of a distinct physical culture, drawing freely on subversive acts and words to challenge offenders, can be related to the Euro-American feminist project. Ardener shows that in a situation where the public cultural lexicon allows no room for women's experience, the reproductive and sexual body provides a coherent language with which to speak back. When expressed subversively, by turning categories of desire and access on their head, this language offers a powerful counter to male physical and cultural experience.

Ardener's study from late-colonial West Africa bears on our theme at two levels. Clearly located in its own space and time, and shaped by its own concerns and context (including that of second-wave feminism in the wider public culture), it nonetheless demonstrates on a theoretical plane the generic potential of detailed ethnography to illuminate more universal questions, such as those surrounding human origins. Substantively, placed alongside new and other historic analysis of women's symbolic strategies collected in this volume

(Finnegan, Knight and Lewis, Power, Watts, Joseph, James), Ardener's work communicates a powerful lesson here. Valid on its own terms, scholarship such as this can also be fruitfully related to data on female coalitionary behaviour that has emerged within primatology, biological anthropology and evolutionary psychology in recent decades. In turn, this suggests that the 'languages' of women's corporeal experience revealed to the contemporary 'ethnographic gaze' – whether in the form of speech, song, dance, gesture or protest – have a deep evolutionary rationale.

Sociobiology and its Critics

But this was not the direction in which discussions developed at the time. During the early 1970s, the implications of essays such as Ardener's, and the chances of *rapprochement* with the evolutionary side of the discipline for interrogating 'Man the Hunter' or 'sexual contract' models, were sidelined by the reaction from the social sciences to the emergence of sociobiology. This entailed accusations – sometimes ill-considered – of biological determinism, assumptions of sexism and racism, and comparisons with social Darwinism (Segerstråle 2000).

From her viewpoint forty years later, Callan selects a moment of comprehensive shift in the rise of human ethology in the old 'Manwatching' school, then rather rapidly overshadowed by a Hamiltonian gene's eye view of the evolution of social behaviours. This shift had a strongly gendered aspect, the ironic undercurrent being that 'selfish' genes ushered in a sexual political emancipation of evolutionary science. The new cohort of feminist evolutionary anthropologists and primatologists began to observe the complex lives of female primates, their interactions, behaviour and strategies. Women like Sarah Hrdy, Barbara Smuts, Shirley Strum, Jeanne Altmann, Adrienne Zihlmann and Joan Silk turned the earlier primatology depicted by Callan upside down by paying attention to female sociality, sexuality and reproductive fitness.

Before sociobiology, the prevailing paradigm of animal social behaviour had been functionalist, assuming that traits had evolved for the good of the 'group' or 'species'. As long as primate groups were viewed as functional wholes, it was not possible to see the conflicts of interest between males and females, parents and offspring, or any members of those groups (Trivers 1985: 78). Sociobiological perspectives 'destabilized the centrality of male behavior for defining social organization' (Haraway 1989: 176). Instead of females being considered as possessions or adjuncts of dominant males organizing them from the top down, under the genetic calculus of sociobiology they became strategists fighting for their own genetic goals. Even 'mother-infant units' dissolved under the scrutiny of sociobiology's methodological individualism. This led sociobiology to be '"female-centred" in ways not true for previous paradigms, where the "mother-infant" unit substituted for females' (Haraway 1989: 178). The female, she continues, 'becomes the fully calculating, maximizing machine that had defined males already ... [She] ceases to be a dependent variable when males and females are both defined as liberal man, i.e. rational calculators' (1989: 178–179).

In *The Use and Abuse of Biology*, Sahlins attacked the transfer of ideology and metaphor from the competitive marketplace – of cost-benefit analysis, and optimization of profit in genes as the ultimate currency – as characteristic of sociobiology, and of a 'late and historically specific development of Euro-American culture' (1977: xiv). Sahlins traced the tradition from Hobbes of placing 'bourgeois society into the state of nature' where nature as a market system is used to explain human social order, and *vice versa* (1977: xv). Yet in the case of sociobiology, as Haraway makes clear, it appeared to be bourgeois feminism that was bursting the bounds and refracting women's newfound sexual and entrepreneurial freedoms through the natural world. The pioneering feminist counternarratives of human evolution of proactive sexuality, with concealed ovulation evolving to confuse males about female fertility, came with Hrdy's *The Woman that Never Evolved* (1981) and Patty Gowaty's 'sexual dialectics' (1997) where female counterstrategies of resistance co-evolve with male strategic attempts to control female fertility.

Fragmentation, Intellectual and Institutional

A sworn enemy of evolutionary biology in its forms of sociobiology, evolutionary psychology and memetics, Tim Ingold emphasizes 'a principled refusal to accept on trust the dominant terms of the debate' (2007: 14) as the cogent response of social anthropologists to Darwinian exploration of human nature. He has often prominently led debates arguing that there is no such thing as human nature. Of course, it is the work of social and cultural anthropologists to act as critical conscience of the stories we tell ourselves about our origins. But Ingold also acknowledges 'a collective loss of confidence'. To outsiders, social anthropology has recently appeared as a branch of hermeneutics, its practitioners taking refuge in a 'jungle of largely incoherent scholarese' (2007: 14).

If social anthropology's search for complexity in particular cultural contexts is opposed to evolutionary scientific model-building aimed at capturing generality, does that inevitably leave us with nothing to say? While large projects on human origins, such as *From Lucy to Language* (Dunbar, Gamble and Gowlett 2010, 2014, and see James, Chapter 12 in this volume), have reached out to social anthropologist contributors, the response has been fairly limited with little attention to the African Middle Stone Age (MSA) in particular. There were no social anthropologist contributors among seventy-four participants to the *Rethinking the Human Revolution* volume (Mellars et al. 2007), nor in the *Homo Symbolicus* collection (Henshilwood and d'Errico 2011). No social anthropologists were invited to speak at the European Palaeolithic conference early in 2013, held in concert with the major Ice Age Art exhibition at the British Museum. On the other hand, a popular social anthropology collection, *Questions of Anthropology* (Astuti, Parry and Stafford 2007), while stimulating and broad-ranging, paid no attention to human origins. There is clearly a glaring and serious omission of social or cultural anthropological input to some of the most important questions about how we became human, but equally a failure to encourage social anthropologists to engage.

In *Fragments of an Anarchist Anthropology*, David Graeber probes the agonizing of contemporary anthropologists over the history of their discipline 'made possible by horrific schemes of conquest, colonization and mass murder' (2004: 96). This has led to a paradoxical result, according to Graeber: 'While anthropologists are, effectively, sitting on a vast archive of human experience, of social and political experiments no one else really knows about, that very body of comparative ethnography is seen as something shameful'. He continues: 'There's more to it though. In many ways, anthropology seems a discipline terrified of its own potential. It is, for example, the only discipline in a position to make generalisations about humanity as a whole ... yet it resolutely refuses to do so' (2004: 97). This leaves the field to philosophers and psychologists whose experience is preponderantly Euro-American and whose pronouncements may carry unconscious ethnocentrism. The discipline which is the most reticent turns out to be the one 'that actually takes all of humanity into account' (2004: 97). Graeber's uncompromising comments present a real challenge to the subdiscipline.

Countercurrents and Change in the Air

Undoubtedly, many social anthropologists have rejected developments in evolutionary biology for spurious reasons. But the communication failure has worked both ways; evolutionary anthropologists have also neglected to take account of important areas of understanding provided by social and cultural anthropologists. Today many social and cultural anthropologists consider their discipline as belonging within the interpretive humanities. They remain the experts in the domains of ideology and symbolism; to understand humans as the symbolic species, this expertise cannot be ignored. The consequence is that few have taken up the task of scientific research on symbolism as an adaptation (but see Deacon 1997; Dunbar, Knight and Power 1999).

Towards the last two decades of the twentieth century, a few mavericks among French, British and US social anthropologists resisted the prevailing antagonism to evolution. Among them are Alain Testart and Chris Knight – both Marxists and structuralists – as well as two major thinkers on ritual, Roy Rappaport and Maurice Bloch. Testart (1988) defended the legitimacy of investigating how social forms change, and of the laws governing that change, producing some of the most careful reconstructions of hunter-gatherer – primarily Australian – kinship systems. His 'reasoned evolutionism' insisted on basing modern inquiry on the 'considerable findings of prehistoric archaeology' (1988: 1). Knight (1991) integrated work on hunter-gatherer symbolism and cosmology, again mainly Australian, with selfish-gene models for the evolution of co-operation. Rather than accept the Sahlins line on sociobiology, he recognized selfish-gene thinking as the 'science of solidarity', with the power to account for unique human forms of collective action. Coming from the holistic cultural ecology tradition, Rappaport (1979, 1999) detested so-called 'selfish' genes. Yet his model of ritual as central to human origins has been readily adopted by behavioural ecologists working on religion (e.g. Sosis and Alcorta 2003), and aligned especially with Zahavi's 'Handicap principle' (Zahavi and Zahavi 1997). Bloch (1992, 1998), a classic social anthropology theorist of ritual as politics, has explored connections with developmental and cognitive psychology, linguistics and theory of cultural transmission.

There are new signs of change in the air. In two recent volumes, *Social Anthropology and Human Origins* (2011) and *The Genesis of Symbolic Thought* (2012), Alan Barnard sets out to carve a subdiscipline within social anthropology, bridging the gap to evolutionary biology and archaeology, and drawing on a century and a half of accumulated ethnographic and theoretical experience. He argues that whereas it was not possible to address the origin of symbolism in the mid-century when Lévi-Strauss wrote, nor at the turn of the nineteenth-twentieth century, when Durkheim attempted it, today, with developments in evolutionary theory, palaeontology, primatology, population genetics, archaeology and hunter-gatherer anthropology, it is. Social and cultural anthropology in fact should stake the claim that 'Symbolism is our subject matter'. No other discipline has the necessary expertise.

A signal of bolder ambition came with the delivery of the 2014 Royal Anthropological Institute Henry Myers lecture on 'Ritual, Seasonality and the Origins of Inequality', in which comparative archaeologist David Wengrow collaborated with social anthropologist David Graeber. They applied a model of alternating political modes, with deliberate switching between hierarchy and egalitarian organization, to hunter-gatherers of the European Upper Palaeolithic, drawing on classic anthropological sources such as Mauss and Beuchat's *Seasonal Variations of the Eskimo* (1979). Wengrow and Graeber (2015) adopt a long-held position in social anthropology, going back to Mauss's total social facts, through Sahlins's idea of a single consistent system of relationships mapped onto all planes of social action – kinship, economics, ritual and politics – to Bloch on sacred and political power being originally fused: religion is not to be treated as a separate analytic category, nor is it epiphenomenal. They argue that current archaeological concepts like 'behavioural modernity' contain the same notion that 'the earliest evidence for what we might now distinguish as "religious", "political" or for that matter "artistic" behaviour is all of a piece, appearing together in striking configurations' (Wengrow and Graeber 2015: 2). Invoking Lévi-Strauss (1968) against concepts of the 'primitiveness' or the 'childlike simplicity' of hunter-gatherers, they favour an approach that sees no difference between hunter-gatherers, horticulturalists or members of state societies in terms either of cognition or political complexity. We examine their argument in more detail under the key theme of egalitarianism and origins of inequality below.

Key Themes in Human Origins Models Ripe
for Input from Social Anthropology

Egalitarianism and the Origins of Inequality

Over the past two decades, there has been a focus on the role of egalitarianism in the emergence of distinctively human society. Surprisingly, in an area where social anthropologists would be well placed to contribute (cf Barnard 2010), to date, it has been evolutionary psychologists and anthropologists who have paid most attention to this issue. David Erdal and Andy Whiten (1994, 1996, Whiten and Erdal 2012), working in an evolutionary psychology framework, viewed typical immediate-return hunter-gatherer egalitarianism as a puzzle to be explained from the perspective of Machiavellian ape-like ancestors. Their intriguing dialectical account of counterdominance behaviours emerging out of an increasingly Machiavellian ability to form alliances belies the common social science perception of reductionist bias in evolutionary 'rational maximizer' models.

Erdal and Whiten made scholarly use of hunter-gatherer ethnography in supporting their arguments, and engaged in lively debates with evolutionary anthropologist Christopher Boehm whose *Hierarchy in the Forest* (1999) proposed a more collective model of 'reverse dominance'. Boehm, observing that weapons were a great leveller, argued that egalitarianism of both reproduction and status would promote effects of group selection in human cultural evolution. While having plenty to say about differing strategies of male and female chimpanzees, when it came to hunter-gatherer ethnography, he said nothing about gender. With a focus on weaponry, dominance and aggression as a male reproductive problem, this implied predominantly male strategic solutions.

Wengrow and Graeber (2015) note Boehm's work on the political complexity of strategies for resisting domination among humans compared with nonhuman primates, but criticize him for assuming that early humans were egalitarian for thousands of generations before hierarchy emerged some 5000 years ago. They ask: 'Why ... should our species' engrained capacity for political complexity have been held in suspense for the greater part of human (pre)history? Sociobiology poses the question, but offers no clear answers' (2015: 3). We respond that sociobiology offers a direct answer with its focus on differential strategies and reproductive trade-offs between the sexes, especially as brain sizes reached their maximum when we became modern humans from 200,000 to 100,000 years ago. The egalitarianism that counts from an evolutionary standpoint is equality in reproductive success. Mothers of very large-brained, costly offspring had increasing motives to share chances of reproduction more equally among males so that more men would invest in offspring; both mothers and investing men should resist any form of dominance that allowed male harem monopoly of female fertility. To meet the material female costs as brain sizes maximized in early modern humans, we can predict the greatest degree of reproductive levelling among males. Female 'reverse dominance' strategies – disregarded by either Boehm or Wengrow and Graeber, but echoed in Ardener's ethnography – can be located here.

Wengrow and Graeber contest the contrast of hunter-gatherer egalitarianism to agropastoralist hierarchy. They argue that the Upper Palaeolithic landscape of ritual burials in particular can be decoded in terms of a deliberate and conscious ritual switching between modes of hierarchical and more egalitarian organization, aligned with seasonal changes in social morphology (cf Mauss and Beuchat 1979). They are at pains to demolish an evolutionist picture of a 'childhood of man'. In making their intriguing argument for political complexity in the Upper Palaeolithic, they critically examine Renfrew's 'sapient paradox'. This is the Eurocentric perspective that humans appear to be 'anatomically modern' *Homo sapiens* by 200,000–150,000 years ago, yet not 'all there' culturally until the last 50,000 years. There is now broad consensus (d'Errico and Stringer 2011) that symbolic culture appears consistently from South to North Africa and into the Middle East over 100,000 years ago, with evidence from sites like Pinnacle Point and Border Cave extending that back to the time period of modern human emergence (Watts 2014). Convincing evidence of ritual activity stretches back even before modern humans into the southern African Fauresmith over 500,000–300,000 years ago (Watts, Chazan and Wilkins 2016). The more we see of the African record, the more the sapient paradox dissolves. The parsimonious view is that archaic human ancestors in Africa were on the cutting edge; humans became 'modern' in Africa, anatomically and behaviourally, all-singing, all-dancing, speaking, laughing, healing, bodies and minds in step. In fact, the paradox could switch the other way: ritual performance among late archaic populations precedes, and may foster the evolution of, modern bodies (see Low on bodily practice as source of human cognition in Chapter 9 of this volume).

The perspective of the sapient paradox could suggest that humans are less interesting, not fully cultural or complex enough until they become unequal. This then runs the risk of relegating the African MSA, where seasonality factors would not be so decisive as in Ice Age Eurasia, to the stage of 'childhood of man'. If Wengrow and Graeber's model of conscious alternation of 'moral, legal and ritual organization' of society is to be applied to human cognitive origins, we need to situate their picture of seasonal social morphology of the Upper Palaeolithic in a wider evolutionary context. We are not likely to understand the Upper Palaeolithic without also understanding what happened in Africa with the origins of symbolism. Wengrow and Graeber refer to Bloch's (2008) framework of transactional vs. transcendental social relations. Whereas all other apes are trapped in a transactional world, humans create a transcendental social world by collectively imagining social roles that extend in space and time beyond the individual. Wengrow and Graeber's social dynamic of regular political reversal could help explain how this transition came about.

Collective/Co-operative Childcare

A recent reworking of Boehm's modelling in collaboration with evolutionary economist Herbert Gintis and primatologist Carel van Schaik (Gintis, van Schaik and Boehm 2015) still stresses the role of weaponry in establishing egalitarian relations, but, through van Schaik, addresses the issue of reproductive costs and co-operative mothering. In the past few decades, Darwinian feminism has matured to produce some of the most influential theory on human evolution, in particular the Grandmother hypothesis (Hawkes et al. 1998). In *Mothers and Others* (2009), Sarah Hrdy argued that co-operative childcare centred on female kin coalitionary networks is fundamental to human 'emotional modernity'. The growing influence of Hrdy's work is producing an expanding evolutionary and biosocial literature on allomothering and collective childcare as the basis for humanlike prosociality. In our current understanding, co-operative breeding allied to great ape cognitive capacity offers the most convincing explanation of the differences between us and the other great apes in terms of intersubjectivity and motivation to share intentions, providing the basis for human 'cultural cognition' (Burkart et al. 2009, 2014, Tomasello et al. 2012, and Ellen, Chapter 2 in this volume). We are the product of natural selection for intersubjectivity and joint attention facilitated by our 'co-operative' eyes, which other apes decidedly are not. To that extent, our capacity for egalitarianism is engrained in our bodies. James (Chapter 12 in this volume) reminds us of the rhythmic give-and-take and sophisticated game-playing that characterize the interactions of even very young children everywhere: 'Over and above the spontaneous, innovative engagements of two or three individuals, among youngsters there will always be movement towards a recognition that social consensus has to depend on rules, reciprocities, categories, conventions and notions of fairness – or shared rejection and protest against these'.

While Hrdy highlights the demographic flexibility of hunter-gather bands and residence patterns and how that can operate as an elastic safety net for childcare, her work (2009) essentially combines the argument of the Grandmother hypothesis with Michael Tomasello and colleagues' Vygotskian intelligence hypothesis, drawing on the evolutionary biology of co-operative breeding systems. Her model of 'emotional modernity' applies to the emergence of genus *Homo/H. erectus* (timeframe 2–1.5 ma). This concurs with the timeframe of O'Connell, Hawkes and Blurton Jones (1999) on shifts in life history, Key and Aiello's (1999) modelling of the emergence of male-female co-operation, and Isler and van Schaik's (2012) recent arguments on breaking through the 'gray ceiling' of encephalization (when genus *Homo* regularly attains twice the volume of the chimpanzee brain). Kramer and Otárola-Castillo (2015) emphasize the role of mother-oldest child co-operation for engendering early human life-history shifts. These interdisciplinary models then are achieving a degree of consensus on key aspects of the evolution of human sociality, sexual and reproductive co-operation. Hrdy has not attempted to push her argument into the symbolic domain or the symbolic era of modern *Homo sapiens* (timeframe within the past 200,000 years), yet it surely has implications which social anthropologists should be attentive to. If the evolutionary priming of the ancestors of early modern humans was for mutual mindreading and co-operation, then the intense physicality of contemporary hunter-gatherer communities begins to make sense, as does the transmission of important ritual information through both the biological and social body. The failure of feminist social and biological anthropologists to communicate across disciplinary divides has resulted in an unwarranted distancing from the reproductive body in mainstream feminist scholarship.

Residence Patterns and Kinship

The basic idea that collective forms of allomothering are fundamental to humanity has haunting resonance with Lewis Henry Morgan. Hrdy herself was persuaded to pursue her argument when Helen Alvarez (2004) re-examined Murdock's cross-cultural assessment of hunter-gatherer residence patterns. There have been robust arguments in support of early human kinship being matrilineal (Knight 2008). Yet the opposite viewpoint of male kinbonding with consequent male control over resources still prevails as a default (e.g. Foley and Gamble 2009). Data is now emerging in population genetics (e.g. Verdu and Austerlitz 2015) which can test these differing positions and combine with ethnographic material on residence and kinship to begin to answer these old questions. That data supports the view that in the timeframe of modern human emergence in Africa matrilocal residence with bride-service should stand as default among African hunter-gatherers.

Suzanne Joseph seeks to contribute to a resurgence of scholarship on early human kinship by examining the specific case of early Bedouin kinship, considering early ethnological accounts from McLennan and Robertson Smith – both matrilineal prioritists – in the light of more recent ethnography. Both Joseph and Ellen (Chapters 11 and 2, respectively) advocate a cautious use of nonhunter-gatherer materials in model-building. Nomadic Bedouin pastoralists show similarities with nomadic foragers sociopolitically, economically, ecologically, in terms of ethnobotanical classification (see Ellen, Chapter 2 below) and demographically. By contrast with non-Bedouin Arab patrilineal kinship structures, Bedouin kinship reveals non-agnatic features which may be explained by a focus on uterine (brother-sister) connections. A Bedouin woman at marriage does not lose her patriline affiliation, which would place her in a different lineage to that of her children if she marries exogamously. Instead, Bedouin systems of kinship hold onto the woman by marrying her within the patriline, with a preference for patriparallel cousin marriage.

Joseph brings out the impact of maternal contribution to kinship inside such a system. Women may remain in residence with their close kin at marriage. A woman's bond with her husband does not come at the expense of her bond with her brother. Male and female lineages are merged in the grandparental generation. Joseph investigates Robertson Smith's thesis that this represented a transitional phase between original matrilineal and present patrilineal systems. Exchange marriages, generally sister-exchange as in Lévi-Strauss' model, do occur, but coercion into exchange marriage, often by male kin, is 'strongly contested by Bekaa Bedouin women' says Joseph, extrapolating from this to the likely gender relations and similar resistance to losing touch with close kin in early human societies. The frequency of divorce in traditional Bedouin communities also parallels the autonomy of hunter-gatherer women in leaving a marriage. In exposing the fallacy of the Bedouin as an 'archetypal patrilineal social system', Joseph recommends that we subject our assumptions about kinship to careful questioning.

For James, also, borrowing a phrase from Marilyn Strathern, kinship is 'at the core'. She adds a structural dimension that is distinctly social-anthropological: 'Human sociality as we should understand it includes consciously co-ordinated principles governing the way maturing individuals gradually learn to place each other in a wider context'. Referring to Nicholas Allen's tetradic model of early kinship (2008), she considers the possibility of an abstract, sociocentric system being invented as a whole in Africa at some point before the global migrations of around 60,000 years ago, and leaving its mark on later structures found in different parts of the world.

Evolutionary hunter-gatherer models highlight egocentric fluidity. In a cross-cultural study of thirty-two hunter-gatherer groups, Hill et al. (2011) identified a 'unique social structure' with both sexes able to remain or disperse from natal groups, frequent co-residence of brothers and sisters, and most individuals being unrelated in residence groups. Dyble et al. (2015) argue from agent-based modelling that such a situation of largely non-relatives living together arises where members of each sex have equal influence in deciding where to go and who to live with. Their models match observed residence data among the egalitarian BaYaka and Agta.

We do not need to adjudicate here absolutely between the various egocentric and sociocentric models of early kinship. What seems clear is the need to question the primacy of 'patrilocal' bands, or the exchange of women, as fundamental to human society.

Gendered Dynamics of Ritual Power

Ardener, as we have seen, dissects in a Cameroonian context women's capacity for protest and solidarity through imageries of the body such as *titi ikoli*, and suggests that this connection may be more widespread. Several more chapters in this book (Finnegan, Knight and Lewis, Power, Watts, Low, Barnard) focus or touch on the dynamics of egalitarianism. Some see the role of gender politics as central in mobilizing symbolic culture and ritual power among egalitarian hunter-gatherers. Can social anthropologists meet these evolutionary perspectives with ethnographic material on gendered symbolic agency in ritual, cosmology and dance?

In their work on gendered secret societies among Central African Yaka people, Morna Finnegan (2013; 2015) and Jerome Lewis (2002) develop a pendulum model with pulses or switches of dominance/ counterdominance between male and female collectives. This strikingly prefigures the model of alternation between hierarchy and egalitarianism offered by Wengrow and Graeber (2015). But it works symbolically on a swifter lunar cycle length, rather than on a seasonal basis. In fact, Finnegan has argued that this pendulum motion is kept swinging continually in micro-scale among peoples such as the Mbendjele, driven by women's constant simmering of song and dance. This 'communism in motion' (cf Morgan's 'communism in living' [1877: 446, 453]) ensures that no group or individual is able to monopolize ritual power, and in turn creates a dynamic social milieu within which power is always in the process of being negotiated. Contexts defined by hierarchy, by contrast, demand the stoppage or privatization of power in order to carve out levels of entitlement and authority. This collective movement against hierarchies of power is dependent on motion – social, ritual and physical. And it is what we should expect from communities in which communal childcare, and consequently high levels of female co-operation and solidarity, are the norm. Attention to male reproductive strategies, subsistence and warfare have too often distracted scholars of hunter-gatherer politics from this pivotal intra-group dynamic.

Warfare in Human Evolution: Between Groups or Between the Genders?

Evolutionary psychologists (e.g. Pinker 2011; Bowles 2009; Alexander 1989), primatologist Richard Wrangham (1999), and most recently mathematical modeller Sergei Gavrilets (2015) look to warfare as the generator of moral cohesion in human evolution, through creation of in-group solidarity against hostile outgroups. In these recent analyses, male warfare appears somehow more compelling than alternative models highlighting the cultural energy released through intersexual ritual conflict. It is as though the increasingly rounded conception of early society as egalitarian and child-centred is less persuasive than the bloodthirsty tribe defending its vulnerable females. As Callan notes, this essentially feeds back into evolutionary scenarios of a particular cultural preoccupation with war and territory.

Even Tomasello et al. (2012) resort to explaining 'group-mindedness' and the enforcement of norms by increasing competition between groups. Recent evolutionary scenarios have given us an alternative to that stubborn assumption. A more universalizing model of group-on-group conflict is of gender ritual as 'warfare', generating solidarity within each gender group (Knight and Lewis 2014). Where female agency becomes a significant driver in human evolution, male violence as structural force is seen as a later development within societies increasingly focused on ownership at the cost of autonomy. The traditional evolutionary picture, skewed by excessive focus on war, raiding, ownership and paternity, in which male group interests are the driving force, runs up against a competing vision of female interests: solidarity based on co-operation, labour-sharing, relationship, and the aggressive cultural defence of fertility and reproductive rights. It is no coincidence that in societies such as the Efe or BaYaka children receive more contact, are breastfed more continuously and weaned later than in any other known society (Hewlett and Lamb 2005). Nor is it a coincidence that in these societies fathers are woven into the cultural *habitus* of open and collective parenting. The vocabulary of female biological interest here is a public one.

Yet the prejudices of scientific populism found in the accessible texts of evolutionary psychology prove hard to shift. Raiding archaeology and ethnography for 'snippets of information about sex and violence', as Kuper and Marks (2011: 167) put it, the evolutionary psychologists know how to sell books, their arguments finding resonance in the age of the 'war on terror'. Can we address the evidence to test between alternative views? Did we become human through the warring of groups on each other or through defusion of such violence and its replacement by widespread networks of connection between groups? Which pathway is most likely to generate language and indeed multilingualism, or universal systems of kinship (see Barnard, Afterword in this volume)? As noted in Callan's chapter, the 1960s and 1970s saw many claims and counterclaims about the supposed universality of 'human aggression'. Douglas Fry's interdisciplinary collection on *War, Peace and Human Nature* (2013), involving both evolutionary biologists and cultural anthropologists, has carefully examined sources of evidence.

Firemaking, Community and the Division of Labour

A prominent current focus in human evolution studies is on the impact of fire on human society. Wrangham (2009) highlighted cooking, making arguments for a relatively early date in relation to increasing brain size and reducing gut size (in *H. erectus*). Recently, archaeologist John Gowlett has examined the evidence on differing levels of fire exploitation and control from c.1.5 ma. This has informed 'social brain' models of expanding group size in genus *Homo* (Dunbar and Gowlett 2014). Fire is expensive to keep going, requiring significant collaboration; yet the extra hours of light, warmth and sociality after twilight became vital to keeping cohesion in social groups. By extending the normal primate equatorial day of twelve hours into the night, hominins could break through the constraints on social time budgets. Wiessner's analysis (2014) of firelight conversations among Ju/'hoansi Bushmen highlights the different kinds of interaction during the hours of darkness compared to 'day talk'. By the fire, people have time for more imaginative and creative exploration of music, song, ritual, story, cosmology and each other's thoughts and feelings. What night talk enables is extension of cultural institutions across time and space to link people from different bands into 'imagined communities', while stories within the band enhance and entrain people's moods.

The mid Middle Pleistocene (c. 500–300 ka) offers a general picture of social developments including homebases, hearths and stone-tipped spear-hunting in conjunction with evidence for ritual display (Watts, Chazan and Wilkins 2016). Gendered social roles, similar to those we know among contemporary hunter-gatherers, may be emerging at this period. Social anthropologists have long debated the causes of the sexual division of labour, and its impact on gender relations. Are women excluded from hunting for biological, social and political reasons or is this a strategic choice for women juggling high reproductive costs with labour demands? While the issue of women's labour roles can be understood through energy budget analysis, Finnegan shows in her chapter that the solution to intensifying workloads among hunter-gatherers lies in collective action. A mechanistic approach to gender roles will miss key examples of women's ritual 'work', which governs and directs hunting success. This work gives women considerable authority when meat is returned to camp. Ethnographic blindness to the cosmological field written around male hunting labour, in which women are both metaphorical and physical co-workers, has often led to a simplistic view of hunting as bringing male prestige alone. In any normal labour scenario those compelled to do the hard physical work on behalf of others (others who collectively claim ritual expertise and control) are clearly not the 'ruling class'. Metaphorically Biaka women become the 'arms' of the *dibouka*, the throw of nets during the collective hunt following women's summoning of *bobanda* spirit (McCreedy 1994). In *Yele*, BaYaka initiates in trance 'tie up' the elephant's spirit, and send men to get it (Lewis 2002). There are numerous other examples cross-culturally of women's essential interventions in hunting labour. To succeed, the hunt happens first in the imagination of the women.

Metaphor, Story, Shaking, Healing

What governed the ability to share fictions, i.e. be tolerant of literal untruths? As Wiessner notes (2014: 14030), egalitarianism is the fundamental framework for the journey into the night-time world. Reverse dominance has been central to the work of Knight and Lewis on the evolution of language through the human ability to engage with metaphor. Language, in this view, emerges as the 'honest' redeployment, internal to the group, of capacities used in the deception of outsiders (trickery by men of animals, and by women of both animals and men!). This inside/outside structure of communicative signals may parallel Wiessner's night-talk/day-talk opposition.

In Andrew Smith and Stefan Hoefler's analysis metaphor utilizes the same cognitive processes to generate both symbols and grammar. Based in our evolved capacity to recognize each other as intentional beings, human communication works through processes of ostension and inference, the production and interpretation of evidence for the speaker's informative and communicative intentions (Sperber and Wilson 1995). Ostensive-inferential communication requires common ground between speaker and listener, including understanding of the goal of the communicative episode, of what is relevant in the interaction, and knowledge of existing conventions. This enables shared meanings but because inferential construction of meaning is inherently approximate, this also allows innovation in use by stepping from a previously agreed meaning to establish a new, shared meaning.

Metaphor is a ubiquitous principle in language, the creative use of an existing linguistic form to express a meaning similar to, but not identical to, its conventional meaning. Using a ratchet model of cumulative cultural evolution, Smith and Hoefler outline how metaphor creation is initially ad hoc and ephemeral, but if it works successfully, will spread in a community. The memorization of successful communicative experience strengthens the metaphoric association for speakers and listeners, leading to entrenchment and automatic inference of meaning. Once the metaphor has a life of its own, independent of any original association, it can then be invoked for the formation of new associations, as a stepping stone in an oscillatory process of innovation followed by conventionalization. Through this ratcheted ostensive-inferential process, initially iconic and non-arbitrary associations of form and meaning will evolve towards purely arbitrary ones – symbols – with no apparent history of the original connections of form and meaning.

In her discussion on Ju/'hoan metaphor (1993: 23–27), Biesele describes a virtual second language of respect words, particularly used in dangerous circumstances. Words as metaphors have powerful and transformative effects when deployed by a skilled storyteller. Puberty rites, storytelling and healing dances all serve in the 'hunt' for *n/om* (Keeney and Keeney 2013). Stories emphasize shapeshifting and transformation, and so awaken *n/om*: 'the stories themselves shake and are capable of sending arrows of *n/om* to the listeners' (Keeney and Keeney 2013: 11). This metaphor stems from the physical shaking that stimulates and awakens *n/om* in healing.

In his chapter on the role of shamanic healing in the so-called cognitive revolution, Chris Low looks for evolutionary continuity from skilful animal to human capacities of bodily performance rather than sudden macro-mutations producing 'symbolic thought'. He examines San healing experience in terms of Winkelman's 'false stress' hypothesis. Rejecting a model of complicated stages of increasing abstraction in symbolism for a simplifying view of metaphor that either works or does not work, Low roots this in essentially physiological experience, feeling, mood and emotion. He points to the role of sensory stimuli, especially smell, and mechanisms of stress applied to the body of a dancer during healing. Singing – 'hypnotic but regularly irregular' – rhythm and movement re-orientate the body. Low describes very concrete physiological effects of clonus-like shaking and boiling potency (cf Katz 1982). The remapping and hyperstimulation of muscle and nerve relationships encourage the body to shake, simulating stress responses of fear – sweating, heat, increased heart rate, hypervigilance and hypersensitivity – which, as the dance progresses, may give way to feelings of power and empathy. Low resists the mystification of Bushman religiosity, and sees practical usage, body posture and focus on 'doing things nicely' as critical to knowledge and truly embodied cognition. Tracking spoor is seen here as a fundamental hominin skill fostering abilities to link signs to things in different space and time.

Africa vs. Australia

One of the strengths of this book is its detailed focus on African hunter-gatherers with several chapters attentive to cosmology, ritual and healing experience (Finnegan, Knight and Lewis, Low, Power, Skaanes, Watts, and finally Barnard). These authors have between them many years of fieldwork with different Khoisan groups and among the BaYaka, as well as significant experience with the Hadza. Given the timeframe of modern human emergence, there is some justification in viewing African cosmologies as the oldest rooted we have.

Testart and Knight both used Australian Aboriginal material in their model-building, following the tracks of Durkheim (1912). The strong argument for this is that farming did not impact on Australian traditions until the relatively recent invasion by Europeans, so they offer evidence of continent-wide kinship, economic, moral and religious systems. Current archaeological and genetic evidence supports modern human entry into Australia earlier than the European Upper Palaeolithic. This offers the longest continuity we know of untrammelled hunter-gatherer subsistence practice. Testart proposed Australia as the best model for Upper Palaeolithic reconstructions on the grounds that their 'social form of production', totemic or exogamous law, 'according to which one may not dispose of what is one's own (or what one is "closest" to) seems to me to represent something like *the principle of intelligibility* of Australian society *conceived as a whole*' (1988: 10, emphasis in original). Making the case for why Bushmen, rather than Australian Aborigines, are more appropriate for thinking about early human society, Barnard (1999: 60) describes the Australian worldview as 'the most structurally evolved ... the world has yet seen'. Characteristic Bushman flexibility, rather than Australian total coherence, offers the more promising starting point, in Barnard's view. Among six differences between Aboriginal and Bushman systems, Barnard identifies belief in the Rainbow Serpent and the Dreaming. Ian Watts contests this assessment, asking whether Rainbow Snakes on each continent could have features in common, indicating a deep-time shared ancestry. He meticulously compares the historic ethnography of initiation myths and ritual associated with serpent-like beings.

Watts rounds up the sources of evidence suggesting that snakes and pythons shared a fundamental identity in Khoisan conception with the eland, the most desired prey animal, described by David Lewis-Williams as *animal de passage*, implicated in initiation and healing rites among many Khoisan groups. A snake is said to reside in the eland's red forelock. Both a physiological and symbolic signal of potency, the forelock is part of the design painted onto a Ju/'hoan girl at the menarcheal ceremony and a Ju/'hoan boy at his first kill.

Providing fascinating comparative material is the chapter by Thea Skaanes, drawing on rich new ethnography of the Hadza. The ankle bells (*!'iŋgiribi*) used by *epeme* dancers when they stamp rhythmically invoke the presence of a bull eland by mimicking the distinctive clicking of its walk. A human-eland therianthrope appears to be central to the Hadza healing dance just as has been documented in Bushman ethnography and rock art studies. The remarkable interviews by Skaanes reveal further precise similarities in practice and belief around the eland between Hadza and Bushman cosmology. While they are click-language speakers, the Hadza are known as an isolate group, not related linguistically to Khoisan languages. However, they have subsistence practices of hunting with poisoned arrows in common with Bushman groups, as well as sharing ancient genome sequences tracing to source Khoisan populations (Power, in this volume). The parsimonious inference must be that these highly specific concepts surrounding eland stem from a Middle Stone Age heritage shared by early African hunter-gatherers. The Hadza !'*iŋgiribi* resonate with the 'eland-headed' people of First Creation.

Chris Knight and Jerome Lewis begin in Australia with Durkheim's understanding of totemism as the root metaphor. If 'man is a kangaroo', it is because they are conceived as sharing the same clan blood. For Durkheim (1912), all creative, conceptual leaps of thought, underlying language and reason, consist in forcibly identifying contraries. In his early origins theory (1963 [1897]), the clan blood issued from women at menstruation, establishing a taboo on sex with any man who shared that blood. Women's identity with totemic game animals was metaphoric, establishing their blood as the blood of the wounded game. Taking this as the fundamental metaphor in their 'Theory of Everything', Knight and Lewis transfer this principle from Central and Northern Australia to the Central African BaYaka and their permeating concept of *ekila*, demonstrating the basic unity of the idea. They extend that to other African hunter-gatherer female initiates who bleed as the game animals men hunt, exploring how this metaphor generates ritual, economic and sexual exchange all at once.

Camilla Power restricts her comparative analysis to African hunter-gatherers. Genetic markers indicate long-term separation of populations, reaching back into the MSA and even to the time period of the earliest evidence for symbolism itself. If there are shared and non-trivial features of cosmology between Khoisan groups, Central African Western and Eastern Pygmies and the Hadza of Tanzania, these could be very ancient. Potentially they offer data for reconstructing the earliest cosmologies. Such shared structures are still likely to be found in non-hunter-gatherer populations. But the argument for antiquity rests on the genetic markers that allow ancient migrations to be tracked – and even dated. Since these groups share many features of social organization, material culture, politics and economics, probably inherited from shared source cultures, it is reasonable to understand the overlapping core of their cosmological systems as archaic and highly conservative. Power argues that this data should be taken into account alongside archaeological data in building models for the African Middle Stone Age emergence of symbolic culture.

Cultural Cognition of Environments

Roy Ellen argues eloquently against too narrow a focus on African hunter-gatherer models, emphasizing the capacity to diversify behaviours through cultural transmission as what makes us human. He examines one critical adaptation: hominin and human organization of knowledge of the natural world. At certain points in time, he argues, we should find a 'meeting place', with evolutionary models projecting forward and social models projecting back from the present into the past. How these two approaches interrelate will depend on the period and focus of investigation. The interdisciplinary discussion here ranges over archaeological evidence for use of plant products in the Pleistocene, ontogeny-phylogeny models of classification, and modular views of evolved specialist intelligence. Ellen contests Steve Mithen's (1996, 2006) model of the relationship of social and natural history intelligences, as separate cognitive domains only joined up through cognitive fluidity among recent modern humans, arguing against the reification of modules in favour of a gradualist model of co-evolution. Social and ecological intelligences could emerge in mutual interaction, with specialized human social skills enabling cultural transmission of ecological knowledge.

Ritual and the Human Moral Community: What Social Anthropology Brings to Human Origins Research

If, as Graeber argues (2011: 54), the thing we care most about is always other people, it is useful to identify who these other people might have been in evolutionary time. The kind of morality of interest here, and commonly found among Central African hunter-gatherers, is neither repressive nor divisive and cannot be hijacked by charismatic individuals for their own purposes. It is a morality seeded in the body after birth when infants first begin to experience the shared contact valued by the adults around them (see Finnegan and James, this volume), and cultivated subsequently through early childhood and into adulthood by corporeal metaphors and practices such as *ekila*, *n/om* or *epeme*. Community dances and the spirits which sustain them reinforce the collective body through which the morality of sharing power is carried and expressed.

People become powerful in societies such as the BaYaka or the Ju/'hoansi through adherence to shared moral constraints rather than through the violation of them. As the work of Lewis demonstrates, egalitarian societies do play routinely with a kind of shadow hierarchy, where intersexual conflict and the threat of collapse serve as a powerful motor for the movement of power across the social landscape. But a fundamental difference between egalitarianism and hierarchy is that under structural hierarchy individuality is sealed off from others (and considered best developed at the expense of those others) while complex egalitarianism cultivates individuality and autonomy through the communal labour of distribution of social power. The grain of community morality is stored in the metaphorical and somatic domain. In that sense – in the ability of a culture to progress and balance without the use of concrete structure, without fences, walls, or icons – hunter-gatherers possess sociopolitical complexity and skills that make 'developed' societies seem clumsy by contrast.

Social anthropology has a long history of theorizing the role of ritual in relation to human origins, the emergence of language, symbolism and morality. Durkheim, Turner, Lévi-Strauss, Douglas, Bourdieu, Bloch and Rappaport all offer important contributions. But in recent years, as with egalitarianism (above), it has been Darwinians who have paid attention to the centrality of ritual (e.g. Maynard Smith and Szathmáry 1995; Deacon 1997; Sosis and Alcorta 2003). Durkheim, Turner and Rappaport, after all, were fundamentally concerned with the interactive relationship of individual to collective, which accords with recent work in behavioural ecology on the evolutionary origin of co-operation and collective action problems. How can their classic models, allied with those of today, illuminate issues of language and morality, and current debates on the archaeology of modern human behaviour? In particular, how does ritual performance generate the morality inherent in hunter-gatherer communities where collective childcare is the prime mode of reproduction? What are the implications for our understanding of the genesis of moral systems more universally?

James's concluding chapter carries forward the work of building bridges. Focusing on the British Academy Centenary Project, 'From Lucy to Language: The Archaeology of the Social Brain' which ran from 2003 to 2010, James discusses ways in which the characteristic discourses of evolutionary and social anthropology can be brought into closer alignment. In doing so, she pinpoints some areas where 'slippage of language' (see also Callan, this volume) can mislead us; examples she dissects include the concepts of 'social bonding', 'fission-fusion' and 'sociality'. Each of these looks the same typographically when deployed in Darwinian and in social anthropological discourses, but a deeper study of their provenance reveals the disconnections. 'Fission-fusion' as a social anthropological concept, for example, derives from Evans-Pritchard who himself drew on an analogy from nuclear physics, and presupposes an enveloping political structure and a shared understanding of it; whereas it is used by the evolutionary anthropologists as straightforward description of patterns of congregation and dispersal within a population.

Notwithstanding James's critical observations on language usages, her overall message is full of encouragement. Focusing on kinship, fire and politics as key themes around which the conversation can move forward, she emphasizes the performative, game-like mutuality that is characteristic of our human engagements with one another; and she invites thought on how and when this came into being. For James, 'this emergence is not simply a matter of "symbolism" or "ritual" as against the pragmatic requirements of survival. It is rather a matter of growingly complex communications with those around us, drawing both on reason and on feeling which may give rise to new mutual understandings not always transparent to an observer'. For generating this human capacity of many-layered moral engagement, Smith and Hoefler's oscillatory 'ratchet' model for human communication can have general application.

Rethinking human origins calls for a rigorous, scientific and also heuristic exploration of the original (and largely misunderstood) moral community. Without understanding the evolutionary foundations of – for example – sexual and reproductive conflict and co-operation, we cannot make that step. As exemplified in Ardener's work and other classic writings to which we make reference here, the wider canon of social anthropology itself offers clues in sometimes surprising places. The field is open; and this book aims to chart some of the routes our thinking might take.

References

Alexander, R.D. 1989. 'Evolution of the Human Psyche', in P. Mellars and C. Stringer (eds), *The Human Revolution. Behavioural and Biological*

Perspectives in the Origins of Modern Humans. Edinburgh: Edinburgh University Press, pp. 455–513.

Allen, N.J. 2008. 'Tetradic Theory and the Origin of Human Kinship Systems', in N.J. Allen et al. (eds), *Early Human Kinship.* Oxford: Blackwell, pp. 96–112.

Alvarez, H. 2004. 'Residence Groups among Hunter-gatherers: a View of the Claims and Evidence for Patrilocal Bands', in B. Chapais and C. Berman (eds), *Kinship and Behavior in Primates.* New York: Oxford University Press, pp. 420–442.

Ardener, E.W. 1975. 'Belief and the Problem of Women', in S. Ardener (ed.), *Perceiving Women.* London: Malaby, pp. 1–18.

———. 1975. 'The "Problem" Revisited', in S. Ardener (ed.), *Perceiving Women.* London: Malaby, pp. 19–28.

Ardener, Shirley. 1987. 'A Note on Gender Iconography: the Vagina', in P. Caplan (ed.), *The Cultural Construction of Sexuality.* London: Tavistock, pp. 113–142.

Astuti, R., J. Parry and C. Stafford (eds). 2007. *Questions of Anthropology.* Oxford and New York: Berg.

Aunger, R. (ed.). 2000. *Darwinizing Culture.* Oxford: Oxford University Press.

Barnard, A. 1999. 'Modern Hunter-gatherers and Early Symbolic Culture', in Robin Dunbar, Chris Knight and Camilla Power (eds), *The Evolution of Culture: an Interdisciplinary View.* Edinburgh: Edinburgh University Press, pp. 50–68.

———. 2010. 'When Individuals do not Stop at the Skin', in R. Dunbar, C. Gamble and J. Gowlett (eds), *Social Brain, Distributed Mind.* Oxford: Oxford University Press, pp. 249–267.

———. 2011. *Social Anthropology and Human Origins.* Cambridge: Cambridge University Press.

———. 2012. *Genesis of Symbolic Thought.* Cambridge: Cambridge University Press.

Biesele, M. 1993. *Women Like Meat. The Folklore and Foraging Ideology of the Kalahari Ju/'hoan.* Johannesburg: Witwatersrand University Press.

Bloch, M. 1992. *Prey Into Hunter.* Cambridge: Cambridge University Press.

———. 1998. *How We Think They Think.* London: Westview Press.

———. 2000. 'A Well-disposed Social Anthropologist's Problem with Memes', in Robert Aunger (ed.), *Darwinizing Culture.* Oxford: Oxford University Press, pp. 189–204.

———. 2008. 'Why Religion is Nothing Special but is Central', *Philosophical Transactions of the Royal Society, Series B* 363: 2055–2061.

Boehm, C. 1999. *Hierarchy in the Forest: The Evolution of Egalitarian Behavior.* Cambridge, MA: Harvard University Press.

Bowles, S. 2009. 'Did Warfare among Ancestral Hunter-gatherers Affect the Evolution of Human Social Behaviors?', *Science* 324: 1293–1298.

Burkart, J.M., S.B. Hrdy and C.P. van Schaik. 2009. 'Cooperative Breeding and Human Cognitive Evolution', *Evolutionary Anthropology* 18: 175–186.

Burkart, J. M. et al. 2014. 'The Evolutionary Origin of Human Hyper-cooperation', *Nature Communications* 5: 4747.

Chapais, B. 2008. *Primeval Kinship: How Pair Bonding Gave Birth to Human Society*. Cambridge, MA: Harvard University Press.

Deacon, T. 1997. *The Symbolic Species: The Co-evolution of Language and the Human Brain*. London: Penguin.

d'Errico, F. and C. Stringer. 2011. 'Evolution, Revolution or Saltation Scenario for the Emergence of Modern Culture', *Philosophical Transactions of the Royal Society, Series B*. 366: 1060–1069.

Dunbar, R., C. Gamble and J. Gowlett (eds). 2010 *Social Brain, Distributed Mind*. Oxford: Oxford University Press.

———. 2014. *Lucy to Language: the Benchmark Papers*. Oxford: Oxford University Press.

Dunbar, R. and J. Gowlett. 2014. 'Fireside Chat: the Impact of Fire on Hominin Socioecology', in R Dunbar, C. Gamble and J Gowlett (eds), *Lucy to Language: the Benchmark Papers*. Oxford: Oxford University Press, pp. 277–296.

Dunbar, Robin, Chris Knight and Camilla Power (eds). 1999. *The Evolution of Culture: An Interdisciplinary View*. Edinburgh: Edinburgh University Press.

Durkheim, E. 1912. *Les formes élémentaires de la vie religieuse*. Paris: Alcan.

———. 1963 [1897]. 'La Prohibition de L'inceste et ses Origines', *L'Année Sociologique* 1: 1–70. Reprinted as *Incest: The Nature and Origin of the Taboo*, trans. E. Sagarin. New York: Stuart.

Dyble, M. et al. 2015. 'Sex Equality Can Explain the Unique Social Structure of Hunter-Gatherer Bands', *Science* 348: 796–798. doi: 10.1126/science.aaa5139.

Engels, F. 1986 [1884]. *The Origin of the Family, Private Property and the State*. Harmondsworth: Penguin Books.

Erdal, D. and A. Whiten. 1994. 'On Human Egalitarianism: an Evolutionary Product of Machiavellian Status Escalation?', *Current Anthropology* 35: 175–183.

———. 1996. 'Egalitarianism and Machiavellian Intelligence in Human Evolution', in P. Mellars and K. Gibson (eds), *Modelling the Early Human Mind*. Cambridge: McDonald Institute Monographs, pp. 139–150.

Eriksen, Thomas Hylland. 2006. *Engaging Anthropology: the Case for a Public Presence*. Oxford and New York: Berg.

Finnegan, M. 2013. 'The Politics of Eros: Ritual Dialogue and Egalitarianism in Three Central African Hunter-gatherer Societies', *Journal of the Royal Anthropological Institute* 19: 697–715.

———. 2015. 'Dance, Play, Laugh: What Capitalism Can't Do', *Hunter-Gatherer Research* 1: 85–105.

Foley, R. and C. Gamble. 2009. 'The Ecology of Social Transitions in Human Evolution', *Philosophical Transactions of the Royal Society of London Series B Biol Sci*. 364: 3267–3279. doi: 10.1098/rstb.2009.0136.

Fry, D. (ed.). 2013. *War, Peace and Human Nature*. Oxford: Oxford University Press.

Gavrilets, S. 2015. 'Collective Action and the Collaborative Brain', *Journal of the Royal Society Interface* 12: 20141067. http://dx.doi.org/10.1098/rsif.2014.1067.

Gintis, H., C. van Schaik and C. Boehm. 2015. '*Zoon Politikon*: The Evolutionary Origins of Human Political Systems', *Current Anthropology* 56: 327–353.

Gowaty, P.A. 1997. 'Sexual Dialectics, Sexual Selection, and Variation in Mating Behavior', in P.A. Gowaty (ed.) *Feminism and Evolutionary Biology: Boundaries, Intersections, and Frontiers.* New York: Chapman & Hall, pp. 351–384.

Graeber, D. 2004. *Fragments of an Anarchist Anthropology.* Chicago: Prickly Paradigm Press.

———. 2011. *Revolutions in Reverse.* New York: Minor Compositions.

Haraway, Donna. 1989. *Primate Visions: Gender, Race and Nature in the World of Modern Science.* New York and London: Routledge.

Harris, M. 1969. *The Rise of Anthropological Theory.* London: Routledge.

Hawkes, K. et al. 1998. 'Grandmothering, Menopause, and the Evolution of Human Life Histories', *Proceedings of the National Academy of Sciences* 95: 1336–1339.

Henshilwood, C.S. and F. d'Errico. 2011. *Homo Symbolicus.* Amsterdam: John Benjamins.

Hewlett, B.S. and M.E. Lamb (eds). 2005. *Hunter-gatherer Childhoods.* New Brunswick, NJ: Transaction.

Hill, K. et al. 2011. 'Co-Residence Patterns in Hunter-Gatherer Societies Show Unique Human Social Structure', *Science* 331: 1286–1289.

Holden, C.J., R. Sear and R. Mace. 2003. 'Matriliny as Daughter-biased Investment', *Evolution and Human Behavior* 24: 99–112.

Hrdy, Sarah Blaffer. 1981. *The Woman that Never Evolved.* Cambridge, MA: Harvard University Press.

———. 2009. *Mothers and Others: the Evolutionary Origins of Mutual Understanding.* Cambridge, MA: Belknap Press of Harvard University Press.

Hughes, A. 1981. *Evolution and Human Kinship.* Oxford: Oxford University Press.

Ingold, Tim. 2007. 'The Trouble with "Evolutionary Biology"', *Anthropology Today* 23: 13–17.

Isler, K. and C. van Schaik. 2012. 'How our Ancestors Broke through the Gray Ceiling: Comparative Evidence for Cooperative Breeding in early *Homo*', *Current Anthropology* 53, S6, Human biology and the origins of *Homo* (December): S453–S465.

Katz, R. 1982. *Boiling Energy. Community Healing among the Kalahari Kung.* Cambridge, MA: Harvard University Press.

Keeney, B. and H. Keeney. 2013. 'Reentry into First Creation: A Contextual Frame for the Ju/'hoan Bushman Performance of Puberty Rites, Storytelling, and Healing Dance', *Journal of Anthropological Research* 69: 65–86.

Key, C.A. and L.C. Aiello. 1999. 'The Evolution of Social Organisation', in R.I.M. Dunbar, C. Knight and C. Power (eds), *The Evolution of Culture.* Edinburgh: Edinburgh University Press, pp. 15–33.

Knight, C. 1991. *Blood Relations. Menstruation and the Origins of Culture.* New Haven and London: Yale University Press.

———. 2008. 'Early Human Kinship was Matrilineal', in N.J. Allen et al. (eds), *Early Human Kinship: From Sex to Social Reproduction.* Oxford: Blackwell Publishing Ltd, pp. 61–82.

——— and J. Lewis. 2014. 'Vocal Deception, Laughter and the Linguistic Significance of Reverse Dominance', in D. Dor, C. Knight and J. Lewis (eds), *Social Origins of Language.* Oxford: Oxford University Press, pp. 297–314.

——— and C. Power. 2005. 'Grandmothers, Politics, and Getting back to Science', in E. Voland, A. Chasiotis and W. Schienfenhövel (eds), *Grandmotherhood.* New Brunswick, NJ: Rutgers, pp. 81–98.

Kramer, K.L. and E. Otárola-Castillo. 2015. 'When Mothers Need Others. Life History Transitions Associated with the Evolution of Cooperative Breeding', *Journal of Human Evolution* 84: 16–24.

Kuper, A. and J. Marks. 2011. 'Anthropologists Unite!', *Nature* 470: 166–168.

Lakoff, G. and M. Johnson. 1980. *Metaphors We Live By.* Chicago: University of Chicago Press.

Leacock, E.B. 1978. 'Women's Status in Egalitarian Society: Implications for Social Evolution', *Current Anthropology* 19: 247–275.

Lee, R.B. and I. DeVore (eds). 1968. *Man the Hunter.* Chicago: Aldine.

Lévi-Strauss, C. 1968. 'The Concept of Primitiveness', in R.B. Lee and I. DeVore (eds), *Man the Hunter.* Chicago: Aldine, pp. 349–352.

Lewis, J. 2002. 'Forest Hunter-Gatherers and Their World', PhD dissertation. London: University of London.

Mauss, M. and H. Beuchat. 1979 [1904–1905]. *Seasonal Variations of the Eskimo: a Study in Social Morphology.* London: Routledge & Kegan Paul.

Maynard Smith, J. and E. Szathmáry. 1995. *The Major Transitions in Evolution.* Oxford: Freeman.

McCreedy, M. 1994. 'The Arms of the Dibouka', in E. Burch and L. Ellanna (eds), *Key Issues in Hunter-Gatherer Research.* Oxford: Berg, pp. 15–34.

Mellars, P. et al. (eds). 2007. *Rethinking the Human Revolution: New Behavioural and Biological Perspectives on the Origin and Dispersal of Modern Humans.* Cambridge: McDonald Institute.

Mithen, S. 1996. *The Prehistory of the Mind.* London: Thames and Hudson.

———. 2006. 'Ethnobiology and the Evolution of the Human Mind', in R. Ellen (ed.), *Ethnobiology and the Science of Humankind.* Blackwell: Oxford, pp. 55–75.

Morgan, L.H. 1871. *Systems of Consanguinity and Affinity.* Washington, D.C.: Smithsonian Institution.

———. 1877. *Ancient Society.* New York: Henry Holt.

O'Connell, J.F., K. Hawkes and N.G. Blurton Jones. 1999. 'Grandmothering and the Evolution of *Homo erectus*', *Journal of Human Evolution* 36: 461–485.

Pinker, S. 2011. *The Better Angels of our Nature*. New York: Viking.

Rappaport, R.A. 1979. *Ecology, Meaning, and Religion*. Berkeley, CA: North Atlantic Books.

———. 1999. *Ritual and Religion in the Making of Humanity*. Cambridge: Cambridge University Press

Rosaldo, M.Z. and L. Lamphere (eds). 1974. *Woman, Culture and Society*. Stanford, CA: Stanford University Press.

Sacks, K. 1975. 'Engels Revisited: Women, the Organisation of Production, and Private Property', in R. Reiter (ed.), *Toward an Anthropology of Women*. London: Monthly Review Press, pp. 211–234.

Sahlins, Marshall. 1977 [1976]. *The Use and Abuse of Biology: An Anthropological Critique of Sociobiology*. London: Tavistock.

Segerstråle, Ullica. 2000. *Defenders of the Truth. The Battle for Truth in the Sociobiology Debate and Beyond*. Oxford: Oxford University Press.

Service, E. 1962. *Primitive Social Organization: an Evolutionary Perspective*. New York: Random House.

Sosis, R. and C Alcorta. 2003. 'Signaling, Solidarity, and the Sacred: The Evolution of Religious Behavior', *Evolutionary Anthropology* 12: 264–274.

Sperber, D. and D. Wilson. 1995. *Relevance: Communication and Cognition*. Oxford: Blackwell.

Testart, A. 1988. 'Some Major Problems in the Social Anthropology of Hunter-gatherers', *Current Anthropology* 29: 1–31.

Tomasello, M. et al. 2012. 'Two Key Steps in the Evolution of Human Cooperation: The Interdependence Hypothesis', *Current Anthropology* 53(6): 673–692.

Trivers, R.L. 1985. *Social Evolution*. Menlo Park, CA: Benjamin/Cummings.

van den Berghe, Pierre L. 1979. *Human Family Systems: An Evolutionary View*. New York: Elsevier.

Verdu, P. and F. Austerlitz. 2015. 'Post-Marital Residence Behaviours Shape Genetic Variation in Hunter-gatherer and Agricultural Populations from Central Africa', *Hunter Gatherer Research* 1(1): 107–124.

Watts, I. 2014. 'The Red Thread: Pigment Use and the Evolution of Collective Ritual', in D. Dor, C. Knight and J. Lewis (eds), *The Social Origins of Language*. Oxford: Oxford University Press, pp. 208–227.

———, M. Chazan and J. Wilkins. 2016. 'Early Evidence for Brilliant Ritualized Display: Specularite Use in the Northern Cape (South Africa) Between ~500 ka and ~300 ka', *Current Anthropology* 57(3): 287–310: doi: 10.1086/686484

Wengrow, D. and D. Graeber. 2015. 'Farewell to the "Childhood of Man": Ritual, Seasonality, and the Origins of Inequality', *Journal of the Royal Anthropological Institute* 21: 597–619.

Whiten, A. and D. Erdal. 2012. 'The Human Socio-cognitive Niche and its Evolutionary Origins', *Philosophical Transactions of the Royal Society B* 367: 2119–2129. doi:10.1098/rstb.2012.0114.

Wiessner, P.W. 2014. 'Embers of Society: Firelight Talk among the Ju/'hoansi Bushmen', *Proceedings of the National Academy of Sciences* 111: 14027–14035. doi: 10.1073/pnas.1404212111

Wrangham, R.W. 1999. 'Evolution of Coalitionary Killing', *Yearbook of Physical Anthropology* 42: 1–30.

———. 2009. *Catching Fire: How Cooking Made us Human.* New York: Basic Books.

Zahavi, A. and A. Zahavi. 1997. *The Handicap Principle. A Missing Piece in Darwin's Puzzle.* New York and Oxford: Oxford University Press.

Camilla Power is Senior Lecturer in Anthropology at the University of East London. Her research has focused on the evolutionary emergence of symbolic culture, language, art and religion. She has published numerous articles on hunter-gatherer cosmology, gender ritual and rock art, and co-edited *The Evolution of Culture* (1999, Edinburgh University Press).

Morna Finnegan is an independent researcher who has published on the sexual egalitarianism of Central African hunter-gatherers. Her writing has focused on the relationship between ritual and political domains, and on BaYaka women's dance collectives as structuring principles. She gained her doctorate from the University of Edinburgh in 2010.

Hilary Callan is Director Emerita of the Royal Anthropological Institute, having served as Director from 2000 to 2010. She has held various academic positions in anthropology and international education. In addition to single-authored publications including *Ethology and Society: Towards an Anthropological View* (1970, Oxford University Press), she has co-edited *The Incorporated Wife* (1984, Croom Helm), *Early Human Kinship* (2008, Blackwell), and *Introductory Readings in Anthropology* (2013, Berghahn). She is Editor-in-Chief of the *International Encyclopedia of Anthropology*, scheduled for publication by Wiley-Blackwell in 2018.

Chapter 1

FORTY YEARS ON

BIOSOCIAL ANTHROPOLOGY REVISITED

Hilary Callan

Introduction

Recent years have seen a tendency for discussions of social anthropology and human origins to take place in a somewhat ahistorical conceptual space: a space in which the subdisciplines encounter one another in a timeless theoretical present; even, one might almost say, an 'ethnographic present'. This is not to deny that model-makers have made abundant reference to preceding literatures; the opposite is of course the case. Rather, in some cases, totalizing claims about the biological roots of culture have been made in isolation from the historical contexts in which the claims themselves are embedded. This is an irony of course, as we are dealing with inherently historical questions about the human past and present. A parallel tendency has been to conduct the academic exchanges in an asocial *conceptual* space, in which the cultural embeddedness of the theorizing itself is ignored or played down. Recent work has broken away from this pattern to some extent (see e.g. Allen et al. 2008); and other chapters in this volume share a renewed attention to our founding figures, and the deeper history of ideas within anthropology. This chapter has a complementary aim. Using a case study, I set out to locate the debates on anthropology and human origins within a continuing flow of ideas; and specifically within a history and anthropology of representations and imageries.

A Case Study: *Biosocial Anthropology*

As a convenient anchoring moment I take the publication in 1975 of *Biosocial Anthropology* edited by Robin Fox, with papers delivered at the 1973 Decennial Conference of the Association of Social Anthropologists of the United Kingdom and Commonwealth (ASA) on the theme 'New Directions in Social Anthropology'.[1] The individual chapters in this collection have had, in terms of their content, very diverse receptions and impacts on later developments in the field. For the purpose of this chapter, however, my concern is less with content than with context: to place *Biosocial Anthropology* within a nexus of transactions going on at that time and since.

Transactions: Conversations and Trading Zones

Biosocial Anthropology is itself an intentionally cross-disciplinary exercise, with contributions from anthropology (Robin Fox), sociology (Lionel Tiger), behavioural biology (Norbert Bischof), primatology (Michael Chance), ethology (Nicholas Blurton Jones) and evolutionary genetics (W.D. Hamilton). For the purpose of this chapter I shall focus on just three of these: those of Blurton Jones, Hamilton and Fox, which seem with hindsight to fit within distinct strands of theory and research that led later in somewhat different directions. Taken as a whole, the collection presents one snapshot or transect of that moment's thinking about how social anthropology could and should take account of the biological in relation to human society. The converse relationship was not seen at the time as focal: an asymmetry that has continued up to the present. The contributions reflect, as one would expect, the predominant themes of the academic writing of the time, what was known empirically, and the literatures and research communities in which they were embedded. Less obviously, I suggest, several of them derive persuasive force from, and in turn inform, a hinterland of more public vocabularies and ways of thinking about the world. Thus we are dealing with 'conversations' of more than one kind: across disciplines and subdisciplines certainly, but also between academic, and the many domains of public, discourses. And this is likely to be generally true of encounters across schools of thought at other times and contexts, in respect of questions as fundamental (and perennially fascinating) as the nature of the human. In a previous paper (Callan 2008: 257), I called up the image of 'trading zones', originally put forward in a different context (Mills and Huber 2005) as an apt one to describe how images and organizing constructs may travel back and forth, often unrecognized, across ostensibly different spheres. I suggested that this idea could encourage a 'flexible articulation between traditions and discourses', and that 'such play in the system ... could allow vocabularies and [representations] to slide across one another in mutually enlightening ways, without being reductively ... locked together'. Here, using *Biosocial Anthropology* as a case study, I want to argue that this 'trading relationship', while it may only recently have come to theoretical attention, has been going on – sometimes on the surface but more often tacitly – over a long period.

Transactions: Disciplinary Boundaries and Territories

A recurring theme in the traffic in ideas leading up to, and following, *Biosocial Anthropology*, is one of negotiation over the boundaries between (broadly) Darwinian and (broadly) superorganic approaches to the human: a negotiation whose terms have themselves altered in line with successive shifts of emphasis within each area. At its crudest, this relationship has sometimes been framed as an attempt at takeover or colonization of social and human science within a Darwinian or neo-Darwinian synthesis,[2] and the many resistances that this perceived colonization has provoked. But the engagement has not always been as confrontational as these battles would suggest, and there have been undercurrents throughout of a more open and mutually receptive kind (see e.g. Barkow and Silverberg 1980). Most recently, some of the undercurrents have become overcurrents, now firmly established in the mainstream. A good example is the British Academy's Centenary project *From Lucy to Language: The Archaeology of the Social Brain* (Gamble, Gowlett and Dunbar 2014; see also James, this volume).

Transactions: the Academic and the Popular

In one sense 'academic' and 'popular' are terms of art, lacking precise application. But at a different level they do point to something real, at least for anthropology. Thus we have a debate going on now about the rights and wrongs of 'popularizing' the discipline (McClancy and McDonaugh 1996); and Thomas Eriksen's *Engaging Anthropology: the Case for a Public Presence* (2006) has had an enduring resonance. But questions about an evolutionary dimension to the human condition

– and whether this dimension is important for our contemporary self-understanding – have been a matter of intense public interest at least as far back as the reception of Darwin's *Origin of Species* and *The Descent of Man*. The debates among specialists have taken place within – and to a greater or lesser extent been coloured by – the ebbs and flows of far broader public concerns.

Biosocial Anthropology did not itself find a large general readership, so far as I am aware. But it is positioned historically within a broad, as well as a narrow, environment of thought. It appeared a few years after a cluster of works that appealed to general readers as well as specialists, and that put forward in different ways the case for an evolution-based interpretation of what were claimed to be universals of human life. The best-known English-language examples from the time are Konrad Lorenz's *On Aggression* (1966, translated from the original German), Tiger and Fox's *The Imperial Animal* (1971) and Tiger's *Men in Groups* (1969); but there were others, such as Tiger's somewhat later *Optimism: the Biology of Hope* (1979), and works further along the scale of populism by authors such as Robert Ardrey, a playwright (1966, 1970), and Desmond Morris (1967, 1969, 1971, 1977). Both Lorenz and Morris were prominent scientific ethologists in the classical tradition who believed that the discoveries coming from ethology about the evolution of behaviour could be applied directly and sweepingly to the contemporary human condition. Their books for a general audience were written in a lively, gripping way, while appealing to the authority of science to make grand claims about our 'animal nature'. But at many points the very constructions of animality, from which these claims were drawn, already enshrined particular models, sometimes unconsciously held, of the human societies the writers inhabited and took for granted. Not surprisingly, the grand claims were widely taken up by the popular media of the time and by some more serious cultural commentators, who saw the findings of animal studies as models – and sometimes as moral lessons – for ourselves. Comments on what we might call this spiral of representations were made at the time; and my own *Ethology and Society* (1970) was an early attempt to map these debates and to highlight the reciprocal trade in images on which they substantially rested.

For a time at least, some of these authors attained the standing of public intellectuals in the English-speaking world. But there was also opposition. In the case of Lorenz, an early association with National Socialism – which he came to regret – was widely cited against him during the 1970s and 1980s. This made Lorenz a suspect figure in the eyes of many on the (broadly speaking) academic and political left, contributing to a widespread feeling among many intellectuals around this time that to be a bona-fide social progressive, you had to reject out of hand *any* evolutionary component to an understanding of the human condition. Critical feminist scholarship at the time, much of which rightly challenged the 'hunting model' as sole driver of early human evolution, also contributed to a wholesale rejection of biologically influenced models of human nature, all of which feminist critics tended to lump together under the fatalist anti-slogan that 'biology is destiny'. Lorenz himself was not a particular target of these critiques, but others among the public intellectuals prominent at the time, such as Tiger, Fox, and Dawkins a little later, certainly were. Later in this chapter I shall return to the positioning of the 'public intellectual' more generally.

Shifting Perspectives: Gender

These debates have of course continued, and gender offers a particularly revealing case of the interplay of academic vision with surrounding currents of social and political thought. Looking back to the period in question it is fairly easy to see how deeply unrecognized observational biases within the science, as much as gendered assumptions inscribed in the grand theories of human nature that were based on it, contributed to the skewed models of both animal and human social structure that drew justified feminist criticism (cf Callan 1978). In these models, by default, agency was largely seen as definitionally male, and male interest was taken to be the driving evolutionary force in areas such as dominance, aggression and competition, social control, coalition, hunting and sex. Thus the nonhuman primate studies available at the time, on which the public intellectuals mainly rested their case about the evolutionary drivers of the human condition, were ones in which the observers in field or zoo had already taken for granted that male behaviour and inter-male relations were the primary object of study. Such assumptions were faithfully reproduced in the hunting-led models of early human life that were current through this period.[3]

A later generation of – often female – primatologists and theorists of human evolution, such as Sarah Blaffer Hrdy (*The Woman that Never Evolved*, 1981; and see her later *Mothers and Others*, 2009) and Nancy Tanner (*On Becoming Human*, 1981), brought a strong corrective voice to these early gendered biases of observation and interpretation. Once again, this counter-narrative had a popular counterpart in works such as Elaine Morgan's lively *The Descent of Woman* (1972). And, of course, the subsequent literature – including, notably, Hrdy's continuing work (2009) – has been both massive and rich in gender-inclusive evolutionary models incorporating female as well as male agency, reproductive strategy, and their significance for our understanding of human origins. Donna Haraway's *Primate Visions* (1989) marked a critical moment in this shift. Other scholars such as Small (1995) and Gowaty (1997) – like Hrdy, also coming from evolutionary theory - have further aligned the logic of Darwinian selection with a feminist spotlight on female strategies and choices, and in doing so have added immensely to our understanding of human evolution, gender and kinship. Here, space limitation makes it impossible to give recognition to the many contemporary scholars whose work has illuminated this area over the past two decades. Suffice it to note that co-operative childcare, female coalitions, counter-dominance, concealed ovulation and helpful grandmothers, topics which encompass female as well as male socio-reproductive interests and strategies, have come increasingly to the fore in models of 'becoming human'.[4] Finnegan (this volume) offers a persuasive discussion of how this latter-day theorizing is bearing fruit for our contemporary understanding of human origins; see also Knight and Lewis, this volume; and Watts, this volume.

Yet it is still worth looking back at the hinterland of thinking around the moment of publication of *Biosocial Anthropology*, exhibiting as it does the multidirectional travel of images and assumptions across the supposedly objective conduct of scientific studies; the often unconscious social assumptions that went into the science; and the grand theories of human nature that were then circularly derived from it. Nor is this interplay of representations necessarily confined to the intellectual moment at issue here. It would not be surprising to find a comparable pattern present in contemporary models of the 'biology of human nature' – but perhaps we will have to wait another forty years for it to become as visible.

Avoiding Grand Claims: Ethology and Human Ethology

Returning to classical ethology and its connections to social thought around the time in question, we can discern three strands of influence, which were in practice closely interwoven in the writings of the period. The first was the rise to broad academic notice (particularly in Europe) of scientific ethology, which had its origins much earlier in the century, and had come to be seen as a naturalistic corrective to the more doctrinaire forms of behaviourism coming from the US. The second was a more inchoate set of assumptions surrounding the kinds of truth – and reality about the human condition – that ethology might yield. Overarching these was, once again, the 'public voice' in which, alongside their professional works, many of the most influential figures of the period also wrote.

From the 1960s onward, a cautious view of the discipline and its human implications came from ethologists such as Robert Hinde in Britain (Hinde 1982), the Austrian Irenäus Eibl-Eibesfeldt, whose writings first appeared mainly in German with a few in English (Eibl-Eibesfeldt 1979), and Lorenz's Dutch colleague Nikolaas Tinbergen. The latter, despite sharing the 1973 Nobel Prize for Physiology or Medicine with Lorenz (and also with Karl von Frisch) had for a time a slightly strained personal relationship with him, having himself faced difficult conditions in Nazi-occupied Holland. Tinbergen held a post-war Chair at Oxford, where he nurtured a generation of European (mainly British and Dutch) ethologists rigorously schooled in the zoological tradition. He and his students avoided in the main grand claims about humanity. They argued that the value of ethology for human studies lay in its insistence on careful observation of behaviour in naturalistic (as distinct from controlled laboratory) settings, under the guidance of fundamental evolutionary questions about the causation, phylogeny, ontogeny and evolutionary function of what is observed. Tinbergen himself wrote for general readers as well as specialists – as also has Eibl-Eibesfeldt (1971). Through that conversation, Tinbergen in particular did much to stimulate public interest in the evolutionary science of behaviour while remaining personally wary, in contrast to the more 'prophetic' style of some contemporaries, of grand theories of human nature (Tinbergen, pers. comm. to me, c.1962). His *The Study of Instinct* (1951) has remained a landmark scientific work, while his *Curious Naturalists* (1958) achieved lasting popularity, and was republished in paperback in 1984.

Some of these younger scholars, together with Eibl-Eibesfeldt and his students in Austria and Germany, went on to adapt the observational methods of classical ethology to the study of people. They were among the pioneers of a movement, beginning in the late 1960s, to establish human ethology as a legitimate subdiscipline within scientific ethology, itself a branch of zoology (see e.g. von Cranach et al. 1979).

Yet again, there was a conspicuously populist end to this, exemplified in a series of works by Desmond Morris appealing to a popular imagination: *The Human Zoo* (1969); *Intimate Behaviour* (1971); *Manwatching: A Field Guide to Human Behaviour* (1977) (a revealing title in itself) and many others, together with some much-viewed television programmes. And in contrast to the cautious stance of most scientific ethologists of the time, these more popular works have in common a (sometimes tacit but often explicit) claim to touch a deeper and truer reality about ourselves than is reached through the interpretative methods of the humanities – or indeed through ordinary human self-reflection. In other words, much of the popular writing of this period enshrines an implied or expressed claim that we can know 'truer truths' about people from what we can 'see' them doing using the methods of natural history, than from what they or others say or think they do.

Writing in a scientific mode, the human ethologists of the time did not on the whole make such claims explicitly; their aims were more modest. However, human linguistic competence and capacity for conscious self-reflection made for complications at the scientific end of human ethology as well. Thus it is noticeable that the human ethology of this period frequently relied on pre-school children and psychiatric patients as subjects (see e.g. Chance and Larsen 1976; Grant 1972).[5] While a clinical concern about the growth (and sometimes the failure) of 'attachment' was a strong rationale for the ethological study of human infants, it was also true that both they and psychiatric patients could be seen implicitly as incomplete persons, more revealing of a biologically inscribed 'nature' than are fully functioning human adults. Alongside this, whether dealing with 'full', 'incomplete' or 'impaired' persons, human ethologists frequently relied on methodologies such as very fast frame-by-frame recording of slices of behaviour ('leakage') thought to be too quick to come under conscious awareness or control (Birdwhistell 1970; Ekman 1979) and therefore, by implication, closer to the 'natural' than behaviour that can be consciously known and talked about. Of course, the belief in 'leakage' as the truest cue to a person's 'real' state of mind, detectable by appropriate training or technology, is still firmly entrenched in public discourse, as well as in management and forensic practices – as demonstrated in innumerable 'revelatory' TV programmes and interview manuals today. Leakage has itself leaked across the scientific/popular boundary. And 'finding the mind's construction in the face' is a motif that already has deep roots in European cultural history.

In this way, it can be argued, despite scientific cautions and disclaimers, some of the human ethology prominent during the period in question succeeded in bypassing by default what is actually most human in the human condition. As S.L. Washburn remarked at the time, '*Human ethology might be defined as the science that pretends humans cannot speak* .... [A] rich study of *human behaviour must start off with human beings*; otherwise, critical behaviours are lost. Human ethology is an extreme example of a science not adjusting to uniquely human problems' (Washburn 1980: 273, author's emphasis).[6] And the implied claim to reveal a deeper truth (or to reach what would once have been understood as 'the natural man'), made strongly or weakly across the spectrum of rigorous and popular science of the time, threads forward rather clearly into the more abrasive claims to privileged knowledge about the 'true' motors of human action that were made later, within what came to be called human sociobiology.

The Tinbergen Legacy: Blurton Jones

But this did not happen everywhere. The generation of scholars who studied under Tinbergen, and went on to apply the guiding principles of ethology to people, is well represented in *Biosocial Anthropology* by Nicholas Blurton Jones. His chapter 'Ethology, anthropology and childhood', falls squarely within the observational tradition laid down by Tinbergen and others. But unlike some of the research in human ethology going on elsewhere at the time, neither here nor in Blurton Jones's later work (see e.g. Blurton Jones 1993) do we find particular reliance, even implied, on the notion of children as 'closer to nature' than other human persons. Instead, we find a clear developmental perspective on the recording of child behaviour, as well as a closely argued rationale for the value of ethological methods in illuminating areas of sameness and difference across cultures.

Along the way, Blurton Jones comments perceptively on what he sees at that moment as a tense relationship between biologists and anthropologists, which he compares unfavourably to what he sees as a growing *rapprochement* between biologists and psychologists. He attributes this contrast to differences in what biologists were then offering to psychology and to anthropology respectively: 'Ethologists and psychologists are getting together primarily about methods, and to a lesser extent about theories and data on development of behaviour. Ethologists and anthropologists have met on the more complex issues of man-animal comparisons, and the implications of the evolutionary history of human behaviour' (1975: 69). This caution notwith-standing, Blurton Jones's own work and that of anthropologists he works with and cites, such as Melvin Konner (see e.g. Konner 2010, and other references cited in Hrdy 2009), demonstrate that real conversations were happening both at that time and since, grounded in observational methods, between ethologists and anthropologists interested in cross-cultural comparison, parent-child interactions, and child development. These conversations have continued up to the present; and I suggest that, unlike some of the more reductionist work going on at the time, the representations of the human which they enshrine sit comfortably alongside parallel developments within social anthropology, in which children have increasingly come to be seen as social actors and full persons in their own right (see e.g. James 1993; Montgomery 2008). I further suggest that in the context of the present book's overall aim, these conversations between human ethology and ethnography in the area of childhood and childcare have a solid and specific contribution to make to our understanding of human origins (see e.g. Hrdy 2009).

For an anthropologist – and perhaps also for biologists – revisiting Blurton Jones's 1975 essay now is a particularly revealing exercise, and, I would argue, a demonstration of the ethological approach at its best. His dissection of the kinds of knowledge that ethological methods can contribute to understanding cultural universality and diversity points to issues that remain topical today. His critique of large categories of explanation such as 'aggression' or 'generosity' (read 'altruism') is an effective counter to the sweeping claims about human nature made by other writers then and since. And his assessment of features common to ethology in the classical mould and anthropology – such as respect for an inductive approach in both domains – proffers a scenario of *conversationality* across porous disciplinary boundaries that equates to what I call 'trading zones' above, and stands in deep contrast to the confrontations that drew rather more noise and fury.

Metaphors, Representations and Polemics

Biosocial Anthropology appeared the year before Richard Dawkins' *The Selfish Gene* (1976) which, partly through the power of brilliant writing, precipitated the debate on genes and human nature into the public imagination in new ways throughout the English-speaking world. As a writer and polemicist, Dawkins is, of course, a key figure now in the trade in representations across domains of academic and public culture. I leave aside here his stature as a public spokesman for the 'new atheism' in the current wars of religion and the narrative imagination, and the sometimes shifting positions he has taken on whether the proposition that 'we' are the unwitting dupes of 'our' selfish genes is an elaborated analogy or a claim of substance. Of interest for this discussion is how the 'meme' concept has travelled since he first introduced it at the end of *The Selfish Gene*. At that moment, the 'meme' as a unit of cognition carried a poetic resonance with other linguistic tropes in circulation: emic/etic, phonemic/phonetic, and so forth, and the word was evidently chosen for that very resonance. Travelling rapidly into academic discourses, in the works of authors such as Susan Blackmore (1999), as a fully-fledged theory of reality, it drew controversy and intellectual opposition from many within social anthropology who have pointed out that the ontological status of the meme is thoroughly obscure.[7] It remains a contested construct. At the same time, and fuelled by the popular writings of the meme theorists, the meme travelled equally quickly into the public imagination – its rhetorical power helped along by sub-imageries derived from people's knowledge of epidemiology: 'viruses of the mind' and the like. While memes were embraced by some as a new kind of fundamental entity, and 'memetics' as a new science analogous to 'phonetics', this picture may again be shifting. My impression is that in the journalism of today, the meme construct has largely turned quieter, usually appearing now as quite a light term interchangeable with 'idea'.

Memes may be the most spectacular, but are not the only constructs within the biosocial field to have travelled this route across scientific and public landscapes in recent times. Taking a history-of-ideas view, the best parallel I can think of is 'pecking order'. This had its origins in early ethology, in the work of Schjelderup-Ebbe (in his 1921 doctoral thesis, unpublished) on domestic chickens. The term, and the concept, were rapidly absorbed into scientific ethology and incorporated into methodologies and theories of dominance in many species. At the same time, like memes, and carried by the power of vivid popular writing, pecking orders too soon became and remain part of a widely available folk lexicon, in English at least.

Hamilton, Evolutionary Genetics and the Language of 'Sociobiology'

Biosocial Anthropology also appeared in the same year as the first edition of Edward Wilson's monumental *Sociobiology: the New Synthesis* (1975) whose final chapter 'Man: from sociobiology to sociology' notoriously heralded what later acquired the character of a culture war in public as well as academic spaces. Wilson himself is referenced only peripherally in *Biosocial Anthropology*, and Dawkins not at all, although their ideas were clearly very much in circulation as the conference session – and later the book – took shape.[8] W.D. Hamilton's chapter on 'Innate social aptitudes of man: an approach from evolutionary genetics' sets out the ground of his transformative kin-selection model, as well as positing some applications of that model in human evolution. While the thrust of Hamilton's thesis is mathematical, here too it is worth noticing the hinterland of ideas on which the argument also draws. For example, amid the huge impact of the kin-selection model within biology, and the controversies surrounding some of the human claims that were drawn from it (Sahlins 1976), it is easy to overlook the fact that in *Biosocial Anthropology* Hamilton himself appeals to contemporary ideologies to account for the long persistence of group-selection arguments within evolutionary theory:

> With facts mostly neutral and theory silent it seems that we must look to the events and 'isms' of recent human history to understand how such a situation arose. Marxism, trade unionism, fears of 'social Darwinism', and vicissitudes of thought during two world wars seem likely influences. ... [N]atural selection is easily accused of divisive and reactionary implications unless 'fittest' means the fittest species (man) and 'struggle' means struggle against nature (anything but man). 'Benefit-of-the-species' arguments, so freely used during the period in question, are seen in this light as euphemisms for natural selection. They provide for the reader (and evidently often for the writer as well) an escape from inner conflict, exacting nothing emotionally beyond what most of us learn to accept in childhood, that most forms of life exploit and prey on one another. (1975: 135)

I find this observation of Hamilton's revealing, exposing as it does a tension in both the scientific and public imaginations at the time, between the idealized representations of nature offered by some of the public intellectuals I referred to above, and the contradictory one of 'nature red in tooth and claw' which is known to have disturbed Darwin profoundly – although the phrase is actually from Tennyson (*In Memoriam*, 1849). The Enlightenment and opposing Hobbesian visions of the 'state of nature' once again cast long shadows here. More immediately, Hamilton offers an account of early human warfare, and its selective advantages in the short but not the long term, into which I think we can read something of the Cold War anxieties of the time.[9]

Hamilton was of course a founding figure, and his celebrated Rule, together with Trivers' parallel models of reciprocal altruism and parent-offspring conflict (1971, 1972), were pillars of what came to be known as sociobiology. But 'sociobiology' itself was and is a term carrying a great deal of definitional slippage, as I argued in an article published in 1984. At that time and for some writers, sociobiology was taken to include the human within an all-encompassing neo-Darwinian synthesis; while for others it was not. There were also broad and narrow conceptions of what was covered under the label of 'sociobiology', whether or not claims were made to include the human in its scope. Much of this variation came to be ignored or obscured, amid the controversies that quickly erupted.[10] In the aforementioned 1984 article, written when the battles over human applications of sociobiology were at their height, I argued that metaphors of choice, strategy, costs, payoffs and the like – encapsulated in the requisitioning of von Neumann's mathematical theory of games such as Prisoner's Dilemma – played a constitutive, not just a decorative, role in the claims made by sociobiologists to offer a consistent new paradigm. Areas of indistinctness in the grounding concepts, I suggested, were given a misleading coherence by fluency in the language:

> [U]ndisciplined imagery, rather than consciously held ideology, has been responsible for much that critics have found morally and politically objectionable in sociobiology. This applies particularly to the apparently reductionist and fatalist implications of sociobiology for man. If our genes are represented as exercizing 'choice' in an imprecise metaphoric sense, it can more easily look as if 'we' don't. Where 'we' are vividly but wildly cast as mere tools of our DNA, our sociability both created and limited by 'strategies' of genetic self-interest, people can easily find themselves locked by the metaphor's own power into a position which seems to deny the reality and authority of human choice. ... The trap is an artefact of language, but it is not easily unsprung where the energizing metaphor itself remains inchoate. (Callan 1984: 413)

Part of the mix, here again, were semi-popular book titles and cover designs (powerful visual imagery) that carried with them a seductive whiff of fatalism, as in *Sociobiology: The Whisperings Within* (Barash 1979).

In trying to map the situation as it appeared at that particular moment, I suggested that we should move away from 'a restricted conception of [sociobiology] as defined by its own formulation of its subject matter (the systematic study of the biological basis of all social behaviour) ... [and] ... view it instead as an emergent blend of community and practice, which is coming to have its own sub-histor[ies], subculture[s] and array of platforms and publics' (ibid: 414).

In the years since that period, definitions have shifted again and become, if anything, more fluid. The term 'sociobiology' has filtered into some parts of public consciousness as code for particular hardline,

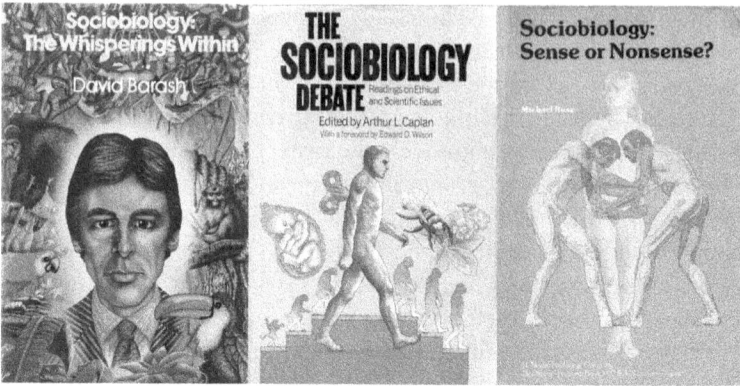

Figure 1.1: These book cover designs speak volumes about the public representation of 'human sociobiology', in works by its supporters and its critics, during the mid- to late 1970s. From left to right: Barash, David, 1979, *Sociobiology: The Whisperings Within*. NY, Harper & Row; Caplan, Arthur (ed.), 1978, *The Sociobiology Debate*. NY, Harper & Row; Ruse, Michael, 1979, *Sociobiology: Sense or Nonsense?* Boston & London, Reidel.

selfish-gene doctrines of the contemporary human condition, while in other places it retains its original, broadly grounded reference to the evolutionary study of the social (Hrdy 2009).[11] The culture wars over 'human sociobiology' have abated somewhat, and newer configurations, such as socioecology and behavioural ecology, have come to the fore. Older versions of 'sociobiology' have morphed into the newer 'evolutionary psychology' with its own community of practice, institutional infrastructure and texts (see e.g. Barrett, Dunbar and Lycett 2002). E.O. Wilson himself has modified his earlier position on gene- and group-level selection and the evolution of altruism (Wilson 2012; see especially p.171ff).[12] Linkages between evolutionary processes and cultural forms are more circumspectly drawn, in the main, by the more recent dual inheritance theorists than by their predecessor sociobiologists; and the (probable) conditions of human evolution in deep time are given a stronger presence as the selection pressures of the past. We hear less of genes 'for' a particular 'trait' arbitrarily lifted from the flow of human action, and more of 'the process of selection [acting] on the organism as a whole and not on genes in isolation' (Barrett, Dunbar and Lycett 2002: 23). Versions of evolutionary psychology can now make non-reductive space for models of cultural evolution and gene-culture co-evolution (Durham 1991, cited in Barrett, Dunbar and Lycett 2002: 372; Mesoudi, Laland

and Whiten 2006). New conversations – not necessarily consensual ones of course – have become possible across the disciplinary divisions. At the same time, the game-theory image and related organizing constructs have been taken forward from early sociobiology, have been elaborated further, and are well entrenched in the evolutionary psychology of today. And, as at earlier moments, some ideas coming from evolutionary science have travelled readily into the public imagination. One of the best up-to-date examples is 'Dunbar's [famous] Number' 150 as the theoretical maximum for human stable social relationships, based on correlations of brain and group sizes in primates and hominins (Dunbar 1993; see also Ellen, this volume). These correlations were germane to the Social Brain construct and the 'Lucy to Language' British Academy project mentioned above (Gamble, Gowlett and Dunbar 2014; James, this volume); but 'Dunbar's Number' has also entranced an impressive public audience.[13]

Kinship and Incest: Fox

Robin Fox's chapter 'Primate kin and human kinship' in *Biosocial Anthropology* fits within a strand that encompasses, of course, his own authoritative *Kinship and Marriage* (1967), *The Red Lamp of Incest* (1980) and many other works, but also reaches forward to later work by others, of which the collection *Early Human Kinship* (Allen et al. 2008) is an example. His point of departure in the chapter is a presumed argument between what he terms 'biosocial' and 'superorganic' approaches, echoing the polarization first set out in his and Tiger's earlier article 'The zoological perspective in social science' (Tiger and Fox 1966) which became a manifesto call for a Darwinian shift in social anthropology. This polarization has certainly persisted in some quarters, as in some of Steven Pinker's work (see for example Pinker 2002); but more nuanced approaches were present at the time and have also since come to the fore. In his *Biosocial Anthropology* chapter, Fox himself quite quickly moves away from a polarizing standpoint to develop a rather more subtle position: that complex structures based on biological kinship exist in nonhuman primates; and that in the transition to a rule-governed human universe, 'even in the absence of cultural rules and the logic of human imagination there would be kinship systems anyway, and that much of the rule-making and imaginative logic is simply (or complexly) playing games with a quite elaborate raw material' (Fox 1975: 10). Fox's central empirical claim in the chapter, based on a summary of what was then known of primate breeding systems, is a bold one: that the characteristically human pattern of kinship organization arose in evolution from putting together elements of 'alliance' and 'descent' found separately, but never together, in nonhuman primates. In the light of the explosive growth in long-term field studies of nonhuman primates happening at the time and later, Fox's claim may now seem an over-interpretation of the data, and his 'never' a hostage to fortune. Yet his core theoretical postulate has proved to be one we can continue to debate to this day: that

> [k]inship groups and the alliances between them are not merely matters of rules, categories, laws, prescriptions, etc. They are more than results of the free play of human imagination. They are embedded in natural processes ... [and] ... are not peculiar to human society. They do not depend for their existence on the equally natural ability to classify and name which characterise our species; in the absence of language and rules, they would still occur. (Fox 1975: 30)

Fast forward to 2008, and the publication of the aforementioned *Early Human Kinship* (Allen et al. 2008): a multidisciplinary volume in which Fox's contribution to the biosocial understanding of kinship is, I now think, under-recognized. His *Kinship and Marriage* and *The Red Lamp of Incest* are referenced and indexed, but not his chapter in *Biosocial Anthropology*. Yet the biosocial questions raised and explored in this 2008 collection, approached from perspectives of biological and social anthropology, primatology, archaeology and historical linguistics, are strikingly consonant with those posed by Fox in *Biosocial Anthropology*. As Wendy James says in her introductory essay to the 2008 volume, 'Why kinship: new questions on an old topic':

> The conversations in this book revolve around the possible ways in which we could re-engage discussion between those coming from the science side, and those from the humanities, on the very important question of how evolutionary theory could or should take account of the *ordered character* of human organization, specifically in respect of how we try to manage patterns of male-female and parent-child relations, and thus the purposeful outcomes of our own reproduction. (James 2008: 3, author's emphasis; see also James, this volume)

In Conclusion: 'Then' and 'Now'

In a review article published in 1977, I questioned the term 'biosocial anthropology'. I suggested then that both the label and the book title conveyed a solidity that was in fact spurious, and that it would be premature to ascribe a settled paradigm to either. *Biosocial Anthropology* the book, I then argued, was 'a good documentation of an incomplete phase in what may yet turn out to be a valuable synthesis of different research areas' (Callan 1977: 112). After almost forty years, I think this judgment still holds, except that the 'incompleteness' will probably prove permanent.

Very clearly, the landscape of research and debate on evolution and the human social world has changed massively in all manner of ways since the publication of *Biosocial Anthropology* in 1975; and I make no attempt to address these changes here. *Biosocial Anthropology* marks a moment of juxtaposition between strands of thought which later took somewhat separate directions. On one view, it might be thought that its content has been largely superseded, even eclipsed, by the noise and fury of later culture wars and by the mass of new knowledge and theory that have accumulated since its publication. I would argue a different case however. Seen with the hindsight of forty years, and notwithstanding the mass of newer knowledge not available at the time, I think *Biosocial Anthropology* stands up well; rather better, I would argue, than some of the approaches that have risen to fashionable prominence between then and now. We can read into it the seeds – or landmarks in the evolution – of a good many of our current concerns and questions. We can also map some of the underground travel of languages and imageries across what are sometimes taken to be disciplinary silos, and across the boundaries of 'scientific' and 'public' imaginations.

New imageries have been, and are being, devised and elaborated in response to new configurations of knowledge, and redrawn understandings of biosocial processes. For example, Lionel Tiger's chapter 'Somatic factors and social behaviour' (not discussed here) in *Biosocial Anthropology* (Tiger 1975) placed heavy reliance on an analogy of 'programs', reflecting no doubt the emerging 'computer-culture' of the mid-1970s. In telling contrast to this static (even deterministic) vision of life, Wendy James has more recently (2003, 2008 and this volume) offered a much more fluid and dynamic set of images around the notions of 'figures in a dance' and 'coming to agreement on the rules of a game'; see also Clive Gamble's metaphor of human emergence as like 'movements' in a symphony, cited in James (this volume). And of course the present chapter, in its appeal to the notions of trading zones and transactions in knowledge, is itself an exercise in image making. Imageries, together with their public resonances, there will unquestionably continue to be in future. The difference perhaps is that we are now able to be more self-conscious and reflexive in our use of them than was possible or easy forty years ago.

The public intellectual remains a liminal figure in the biosocial landscape, as he or she was throughout the period encompassing *Biosocial Anthropology*. As we have seen, those years saw figures such as Lorenz and Morris step beyond the bounds of a particular specialism, and lay claim to the authority of science in support of more universal social diagnoses and prescriptions. The same pattern has been repeated, with variations, many times since, for example by some (not all) sociobiologists, meme theorists, and evolutionary psychologists. Other instances can be found in related fields: see for example Raymond Tallis's powerful critique (2011) of some of the reductionist claims about 'who we are' that have been coming out of neuroscience.[14] At the time of writing (2015) Richard Dawkins is probably the most prominent instance of a public intellectual who has travelled the road from scientific eminence to prophecy in this field. But one conclusion we might draw from the foregoing discussion is that the idea of 'academic' and 'public' spheres as separable domains, which someone could step across, is itself problematic. In any of the fields touching on human origins or the human condition, the scientific and the public are mutually embedded from the start. On this view, then, the public intellectual is someone who does more than merely step outside his or her field of peer-reviewed competence to pronounce on public affairs with the authority of science. Rather, he or she is someone who succeeds – for a while, perhaps – in surfing the infinitely more complex waves, currents, ebbs and flows of scientific *and* popular understandings, and in giving public voice to the result.

In anthropology, amid the many debates going on now about 'popularizing' the subject, we frequently hear regrets about the absence of contemporary public intellectuals since the generations of Malinowski, Mead and Leach. I suggest that it could be just as much the task of anthropology to chart what goes into the emergence of the public intellectual, and the flow of influences across domains in which he or she is multiply enmeshed. And nowhere, surely, might this be more important than in consideration of what it is to be human. A starting-point of the present volume is the question of why social anthropologists have been strangely absent from debates on what made us human. In this chapter I have sought to show that beneath this apparent absence, there lies a deeper story of engagement, disengagement, appropriation, negotiation, poetics and trading of imageries and rhetorics that has a long past, but that we can also begin to locate within a history and an anthropology of ideas of the biosocial, spanning the past half-century and more.

Acknowledgments

I would like to thank Morna Finnegan, Camilla Power and an anonymous reviewer for valuable feedback on drafts of this chapter. I also thank fellow contributors to this collection for helpful advice given during discussions. Responsibility for any errors or omissions is mine.

Notes

1. The 1973 conference did have an explicitly historical frame, clearly brought out by its convenor Edwin Ardener in his general Editor's Note, in which he described the event as in part a stock-taking exercise placed within the ASA's own biography and the rhythm of its Decennials.
2. See for example Dennett's 'universal acid' image (Dennett 1995).
3. Nor was this observational skewing confined to ethology and primatology, as witness Ardener's critique (1972) of some of the functionalist ethnography of the time.
4. A reading of recent literature, written for general audiences as well as specialists, on the 'social brain' and 'co-operative breeding' models of early human origins (Gamble, Gowlett and Dunbar 2014; Hrdy 2009) gives an impression of some disconnection between them. For example, cross-referencing between the above works and their supporting literatures is minimal. This is surely unnecessary, as the models are not mutually incompatible. A deep conversation between them would now seem both informative, and timely.
5. A declaration of interest: between 1968 and 1970 I took part in a project at the University of Birmingham, funded by the then Social Science Research Council, that sought to investigate human homologues of M.R.A. Chance's theory of 'attention structure' as an organizing principle of nonhuman primate societies. Long-tailed macaques (*Macaca fascicularis*) were the subjects of nonhuman observations, while on the human side there was indeed a concentration on psychiatric patients and nursery-school children. Some of this work is described in Chance's chapter in *Biosocial Anthropology* (1975; see also Chance and Larsen 1976). As a young social anthropologist working within a department of human ethology, I had direct experience of the challenge of 'conversing across' discrepant paradigms and frameworks of explanation.
6. I thank Camilla Power for drawing this quotation to my attention.
7. Thus one commentator (Lanier 1999, cited in Aunger 2000: 2) asks 'Are memes a rhetorical technique, a metaphor, a theory, or some other device?' For contrasting examples of the careful use of 'traits' in support of models of early human symbolic life, see Power, this volume.

8. Hamilton's definitive article, setting out the principles of kin selection and his famous 'rule', had appeared some ten years before the publication of *Biosocial Anthropology* (Hamilton 1964).
9. Camilla Power (pers. comm.) has suggested a parallel between the Cold War anxieties colouring biosocial thinking in the 1970s, and contemporary tensions. While there is a persistent tradition in sociobiology and evolutionary psychology to link warfare to the genesis of morality and group solidarity, it is arguable that a focus on warfare in human evolution has been resurrected in the era of the so-called 'war against terror'.
10. Sahlins (1976) is a well-known anthropological critic of the 'harder' versions of the human sociobiology of the period in question. For critical essays written at roughly the same time from the perspectives of other disciplines as well as anthropology, see for example Montagu 1980.
11. For an excellent present-day assessment of sociobiology and its claims with reference to social anthropology, see chapter 8 of Alan Barnard's *Social Anthropology and Human Origins* (Barnard 2011: 128 ff).
12. I thank Emily Flashman for drawing this reference to my attention.
13. Dunbar's own *How Many Friends Does One Person Need?* (2010) has been featured in the *Sunday Times, Daily Telegraph, New York Post* and on the BBC's *Today* programme.
14. There are also many examples of crossover between science and literature, where authors have creatively drawn on the scientific ideas of their time to explore aspects of the human condition but without, on the whole, offering authoritative pronouncements on it. Such restraint has not, of course, stopped others from doing so. Instances abound, from Mary Shelley's day to this. A powerful up-to-the-minute example (at the time of writing) is Tom Stoppard's *The Hard Problem* (2015): a brilliant riff on brain science, Darwinism, game theory, investment banking and morality.

References

Allen, Nicholas J., et al. (eds). 2008. *Early Human Kinship: from Sex to Social Reproduction.* Malden, MA and Oxford: Blackwell.
Ardener, E.W. 1972. 'Belief and the Problem of Women', in J. La Fontaine (ed.), *The Interpretation of Ritual.* London: Tavistock. Reprinted 1975 in S. Ardener (ed.), *Perceiving Women.* London: Malaby, pp. 1–17.
———. 1975. 'General Editor's Note', in R. Fox (ed.), *Biosocial Anthropology.* London: Malaby, pp. ix–xii.
Ardrey, Robert. 1966. *The Territorial Imperative.* London: Collins.
———. 1970. *The Social Contract.* New York: Atheneum.
Aunger, R. 2000. 'Introduction', in R. Aunger (ed.), *Darwinizing Culture.* Oxford: Oxford University Press, pp. 1–24.

Barash, David. 1979. *Sociobiology: The Whisperings Within.* New York: Harper & Row.

Barkow, G. and J. Silverberg (eds). 1980. *Sociobiology: Beyond Nature/Nurture?* Boulder: Westview Press.

Barnard, A. 2011. *Social Anthropology and Human Origins.* Cambridge: Cambridge University Press.

Barrett, Louise, Robin Dunbar and John Lycett. 2002. *Human Evolutionary Psychology.* Basingstoke and New York: Palgrave.

Birdwhistell, R. 1970. *Kinesics and Context: Essays on Body Motion Communication.* Philadelphia: Pennsylvania University Press.

Blackmore, Susan. 1999. *The Meme Machine.* Oxford: Oxford University Press.

Blurton Jones, N. 1975. 'Ethology, Anthropology and Childhood', in R. Fox (ed.), *Biosocial Anthropology.* London: Malaby, pp. 69–92.

———. 1993. 'The Lives of Hunter-gatherer Children', in M. Perreira and L. Fairbanks (eds), *Juvenile Primates.* Oxford and New York: Oxford University Press, pp. 309–326.

Callan, Hilary. 1970. *Ethology and Society: Towards an Anthropological View.* Oxford: Clarendon Press.

———. 1977. 'Biosocial Anthropology: Review Article', *Journal of the Anthropological Society of Oxford* (ISCA Archive).

———. 1978. 'Harems and Overlords: Biosocial Models and the Female', in S. Ardener (ed.), *Defining Females: the Nature of Women in Society.* London: Croom Helm, pp. 200–219.

———. 1984. 'The Imagery of Choice in Sociobiology', *Man* (NS) 19: 404–420.

———. 2008. 'Epilogue: Reaching Across the Gaps', in Nicholas J. Allen et al. (eds), *Early Human Kinship: from Sex to Social Reproduction.* Malden, MA and Oxford: Blackwell, pp. 247–258.

Chance, M.R.A. 1975. 'Social Cohesion and the Structure of Attention', in R. Fox (ed.), *Biosocial Anthropology.* London: Malaby, pp. 93–114.

——— and R. Larsen (eds). 1976. *The Social Structure of Attention.* London and New York: Wiley.

Cranach, M. von, et al. (eds). 1979. *Human Ethology: Claims and Limits of a New Discipline.* Cambridge: Cambridge University Press and Maison des Sciences de l'Homme.

Dawkins, Richard 1976. *The Selfish Gene.* London: Oxford University Press.

Dennett, Daniel C. 1995. *Darwin's Dangerous Idea: Evolution and the Meanings of Life.* New York: Simon & Schuster; republished by Penguin.

Dunbar, R. 1993. 'Coevolution of Neocortical Size, Group Size and Language in Humans', *Behavioural and Brain Sciences* 16: 681–735.

———. 2010. *How Many Friends Does One Person Need?* London: Faber.

Durham, W.H. 1991. *Coevolution: Genes, Culture and Human Diversity.* Stanford: Stanford University Press.

Eibl-Eibesfeldt, I. 1971. *Love and Hate* (translated from the German original, 1970). London: Methuen.

————. 1979. 'Ritual and Ritualization from a Biological Perspective', in M. von Cranach et al. (eds), *Human Ethology: Claims and Limits of a New Discipline*. Cambridge: Cambridge University Press, pp. 3–55.

Ekman, Paul. 1979. 'About Brows: Emotional and Conversational Signals', in M. von Cranach et al. (eds), *Human Ethology: Claims and Limits of a New Discipline*. Cambridge: Cambridge University Press, pp. 169–202.

Eriksen, Thomas Hylland. 2006. *Engaging Anthropology: the Case for a Public Presence*. Oxford and New York: Berg.

Fox, Robin. 1967. *Kinship and Marriage: An Anthropological Perspective*. Harmondsworth and Baltimore: Penguin.

———— (ed.). 1975. *Biosocial Anthropology*. London: Malaby.

————. 1975. 'Primate Kin and Human Kinship', in R. Fox (ed.), *Biosocial Anthropology*. London: Malaby, pp. 9–36.

————. 1980. *The Red Lamp of Incest*. London: Hutchinson.

Gamble, Clive, John Gowlett and Robin Dunbar. 2014. *Thinking Big: How the Evolution of Social Life Shaped the Human Mind*. London: Thames & Hudson.

Gowaty, P.A. (ed.). 1997. *Feminism and Evolutionary Biology: Boundaries, Intersections and Frontiers*. New York: Chapman & Hall.

Grant, E. 1972. 'Non-verbal Communication in the Mentally Ill', in R.A. Hinde (ed.), *Non-verbal Communication*. Cambridge: Cambridge University Press, pp. 349–358.

Hamilton, W.D. 1964. 'The Genetical Evolution of Social Behaviour', *Journal of Theoretical Biology* 7: 1–52.

————. 1975. 'Innate Social Aptitudes of Man: an Approach from Evolutionary Genetics', in R. Fox (ed.), *Biosocial Anthropology*. London: Malaby, pp. 133–156.

Haraway, Donna. 1989. *Primate Visions: Gender, Race and Nature in the World of Modern Science*. London and New York: Routledge.

Hinde, Robert. 1982. *Ethology: Its Nature and Relations with other Sciences*. London: Collins.

Hrdy, Sarah Blaffer. 1981. *The Woman That Never Evolved*. Cambridge, MA and London: Harvard University Press.

————. 2009. *Mothers and Others: the Evolutionary Origins of Mutual Understanding*. Cambridge, MA: Harvard University Press.

James, Allison. 1993. *Childhood Identities: Self and Social Relationships in the Experience of the Child*. Edinburgh: Edinburgh University Press.

James, Wendy. 2003. *The Ceremonial Animal: A New Portrait of Anthropology*. Oxford: Oxford University Press.

————. 2008. 'Why Kinship? New Questions on an Old Topic', in N. Allen et al. (eds), *Early Human Kinship: from Sex to Social Reproduction*. Malden, MA and Oxford: Blackwell, pp. 3–20.

Konner, Melvin. 2010. *The Evolution of Childhood: Relationships, Emotion, Mind*. Cambridge, MA: Harvard University Press.

Lanier, J. 1999. 'On Daniel C. Dennett's "The Evolution of Culture"', *Edge* 53, 8 April 1999 and http://www.edge.org/documents/archive/edge53. html.

Lorenz, Konrad. 1966 [1963]. *On Aggression*. London: Methuen.

MacClancy, Jeremy and Chris McDonaugh (eds). 1996. *Popularizing Anthropology*. London and New York: Routledge.

Mesoudi, Alex, Andrew Whiten and Kevin Laland. 2006. 'Towards a Unified Science of Cultural Evolution', *Behavioural and Brain Sciences* 29: 329–383.

Mills, D. and M.T. Huber. 2005. 'Anthropology and the Educational "Trading Zone": Disciplinarity, Pedagogy and Professionalism', *Arts and Humanities in Higher Education* 4: 9–32.

Montagu, Ashley (ed.). 1980. *Sociobiology Examined*. New York and Oxford: Oxford University Press.

Montgomery, Heather (ed.). 2008. *An Introduction to Childhood: Anthropological Perspectives on Children's Lives*. Oxford: Wiley-Blackwell.

Morgan, Elaine. 1972. *The Descent of Woman*. London: Souvenir Press.

Morris, Desmond. 1967. *The Naked Ape*. London: Cape.

———. 1969. *The Human Zoo*. London: Jonathan Cape.

———. 1971. *Intimate Behaviour*. London: Jonathan Cape.

———. 1977. *Manwatching: a Field Guide to Human Behaviour*. London: Abrams.

Pinker, Steven. 2002. *The Blank Slate*. London and New York: Penguin.

Ruse, Michael. 1979. *Sociobiology: Sense or Nonsense?* Boston & London: Reidel.

Sahlins, M. 1976. *The Use and Abuse of Biology: an Anthropological Critique of Sociobiology*. Ann Arbor: University of Michigan Press.

Schjelderup-Ebbe, T. 1921. 'Gallus domesticus in seinem täglichen Leben', Ph.D Dissertation Greifswald: Universität Greifswald.

Small, Meredith F. 1995. *Female Choices: Sexual Behaviour of Female Primates*. Ithaca, NY: Cornell University Press.

Stoppard, Tom. 2015. *The Hard Problem*. London: Faber & Faber. Original production January 2015 at the National Theatre, London.

Tallis, Raymond. 2011. *Aping Mankind: Neuromania, Darwinitis and the Misrepresentation of Humanity*. Durham and Bristol, CT: Acumen.

Tanner, Nancy Makepeace. 1981. *On Becoming Human*. Cambridge: Cambridge University Press.

Tiger, L. 1969. *Men In Groups*. London: Nelson.

———. 1975. 'Somatic Factors and Social Behaviour', in R. Fox (ed.), *Biosocial Anthropology*. London: Malaby, pp. 115–132.

———. 1979. *Optimism: The Biology of Hope*. London: Secker & Warburg.

Tiger, L. and R. Fox. 1966. 'The Zoological Perspective in Social Science', *Man* (NS) 1: 75–81.

———. 1971. *The Imperial Animal*. New York: Holt, Rinehart & Winston.

Tinbergen, Nikolaas. 1951. *The Study of Instinct*. Oxford: Oxford University Press.

————. 1958. *Curious Naturalists*. New York: Basic Books.

Trivers, R. 1971. 'The Evolution of Reciprocal Altruism'. Reprinted in T. Clutton-Brock and P. Harvey (eds), 1978, *Readings in Sociobiology*. Reading and San Francisco: Freeman, pp. 189–226.

————. 1972. 'Parental Investment and Sexual Selection', in B. Campbell (ed.), *Sexual Selection and the Descent of Man*. Chicago: Aldine, pp. 136–179.

Washburn, S.L. 1980. 'Human Behaviour and the Behaviour of Other Animals', in A. Montagu (ed.), *Sociobiology Examined*. Oxford and New York: Oxford University Press, pp. 254–282.

Wilson, E.O. 1975. *Sociobiology: the New Synthesis*. Cambridge, MA: Harvard University Press.

————. 2012. *The Social Conquest of Earth*. New York and London: Liveright Publishing Corporation.

Hilary Callan is Director Emerita of the Royal Anthropological Institute, having served as Director from 2000 to 2010. She has held a number of academic positions in anthropology and international education. In addition to single-authored publications, she has co-edited *The Incorporated Wife* (1984, with Shirley Ardener), *Early Human Kinship* (2008, with Nicholas Allen, Robin Dunbar and Wendy James), *Introductory Readings in Anthropology* (2013, with Brian Street and Simon Underdown) and the present volume. She is Editor-in-Chief of the *International Encyclopedia of Anthropology*, scheduled for publication by Wiley-Blackwell in 2018.

Chapter 2

RETHINKING THE RELATIONSHIP BETWEEN STUDIES OF ETHNOBIOLOGICAL KNOWLEDGE AND THE EVOLUTION OF HUMAN CULTURAL COGNITION

Roy Ellen

Introduction

Recent projects reclaiming social anthropology for the study of human origins have relatively little to say about cognition of the natural world. Yet, how early humans organized their knowledge of biota must have been crucial for key adaptations at successive thresholds of evolutionary change. Drawing on a growing body of work comparing the perception, engagement and management of biotic forms among peoples living in a diversity of environmental and social contexts, this chapter offers a critical review of how it might be applied to our understanding of human evolution.

Models

Anthropologists have long reflected on the legitimacy of applying theory developed in relation to contemporary ethnography to the study of human origins. As we move backwards in time differences in biology, behaviour, cognition and ecology make it decreasingly plausible that such theory is relevant. For peoples who preceded the historical record by a few millennia it is reasonable to assume 'continuity thinking': that these are 'people like us' (Ingold 2000). But to what extent can we be confident for human and pre-human populations at 20,000 BP, or 200 ka or 2.0 ma? When we find evidence of red ochre use at 100 ka (Watts 2014) what assumptions can we make about behaviour that accompanied it?

The big epistemological and methodological issue for evolutionary biology is different. In dealing with the earlier period of human evolution, biologists assume humans to be like other species for which the modern synthesis of genetics, palaeontology and socioecology is our best source of models and evidence. However, there are varying views as to the extent to which this approach might apply to more recent phases of human evolution, and Mithen (1996) has argued that comparison with living nonhuman primates for species closer phylogenetically to *Homo sapiens* than early African *Homo erectus* (sometimes called *H. ergaster*) is problematic. Up until the 1960s - and still in some quarters - there was a view that evolutionary theory was unhelpful because of the overarching dominance of 'culture' and the human capacity to self-consciously control the conditions of its own change. We would now want to qualify this, and note the usefulness of primate models when examining, for example, sexual signalling in descendants of *Homo heidelbergensis* in the past half-million years (Power, Sommer and Watts 2013). Indeed, the rise of human ethology, and then behavioural ecology, evolutionary psychology and most recently cultural phylogenetics (Callan, this volume), has undermined the notion that the dominance of 'culture' is always inconsistent with evolutionary explanations.

We therefore have two types of model: those from social anthropology looking from the present towards the past, and those from evolutionary biology looking forwards from the past, a distinction mirroring anthropology's uncomfortable relationship with the concepts of history and evolution. To this we might add a third type: Darwinian modelling testing hypotheses using data drawn from archaeology or ethnography. At some point in geological time, the explanatory power of evolutionary models meets that emerging from anthropological and other forms of socio-cultural theory coming in the other direction. At the meeting point there is a horizon where both might plausibly operate. Thus, depending on whether we focus on the emergence of 'symbolic culture' (learned behaviour socially transmitted through symbols) at 100 ka or earlier, on modern humans at 200 ka, or fire and homebases at 400 ka, there are major differences in how modelling based on either might work. Archaeologists have been caught between these two kinds of theory, reliant on biological theory to understand the early parts of the human story but on comparative social anthropology and history to understand the recent past. But while biological models are at their weakest in explaining the specific present, and social anthropology at its weakest in explaining the distant past, each operates at different explanatory levels and they should not in any fundamental sense compete, both contributing to explaining behaviour that is ostensibly the same.

One argument in favour of ethnographic analogies and theory drawn from social anthropology is that while they generate models that might be wrong, at least they are explicit and testable. The same applies to behavioural ecology based on fieldwork with modern peoples. By contrast, one of the criticisms of evolutionary psychology is its underlying teleological notions about 'basal humanity', often dependent on studies from WEIRD (Western, Educated, Industrialized, Rich, Democratic) populations (Henrich, Heine and Norenzayan 2010). While apparently drawing on modern hunter-gatherer studies, evolutionary psychologists are often insufficiently explicit and selective in analogy, and disregard many findings from contemporary ethnography and comparative anthropology (e.g. Confer et al. 2010).

It is unsurprising that the study of human origins has been especially concerned with hunter-gatherers. Since Lee and DeVore (1968) more care has been taken in defining what kind of model we are talking about, and the view that the lives of the ever-dwindling number of African hunter-gatherers might tell us something about the socio-cultural contexts in which humans evolved has been reinforced by what we now know of sub-Saharan Africa as the home of 'basal humanity' through the fossil, archaeological and genetic evidence. However, the extent to which early foragers were 'hunter-gatherers' as we currently understand the term, or that 'hunter-gatherers most closely represent *natural* humanity' (Barnard 2011: 106) [my emphasis], remains controversial. If we accept that what has made humans is a capacity to diversify behaviour through cultural transmission on a scale not found among great apes and early hominins, in order to deal with the widest possible set of environmental conditions, then the African hunter-gatherer model alone is insufficient to allow us to properly understand not only later transformations but human origins as well. Given ecological differences and cultural change through geographic separation, we might expect considerable variation among palaeolithic hunting and foraging groups. In placing so much weight on the significance of contemporary African hunter-gatherers we risk missing evidence from other hunter-gatherers, or indeed other subsistence populations, and adopting a very restricted interpretation of the relevance of social anthropology.

Cognizing the Biological World

Alan Barnard (2011) invites palaeoanthropologists to engage with 'social anthropology', meaning an intellectual tradition that had come to be recognized by 1965 as the 'British School', with its particular focus on kinship. But social (socio-cultural) anthropology in its wider sense refers to all that social anthropologists do, and increasingly this has been outside the narrowly defined canon of work. Given how social anthropology developed until the 1970s, and the main concerns of behavioural ecology and evolutionary psychology, it is understandable that there has been a primary focus on hunter-gatherer studies, and also on social cognition and kinship in seeking to apply its findings to human origins. But we cannot comprehend the evolution of sociality without attending to how early hominins and humans perceived their environment, organized the information necessary to evaluate it and used it to adapt to changing circumstances.

While it is recognized that hunting requires knowledge of animal behaviour (Barnard 2011: 100), there has been less focus on how that capacity developed. And while much of the mind has evolved to identify, harvest, process and digest biota in the widest sense, comparatively little has been published on the use of plants by early hominins and humans, as food, indicator species, tools and medicines. Many of the cognitive characteristics underpinning the sharing and transmission of this knowledge humans share with other apes, for example in regard to tool-making or nut-cracking.

There are many similarities between human and nonhuman primates in terms of categorical perception (e.g. Harnad 1987; Zentall et al. 2008). Comparative studies have demonstrated the importance of abilities to compose two or more objects into sets, and make distinctions of the kind food–non-food, same species–different species, toxic–non-toxic, male–female, predator–prey, though we have yet to find good evidence of more advanced hierarchic cognitions such as taxonomizing or synchronous notions of causality. Abstract categories seem to require the kind of training that some chimpanzees have undergone, though some can achieve the same end using memorized images. Chimpanzees can also classify functionally, grouping, for example, pips and fruit rather than apples and pears, though it remains unclear whether these operations are routine behaviours in natural settings or simply potential evident in experimental situations. In the realm of social intelligence too, nonhuman primate studies yield evidence that individuals can group others according to their pattern of association (e.g. Premack 1986; Cheney and Seyfarth 1990: 86; Clay and Zuberbühler 2014; Pika 2014).

There is evidence for genetically encoded prototypes in nonhuman vertebrates triggering behavioural responses, such as aversion behaviour with respect to predator-like images. That these latter are strongly selected for may explain why animacy as a phenomenon and certain animal life forms (e.g. 'birds') are more perceptually salient than plants (e.g. 'vines'). However, Herrnstein (1985) has shown that pigeons exposed to pictures of all kinds of trees, as well as trees in different contexts, could differentiate these from non-trees. This has been interpreted as indicating the existence of a concept of 'treeness' as a prototype (Cheney and Seyfarth 1990: 87; Orians and Heerwagen 1992: 4559).

However we interpret the evidence, categorical thinking does not in itself separate humans from other animals (Harnad 1987), and we share many biological prompts which help make sense of the world, combined with more specific genetically encoded image-response patterns. Therefore, the tendency to categorize the world and then act on the reconfiguration is an evolved and ancient function (Tallerman and Gibson 2011), while in all apes and hominins the processes of categorization in both natural history and social intelligence are achieved through advanced neural plasticity of the prefrontal cortex.

Physical Evidence for Biological Knowledge During the Pleistocene

A problem in reconstructing the evolution of human biological knowledge capacity is lack of physical evidence. Macroscopic organization of the brain inferred from fossil crania, and the post-cranial skeleton, tell us something about the ability of early hominins (e.g. *Australopithecus*) and early humans (that is *Homo*) to perceive, interact with, and manipulate biota around them. Contextualized animal bones permit identification of butchering sites, hearths, waste areas and processed objects. For the Upper Palaeolithic the significance of animals is apparent from artistic representations. Evidence for plant knowledge and use is, however, comparatively poor. For 10,000–27,000 BP we have data on various plants as food, psychoactive substances, poisons, cordage and textiles; and for plant processing tools (mortars and pestles, needles, awls, and loom shuttles that suggest plant fabrics) (e.g. Soffer 2004; Shepard 2005; Mercader 2009; d'Errico et al. 2012). Recent Spanish evidence (Sistiaga et al. 2014) suggests greater Neanderthal plant consumption than previously assumed, while Henry, Brooks and Piperno (2014) have shown Neanderthals and early modern humans consuming equal quantities of plant matter, including seeds and storage organs. From ~77,000 BP we have sedges and rushes from South Africa, particularly *Crypocarya woodii* for bedding and as insecticide, regularly being burned (Wadley et al. 2011). From 300 ka we have wooden artefacts (e.g. Thieme 2000), and at 790 ka burned seeds, including olives, barley and grapes from Israel (Goren-Inbar 2011).

The shift between early hominins and early humans incorporated significant dietary change, but available physical evidence has possibly skewed our interpretations. Hunting and scavenging as practices, and meat as food, have received more attention than use and knowledge of plants. While modern hunter-gatherers (and not only hunter-gatherers) prioritize animals and meat in ritual and cosmology, apart from polar and sub-polar peoples, there is often a disconnect between the importance attached to hunting and the fact that bulk food is plant-sourced. However, even where we can demonstrate from the archaeological record levels and kinds of plant use, it is difficult to know how these impinge on the capacity for environmental perception and classification.

Controlled fire use is a crucial step in an evolving capacity for biological knowledge, as it requires collecting phytomaterials and an understanding of their properties as fuel. In Eurasia, fire control becomes general by 300–400 ka (Roebroeks and Villa 2011). In Africa, the picture remains unclear, though there is evidence from 1.0 ma at Wonderwerk (Berna et al. 2012). Fire is a pre-condition for cooking and Wrangham (2009) has suggested that the ability to cook both meat and vegetables had a major impact on subsequent human evolution, altering the apparatus of mastication, digestion and nutrition. For Wrangham, the most likely threshold is the transition to *Homo erectus* at 1.8 ma, where we find shrivelling of the gut, dental changes and other features consistent with processing food. But there are doubts concerning the early dates for cooking and the social difficulties and costliness of its use, for example the likely requirement for homebase organization and fire-tending. Others have suggested that cooking is better associated with the appearance of *H. heidelbergensis*, between ~500 and ~300 ka (e.g. Watts 2014). In this case, cooking cannot account for the anatomical changes mentioned by Wrangham, though it doubtless made food more palatable, easier to digest, and calorifically efficient, releasing nutrients and removing toxins. Moreover, cooking requires knowledge of raw materials, their preparation and the effects of their transformation, and may have made a big difference in terms of the role of seeds and plant storage organs in the diet.

Further clues as to how biological knowledge-making evolved are found in comparative primatology. We have increasing evidence for the social transmission of plant and animal use among anthropoid apes and monkeys: for food (including nut-cracking, geophagy and the seeking out of fermented biomass), for medicines (including de-wormers and insecticides), and for tool selection and nesting tree preference (e.g. Nishida et al. 1983; Badrian and Malenky 1984; Huffman 1997; Krief et al. 2006). We know that chimps think about the spatial distribution of resources, and about fruit ripening times (e.g. Wrangham 1977), but have no way of inferring the likelihood of the existence of food patches based on the generalization of knowledge. They rely on memory alone. Chimps can, however, measure distance between paired locations and make harvesting decisions on this basis (Boesch and Boesch 1984), and co-operate in hunting.

We can make a fair claim that the basal hominin diet was plant-based (Milton 1999), and that omnivory was integral to an eclectic diet and generalist feeding strategy (Teaford and Ungar 2000) in an environment where competing primate species were leaf-eating and more specialized. But although Darwinian theory goes some way in explaining how biological knowledge further evolved within human phylogeny, we need to turn to the anthropology of living human populations to find better clues as to how this happened.

The Ethnobiological Turn and Modelling Modularity

Anthropological studies of biological knowledge emerged from the Boasian ethnolinguistic tradition associated with Edward Sapir and Benjamin Lee Whorf. Initially, this was concerned with demonstrating what people knew and how they organized that knowledge at the level of individual 'cultures'. The prime exponent of this approach within ethnobiology was Harold Conklin. But by the early 1960s Brent Berlin was showing how cross-language data could provide evidence of the way in which colour terms were added to languages (Berlin and Kay 1969), and suggesting principles that could be applied to other domains. This guided his work on ethnobiological classification, and underpinned his universalist-evolutionist approach. In the Berlin model (1970, 1972), the ontogenetic order in which ranks are acquired in the growing child mirror the order of their evolution (e.g. generics > 'higher order' taxa > sub-generic taxa > kingdom). Similar claims were later made by Brown (1984, 1986) for the order in which life forms (e.g. trees and birds before herbs and mammals) are added to language. Such mutually-reinforcing ontogeny-phylogeny models have been common in anthropology since the nineteenth century. While not accepted by all, the approach has been influential among not only ethnobiologists, but also psychologists (Rosch 1978; Medin and Atran 1999), cognitive scientists (Boden 2006), linguists and even social anthropologists (e.g. Bloch 1998). With its endorsement through the work of Atran (e.g. 1990), it has acquired the status of a new orthodoxy.

The Berlin–Atran consensus has fed into the archaeology of human origins through the work of Stephen Mithen. In his *Prehistory of the Mind* Mithen (1996) uses the modular model of multiple intelligences popularized by Fodor (1983) and others, distinguishing variously, mathematical, social, linguistic, technical (intuitive physics) and natural history intelligence, in addition to general intelligence. In this chapter I confine myself to natural history intelligence in relation to social cognition.

Mithen (2006) accepts the existence of a strong module of natural history intelligence, which he argues comprises the principles for organizing knowledge of plants, animals, landscapes and (perhaps we should now add) fungi. The key features of natural history intelligence are the universality of the species concept, sequential patterns of naming (mainly use of binomials implying kind-of relationships), 'taxa' based on morphological regularity, life-form recognition, an underlying principle of 'hierarchy' or ranking, and a propensity to categorize and name regardless of the usefulness of a species.

In the Mithen model the trajectory of human evolution moves from general cognitive flexibility in pre-hominins, to increasing specialization and modularization among early humans (*H. erectus*, *heidelbergensis* and *neanderthalensis*), to cognitive fluidity through inter-modular connection in modern humans. This model finds some role for a distinctive natural history intelligence in nonhuman apes. Modules for both social and natural history intelligence are predicted to have grown considerably by the time we reach early *Homo*, where a separate technical intelligence module first appears, and is exceeded in size by social intelligence. In *Homo erectus*, social, technical and natural history modules have all grown further but are of equal size, and social intelligence appears to have propagated a new smaller and overlapping language module. The same is true of *Homo neanderthalensis*, but with a larger language module. Among modern humans, early forms are presented as merging natural history with social intelligence but without full cognitive fluidity, this being finally achieved in the Upper Palaeolithic.

I have put it this way to emphasize the reification of the idea of 'module', the proliferation of types, the difficulties of measurement and of delineating boundaries in Mithen's approach, let alone establishing a neurobiological basis. There are good reasons to be sceptical of models of 'massive modularity' (e.g. Buller 2005): the arbitrary separation of capacities, a methodology of 'reverse engineering' from the vantage of the Pleistocene that is prone to circularity, and insufficient attention to the potential of cultural cognition. Mithen's mapping of modules on to the fossil evidence is particularly unsatisfactory. I suggest here that a gradualist model, in which social intelligence co-evolves with natural history intelligence, is more consistent with current evidential and theoretical resources.

Nature-social Mutuality

Biological knowledge systems do not stand outside society, but are culturally and socially-embedded. For example, because the environments of early *Homo* were more risky than those of present-day hunter-gatherers, and food resources irregularly distributed, this likely exerted selective pressure in favour of new ways of using social links and increasing group numbers. On the basis of observed correlations between group size, neocortex size and grooming time among primates, Dunbar (1993) hypothesizes that as hominin group size increased so manual grooming alone was insufficient to maintain social relationships. The initial pressure for larger groups may have been predation risk in more open habitats, and a broad-spectrum food-getting strategy. Increased sociability and the need to handle 'social complexity', perhaps through pre-linguistic vocal-auditory signalling rather than language capacity, was a possible consequence (Freeberg et al. 2012), as were greater cognitive resources to underpin foraging strategies, including the sharing and transmission of biological knowledge. A corresponding increased capacity among potential sharers to construct categories, mind-read and empathize would have supported this (Hrdy 2009). Dunbar (2003: 175) puts the threshold for this transition at ~500 ka. Others (e.g. Isler and van Schaik 2014) have argued that the ability to solve ecological problems correlates better with brain size, and that big brains then permitted the solving of social problems. One way of resolving this dispute would be to assume progressive mutual reinforcement between social and ecological intelligence. While great apes are equal to young children in technical matters (Herrmann et al. 2007), humans have been most selected for in terms of social skills. This would have permitted an increased role for culture in connecting domains, transmitting knowledge, and placing general intelligence into learning contexts (e.g. Tomasello 1999).

For nonhuman primates (and early hominins), Mithen implies (2006: 61–63) that natural and social intelligence work independently. However, the partial integration of social and natural intelligence must have happened before the development of full language. Since Lévi-Strauss (e.g. 1964) it has been recognized that at the core of human cognition is a necessary duality and tension whereby humans understand the natural world through their experience of social relations with other humans, and the social world through their experience of nature. This is why despite repeated attempts to counter naive dualism and challenges to the culture-nature divide, the divide keeps on re-emerging (Astuti 2001). Related to this is a proclivity to attribute and represent the inanimate world in organic terms, and to attribute inanimate objects with the properties of living things. It happens because we are bound to model our world directly on those experiences of our own body and we employ this same model as a source of labels and concepts to interpret the world outside the body. We attribute human-like minds to animals, while the lexicon of animal parts is for the most part that of human anatomy. Botanical nomenclature is less anthropomorphic, and that of inanimate objects less still, but body terms – or at least terms that appear concurrently in anatomical lexica – are still crucial (Ellen 2005: 90–116). How much of this is possible without symbolic culture is a matter for continuing debate.

Sharing and Knowledge Distribution

The evolutionary significance of social intelligence is that, ultimately, it improves food-getting, mating and therefore reproductive efficiency. Individual animals of many species learn to recognize different species and utilize their properties. Similarly, repeat discovery of the same properties by ecologically separated human groups is evidence for convergent patterns of organizing biological knowledge (e.g. Moerman et al. 1999). However, what characterizes humans is how information about the natural world acquired by individuals is shared with others and transmitted inter-generationally through socially distributed storage and 'external memory' supported through language (Donald 1991). But this does raise the issue of why, if culture in the sense of socially transmitted practice is common among many species, it evolved so rarely into more elaborate patterns (Boyd and Richerson 1996). This is why data on knowledge sharing as documented in ethnobiological research is instructive. Early attempts to collect data relied heavily on aggregate figures for numbers of organism names and the omniscient speaker-hearer assumption. We now know that biological knowledge does not exist in its totality in any one place or individual (despite cases of individual encyclopedism: e.g. Berlin 2003), that it is much more distributed, while its movement between individuals is rarely regulated by what we would normally understand as exchange, though exchange relations may improve access to resources.

But for sharing of biological material and knowledge to be routinized and dependable required the recognition of individuals as intentional agents, and arising from this the development of those norms of trust that we now accept were crucial to the evolution of sociality itself, and which are now such an issue in the study of great apes, and critical for understanding the emergence of symbolic culture and language. The concept of 'sociality' is further addressed by James (this volume). Where knowledge is shared there is always a tension between literal acceptance and distrust, as in those social relations more generally that are the context for material transactions and knowledge exchange. Among hunter-gatherers, as in most acephalous societies, there are fewer robust social means for establishing authority and for standardizing what is known and adjudicating in disputes than in complex centralized systems (Sillitoe 2002).

In understanding how distributed and shared cognition evolved, other parts of the body in addition to the brain were integral (see Low, this volume). Category mechanisms work through mapping, involving our whole bodies and personal histories. The evolution of the hand in particular, and with it the tool, brought about a transformation in the relationship between hominins and their own body, a greater level of physical self-awareness and sense of self, arising from use of the hands in communication, as sensory organs, and through recognition of their manipulative capacity. The development of physical motor skills also improved the potential utility of biota and therefore encouraged selection for more sophisticated classification skills. Similarly, transmission was not simply the passing of information from one brain to another but required complex interactive rediscovery (Ellen and Fischer 2013).

Episodic and Mimetic Memory

Key to understanding the growth in human sharing is the relationship between episodic and mimetic memory: memory based on remembering occasions in the past when significant events occurred, and remembering general principles distilled from what may have occurred on one or more occasions. It is sometimes supposed that there was a shift from cultural accumulation and transmission based predominantly on the first to one predominantly based on the second (Donald 1991, following Tulving). But the assumption that nonhuman animals have episodic recall in the sense described has been challenged, and the term 'episodic-like' may be preferable (Crystal 2010). Whether or not nonhuman animals have temporal processing or can recall 'events', they are able to associate particular contexts with experiences. In terms of plant knowledge, 'episodic-like' memory provides a basis for distinguishing predator from non-predator, toxic from non-toxic, fermented from non-fermented matter, for storing plant foods and for distinguishing medicinals. But only mimetic memory would have permitted the more abstract grouping of plants and animals necessary for sharing large numbers of types of biota among larger numbers of individuals.

The shift from episodic-like to mimetic also reflects a shift from recognition of broad use categories and similarity judgments to something resembling what Berlin, Atran and others call 'natural classification', and an ability to infer properties of one type of organism on the basis of physical similarity to another. In other words, classification reduces the 'thought load', expedites new learning and allows inference. For example, if plant (A) has property (a), and if plant (A) is similar to (B) then it is also likely to share property (a), e.g. be edible, toxic, useful in some other way, and so on. Similarity judgments can be based on morphological similarity or ecological similarity (Atran and Medin 2008), thus if (X) is in flower then (Y) will be in fruit. The same kind of reasoning is found in both folk biology and social cognition. Storing knowledge as causal hypotheses is efficient because humans do not have sufficient memory to make the right responses by induction alone, especially where they are relying on oral culture and limited division of labour (e.g. Johnson-Laird 1982).

A central element of mimetic thinking as applied to natural history knowledge is a universal concept of basic category or essence applied to all biological types (e.g. 'dog', 'cat', 'willow', 'oak'). This is often described as a 'species' concept, though confusingly it maps mainly on to what Berlin calls 'folk genera'. The notion of basic biological category was early identified in both anthropology (Lévi-Strauss 1966; Bulmer 1970) and psychology (Rosch 1978), based on a cognitive simplification through which living objects of sufficient similarity were recognized as being the same 'natural kind'. It is difficult to imagine the concept of shared basic category except when linked to proto-linguistic 'mental representations' and proto-names comprising arbitrary tokens standing for something else (Penn et al. 2008; Bickerton 2011) or perhaps onomatopoeia.

Experience of their own bodies enabled early humans to model the world around them and to understand inferentially how the bodies of other organisms worked. The hands in particular served not merely as sensory and motor organs, but as a strong model for binary strategies in dividing up the natural world through incipient naming. The introduction of proto-names for categories meant that while cognitive prototypes might still serve as the main way by which members of a category were identified, the act of sharing through language meant that boundaries around categories needed to be agreed, and this had to be based on a rudimentary scheme of distinctive features (e.g. colour, shape, size, smell, taste).

Language, Naming and Symbolic Culture

It is now widely accepted that language (primarily speech-based and using words in a structured and conventional way) evolved primarily to enhance sociality rather than technical communication (Barnard 2011; Dor, Knight and Lewis 2014), and co-evolved with symbolic culture more generally. By symbolic culture I understand sharing and transmission mediated through the use of symbols: concepts or things standing for each other, often in an arbitrary relationship. Using a system of social categories, for example, this allowed for kin connections and extended social links beyond the immediate present, even when relevant individuals were physically absent. However, the evidence of macro-anatomy indicates that symbolic capacity evolved before any archaeological evidence is found in early *Homo* to support it. This suggests that it did not immediately translate into symbolic culture. The mimetic culture that developed during this period would have likely been sufficient to support proto-language capacity that involved categorization and proto-naming of the natural world in the way I have already outlined (c.f. Mithen 2006: 66–67).

While sharing practices and cognitive skills can improve without language, progressive language skills improve both. Language depends upon and fosters the ability to imagine what is in other people's minds, to make assumptions as to how they will cognize shared data. This is achieved through treating shared fictions as objective facts, using names that can stand for generalized abstract entities in an environment and mean sufficiently the same for both parties in a conversation. Some simple names may well have been onomatopoeic, and onomatopoeia is still strongly represented for certain groups of animals (e.g. birds and frogs), but the process of agreeing shared meanings in itself can lead to lexemes becoming arbitrary. In some cases, as Berlin (2006) has shown, the non-arbitrariness of the relation of sounds to animals they represent can be remarkably consistent. But it is not only names for things that are required for this process to work, but descriptions of attributes of things, for example taste in the case of plants and animals used for food, as distinctive features become increasingly important for enforcing category boundaries.

Agreeing names and thereafter a consistent semantic association between names and generalizations about entities in an environment requires shared acceptance of a set of rules for making meaning. Most ethnobiological data is collected by asking informants what they call things. Although there are methodological dangers here, names are a reasonable proxy for knowledge. And in recognizing this we identify the reasons why names were introduced in the first place, not only to increase the reliability of sharing knowledge, but as better triggers for inference. While it is possible to imagine the collective imposition of rules without language (e.g. Searle 1996: 60–61), rules are more effectively recognized (and enforced) with a language that facilitates sharing knowledge, generalizing it, agreeing on notions of right and wrong and encoding this into a moral framework. Thus, one-way rule behaviour is embedded by introducing an emotional charge to our interpretation of what is embedded in long-term memory. By making something 'right', shared rules of recognition and behaviour are reinforced; authority is established. There is, therefore, a link between enculturation of the mind, classification and social morality.

Speech acts concerning aspects of the biological world occur not only in particular physical contexts that reinforce the meaning of names, but in the context of different kinds of social relations. In some cases there is a mutual exchange of words, but sometimes it is deliberately instructional. Pedagogy, therefore, becomes an increasingly efficient form of cultural transmission with the development of language and higher orders of intentionality, but not at the expense of self-learning.

Symbolic language also makes possible environmental narrativity, the ability to recall events and processes, and tell stories about plants, animals and their maturation in particular places, both in the specific and in the general. This has an obvious positive effect on harvesting efficiency. The idea of narrativity as an essential component of symbolic culture was first introduced by Michael Carrithers (1990), but has been elaborated by Alan Barnard (2013) in what he calls his 'second theory'. What is interesting about narrativity in terms of the evolution of biocognition is that it involves a significant role for episodic memory in the organization of resource and spatial knowledge, but in the context of a linguistic capacity that allows for generalization about particular kinds of environment, and an ability to infer what kinds of resources might be found in what kind of habitat. It also permits abstract narratives that combine biological and social knowledge in imaginative ways of the kind we call myths. Such narratives can only work by using names to generalize about species and habitats, but it is notable that with ethno-ecological categories we do not find the same kinds of complex lexically embedded classifications that we find for the separate domains of plants and animals. Instead, we find that knowledge of physical landscape is culturally embedded by using narratives of particular places and myth that enhance memorability and provides moral reinforcement. Moreover, this integration of culture and environment is all the more powerful because even before the Holocene human groups were self-evidently making their environment physically cultural, for example by creating resource rich patches through inadvertent dropping of seed, selective extraction, and camp and trail-making (Ichikawa 1996; Ellen 2007). Non-linguistic episodic memory is thus transformed through language into more effective edited accounts that can be better shared.

With the ability to convey and store messages about abstract 'natural kinds', it becomes in principle possible to construct categories of increasing inclusiveness (through aggregation) or decreasing abstraction (through segregation). Berlin (1972) showed that classification, in terms of shared named basic categories, evolves from the middle outwards, both ontogenetically and historically. This core, as Berlin (1992: 96–101 has also shown, comprises around 500–600 'generic' categories in all recorded ethnobiological classification systems, with the total number of taxa altogether reaching approximately 2000. The process depends on notions of ranking and taxonomy that may have evolved independently of biocognition, as a means of contrasting and grouping various kinds of entity, and as a response to the difficulties of recalling large numbers of similar items (Miller 1956). Such procedures are enabled by a syntax that can repeatedly embed adjectives and phrases, and a recursiveness that gives form to more complex classificatory structures.

The convergence of language, social-natural mutuality, imagination and abstraction permitted plants and animals to be spoken of in multi-referential ways as parts of networks of meaning. This reinforced knowledge about them but also increased their symbolic functionality in other social contexts: through analogical reasoning (e.g. use of male/female), genealogical metaphors ('families', 'brothers', 'mother of'), the very notion of 'hierarchy', animation and the personification of biological types.

Naming and the Influence of Environment and Subsistence

What constitutes a name? Conklin and Berlin showed in the 1960s that though we can treat some names as semantically 'unanalysable' or primary (e.g. 'oak', 'cat'), many are secondary (e.g. 'turkey oak', 'house sparrow'), have obvious histories, and allude to other domains (colour, social, places, other animals and plants, human anatomy). Secondary names take on a kind-of or part-of relationship, and are a feature of all known languages, a nomenclatural consequence of marking behaviour: 'A : not A', where 'not A' is the marked term.

Systematic binomialism, however, is rare in the nomenclatures of hunter-gatherers compared to farmers (Morris 1976; Ellen 1999). Binomials only become predominant with domestication, where it is necessary to (firstly) distinguish cultivated from non-cultivated forms, and thereafter numerous cultivars (varietals). In contexts of proto-domestication the basic categories that are marked are those for the cultivated form of the same natural kind found outside of cultivation (Nabhan and Rea 1987). For populations where cultivation is the default mode, as among the Nuaulu, adjectival qualifiers that mark non-cultivated habitats tend to predominate e.g. 'forest, 'mountain' rather than 'garden', 'village' or 'house' (e.g. *munu wesie* ['forest *munu*'], the fish poison *Derris trifoliata*). The more humans managed their environment the more distinctions below the species level became important. Thus, among Nuaulu plant terms, cultivar segregates (e.g. for sago, yams and taro) represent the largest group of binomials.

One problem of the Berlin–Atran scheme of taxonomic biocognition as a default universal model is that we have poor accounts of the ethnobiological classification of contemporary hunter-gatherers, and what we do have challenge this consensus (Morris 1976, 1984; Brown 1986). For example, there are fewer names reported for hunter-gatherers compared with farmers. This is counter-intuitive, given claims that hunter-gatherers have more sophisticated biological knowledge systems than farmers. They also use fewer sequential naming practices, resort less to hierarchies and ranks, have fewer more inclusive categories (e.g. life-forms), rely more on use categories, and are more flexible (e.g. Heinz and Maguire 1974; Terashima and Ichikawa 2003; Bowern et al. 2014). This is also the case for hunter-gatherers whom we often place in a separate category, such as the peoples of the northwest coast of America (e.g. Turner 1974). Because these groups are subject to similar constraints – social, demographic and environmental – we can account for some of the characteristics through small population size and density, widespread distribution, and foraging strategies that tend to be more individual and less social, and that rely on direct experience less easily communicated and encoded in language, or not requiring lexical elaboration. Indeed, hunter-gatherer biological knowledge is more 'substantive' than lexical (Ellen 1999), with wayfinding for example being less about linguistic competence and the application of self-consciously encoded knowledge than about how the body learns to move through familiar landscapes. Complex names (serving as proxies for connected knowledge about specific taxa that cannot easily be expressed lexically) are important once it becomes useful to encode large numbers of differences and share with larger numbers of people, as in farming.

Summary

The problem is: how can we map changes in hominin and human capacity to organize and use biological knowledge on to chronological frameworks, and what theories of cognitive and language evolution most satisfactorily support them? In terms of the first, I rely here on Shulz et al. (2012), which conveniently brings together key data, arguing for punctuated changes in hominin brain evolution at approximately 1.8 ma, 1 ma and 100 ka, plus gradual changes within

H. erectus and *H. sapiens*. In terms of the second, I follow Donald (1991), in distinguishing three major cognitive transitions: (1) 'episodic' to mimetic (involving sharing and social storage); (2) mimetic to 'mythic' (meaning broadly symbolic culture); and (3) external symbolic storage (graphic symbols and pictures). This may oversimplify the picture, especially in relation to language origins, but the diversity of opinion here is considerable, and it has seemed to me wise to engage only in so far as it is necessary to explain key features of the linguistic encoding of natural history knowledge.

Transition 1 is linked to the appearance of *Homo habilis*, and *H. erectus* with a wider geographic distribution (extending to the trans-Caucasus and into Asia). The beginning point corresponds to the appearance of Acheulean tools in Africa from 1.76 ma, apparently associated with a step-change in encephalization. The evidence suggests an ability to hunt large animals, greater performance of social tasks, more dependent young, an extended juvenile learning phase, with more opportunities for improving problem-solving capabilities, and with consequent changes in group structure, foraging behaviour and range use. This would likely correspond with a shift from 'episodic-like' to mimetic thought between 2.0 and 0.5 ma, completed with the arrival of modern humans. This phase is associated with improved (functional) categorization and basic naming skills linked to proto-language.

Transition 2 is associated with *H. heidelbergensis* and *neanderthalensis* after 500 ka, and the need to adapt to a wide range of new species and environments as humans moved both within and out of Africa into Eurasia between 400 and 100 ka. In other words, life-world concepts and natural history knowledge diversified in response to habitat change and a diversity of environments. Indeed, much of what we regard as the essential features of the modern package of ethnobiological classification are probably a consequence of developments arising as humans moved into varied new environments that they were thus able to manage with increased effectiveness, through greater sharing and management of social relations, as reflected – for example – in effective fire control. The important cognitive breakthrough here (as suggested by Mithen) was a predictive model of natural history, emerging through a self-learning process in which as the lexicon grows and proto-sentences are used, categorization of experience leads to more complex proto-syntax (Bickerton 2011). In turn, engagement between ecological diversity, local population histories and ethnobiological classification itself fuelled further cultural diversity (Mithen 2006: 65).

Transition 3 begins with the appearance of the first modern humans in Africa after 200 ka, having evolved a fully modern life-history strategy but with no clear corresponding changes in archaeology. However, a 'cascade of consequences' accompanied increasing evidence of symbolic behaviour after 60 ka as modern humans spread from Africa: cultural variation reflected in technological specialization, art and decoration, and the rapid facilitation of full-language capabilities at 50 ka, involving lexical (rather than phonological) syntax (Knight et al. 2000; Tallerman 2011: 442). Syntactical language made classifying much easier, by enforcing arbitrariness (e.g. category boundaries) through shared rules. It permitted relational similarity, intentionality competences (e.g. number of embedded clauses), metaphor (including 'totemic thinking'), analogy, higher order spatial relations, transitive inference, and hierarchical and causal relations. Words could be introduced for non-basic categories as required in different eco-cultural contexts through a process of progressive aggregation and segregation, finally denoting 'unique beginners' at a kingdom level. The adaptiveness of this system stemmed from the multiplicity of ways in which it could re-organize perceptual data, and from the redundancy built into the process. The classifications that resulted were fluid and negotiable, produced as well as reproduced.

Conclusion

The origins of kinship and religion are big and important issues, but are not the only issues that socio-cultural anthropologists are equipped to explain. I have tried in this chapter to focus more on the role of natural history knowledge in accounts of human evolution, and to pay more attention to plants in particular. In his *Prehistory of the Mind*, Steven Mithen offers us a powerful model based on theories of modularity, and builds his model of natural history intelligence on the basis of the findings of Berlin and Atran. I have suggested that there are difficulties with his appeal to modularity. There are problems in defining the boundaries of modules, and a likelihood of much more continuous interconnection between the elements of different modules, such that we might wish to question the exclusiveness of separate natural history intelligence. On the other hand, the strong evidence for nature–social mutuality implies two cognitive sub-systems that are constantly reinforcing each other. Similarly, what is grouped together in the Berlin–Atran model might be better envisaged as a collection of different cognitive and cultural elements that arose separately, at different evolutionary phases. We need to recognize the difference between semantic domains that we can infer from patterns of linguistic and cultural practice, and neurobiological modules that we can only infer with more circumspection.

Acknowledgments

I would like to thank Hilary Callan, Morna Finnegan, Tatyana Humle, Tracy Kivell, Camilla Power, Carel van Schaik, Hanna Simons, Brandon Wheeler and one anonymous reviewer for their helpful comments and advice.

References

Astuti, R. 2001. 'Are we all Natural Dualists? A Cognitive Developmental Approach', *Journal of the Royal Anthropological Institute (N.S.)* 7: 429–447.

Atran, S. 1990. *Cognitive Foundations of Natural History*. Cambridge: Cambridge University Press.

——— and D. Medin. 2008. *The Native Mind and the Cultural Construction of Nature*. Cambridge, MA: MIT Press.

Badrian, N. and R. Malenky. 1984. 'Feeding Ecology of *Pan paniscus* in the Lomako Forest, Zaire', in R. Susman (ed.), *The Pygmy Chimpanzee*. New York: Plenum Press, pp. 275–299.

Barnard, A. 2011. *Social Anthropology and Human Origins*. Cambridge: Cambridge University Press.

———. 2013. 'Cognitive and Social Aspects of Language Origins', in C. Lefebvre, B. Comrie and H. Cohen (eds), *New Perspectives on the Origins of Language*. Amsterdam: John Benjamins, pp. 53–71.

Berlin, B. 1970. 'A Universalist–Evolutionary Approach in Ethnographic Semantics', in A. Fisher (ed.), *Current Directions in Anthropology*. Bulletin of the American Anthropological Association 3: 3–18.

———. 1972. 'Speculations on the Growth of Ethnobotanical Nomenclature', *Language in Society* 1: 151–186.

———. 2003. 'One Maya Indian's View of the Plant World: How a Folk Botanical System Can be Both Natural and Comprehensive', in G. Sanga and G. Ortalli (eds), *Nature Knowledge: Ethnoscience, Cognition, and Utility*. Oxford: Berghahn, pp. 38–46.

———. 2006. 'The First Congress of Ethnozoological Nomenclature', in R. Ellen (ed.), *Ethnobiology and the Science of Humankind*. Oxford: Blackwell, pp. 29–54.

————— and P. Kay. 1969. *Basic Color Terms*. Berkeley: University of California Press.

Berna, F. et al. 2012. 'Microstratigraphic Evidence of In situ Fire in the Acheulean Strata of Wonderwerk Cave, Northern Cape Province, South Africa', *Proceedings of the National Academy of Sciences* 109(20), E1215–E1220.

Bickerton, D. 2011. 'The Origins of Syntactic Language', in M. Tallerman and K. Gibson (eds), *Oxford Handbook of Language Evolution*. Oxford: Oxford University Press, pp. 456–468.

Bloch, M. 1998. *How We Think They Think*. London: Westview Press.

Boden, M. 2006. *Mind as Machine*. Volume 1. Oxford: Clarendon Press.

Boesch, C. and H. Boesch. 1984. 'Mental Maps in Wild Chimpanzees: An Analysis of Hammer Transports for Nut Cracking', *Primates* 25(2): 160–170.

Bowern, C. et al. 2014. 'Loan and Inheritance Patterns in Hunter-gatherer Ethnobiological Systems', *Journal of Ethnobiology* 34(2): 195–227.

Boyd, R. and P.J. Richerson. 1996. 'Why Culture is Common, but Cultural Evolution is Rare', *Proceedings-British Academy* 88: 77–94.

Brown, C.H. 1984. *Language and Living Things*. New Brunswick, NJ: Rutgers University Press.

—————. 1986. 'The Growth of Ethnobiological Nomenclature', *Current Anthropology* 27(1): 1–19.

Buller, D. 2005. *Adapting Minds*. Cambridge, MA: MIT Press.

Bulmer, R. 1970. 'Which Came First, The Chicken or the Egg-head?', in J. Pouillon and P. Maranda (eds), *Echanges et Communications*. The Hague and Paris: Mouton, pp. 1069–1091.

Carrithers, M. 1990. 'Why Humans have Cultures', *Man (N.S.)* 25: 189–206.

Cheney, D.L. and R.M. Seyfarth. 1990. *How Monkeys See the World*. Chicago and London: University of Chicago Press.

Clay, Z. and K. Zuberbühler. 2014. 'Vocal Communication and Social Awareness in Chimpanzees and Bonobos', in D. Dor, C. Knight and J. Lewis (eds), *The Social Origins of Language*. Oxford: Oxford University Press, pp. 141–156.

Confer, J.C. et al. 2010. 'Evolutionary Psychology: Controversies, Questions, Prospects, and Limitations', *American Psychologist* 65(2): 110–126.

Crystal, J.D. 2010. 'Episodic-like Memory in Animals', *Behavioral Brain Research* 215: 235–243.

Donald, M. 1991. *Origins of the Modern Mind*. Cambridge, MA: Harvard University Press.

Dor, D., C. Knight and J. Lewis (eds). 2014. *The Social Origins of Language*. Oxford: Oxford University Press.

Dunbar, R. 1993. 'The Co-evolution of Neocortical Size, Group Size and Language in Humans', *Behavioural and Brain Sciences* 16: 681–694.

—————. 2003. 'The Social Brain: Mind, Language, and Society in Evolutionary Perspective', *Annual Review of Anthropology* 32: 163–181.

Ellen, R. 1999. 'Modes of Subsistence and Ethnobiological Knowledge: Between Extraction and Cultivation in Southeast Asia', in D.L. Medin and S. Atran (eds), *Folkbiology*. Cambridge, MA: MIT Press, pp. 91–117.

———. 2005. *The Categorical Impulse*. Oxford: Berghahn.

———. 2007. 'Local and Scientific Understandings of Forest Diversity on Seram, Eastern Indonesia', in P. Sillitoe (ed.), *Local Science Versus Global Science*. Oxford: Berghahn, pp. 41–74.

——— and M.D. Fischer. 2013. 'Introduction: On the Concept of Cultural Transmission', in R. Ellen, S.J. Lycett and S.E. Johns (eds), *Understanding Cultural Transmission in Anthropology*. London: Berghahn, pp. 1–54.

d'Errico F. et al. 2012. 'Early Evidence of San Material Culture Represented by Organic Artifacts from Border Cave, South Africa', *Proceedings of the National Academy of Sciences* USA, 10.1073/pnas.1204213109.

Fodor, J. 1983. *The Modularity of Mind*. Cambridge MA: MIT Press.

Freeburg, T., R. Dunbar and T. Ord. 2012. 'Social Complexity as a Proximate and Ultimate Factor in Communicative Complexity', *Philosophical Transactions of the Royal Society B* 367: 1785–1801.

Goren-Inbar, N. 2011. 'Culture and Cognition in the Acheulian Industry: A Case Study from Gesher Benot Ya'aqov', *Philosophical Transactions of the Royal Society B* 366(1567): 1038–1049.

Harnad, S. (ed.). 1987. *Categorical Perception*. Princeton, NJ: Cambridge University Press.

Heinz, H.J. and B. Maguire. 1974. *The Ethno-Biology of the !Kõ Bushmen*. Gaborone: The Botswana Society.

Henrich, J., S. Heine and A. Norenzayan. 2010. 'The Weirdest People in the World?', *Behavioral and Brain Sciences* 33(2–3): 61–83.

Henry, A., A. Brooks and D. Piperno. 2014. 'Plant Foods and Dietary Ecology of Neanderthals and Early Modern Humans', *Journal of Human Evolution* 69: 44–54.

Hernnstein, R.D. 1985. 'Riddles of Natural Classification', *Philosophical Transactions of the Royal Society (London) B*, 308: 129–143.

Herrmann, E. et al. 2007. 'Humans Have Evolved Specialized Skills of Social Cognition: The Cultural Intelligence Hypothesis', *Science* 317: 1360–1366.

Hrdy, S. 2009. *Mothers and Others*. Cambridge: Harvard University Press.

Huffman, M.A. 1997. 'Current Evidence for Self-medication in Primates: A Multi-disciplinary Perspective', *Yearbook of Physical Anthropology* 40: 171–200.

Ichikawa, M. 1996. 'The Co-existence of Man and Nature in the African Rain Forest', in R. Ellen and K. Fukui (eds), *Redefining Nature*. Oxford: Berg, pp. 467–492.

Ingold, T. 2000. '"People Like Us": The Concept of the Anatomically Modern Human', in *The Perception of the Environment*. London: Routledge, pp. 373–391.

Isler, K. and C.P. van Schaik. 2014. 'How Humans Evolved Large Brains: Comparative Evidence', *Evolutionary Anthropology* 23(2): 65–75.

Johnson-Laird, P. 1982. *Mental Models*. Cambridge: Cambridge University Press.

Knight, C., M. Studdert-Kennedy and J. Hurford (eds). 2000. *The Evolutionary Emergence of Language*. Cambridge: Cambridge University Press.

Krief, S. et al. 2006. 'Bioactive Properties of Plant Species Ingested by Chimpanzees (*Pan troglodytes schweinfurthii*) in the Kibale National Park, Uganda', *American Journal of Primatology* 68(1): 51–71.

Lee, R.B. and I. DeVore (eds). 1968. *Man the Hunter*. Chicago: Aldine Press.

Lévi-Strauss, C. 1964 [1962]. *Totemism*, trans. R. Needham. London: Merlin Press.

———. 1966. *The Savage Mind*. London: Weidenfeld and Nicholson.

Medin, D. and S. Atran (eds). 1999. *Folkbiology*. Cambridge, MA: MIT Press.

Mercader, J. 2009. 'Mozambican Grass Seed Consumption During the Middle Stone Age', *Science* 326: 1680–1683.

Miller, G.A. 1956. 'The Magical Number Seven, Plus or Minus Two: Some Limits to Our Capacity for Processing Information', *Psychological Review* 63: 81–97.

Milton, K. 1999. 'Nutritional Characteristics of Wild Primate Foods: Do the Diets of our Closest Living Relatives have Lessons for us?', *Nutrition* 15: 488–498.

Mithen, S. 1996. *The Prehistory of the Mind*. London: Thames and Hudson.

———. 2006. 'Ethnobiology and the Evolution of the Human Mind', in R. Ellen (ed.), *Ethnobiology and the Science of Humankind*. Blackwell: Oxford, pp. 55–75.

Moerman, D.E. et al. 1999. 'A Comparative Analysis of Five Medicinal Floras', *Journal of Ethnobiology* 19(1): 49–67.

Morris, B. 1976. 'Whither the Savage Mind? Notes on the Natural Taxonomies of a Hunting and Gathering People', *Man (N.S.)* 11: 542–557.

———. 1984. 'The Pragmatics of Folk Classification', *Journal of Ethnobiology* 4: 45–60.

Nabhan, G.P. and A. Rea. 1987. 'Plant Domestication and Folk-biological Change: The Upper Piman/Devil's Claw Example', *American Anthropologist* 89(1): 57–73.

Nishida, T. et al. 1983. 'Local Differences in Plant-feeding Habits of Chimpanzees Between the Mahale Mountains and Gombe National Park', *Journal of Human Evolution* 12: 467–480.

Orians, G.H. and J.H. Heerwagen. 1992. 'Evolved Responses to Landscapes', in J.H. Barkow, L. Cosmides and J. Tooby (eds), *The Adapted Mind*. Oxford: Oxford University Press, pp. 555–579.

Penn, D., K. Holyoak and D. Povinelli. 2008. 'Darwin's Mistake: Explaining the Discontinuity Between Human and Nonhuman Minds', *Behavioral and Brain Sciences* 31: 109–178.

Pika, S. 2014. 'Chimpanzee Grooming Gestures and Sounds: What Might They Tell us About How Language Evolved?', in D. Dor, C. Knight and J Lewis (eds), *The Social Origins of Language*. Oxford: Oxford University Press, pp. 129–140.

Power, C., V. Sommer and I. Watts. 2013. 'The Seasonality Thermostat: Female Reproductive Synchrony and Male Behavior in Monkeys, Neanderthals, and Modern Humans', *PaleoAnthropology* 2013: 33–60.

Premack, D. 1986. *Gavagai, or the Future History of the Animal Language Controversy*. Cambridge, MA: Bradford Books.

Roebroeks, W. and P. Villa. 2011. 'On the Earliest Evidence for Habitual Use of Fire in Europe', *Proceedings of the National Academy of Sciences* 108(13): 5209–5214.

Rosch, E. 1978. 'Principles of Categorization', in E. Rosch and B.B. Lloyd (eds), *Cognition and Categorization*. Hillsdale, NJ: Erlbaum, pp. 27–48.

Searle, J. 1996. *The Construction of Social Reality*. London: Penguin.

Shepard, G.H. 2005. 'Psychoactive Botanicals in Ritual, Religion and Shamanism', in E. Elisabetsky and N. Etkin (eds), *Ethnopharmacology, Encyclopedia of Life Support Systems*. Oxford: UNESCO/EOLSS.

Shultz, S., E. Nelson and R. Dunbar. 2012. 'Hominin Cognitive Evolution: Identifying Patterns and Processes in the Fossil and Archaeological Record', *Philosophical Transactions of the Royal Society B: Biological Sciences* 367(1599): 2130–2140.

Sillitoe, P. 2002. 'Contested Knowledge, Contingent Classification: Animals in the Highlands of Papua New Guinea', *American Anthropologist* 104(4): 1162–1171.

Sistiaga A. et al. 2014. 'The Neanderthal Meal: A New Perspective Using Faecal Biomarkers', *PLoS ONE* 9(6): e101045. doi:10.1371/journal.pone.0101045.

Soffer, O. 2004. 'Recovering Perishable Technologies through Use Wear on Tools: Preliminary Evidence for Upper Paleolithic Weaving and Net Making', *Current Anthropology* 45(3): 407–413.

Tallerman, M. 2011. 'What is Syntax', in M. Tallerman and K. Gibson (eds), *Oxford Handbook of Language Evolution*. Oxford: Oxford University Press, pp. 442–455.

——— and K. Gibson. 2011. 'Introduction: The Evolution of Language', in M. Tallerman and K. Gibson (eds), *Oxford Handbook of Language Evolution*. Oxford: Oxford University Press, pp. 1–37.

Teaford, M.F. and P.S. Ungar. 2000. 'Diet and the Evolution of the Earliest Human Ancestors', *Proceedings of the National Academy of Sciences* 97: 13506–11.

Terashima, H. and M. Ichikawa. 2003. 'A Comparative Ethnobotany of the Mbuti and Efe Hunter-gatherers in the Ituri Forest, Democratic Republic of Congo', *African Study Monographs* 24(1–2): 1–168.

Thieme, H. 2000. 'Lower Palaeolithic Hunting Weapons from Schöningen, Germany – The Oldest Spears in the World', *Acta Anthropologica Sinica* 19 (supplement): 140–147.

Tomasello, M. 1999. *The Cultural Origins of Human Cognition*. Cambridge, MA: Harvard University Press.

Turner, N. 1974. 'Plant Taxonomic Systems and Ethnobotany of Three Contemporary Indian Groups of the Pacific Northwest (Haida, Bella Coola, and Lillooet)', *Syesis* 7, supplement no. 1: 1–104.

Wadley, L. et al. 2011. 'Middle Stone Age Bedding Construction and Settlement Patterns at Sibudu, South Africa', *Science* 334(6061): 1388–91.

Watts, I. 2014. 'The Red Thread: Pigment Use and the Evolution of Collective Ritual', in D. Dor, C. Knight and J. Lewis (eds), *The Social Origins of Language*. Oxford: Oxford University Press, pp. 208–227.

Wrangham, R.W. 1977. 'Feeding Behaviour of Chimpanzees in Gombe National Park, Tanzania', in T.H. Clutton-Brock (ed.), *Primate Ecology*. London: Academic Press, pp. 503–538.

———. 2009. *Catching Fire: How Cooking Made us Human*. New York: Basic Books.

Zentall, T. et al. 2008. 'Concept Learning in Animals', *Comparative Cognition and Behavior Reviews* 3: 13–45.

Roy Ellen is Emeritus Professor of Anthropology and Human Ecology at the University of Kent. His main areas of current interest are ethnobiological knowledge systems, cognitive anthropology, ritual dynamics and inter-island trade. He has conducted field research in island southeast Asia over a period of forty-five years. His recent books and editions include *On the Edge of the Banda Zone: Past and Present in the Social Organization of a Moluccan Trading Network* (2003), *Nuaulu Religious Practices: the Frequency and Reproduction of Rituals in a Moluccan Society* (2012) and *Understanding Cultural Transmission in Anthropology: a Critical Synthesis*, edited with Stephen Lycett and Sarah Johns (2013). He was elected to a fellowship of the British Academy in 2003, and was President of the Royal Anthropological Institute between 2007 and 2011.

Chapter 3

TOWARDS A THEORY OF EVERYTHING

Chris Knight and Jerome Lewis

Toward the end of the nineteenth century, when popular Darwinism and evolutionism were still much in vogue, armchair anthropologists invented a rich variety of theories of origin, the assumption being that one theory would be needed to explain the emergence of religion, another the origins of law, another the origins of language and so forth.

It was not until the 1930s that the rise of functionalism put an end to all this. Fieldworkers inspired by Bronislaw Malinowski insisted that in any given community, the system of cosmological beliefs, mode of subsistence, linguistic patterns and so forth all intertwine to form a functional whole, making it impossible to imagine how one component could exist for a moment without all the others (Knight 1995: 50–70). The implication was clear: to explain the origins of, say, language, an adequate theory would have to account simultaneously for all the other things which presuppose language and underpin its use.

The point is as valid today as it ever was. Taken in isolation, there can be no such thing as a theory of the origins of language. There can be no such thing as a theory of the origins of morality, law, totemism, exogamy, kinship or indeed anything else. To explain any one feature, we need to explain the whole – a challenging prospect (Dor, Knight and Lewis 2014: 1–12). For most of the past century, social anthropologists have responded by avoiding biological and evolutionary questions altogether, resulting in a situation in which biological and social anthropologists rarely speak to each other.

When physicists today talk of a 'theory of everything' (ToE), they are wondering whether general relativity (GM) theory and quantum mechanics (QM) might one day be reconciled within a deeper body of theory underlying both (Ellis 1986; Oerter 2006; Weinberg 1993; Hawking and Mlodinow 2010). For anthropologists, the closest parallel might be the hope for an elegant theoretical means of bridging the gulf between the Darwinian paradigm currently prevailing in biological anthropology – sometimes known as 'selfish gene' theory – and the radically different, more holistic approaches adopted by social and cultural anthropologists.

One brilliant armchair anthropologist got tantalizingly close to a theory of everything in the 1890s. Emile Durkheim argued that a certain kind of action – collective ritual action – could establish simultaneously totemism, law, exogamy and kinship in addition to distinctively human language and thought. Everything began, according to Durkheim, when a flow of blood periodically ruptured relations between the sexes. 'All blood is terrible', he observed (Durkheim 1963 [1897]: 83), 'and all sorts of taboos are instituted to prevent contact with it'. During menstruation, females would exercise a 'type of repulsing action which keeps the other sex far from them' (p. 75). This was the origin of the incest taboo. As women bled, it was as if they were wounded game, and since men were related to their own mother through blood, this triggered the idea that the blood of kinship united them equally to the animals they hunted. Thus a single bloodstream ran through the veins of women and animals alike, suggesting the blood's ultimate source in an ancestor who combined human and animal features – the 'totem'. Once menstrual blood had been linked in this way with the blood of the hunt, it became logically possible for a hunter to respect certain animals as if they were his kin, this being the essence of totemism. Within the group's shared blood resided its 'god' or 'totem', 'from which it follows that the blood is a divine thing. When it runs out, the god is spilling over' (Durkheim 1963 [1897]: 89).

Durkheim's case was that distinctively human conceptual thought can be explained on the basis of this one development. Once humans and kangaroos had been constructed as sharing the same clan blood, it became logical for a man of that particular clan to identify himself as a 'kangaroo'. To think in this way, continued Durkheim, might seem paradoxical, violating what he termed 'the principle of contradiction'. Humans and kangaroos are different species: you can be one or the other but not both. And yet, continued Durkheim, the distinguishing feature of human symbolic thought is precisely this:

> Is not the statement that a man is a kangaroo ... equal to identifying the two with each other? But our manner of thought is not different when we say of heat that it is a movement, or of light that it is a vibration of the ether, etc. Every time that we unite heterogeneous terms by an internal bond, we forcibly identify contraries.

Durkheim (1947 [1915]: 238) is here pointing out that human conceptual thought is, above all, metaphorical – an idea which in recent years has become standard (Lakoff and Johnson 1980; Ortony 1993; Goatly 2007). Statements that are true by definition are circular and obvious; to think creatively is to discern truth on a deeper level by means of metaphors – expressions which, interpreted literally, are patent falsehoods (Davidson 1979). The ability to seek out and discern meaning in such falsehoods is the unique distinguishing feature of human conceptual thought. Whereas other species rely heavily on categorical perception – allocating objects and events to either/or categories (Harnad 1987) – humans think conceptually on an additional level by combining opposites, dissolving familiar categories and in the process imaginatively creating new ones.

Just as the Victorians hoped to invent one theory to explain the origins of language, another for religion and so forth, so – until very recently – the evolutionary emergence of language was subdivided into the quite separate challenges of explaining symbols and explaining grammar. The linguist Derek Bickerton, for example, divides language evolution into two steps, the first establishing a 'protolanguage' of grammatically unconnected words while the second conjures grammar into being (Bickerton 2003). In the same vein, evolutionary psychologist Michael Tomasello (2003: 109) suggests that '[l]anguage is a complex outcome of human cognitive and social processes taking place in evolutionary, historical and ontogenetic time. And different aspects of language – for example, symbols and grammar – may have involved different processes and different evolutionary times'.

In contrast to this approach, we endorse Smith and Hoefler (this volume) in claiming that metaphor offers a single solution to the two evolutionary sub-problems. The cognitive mechanisms underlying metaphor, according to these scholars, underpin not only symbols and grammar but all distinctively human communication, both linguistic and non-linguistic, from its prehistorical beginnings to the present. Metaphor is the underlying principle of all that is distinctive about human language and thought (Lakoff and Johnson 1980; Smith and Hoefler 2014). Even scholars such as Dan Sperber and Deidre Wilson – who insist that '"metaphor" is not a theoretically important notion in the study of verbal communication' – do so because they consider the concept too broad, all verbal utterances requiring more than literal decoding: 'We claim that metaphors are not exceptional, and that the linguistic content of all utterances, even those that are literally understood, vastly underdetermines their interpretation' (Sperber and Wilson 2008: 8). Far from being exceptional, saying one thing while meaning another is the norm.

A metaphor is, taken literally, a 'false statement' (Davidson 1979). Faced with this, the hearer must try to work out the speaker's communicative intention, deciding between possibilities on the basis of assumed relevance (Sperber and Wilson 1986). The simple metaphor 'John's a real pig', for instance, might be interpreted in various ways depending on the context: it might mean that John is very messy, that he is very fat, that he is gluttonous or, more generally, that he is badly behaved. The metaphor's less relevant meaning components – for example having a curly tail – must be ignored for communicative success to be achieved (Smith and Hoefler 2014).

Durkheim understood this when faced with the Aboriginal Australian assertion that a man might really be a kangaroo. Instead of dismissing the idea as irrational, he insisted that it reveals to us the workings of man's scientific mind. Durkheim took his illustrations mainly from Australia, where a group of clan members during an initiation ceremony might enact, say, the kangaroo dance, jumping or leaping like kangaroos. With extraordinary insight, he realized that communal activities of this metaphorical kind lie at the basis of all symbolic thinking, including modern science.

In Durkheim's evolutionary narrative, totemism and exogamy emerge together as the earliest form of ritual and social organization. Communal participation in dancing, singing and other ritual performance forges bonds of solidarity while, at the same time, body and mind are seized by a metaphorical representation of their existence as a collective. That metaphor – the 'totem' – is the creature whose movements and appearance are acted out in the dance.

Published in 1897, the earliest version of Durkheim's theoretical model (Durkheim 1963 [1897]) was strongly gendered, with men and women facing each other in opposite camps. Women repulse the other sex with their symbolically potent blood, each dancer's menstrual blood being equated with that of a kangaroo or other game animal. As a result, men jointly perceive their mothers and sisters as active participants in the sacredness of the kangaroo or other emblem of the clan. As sacred beings, these women establish themselves as sexually prohibited, just as meat of the totemic species becomes prohibited flesh. In this way, a powerful communal metaphor enforces a unitary principle of exogamy which applies alike to human and nonhuman kin.

There can be no doubt that Durkheim glimpsed here a theory of everything – a way of explaining the emergence of human society, morality, religion and language in one theoretical move. His ethnographic sources were conscientiously examined and accurately cited, subsequent studies amply confirming his initial insight. Durkheim rightly understood that Aboriginal Australian 'totemic' symbolic equations flow naturally and logically from an initial situation in which women's blood is equated with that of the animals men love to hunt.

Twentieth-century ethnographers have confirmed that this linkage is a constant theme in songs, myths and rock art from across the continent (Berndt 1976; Testart 1978, 1986). An example is David McKnight's (1975: 85) discussion of how meat becomes *ngaintja* – 'sacred' or 'taboo' – among the Wik-Mungkan Aborigines of Cape York Peninsula:

> Any act suggestive of menstrual bleeding makes things *ngaintja*. Thus if blood from an animal falls on a woman's lap, her father and many other male relatives may not eat it. If a young man carries meat on his back or shoulders ... so that the blood runs down between his buttocks this, to the Wik-Mungkan, is too uncomfortably like menstrual blood to be ignored.

It is not surprising, then, to learn (p. 86) that when men cut up the flesh of a recently killed game animal,

> they make certain that women, especially their daughters, stand well away. Men will not even take fish from a daughter if she has caught it with a fishing line and pulled the line so that it falls on her lap. If a daughter should accidentally sit on her father's possessions then they are *ngaintja* to him... I might add that blood from wounds is also considered to be *ngaintja*, though not to the same degree as menstrual blood.

Menstruation is sacred – even taboo – but as a mark of fertility it is especially tempting and difficult to resist. Men fantasize about such women, as these lines from a Western Arnhem Land erotic song-cycle (Berndt 1976: 61) clarify:

> Like blood from a speared kangaroo; sacred blood flows from the uterus...
> They are always there, at the wide expanse of water, the sea-eagle nests...

They are sacred, those young girls of the western tribes, with their
menstrual flow...
They are always there, sitting within their huts like sea-eagle nests,
with blood flowing...
Flowing down from the sacred uterus of the young girl...
Sacred blood flowing in all directions...
Like blood from a speared kangaroo, from the sacred uterus...

Far away in Central Australia, we find similar themes. Among the
most important and powerful figures in Aranda mythology are the
alknarintja women. They are characteristically depicted as
menstruating together. In one song (Róheim 1974: 138–139), the
awesomely powerful women cut their breasts:

On their breasts they make scars.
They slap their thighs...
They are menstruating.
Their flanks are wet with blood.
They talk to each other.

An *alknarintja* may be recognized in a myth by the fact that she is
constantly decorating herself with red ochre, is associated with water
and is 'frequently represented as menstruating copiously' (p. 150).
Alknarintja women possess bullroarers and other symbols of power,
and have solidarity – evoked in one song through the image of a clump
of bushes 'so thick and so pressed against each other that they cannot
move separately' (p. 144). The *alknarintja* are also known as 'women
who refuse men'. The name 'alknarintja' means, in fact, 'eyes-turn-
away'. From another song (p. 141–142) come these lines:

They say, 'I won't go with you'.
'I will remain an alknarintja.'
They whirl their bullroarers.
They stay where they are.
They sit very still.
The man wants them to say, 'I will go with you'.
But they remain where they are.

The strength of Durkheim's origins theory is its parsimony and
simplicity: instead of multiple different theories to explain how symbolic
culture emerged, we are offered just one. Yet it could have been simpler
still. Despite the elegance of his theory, Durkheim offers no simple,
logical explanation for its key feature – the identification of women's
blood with the blood of the hunt. Durkheim marshals ethnographic
details confirming that across Australia, the blood does have this
symbolic significance, but he does not explain how or why hunter-
gatherers across Australia should ever have arrived at that idea.

Durkheim's theories were unfortunately never followed up or appreciated as key to an understanding of how symbolic culture evolved. In recent years, however, hunter-gatherer ethnographers have been able to confirm that his insights about blood were essentially correct. On one level, human or animal blood is just a biological substance. But for traditional hunter-gatherers across the world it is much more than that – it is the primary material from which their most sacred ritual metaphors derive. Anyone familiar with Judaic, Muslim or Christian traditions – as Durkheim certainly was – will realize that things have not changed.

Examples of blood-symbolism abound in virtually all cultures (Buckley and Gottlieb 1988), being especially complex and prominent among Australian hunter-gatherers (e.g. Berndt 1976; Durkheim 1947 [1915]; Knight 1988; Testart 1985, 1986). But sometimes a detailed focus on a particular society can shed light on the wider picture. With this in mind, we turn now to work conducted recently among the BaYaka Pygmy inhabitants of the forests of the Congo Basin. The value of this is that it shows how women actively construct the metaphor of their blood as that of the hunt, thereby turning it into something sacred.

Among these forest people, older women assume primary responsibility for teaching younger ones the importance of dancing and singing, valuing such activity as a primary means of influencing the behaviour of males. The fact that women and men form counterposed communities assertively responding to and thereby shaping one another's sexual strategies sheds a very different light on Durkheim's original argument, from which any hint of conflict or struggle is strangely absent.

For Durkheim, women's blood of its own accord somehow 'repulses' the opposite sex. What's missing in Durkheim's account is an understanding of women's active role in periodically defying male sexual desire. Whereas Durkheim presents menstrual blood as possessing a force which independently repulses males, his theory makes more sense when it is realized that women – like the *alknarintja* sacred beings of Aranda myth – actively refuse men at the moment when they are most desired. Only then does it become clear why metaphorical shape-changing – collectively assuming animal form – is a logical strategy of gender defiance. And only then, finally, does it become clear why and how women establish their own blood as mystically connected with that of the animals men hunt.

To grasp how women achieve this in practice, we may turn to a special word in the lexicon of the BaYaka forest people which, for them, has a host of meanings. *Ekila* can refer to menstruation, blood, taboo, a hunter's meat, good hunting luck, the power of animals to harm humans, and particular dangers to human reproduction, production, health and sanity. As an elderly male informant explained:

> A woman's *ekila* is with the moon. When a woman is *ekila* [menstruating] her husband takes her smell. So he doesn't go hunting or walking in the forest with friends. Animals flee when they smell a woman's *mobeku* (ritual danger). The animals smell her on him. If strong animals, like gorillas, elephants, buffalo, or leopards, smell it they will come, even from far away, charging towards him in a rage, passing other people by just to get him. (Lewis 2008: 298)

Another informant explains:

> *Ekila* is the same as *mobeku*. That's the name of the medicine God *(Komba)* sent women when women put in the moon [menstruate]. The business of *ekila* was first with them. It is all about children. You can see women's tummies swell up at this time. It's the wind. They have to expel their wind as *ekila* [blood]; this cleans out their wombs... Women's biggest husband is the moon.
>   If I'm a hunter, I don't sleep around with different women. If I slept with her, then her, and then her, all the animals would know. They would smell my smell and know 'that hunter has ruined his own *ekila* [ruined his hunting]'. Some will come with great anger. Others, you shoot them, but they won't die. You are very surprised. When you shoot at an antelope from close range and it doesn't die, we call this *ekila*.... (Lewis 2008: 299)

Or again:

> If you are *mobeku*, animals attack you. In big forest full of large game, having sex is *mobeku* – a huge *ekila*. This is because we are in conflict *(bita)* with the animals. If they smell the odour of women, some are frightened and flee you. Others come from far away and follow you, only you. That's why women are frightened in the forest. The animals smell them. (Lewis 2008: 302)

While it is male informants who are speaking here, to understand the logic we must turn to the female community to find out in greater detail what *ekila* really means.

For women and men alike, collective ritual action is fundamental to the day-to-day maintenance of *ekila*. *Ngoku* is women's all-female ritual association, the counterpart of the men's *Ejengi*. After her initiation into the women's secret society, it is only with the onset of her first menstrual flow that a girl is suddenly referred to as *ekila*. This arouses in her a curiosity to delve deeper into the secrets of her sex, learning about procreation and related aspects of cosmology (Lewis

2008). *Ngoku* specifically instructs her in how to use sexual attraction to control men. Women's communal singing and dancing establishes their solidarity so they can band together to resist male violence, periodically withdrawing sex to exert leverage in achieving key goals. Central among these is the proper sharing of meat and respect for egalitarian political norms (Lewis 2008; Finnegan 2009).

While hunters penetrate with their spears and cause dangerous blood to flow, women's priority is to control not only this bloodshed but also their own, rendering it safe and life-bringing to the human group through a range of strategies which include the controlled use of fire – a technology which, as Lévi-Strauss (1970) famously clarified, transforms dangerously raw, bloody meat into desirable flesh (whether human or animal), now safely available or 'cooked'. The gendered rituals of the two sexes balance out and interact, in this way jointly establishing the core metaphorical equivalences of *ekila* – between men killing animals and women birthing children, between the spearing of animals and the penetration of women's bodies in intercourse, between menstrual blood and the blood of the hunt (Lewis 2008; Finnegan 2013).

Among biologists and evolutionary ecologists, it is well understood that for primates in general, it is the females whose foraging and reproductive strategies ultimately determine the direction of evolutionary change (Dunbar 1988; Hrdy 1981; Lindenfors 2005; Lindenfors, Fröberg and Nunn 2004; Lind and Lindenfors 2010; Wrangham 1979, 1980). Regardless of whether or how much they dominate, the fact that 'primate males go where the females are' (Altmann 1990) means that female decision-making is always paramount. This basic understanding of how things work tends to get set aside by modern advocates of 'man the hunter' (e.g. Kaplan et al. 2000, 2001), but we see no justification for this. Even if dominance in our ancestors were so extreme that male control over basic resources characterized all human evolution, as some (e.g. Foley and Gamble 2009) assert, this would not make male decision-making the driver of human evolutionary change. We need to set out from theoretical fundamentals. Since we were once primates, it follows that if males in our case alone came to drive evolution, we would still need to ask at which particular stage – and through which initially female strategies – males stopped going where the females were.

In our view, the best way to avoid these difficulties is to assume theoretical continuity, applying basic primatological understandings equally to evolving humans. The biological background to the scenario we favour – not discussed here – is one in which evolving hominin females had long been mobilizing assistance and support to meet their increasingly costly childcare burdens (Hrdy 2009). They achieved this through a whole range of strategies which included the phasing out of external signs of ovulation, residing where possible with the mother, extending and maintaining female coalitions, raising male levels of commitment, and co-operatively resisting the strategies of dominant male philanderers. Finally, it meant finding new ways of dealing with menstruation which, with ovulation effectively concealed, had become salient as a cue to imminent fertility. The eventual solution involved the use of cosmetic substitutes to prevent real menstrual blood from triggering dangerous levels of inter- and intra-sexual competition and conflict (Power 2009, 2010, 2014; Power and Aiello 1997). Against this background, we attribute the metaphors and equivalences of *ekila* and its cross-cultural variants in the first instance to women's collective action in their own reproductive interests (see Finnegan, this volume).

All this allows us to complete Durkheim's 'theory of everything' in a much more powerful and parsimonious way. Metamorphosing into animal form, bleeding in sympathy with wounded game – such metaphorical equivalences are best seen as signals of defiance aimed at male sexual desire. If women are to use sex to control male behaviour, they must – at the very least – be able to say 'No'. And what better way to do this than to form into a defiant mass, resorting to explicit body language, dancing the way animals dance, bleeding the way animals bleed? Women's strategy is to set out from the fundamental male need for a sexual partner who is female, human and available and, with that in mind, systematically enact an identity that is the reverse:

$$\text{human} \rightarrow \text{animal}$$
$$\text{female} \rightarrow \text{male}$$
$$\text{available} \rightarrow \text{unavailable}$$

By ritually denying men in this way, women demonstrate that they cannot be taken for granted. While welcoming men's capacities for shedding blood, they are able to insist that there are limits. Killing game animals with piercing weapons is not to be confused with using those same weapons against women, or against rival males. Establishing such boundaries is in everyone's long-term interest because otherwise – if males could resort to weapons at will – the consequences might be calamitous. Without powerful ritual inhibitions – without concepts on the model of *ekila* – community survival would be placed at risk.

We can now state the stunningly simple mechanism through which this entire complex is generated. When a menstruating dancer performs the steps and characteristic antics of a game animal, the very fact that she is bleeding now constructs that animal as a wounded one. Metaphorically, her blood is now that animal's blood. Paradoxically, it is this very identification of human with animal blood which keeps the two categories apart. Never laugh at the sufferings of an animal you have killed, insist the BaYaka – it might turn out to be your own unborn child. The Hadza have essentially the same idea:

> The whole process of hunting big game (male productivity) is symbolically linked with the whole process of female reproduction (female productivity). Activities in one process are mystically dangerous for activities in the other. A man whose wife is menstruating cannot hunt big game because the poison of his arrows is believed to lose its efficacy. If his wife is pregnant he cannot walk on the tracks of a wounded game animal because this will cause it to recover from its wounds. Reciprocally, if a man whose wife is pregnant laughs at or mocks the dead but not yet dismembered carcass of a game animal, the unborn baby will be born with defects which resemble the characteristics of the dead animal. (Woodburn 1982: 188)

Identifying the blood of the hunt with that of menstruation forces men to keep their wits about them, using violence with care, aware at all times that recklessly spilled blood might turn out to be their own.

The blood of menstruation, then, is that of the hunt. Whereas Durkheim had to add this all-important feature to his model, in our version it is intrinsic from the outset. Women who mimic an animal at the time of menstruation are by that fact alone constructing Durkheim's Ur-metaphor, the primordial metaphor from which society emerges as a moral entity. Once this conceptual equivalence has been established, it triggers a cascade of subsidiary metaphorical equivalences, as seen above – between men killing animals and women birthing children, between the spearing of animals and the penetration of women's bodies in intercourse, between taboos on menstruation and hunting taboos. These associations are ubiquitous, and it is not easy to imagine how else they might be explained.

There is a background to all this in evolutionary biology, beyond our remit here. Suffice it to say that we routinely expect female reproductive priorities to conflict in key areas with those of males. Females cannot afford to co-operate unconditionally with the opposite sex, any more than males can afford to collude unconditionally with females (Trivers 1972). So it may seem inexplicable why the males in our origins narrative should collude with the female tactics described.

We cannot assume male moral sensibilities here; in an evolutionary account, taking primate sociology and psychology as our point of departure, moral constraints must be explained, not just assumed. The mere fact that women pretend to be game animals is no reason why male onlookers should collude with or join in the make-believe – especially if it means foregoing sex.

It is true that a male could respond to women's pretence with violence, but there are good reasons why this might not work. Although fighting is always an option, it entails risks and costs. A violent male attacking his female partner and her allies might unwittingly endanger his own genetic offspring. Apart from that, he would have no reason to expect his male companions to support him. After all, if he did succeed in imposing his sexual dominance, they, too, would have good reason to feel threatened. In deciding whether to co-operate or fight, we expect the primate male to weigh up the costs and benefits. Provided the costs of violence are made sufficiently high, it may make better Darwinian sense (and so begin to feel logical and emotionally satisfying) for males to nurture their own babies – hence their own genetic future – by acknowledging female solidarity, respecting its message, co-operating in the hunt and bringing back game to camp (Knight 1999). Following this logic, under both pressure and seduction from females, our male ancestors willingly succumb to being fully human (cf Finnegan, this volume).

It is clear that wrong species/wrong sex is on one level pure nonsense. But escaping the confines of literal truth is precisely the secret of symbolism. Saying one thing in order to mean another is the essence not only of metaphor but of all symbolic language and life (Knight 2008; Knight and Lewis 2014). Taken literally, every metaphor is patently absurd, and claiming to be a game animal is no exception. The trickster who plays such a prominent role in hunter-gatherer narratives is endlessly switching gender and species, transforming himself into his own opposite. This trickster is sex-resistant, rebellious and ludicrous – yet also a lustful clown, creator of antelopes and guardian of menstrual taboos. Because trickery is the secret of symbolic culture, the Kalahari Bushmen seem uncannily perceptive in considering a trickster figure such as *//Gauwa* 'the central denizen of the First Order of existence' (Guenther 1999: 96). Each trick provokes laughter because it is such evident nonsense. But behind the hilarity is an egalitarian purpose, which becomes especially apparent when the story is acted out in ritual performance to the accompaniment of laughter. Yes, it looks like nonsense. But when women band together and hilariously insist to men that they are game animals, the implication of this metaphor – 'No sex' – comes over loud and clear.

Our scenario would seem weak if the core metaphor we have described turned out to be confined to just a small range of hunter-gatherer cultures. It is possible that on closer examination, it will turn out to be universal – a core symbolic feature of the hunter-gatherer lifestyle as such. This can be tested.

So far, we have relied on Durkheim's survey of nineteenth-century Australian ethnography augmented with recent work among the BaYaka. But at the southern end of the African continent, among the Ju/'hoansi and other Bushmen, we have perhaps the clearest confirmation of all. Among these groups, the Eland Bull Dance (in some regions the Gemsbok Dance) was the primary initiation rite, fundamental to San cultural identity (see also Low, Watts and Power, this volume).

The dance celebrated a young woman's first menstruation. As she began to bleed, her senior female kin would ensure that she entered a special hut, where she would remain for several days. Inside that hut, she consorted with – or in some accounts metamorphosed into – the great Eland Bull, surrounded outside by female dancers thrusting out their buttocks while holding aloft forked sticks to mimic the horns of rutting eland cows (Guenther 1999; Lewis-Williams 1981; Lewis-Williams and Pearce 2004). At this point, as the performance makes clear, women are consorting not with their usual sexual partner but with their fantasy lover – the Eland Bull (Power and Watts 1997). It would be hard to imagine an enactment which more strikingly confirms the predictions of our model. The women are signalling to any onlooking male their message of playful yet determined defiance: wrong species, wrong sex, wrong time. Males must not probe this signal too closely. /Xam Bushmen warn that staring at a girl during such proceedings might 'turn a man into a tree' (Lewis-Williams and Pearce 2004: 162).

Yet another example is provided by the Hadza of Tanzania, where the same logic is found. The girl's initiation ritual, known as *Maitoko*, re-enacts the story of Mambedeko, the 'Woman With the Zebra's penis' (Power 2015). At the beginning of time, this mythical heroine would metamorphose into a male zebra, using its penis to have sex with all the other women – known as the heroine's 'wives'. During *Maitoko*, women and girls to this day shed blood together in re-enactment of this story, their legs adorned with zebra stripes. Echoing the 'wrong sex' theme, when a Hadza girl first menstruates, she is congratulated for having 'shot her zebra' (*//akakwa dongo* – Mouriki, pers. comm. 2015). Stepping into the role of Mambedeko with her zebra penis, she conveys the message to any onlooking male that she is not available for sex – she is now the one who penetrates. Once again, wrong species, wrong sex, wrong time.

As far away as Australia, we find endless variations on these themes. Testart (1978: 113) perceptively describes the relationship between the Rainbow Serpent and menstrual blood in Aboriginal mythology as 'an association of opposites linked by their very contradiction'. When women dance while menstruating together, they metamorphose into an immense rainbow which is also a snake. Recorded in north-east Arnhem Land, the best-known of all Aboriginal myths – the story of the two Wawilak Sisters – depicts this immense creature as an all-swallowing, shimmering skin enveloping menstruating women whose blood is that of the game animals men hunt. When the snake is aroused by this blood, speared and bleeding animals placed on a fire defiantly jump up, come back to life and dive for protection into the pool (Warner 1957: 234–301). The message 'wrong species, wrong sex, wrong time' is here conveyed by the terrifying image of an immense creature which is gender-ambivalent, species-ambivalent, conjured up by women's blood – and hostile to both cooking and exogamous sex (Knight 1988). Here, as across much of the continent, things have got complicated over time because men have found ways of intentionally subverting women's power. Men understand full well that when shedding one another's blood during rites of initiation, they are modelling themselves on menstruating women:

> But really we have been stealing what belongs to them (the women), for it is mostly all woman's business; and since it concerns them it belongs to them. Men have nothing to do really, except copulate, it belongs to the women. All that belonging to those Wauwelak, the baby, the blood, the yelling, their dancing, all that concerns the women; but every time we have to trick them. Women can't see what men are doing, although it really is their own business, but we can see their side. This is because all the Dreaming business came out of women – everything... In the beginning we had nothing, because men had been doing nothing; we took these things from women (Berndt 1951: 55).

If this indigenous analysis is accepted – and much evidence supports it – we can treat male ritual power across much of the world as modeled on a female template, with concepts reminiscent of *ekila* playing a central role. This sheds fresh light on Lévi-Strauss's extraordinary thesis that the world's most stubbornly surviving narratives are 'One Myth Only'. The stories differ gloriously, but their grammar remains everywhere intact. This long-term conservatism of structure is perhaps still more evident in ritual, whose recurrent forms reflect facts as fundamental as the need to reconcile the priorities of two polar opposite sexes, only one of which gets pregnant. As Bloch (1992: 23) explains: 'It is because the symbolism of ritual is an attempt to solve problems intrinsic to the human condition and based on a similar understanding of life that ritual systems are so similar and produce such similar political results'. Exploring sacrificial bloodshed as 'the irreducible core of the ritual process' across traditional cultures, Bloch in the same essay goes on to remind us that the central notion is reversal – as in the two-way metamorphosis (analysed above) from hunter to hunted and vice versa.

We are brought back again and again to animal metamorphosis as the world's first metaphor, endorsing Durkheim's insightful attempt at a 'theory of everything', first proposed in 1897. We can now see more clearly than ever how a certain kind of action – collective ritual action – could establish simultaneously totemism, law, exogamy and kinship in addition to distinctively human language and thought.

References

Altmann, J. 1990. 'Primate Males Go Where the Females Are', *Animal Behavior* 39: 193–195.

Berndt, R.M. 1951. *Kunapipi*. Melbourne: Cheshire.

———. 1976. *Love Songs of Arnhem Land*. Chicago: University of Chicago Press.

Bickerton, D. 2003. 'Symbol and Structure: A Comprehensive Framework for Language Evolution', in M. Christiansen and S. Kirby (eds), *Language Evolution*. Oxford: Oxford University Press, pp. 77–93.

Bloch, M. 1992. *Prey Into Hunter*. Cambridge: Cambridge University Press.

Buckley, T., and A. Gottlieb (eds). 1988. *Blood Magic. The Anthropology of Menstruation*. Berkeley, Los Angeles and London: University of California Press.

Davidson, R.D. 1979. 'What Metaphors Mean', in S. Sacks (ed.), *On Metaphor*. Chicago: University of Chicago Press, pp. 29–45.

Dor, D., C. Knight and J. Lewis. 2014. 'Introduction: A Social Perspective on How Language Began', in D. Dor, C. Knight and J. Lewis (eds), *The Social Origins of Language*. Oxford: Oxford University Press, pp. 1–12.

Dunbar, R.I.M. 1988. *Primate Social Systems*. London and Sydney: Croom Helm.

Durkheim, E. 1947 [1915]. *The Elementary Forms of the Religious Life: A Study in Religious Sociology*, trans. J.W. Swain. Glencoe, Illinois: The Free Press.

————. 1963 [1897] 'La Prohibition de L'inceste et ses Origines', *L'Année Sociologique* 1: 1–70. Reprinted as *Incest: The Nature and Origin of the Taboo*, trans. E. Sagarin. New York: Stuart.

Ellis, J. 1986. 'The Superstring: Theory of Everything, or of Nothing?', *Nature* 323(6089): 595–598.

Finnegan, M. 2009. 'Political Bodies: Some Thoughts on Women's Power among Central African Hunter-gatherers', *Radical Anthropology* 3: 31–37.

————. 2013. 'The Politics of Eros: Ritual Dialogue and Egalitarianism in Three Central African Hunter-gatherer Societies', *Journal of the Royal Anthropological Institute* (N.S.) 19: 697–715.

Foley, R. and C. Gamble. 2009. 'The Ecology of Social Transitions in Human Evolution', *Philosophical Transactions of the Royal Society of London, B. (Biological Sciences)* 364: 3267–3279.

Goatly, A. 2007. *Washing the Brain: Metaphor and Hidden Ideology*. Amsterdam and Philadelphia: John Benjamins.

Guenther, M. 1999. *Tricksters and Trancers: Bushman Religion and Society*. Bloomington: Indiana Press.

Harnad, S. 1987. *Categorical Perception: The Groundwork of Cognition*. Cambridge: Cambridge University Press.

Hawking, S. and L. Mlodinow. 2010. *The Grand Design*. New York: Bantam Books.

Hrdy, S.B. 1981. *The Woman that Never Evolved*. Cambridge, MA: Harvard University Press.

————. 2009. *Mothers and Others: The Evolutionary Origins of Mutual Understanding*. Cambridge, MA: Harvard University Press.

Kaplan, H. et al. 2000. 'A Theory of Human Life History Evolution: Diet, Intelligence, and Longevity', *Evolutionary Anthropology* 9(4): 156–185.

————. 2001. 'The Embodied Capital Theory of Human Evolution', in P.T. Ellison (ed.), *Reproductive Ecology and Human Evolution*. New York: Aldine de Gruyer, pp. 153–176.

Knight, C. 1988. 'Menstrual Synchrony and the Australian Rainbow Snake', in T. Buckley and A. Gottlieb (eds), *Blood Magic: The Anthropology of Menstruation*. Berkeley and Los Angeles: University of California Press, pp. 232–255.

————. 1995. *Blood Relations: Menstruation and the Origins of Culture*. London and New Haven: Yale University Press.

————. 1999. 'Sex and Language as Pretend-Play', in R. Dunbar, C. Knight and C. Power (eds), *The Evolution of Culture*. Edinburgh: Edinburgh University Press, pp. 228–247.

————. 2008. '"Honest Fakes" and Language Origins', *Journal of Consciousness Studies* 15(10–11): 236–248.

———— and J. Lewis. 2014. 'Vocal Deception, Laughter, and the Linguistic Significance of Reverse Dominance', in D. Dor, C. Knight and J. Lewis (eds), *The Social Origins of Language*. Oxford: Oxford University Press, pp. 297–314.

Lakoff, G. and M. Johnson. 1980. *Metaphors We Live By*. Chicago: University of Chicago Press.

Lévi-Strauss, C. 1970. *The Raw and the Cooked. Introduction to a Science of Mythology 1*. London: Cape.

Lewis, J. 2008. '*Ekila*: Blood, Bodies and Egalitarian Societies', *Journal of the Royal Anthropological Institute* (N.S.) 14: 297–315.

Lewis-Williams, D. 1981. *Believing and Seeing. Symbolic Meanings in Southern San Rock Paintings*. London: Academic Press.

——— and D. Pearce. 2004. *San Spirituality: Roots, Expressions, and Social Consequences*. Cape Town: Double Storey.

Lind. J, and P. Lindenfors. 2010. 'The Number of Cultural Traits Is Correlated with Female Group Size but Not with Male Group Size in Chimpanzee Communities', *PLoS ONE* 5(3): e9241.

Lindenfors, P. 2005. 'Neocortex Evolution in Primates: The "Social Brain" is for Females', *Biological Letters* (1): 407–410.

———. L. Fröberg and C.L. Nunn. 2004. 'Females Drive Primate Evolution', *Proceedings of the Royal Society of London* B (Suppl.) 271: S101–S103.

McKnight, D. 1975. 'Men, Women and Other Animals: Taboo and Purification among the Wikmungkan', in R. Willis (ed.), *The Interpretation of Symbolism*. London: Malaby, pp. 77–97.

Oerter, R. 2006. *The Theory of Almost Everything: The Standard Model, the Unsung Triumph of Modern Physics*. New York: Penguin.

Ortony, A. 1993. *Metaphor and Thought*. 2nd edn. Cambridge: Cambridge University Press.

Power, C. 2009. 'Sexual Selection Models for the Emergence of Symbolic Communication: Why they Should be Reversed', in R. Botha and C. Knight (eds), *The Cradle of Language*. Oxford: Oxford University Press, pp. 257–280.

———. 2010. 'Cosmetics, Identity and Consciousness', *Journal of Consciousness Studies* 17(7–8): 73–94.

———. 2014. 'The Evolution of Ritual as a Process of Sexual Selection', in D. Dor, C. Knight and J. Lewis (eds), *The Social Origins of Language*. Oxford: Oxford University Press, pp. 196–207.

———. 2015. 'Hadza Gender Ritual – *Epeme* and *Maitoko* – Considered as Counterparts', *Hunter Gatherer Research* 1: 333–358. doi:10.3828/hgr.2015.18.

——— and L.C. Aiello. 1997. 'Female Proto-Symbolic Strategies', in L.D. Hager (ed.), *Women in Human Evolution*. New York and London: Routledge, pp. 153–171.

——— and I. Watts. 1997. 'The Woman with the Zebra's Penis. Gender, Mutability and Performance', *Journal of the Royal Anthropological Institute* (N. S.) 3: 537–560.

Róheim, G. 1974. *Children of the Desert*. New York: Basic Books.

Smith, A.D.M. and S.H. Hoefler. 2014. 'The Pivotal Role of Metaphor in the Evolution of Human Language', in J.E. Díaz Vera (ed.), *Metaphor and Metonymy through Time and Culture*. The Hague: Mouton, pp.123–139.

Sperber, D. and D. Wilson. 1986. *Relevance. Communication and Cognition.* Oxford: Blackwell.

———. 2008. 'A Deflationary Account of Metaphors', in R.W. Gibbs (ed.), *The Cambridge Handbook of Metaphor and Thought.* Cambridge: Cambridge University Press, pp. 84–105.

Testart, A. 1978. *Des Classifications Dualistes en Australie.* Lille: Maison des Sciences de l'Homme, Université de Lille.

———. 1985. *Le Communisme Primitif.* Paris: Éditions de la Maison des Sciences de l'Homme.

———. 1986. *Essai sur les Fondements de la Division Sexuelle du Travail chez les Chasseurs-cueilleurs.* Paris: Éditions de l'École des Hautes Études en Sciences Sociales.

Tomasello, M. 2003. 'Different Origins of Symbols and Grammar', in M.H. Christiansen and S. Kirby (eds), *Language Evolution.* Oxford: Oxford University Press, pp. 94–110.

Trivers, R.L. 1972. 'Parental Investment and Sexual Selection', in B. Campbell (ed.), *Sexual Selection and the Descent of Man 1871–1971.* Chicago: Aldine, pp. 136–179.

Warner, W.L. 1957. *A Black Civilization.* New York: Harper.

Weinberg, S. 1993. *Dreams of a Final Theory: The Search for the Fundamental Laws of Nature.* London: Hutchinson Radius.

Woodburn, J.C. 1974. 'The Interpretation of Hadza and other Menstrual Taboos'. Unpublished paper cited in J. Woodburn. 1982. 'Social Dimensions of Death in Four African Hunting and Gathering Societies', in M. Bloch and J. Parry (eds), *Death and the Regeneration of Life.* Cambridge: Cambridge University Press, pp. 187–210.

Wrangham, R.W. 1979. 'Sex Differences in Chimpanzee Dispersion', in D.A. Hamburg and E.R. McCown (eds), *The Great Apes: Perspectives on Human Evolution.* Menlo Park, CA: Benjamin/Cummings, pp. 481–490.

———. 1980. 'An Ecological Model of Female-Bonded Primate Groups', *Behaviour* 75: 269–299.

Chris Knight is best known for his 1991 book, *Blood Relations: Menstruation and the Origins of Culture.* A co-founder with Jim Hurford of the Evolution of Language series of international conferences, he has published many chapters and articles on the origins of language and helped edit six volumes on such topics. Now a senior research associate at University College London, he was until his retirement in 2009 Professor of Anthropology at the University of East London. His most recent book, *Decoding Chomsky: Science and Revolutionary Politics,* analyses Noam Chomsky's impact on linguistics and political activism over the past half century.

Jerome Lewis is Reader in Social Anthropology, UCL. He studies hunter-gatherers and former hunter-gatherers across Central Africa. After researching the impact of the genocide on Rwanda's Twa Pygmies, he worked with Mbendjele Pygmies in Congo-Brazzaville on egalitarian politics, child socialization, play, religion and communication. This has led to publications on egalitarianism, language, music, taboo, property and inter-ethnic relations. Examining the impact of global forces on forest people across the Congo Basin has led to research into human rights abuses, discrimination, economic and legal marginalization, and to applied research supporting conservation efforts by forest people. He is co-director of the Extreme Citizen Science Research Group, and of CAoS, the Centre for the Anthropology of Sustainability.

Chapter 4

SEXUAL INSULT AND FEMALE MILITANCY

Shirley G. Ardener

This article attempts to examine certain manifestations of female militancy in Africa, not only for their own interest, but also to see whether they can throw any light upon the completely independent modern women's liberation movements with which we are now familiar in the West. The African ethnographical material, which is set out first, refers mainly to the Bakweri, the Balong and the Kom of West Cameroon. Besides oral reports collected from Cameroonians about traditional behaviour and on particular occurrences, for the Bakweri there is additional relevant documentation from court records. For the Kom some published material is available, but I rely here mainly upon information collected by a Kom who had an interest in social anthropology, as well as being the son of one of the principal female actors in the drama, which will unfold below. The Cameroon material is followed by some relevant data from other parts of Africa. Discussion is then broadened to include material on the women's liberation movement in America and England.

The Bakweri

The Bakweri live on the slopes and around the base of the Cameroon Mountain, which is a volcano of some 13,500 feet lying on the west coast of Africa. They are the largest autochthonous population in the area, numbering near 20,000 persons. They speak a Bantu language, and they distinguish a category, which they label *titi ikoli* which is relevant to our discussion of female militancy. It is difficult to give a precise translation of the expression. Bakweri explain it in different ways: *titi ikoli* is 'beautiful'; *titi ikoli* means something valuable 'as if one married a woman for £1,000'; yet, 'the word refers to an insult'. As we shall see, it is possible to speak of the 'native law of *titi ikoli*' and of things being 'of the nature of *titi ikoli*'. The expression falls into two parts: *ikoli* has the independent meaning of 'thousand'. *Titi* is said to be a childish word for the female vulva, although the normal term for this is *ndondo*. It is sometimes used to refer to young girls. Everyone is said to 'know the implications in [the combination] *titi ikoli*' and usually mention of the expression brings forth embarrassed laughter. It comprehends the following main associations: 'a woman's underparts' (the genitals, anus and buttocks), and the insult of these; and 'women's secrets' and the revealing of these. At the same time it is associated with certain types of mandatory female sanctions, which follow upon insults.

The insult is typically envisaged in the form of an accusation that the sexual parts of women smell. If such an insult has been uttered to a Bakweri woman before a witness, she is supposed immediately to call out all the other women of the village. The circumstances having been recounted, the women then run and pluck vegetation from the surrounding bush, which they tie around their waists. Converging again upon the offender they demand immediate recantation and a recompense. If their demands are not met they all proceed to the house of the village head. The culprit will be brought forward, and the charges laid. If the insult is proved to have taken place, he will be fined a pig of a certain size for distribution to the group of women, or its money equivalent plus something extra, possibly salt, a fowl or money, for the woman who has been directly insulted. The women then surround him and sing songs accompanied by obscene gestures. All the other men beat a hasty retreat, since it is expected that they will be ashamed to stay and watch while their wives, sisters, sisters-in-law and old women join the dance. The culprit must stay, but he will try to hide his eyes. Finally the women retire victoriously to divide the pig between them.

The songs the women sing are often obscene by allusion, as for instance, in the song:

Na l-umwe njenje, e.
(I prick thorn)

Another kind of song would be:

Titi ikoli, a senje veoli,
molonga na molonga

(*Titi ikoli* is not a thing for insults,
  beautiful beautiful)

Other types of insult are recognized, as we shall see below, but it was said by a youth that offences relating to *titi ikoli* had become less common, since 'people were more clever and would not insult people like that. Not that they would not insult nowadays, but that they were cleverer to do it in the house with no-one to be witness'.

Cases of abuse of the type discussed were reported as having occurred, not only in Bakweri villages, but also in the ethnically mixed immigrant-dominated plantation camps and townships lying between them. For instance, in 1953, at a plantation labour camp, a Balundu boy cursed a woman saying she was 'rotten'. The women were all annoyed and they combined, regardless of tribal origin, and attempted to catch the offender. He managed to escape, but they determined to watch out for him.

Judicial Procedures

During the late colonial period women had largely replaced these traditional direct sanctions by the use of formal court procedures. Looking through notes taken from old court records for a number of Bakweri villages for 1956, several cases of abuse of this type were revealed. The records were kept in English or pidgin English, by court clerks, and give useful examples of situations which could provoke such insults.

In the dispute taken by Mary Ekumbe and other women of Mafanja against Efende Mwendeley of Mafanja, before the Bonjongo Court, the charge was:

> The plaintiff claims jointly for self and other women of Mafanja Bakweri Native Town the sum of £20, being damages for defamation of character and slander on about the 14th February 1956 at about 2 p.m. In that Defendant did on 14th February 1956 at about 2 p.m. meet with Madam Therisia Ese at Mafanja town and used the following words in Bakweri language: '*Ngwete ja varana isasosa imbondo jawu. Eveli ndi varana vase. Ese nyi? Ema linga emna na mende o vewa. Ndi na suu mwango*'. The above speech in Bakweri language means that the women in this village have smelling bottoms and are not washing their bottoms. You are glad that I have gone to prison. I have won the case.

The defendant, Efende, denied the charge. The leading plaintiff, Mary, gave the following evidence:

Some months ago defendant had a case of a cap gun with Carl Bweme. This matter was reported to police and a police constable came [from town] to arrest defendant [and took him away]. A few days later defendant returned rejoicing that he had been acquitted. We all were happy to hear that, and we were trying to welcome [him, and] he turned to us and used the words mentioned above on us. We got offended and reported the matter to the village head Kekele where defendant was found guilty and asked to pay £5.0.0 to the women, [but] he refused. Then we took action in the magistrates' court.

The magistrate's court had then referred the case back to the local village court.

The women's case was much strengthened by the support of the defendant's wife, who after reporting what her husband had said about the Mafanja women, remarked sadly: 'Hearing this I was touched' (that is: upset). The court ruled in favour of the women and awarded them £10 damages, and costs of £4.0.6d. The reasons given by the court for this decision were:

Defendant admits that he used insultive words on the people of Mafanja including women. But has refused to tell court the words on the people. Plaintiff has 3 witnesses to support her statement and defendant's wife is one. Defendant has no witness for his defence. The real damages that would have been awarded to the women according to local customary laws is £5.6.0. The court considers the award of £10.0.0. because defendant has suffered the women by going to Buea Magistrate's Court and to this Court.[1]

In the same court, Namondo Lokita of Ewongo accused another woman of (as a judge put it) insulting 'the lower part of women'. She claimed £3 'being damages for insult that Plaintiff speaks with the anus'. Namondo's evidence went as follows (I paraphrase where not in quotation marks): the defendant, Sundi, is my sister-in-law. She began to talk against me and I reported this to her sister Misis, who then warned her not to do so. Whereupon the defendant Sundi, in front of witnesses, said 'my disgrace of suing people to court had gone far and wide'. Namondo continued:

I asked whether suing people to court was a crime. I told her that she should not forget she is so mouthy that she could not stay with the husband in a house for a long period. Then she said I speak with my Anus. Tondi heard this...

Sundi's side of the story was as follows:

It is true [that the] Plaintiff is my sister-in-law. One day her husband came to ask me that I talked ill of Plaintiff that I asked whether plaintiff was wearing high hill shoes. I refused the fact. [Later I was with the

> Plaintiff and] she began to quarrel [with] me. She said I had a disgrace
> that I would not stay in any house with my husband because of being
> too mouthy. I asked whether she was speaking with her anus...

Namondo had taken Sundi before the village head, Nambele Moka,
who supported her complaint. But Sundi would not accept his ruling
and had then gone to another elder who supported her instead.

After hearing all the evidence the court ruled in favour of the
plaintiff Namondo, awarding 30/- damages and 12/6 costs. The
reasons given were:

1. Defendant admits that she said Plaintiff speaks with the anus.
2. Defendant was found guilty by chief Nambile who heard witnesses.
   The second elder who found the plaintiff guilty [that is, found Sundi,
   our Defendant, not guilty] did not hear any witnesses.

The court then added the general principle, with which we are now
concerned: 'It is unlawful to insult the lower part of women'.[2]

Another case which was brought before the Lisoka Court is useful
because it concerns the definition of *titi ikoli*. The interpretation of the
term made by the women plaintiffs was not upheld by the all-male
court bench. The case was brought by Namondo Keke of 'Wonjia
Women Community' against another woman, Elisah Ngalle, also of
Wonjia. The claim was for £6.10.0 'being compensation for woman
"titi Ikolli"'. The plaintiff, being ill, was represented by another woman
of the same community. Her case was presented thus:

> One day I was in my house and so Defendant and her husband had a
> dispute. She suspected the husband of adultery. That she met a rag on
> the bed owned by one Lyona [= Liengu] Ikome. This rag is what we
> women use for co-habiting. It was a very shameful thing when this was
> brought out. We then decided to call for Lyengu [Liengu] Ikome.
> Defendant disagreed. This is why the community of Wonjia women
> have sued her to Court that she has proven women's secrets.

The rag was produced in court. The defendant, Elisah, did not in fact
deny the circumstances, but said as part of her evidence:

> Very soon woman said I have offended them by native law of 'titi ikoli'.
> This was at my surprise. 'Titi ikoli' means a person who has abused
> another the private part. I did not abuse anybody. I wonder to be sued in
> Court.

Although the plaintiff (acting for the 'women's community') affirmed
that 'any rag of this nature is of "titi ikoli"', the court dismissed the
case against Elisah. Here, however, we meet the element of 'revealing
women's secrets'.[3]

These incidents all involved Bakweri. There are many migrants from other parts of Cameroon in the area, and at Muea Court, in the same year, a woman described as 'Catherine of Yaounde at Muea' sued a plantation worker from the up-country plateau who was known to the court as 'Thomas of Grassfield at Lysoka Camp'. She asked for £15 'being compensation for immoral insult against Plaintiff in that her private part is watery and hollow since 2 weeks'. Thomas did not show up in court. Catherine gave her evidence as follows:

> One day while coming from the farm in company of [two Muea women] the Defendant saw me and called me. I kept mute. He began to abuse me to say my private part is hollow and watery. I then held him. The Molyko C[ameroon] D[evelopment] C[orporation] Manager met us and on inquiry, I told him the whole story. He then advised me to sue to Court. Before suing to Court I first of all approached the Overseer and the headman of [the] Defendant['s plantation work gang] was authorized [to hear the complaint]. The defendant was called for hearing but refused. This is why the case has been brought before this Court.

The two Muea women witnesses confirmed Catherine's story and the court ruled in her favour, awarding her £10 damages and costs. A Free Warrant of Arrest of the defendant Thomas was issued.[4]

The seriousness with which the courts regarded insults of this kind is confirmed when we consider the level of damages awarded at that time in other types of defamation case. In Bonjongo during the year under examination, 206 new cases were heard (plus fifty enforcement cases). Fifteen of these (or approximately 7 per cent of new cases) involved defamation of one sort or another. Apart from the two cases we have considered above there were: defamation by accusation of witchcraft, six cases; by accusation of corruption (also in fact a witchcraft case), one case; one case of false accusation of theft; one case where the plaintiff claimed to have been falsely accused of destroying crops; one defamation case where plaintiff (who was to be a selector in a succession dispute) had been accused of not being a citizen of his village. There was one case each of 'scandalizing' or 'traduction' of name, and one where the plaintiff had been insulted by being called a fool. The damages awarded in the cases that were successful were as follows: false accusation of witchcraft, two cases, damages assessed at £1 and £5; false accusation of theft, £6; and for falsely alleging that plaintiff had destroyed crops, damages 10/-. 'Scandalizing my name' was proved, and a recompense of £1 was given; and damages for suggesting that Plaintiff was a fool were assessed at 5/-.

The fines in the cases that were discussed earlier were as follows: Namondo, who had asked for £3, received 30/- damages from Sundi.

In the case where Efende had to pay damages to the women of Mafanja, the court assessed the customary charge as £5.6.0, but ordered him to pay £10, for putting the women to the trouble of taking him to court (the women had wanted £20). The women of Wonjia asked for, but did not get £6.10.0, since the case was dismissed. Although Catherine did not get all the £15 she asked for, she was awarded £10. These sums may seem paltry by modern English monetary standards, but they were quite high in Bakweri terms at the time, especially compared to damages paid for other insults. They were surprisingly high when one considers that damages demanded of co-respondents in divorce cases were set as low as £2.2.6 (a sum known as 'an adultery fee'), and that where divorce was not involved compensation paid by an adulterer was likely to be in the order of £5: only half the sum which Efende had to pay the Mafanja women.

❊   ❊   ❊   ❊   ❊

What can be teased out of the evidence so far considered? In *titi ikoli* we find a semantic field which includes 'beautiful and above price', the female genitals and, possibly by extension, the neighbouring area of the anus and buttocks, and is associated with 'women's secrets'. It includes the serious offence of stating publicly that the private parts of women smell. Both men and women may commit the offence. Such insults concern not only the woman directly abused, but all women. Mandatory militant action follows which overrides allegiance to kin and tribal groups. Women demonstrate, not on behalf of the victim of the abuse, but on behalf of themselves as a sexual group. Traditionally on these occasions they dress as the 'wild' in green vegetation. Judicial procedures controlled by men may be invoked in both traditional and modern circumstances.

In stressing the particular association of *titi ikoli* with women, the possibility of an association of the term with men has not been excluded. In response to questions it was said that men would resent insults of the kind under discussion, but it was agreed that there would be no question of men coming out to demonstrate *en masse* or to dance or to sing indecent songs. The only alleged evidence of such insults being directed against men that I have was the attempt by Efende to escape the wrath of the women of Mafanja by saying he had 'insulted all people both women and men ... I did not call one's name'. He hoped, it seems, thus to desexualize the insults, but no offence seems to have been taken by the men if he did so. Young brides are particularly warned not to insult their husbands in certain ways:

these include spitting, and a certain gesture made with the hand, but no mention is made of *titi ikoli* insults.

The Balong

The Balong are a people numbered in hundreds only, who live in four villages at the foot of the mountain, about forty miles inland, sharing a boundary with the Bakweri. In all four villages immigrants are very conspicuous. Although there are differences Balong also share many features with the Bakweri. Balong women too are prepared to come out in defence of their sex:

> When a man insults his wife and says 'Your ass de smell' it is like insulting all women, and all the women will be angry. Even if a brother curses his sister like that it will be the same. The women will tell other women and in the evening they will go to that man and demand a fine of £5 and one pig and soap for all to wash their bodies because he has said that women smell. If the man refuses, the women will send a young woman round the village with a bell to warn men to stay indoors. They [the women] will be angry and they will take all their clothes off. They will shame him and sing songs. They will sing *Ndungtu fumwe figa wa* (I knock my toe, it hurts, meaning 'man curse me, I vex').

Usually the man will pay the fine, but if he still refuses the women will go and tell the old men of the village. If they do not get satisfaction there, in the last resort they will take the offender to court.

Balong women told of these events with obvious glee. The chief's sister, a youngish woman, said that she had on one occasion been 'a soldier boy', that is one of the young women chosen as messengers by the older women to do 'the fighting', and she claimed that she had helped to seize a man. The Balong also reported a case of two women who had quarrelled and had insulted each other in the standard way. The women of all Yoke village gathered and fined them £5 each, which they paid. The money was used to buy salt from a town about forty miles away. It is to be noted that this salt was divided among all the women of Yoke village, including the newly born female children. The Balong called this *titi ikoli*-like custom *ndong*. I cannot offer a firm etymology for this, but it resembles Duala *ndon*, 'beautiful'.

The Kom

The Kom (some 30,000 strong) live in a very different environment from the Bakweri and Balong, some 300 miles inland on the rolling mountain tops of the Grassland Plateau. The only immigrants in significant numbers are the transhumant Fulani cattle-herders who, by arrangement with the Kom chief, obtain permission to graze their stock on Kom lands. Descent is matrilineal, and in their traditions of migration and early history females occupy a prominent role. It is recounted that, due to an act of trickery by an enemy, all the active male members of the community were once slaughtered. To defend the group the women decked themselves in their deceased husband's military garb and weapons and camouflaged themselves in vines. The women kept guard and repelled enemy attacks, while the few remaining old men built the houses, hunted for food, and went and paid the required tributes.

The Kom have a female practice called *anlu* with aspects very similar to those associated with *titi ikoli* and *ndong*. *Anlu*

> traditionally referred to a disciplinary technique employed by women for particular offences. These include the beating or insulting (by uttering such obscenities as 'Your vagina is rotten') of a parent; beating of a pregnant woman; incest; seizing of a person's sex organs during a fight; the pregnancy of a nursing mother within two years after the birth of the child; and the abusing of old women (Ritzenthaler 1960: 151).

We should note here Ritzenthaler's term 'disciplinary technique'. Chilver and Kaberry (1967: 141), speaking also of the Kom, say that 'when the women of a village wished to resort to disciplinary action against a man ... they assembled as *anlu*'. *Anlu* they derive from the root -*lu*, meaning 'to drive away'. The term *anlu* itself, then, is not a Kom equivalent for the expression *titi ikoli*. It appears to connote the Kom equivalent of the patterns of militant behaviour associated with *titi ikoli*.

> The invoking of *anlu* is described by a Kom (Francis Nkwain) as follows: 'Anlu' is started off by a woman who doubles up in an awful position and gives out a high-pitched shrill, breaking it by beating on the lips with the four fingers. Any woman recognizing the sound does the same and leaves whatever she is doing and runs in the direction of the first sound. The crowd quickly swells and soon there is a wild dance to the tune of impromptu stanzas informing the people of what offence has been committed, spelling it out in such a manner as to raise emotions and cause action. The history of the offender is brought out in a telling gossip. Appeal is made to the dead ancestors of the offender, to join in with the 'Anlu'. Then the team leaves for the bush to return at the

appointed time, usually before actual dawn, donned in vines, bits of men's clothing and with painted faces, to carry out the full ritual. All wear and carry the garden-egg type of fruit which is supposed to cause 'drying up' in any person who is hit with it. The women pour into the compound of the offender singing and dancing, and, it being early in the morning, there would be enough excreta and urine to turn the compound and houses into a public latrine. No person looks human in that wild crowd, nor do their actions suggest sane thinking. Vulgar parts of the body are exhibited as the chant rises in weird depth.[5]

Until the offender repents, he is ostracized, a punishment said to be worse than death, which seems the more welcome because 'by it a new door is opened into a room peopled by relatives and friends and there are always sacrifices to link the living with the dead', whereas ostracism 'kills and gives no new life'. When he repents, the offender will be taken and immersed in a stream, and any of his cooking pots which had been contaminated by the garden eggs will be cleaned also. After the purification, the incident is regarded as closed, and is not to be referred to again.[6]

Thus the Kom can be seen to have a pattern of female militancy not unlike that of the Bakweri and Balong. Revenge is taken on an offender by corporate action, and typically he is disgraced by a display of vulgarity on the part of the women. The traditional picture is of such militancy being aroused by offences against women of a broadly sexual nature. Although *anlu* could involve the participation of women from more than one village, it used to be said that only very few old men could recall incidents beyond simple boycotts limited to the village where the offender lived. One might easily have been led to assume, therefore, that the practice had become enfeebled and was dying out. Experience elsewhere (for instance, among the Bakweri) has shown the unreliability of such assumptions. The concept of symbolic 'templates' which serve to generate events from time to time in unexpected ways has been set out in Ardener (1970). Something like this process took place among the Kom in 1958, when 7,000 *anlu* women rose up. It must be noted that their grievance was not, in this case, sexual insult, but the 'template' for action was that of *anlu*, and for that reason is of interest here. Events astonished everyone, including the Kom. The following account rests on Nkwain's data, although Ritzenthaler has also published a version (1960).

It may all be said to have started in 1955 when a regulation was brought in to force the women of the Grassfields to build their farm ridges horizontally along the hills instead of vertically, to prevent soil erosion. Not, you might think, a very provocative requirement. It is, however, as I can confirm from experience, much harder to ridge horizontally on a steep slope. Demonstration farms were set up to instruct the women, to no avail: they ignored the order. Some were fined. Despite the unpopularity of the measure with women, the new methods were supported by some 'progressives' (teachers and others) on the all-male Kom local government council. In 1958 a zealous Agricultural Assistant unwisely tried to force the issue by uprooting some farm crops, traditionally an offence in Kom. About this time also, a Sanitary Inspector had been trying to improve hygiene in the market by pouring away tainted liquor and destroying bad food. The chief was also becoming unpopular with the women due to his supposed leniency with Fulani cattle-herders who allowed their stock to wander into the women's farms. Other changes at that time included the development of national party politics. The government party was then led by a Bakweri, Dr Endeley. In Kom his party was associated with the modernizing policy which had resulted in the destruction of food. The party was also unpopular on other grounds.

Matters came to a head on Friday 4 July when the council met to consider two issues: the fining of women for farming offences, and the organizing of a welcome party for the impending visit of the premier, Dr Endeley. A council member, Teacher Chia, was advocating both, in the face of known opposition from the women. The atmosphere became tense. Then Mamma Abula stepped forward from out of the crowd of spectators. She performed some dance steps, and gingerly walked up to Teacher Chia and spat in his face. Suddenly,

> A woman from Tinifoinbi sprinted up to the said Chia and also spat. Then a third woman, Mamma Thecla Neng, doubled over and shrilled the 'Anlu' war cry, which was echoed and re-echoed in a widening circle beginning with the women who had been in attendance at the Council. Fright gripped Chia and he started for his bicycle only to find it covered with twines, around which a growing number of women were dancing and singing. Women started to pick up bits of stones to throw them at him cursing him as they did so. He ran to the Mission House and made for the Father's latrine. The Rev. Father bolted the door and stood with his back to it. The women gathered in dance, and vines and branches were cut and heaped in front of the latrine.

The headmaster tried to disperse the women, but they sang mocking songs about him.

> The women sang and danced and, as emotions grew, told the world Mr Chia belonged nowhere – 'He is excreta'. And they would shrill out 'U-li-li-li-li-li' and inform the ancestors that their culprit sons were on the way to join them. Death wish! Terror! And then they turned and left

the Mission and went up the Yongmbang Hill overlooking the Njinikom
market, there to set up their [own] demonstration farm, with the ridges
running down the hill in a challenge to the new Agricultural
Department's directive. No broadcasting station could surpass the
Yongmbang Hill and soon this hill was black with teeming thousands
of women. When they came down that hill planning had already been
fixed. 'Anlu' had started ... The next day, Saturday, 5th July, saw the
women in Bobe Andreas Ngong's compound where fighting ensued.
Jerome Ngong used a cutlass on one of the women and sticks flew here
and there battlewise. After ruining much property the 'Anlu' marched
on the market beating and driving away such men as had dared to put
up wares... 'The men can't have their fun while we are suffering'.

To cut a long and fascinating story short: the place was in uproar.
Since the teachers and the Catholic Father had determined to send the
school children out to the road to welcome the premier, the women
kept the children away from school, which therefore had to close. The
prominent catholic establishment in Kom was finally forced to concede
the transfer of some unpopular teachers, but not before the notorious
headmaster had died (of, it was said, high blood pressure). Disgusted
with the courts which were prepared to consider fining women, the
anlu leaders even set up their own, and insisted on dealing with all
land cases, in defiance of the chief and the administrative machine.
'"Anlu" raged', there were 'breaches of the peace' and finally the police
had to take notice, and a number of men and women were arrested.
The expatriate police official in Bamenda intervened and ordered their
release on condition that they report for questioning to the police
station in Bamenda, about forty miles from Kom, at a later date. In the
intervening weeks *anlu* operated in a hushed atmosphere that was
said to be more frightening than the more overt demonstrations. The
women took advice from those men who were opposed to Mr Chia and
the government party of Dr Endeley. *Anlu* became highly organized.

On Thursday afternoon, 20 November, 2,000 women left for
Bamenda, wearing vines, and with unwashed bodies painted black.
They were accompanied by two men. Another 4,000 women (the
elderly, suckling mothers and the like) settled down in the Njinikom
market to await their return. The column of women were ordered not
to speak to any man on the way, and to eat only Kom food and drink
only Kom water which they therefore carried with them. No peel, nor
any remains of food were to be left on alien soil. An exception was
made of the settlement just outside Bamenda where they were to
spend the night. They arrived there totally exhausted, their feet
swollen, some never having travelled such a distance before. They
spent the night singing special songs. The next day they marched up

the escarpment to Bamenda, where the leader made a long statement to the police. In the end, however, the police decided to take no further action. The women returned to Kom in triumph – ferried part of the way in two trucks lent by the police.

For some time the opponents of *anlu* were ostracized and prevented from attending public functions and ceremonies, funerals, childbirth feasts and co-operative farming units. They were by these means denied access to some farming lands. These were traditional *anlu* methods of forcing quick penitence. Eventually peace was made and things settled down, although to a new order. The *anlu* leader sat on the local council. The Catholics and the *anlu* women became reconciled. Indeed they teamed up against the American Baptists who were said to have referred to the women as '*anlu*-nuts'. Mr Chia made his peace with the women too. He is now said to be happy when he recalls the day when the women 'cleansed' both him and his compound. 'I felt good after that' he is quoted as saying, 'Be careful with our mothers'.

Comparative African Material

The ethnographic data presented above all comes from West Cameroon. The use of obscenity by women, including exposure (real or implied) of parts of the body which are normally covered, exists elsewhere. Mrs Steady kindly reviewed her material for Sierra Leone and confirmed that 'It is not unusual for signalled references to be made to the genitals or the bottom in disputes'. In what is often regarded as no more than a childish parody, she says, children 'usually accompany the gesture by the characteristic flippant remark "ax mi wes" (ask my bottom)'. 'Between adults it is far more serious. It is more commonly employed by women mainly, I think, because of the greater mobility of women's clothing'. 'Prostitutes are known to employ this form of insult whenever a client refuses to honour his credit'. '[At] least three cases are known where [gestures of vulgarity] were used to counter the husband's physical violence'. Mrs Steady's information all related to instances of individual action, except for one where 'this form of protest was used by a girl and her mother against a man for his breach of promise of marriage'.[7] She stresses that such vulgar behaviour would normally be considered disgusting.

Sir Edward Evans-Pritchard, in a paper about prescribed or ritualized obscenity, cites a case of female exposure which is relevant here. Among the Azande the behaviour of the wives of a man when his sister's son has made a predatory raid on his belongings, for which, according to native law, there is no redress, seems from one aspect to be a custom in the same category as those already described in this paper. These women tear off their grass covering from over the genitals and rush naked after the intruder, shouting obscene insults at him and making licentious gestures. We mention these occasions, but the obscenity, though permitted is neither a prescribed nor a collective response (Evans-Pritchard 1929: 320; 1965: 87–88).

Professor Evans-Pritchard is no doubt correct in stating that the behaviour of the women is not prescribed, but it seems to be a standardized or predictable response. Although he states that such behaviour is not collective, we may notice that he refers to 'the wives of a man', and not merely to 'a wife'.

Kikuyu women, it seems, also expose themselves in certain circumstances. In the Kikuyu data which follows we may note that the notion of 'women's secrets' once again appears in association with the technique:

> It is said that in the Meru group when a girl becomes a woman, that is when her first child is born, a contingent curse is sworn on the amniotic fluid to regulate her future conduct as a woman and to preserve the secrets of the woman's social life; this oath was also used to hide the fact of second circumcisions practised on initiated girls at the time of childbirth. A form of curse employed by women and known throughout the Unit is the deliberate exhibition of the private parts towards the thing or person cursed. To do this is *guturama* in Kikuyu and *futuramira ng'ania* is to curse So-and-So in this way. Quarrelling women sometimes use it, and when co-wives dispute about a garden one of them if she gets thoroughly angry, may put it out of use entirely by uncovering her person and making sexual gestures at the garden in the presence of her rival. It is to be noticed, however, that this is not a recognized and regular form of contingent curse, and Africans, except when they are inflamed by anger, find its use disgusting. But occasions when it has been solemnly employed, even by all the women of a large community, are sometimes mentioned, as when the women of a ridge have gathered together to show their disapproval of another ridge or of some over-bearing personality who has annoyed them. The method is then to remove their under-garments, stand in a line with their backs towards the offender, bend forward, and lift their skirts in unison (Lambert 1956: 99).[8]

Mary Douglas states that among the Lele of the Kasai (Congo), any married woman who ran away with a lover ran the risk of involving her relatives in a blood feud. If this happened she would be blamed, and 'The women, mothers and sisters of the dead men in the village where she had fled, would treat her with every contumely, dancing around her, singing abusive songs, stripping off their skirts, unforgivable in itself, and rubbing her face in the dirty clothes' (Douglas 1963: 137).

These small scraps of comparative material from different parts of Africa do not allow firm conclusions to be drawn, but they do show that some elements in the pattern found in Cameroon are not unique in Africa. Perhaps more similar evidence has been overlooked.

Militant Techniques and their Application in Africa and in the Women's Liberation Movements

Having looked at the African material, can we now see any similarities between the garden-egg throwing women of Kom and the women who threw flour over Bob Hope during the Miss World competition in London? Are the strippers of Balong and the bra-discarders of America motivated alike? Has Germaine Greer anything in common with the Bakweri?

First let us consider the use of obscenity itself. This can best be understood through consideration of respectful, deferential and submissive behaviour. There are a great number of symbolic systems through which degrees of deference towards a superior or the structuring of mutual attention can be manifested, and these may have positive and negative aspects. Thus not only may prescribed modes of address express relationships, but the avoidance of certain terms and phrases may also be significant; certain gestures may be exacted, while others are deliberately suppressed; parts of the body may be revealed, or they may be covered.[9] The existence of an array of signs for demonstrating respect and submission permits the generation of the oppositely marked contraries that express their antitheses: disrespect, or the denial of dominance. It is from such oppositions that the absurdities of obscenity draw their symbolic force, or derive what Mrs Steady has termed the inherent power in vulgarity. When the women of Cameroon subject a man to such a display they demonstrate that they no longer recognize his power to elicit conformity. He is further demeaned to the extent that normal social relations are denied him, and his recognition as a full member of the community may be put in jeopardy ('Mr Chia belonged nowhere'). Thus the obscenities of *anlu* mark the middle stage in the series:

	Respect	→	disrespect	→	no respect
(or:	seemly behaviour	→	unseemly behaviour	→	ostracism
or:	+	→	–	→	0)

Lambert similarly explains that when the Kikuyu women lift their skirts in unison 'they indicate that they will have no further social dealings with the people of the area concerned or that they do not recognize the authority of the man whom they have thus deliberately insulted'. In Sierra Leone, within the domestic unit, as Mrs Steady puts it, such behaviour is 'a retaliatory *threat* to the husband's position of dominance in the household'.

A full examination of why certain symbols are selected to indicate deference, rather than others, is not possible here. Each will no doubt have a different social 'etymology'. We might note, however, that the use of expressions normally taboo (e.g. swear words) seems to be more widespread among the men of some societies (e.g. our own) than among the women. The practice is often intended to symbolize the inability of others to demand deference or exert control over the speaker or group of speakers, and it may be that women do not swear as frequently because their dependent position does not allow them this freedom. Perhaps where women do adopt the habit, they feel themselves to be in relatively independent or secure positions. How far modesty and the preserving of 'women's secrets' rests upon the need to avoid the dangers of molestation, it is difficult to say.[10] If the motive for obscuring parts of the body by women, through verbal avoidance or otherwise, is interpreted as a form of self-defence, this itself implies a position of weakness or inferiority, and the symbolic usages to indicate politeness might be an extension of this. I cannot go into such speculations now, but we can note the need for further discussion.

In moving on to examine the modern women's movements in America and Europe, I stress the distinction between 'women's rights' and 'women's liberation'. Those who concern themselves with the former seek the recognition of a claim to a greater share of valued resources, both tangible and intangible, as contemporarily defined. Those concerned with 'women's liberation' believe that this cannot be achieved without changes in the stereotypes of women, which have supposedly largely been determined by men. Victoria Brittain says of those representing the former movement: 'When they think in feminist terms ... it is about actual discrimination and prejudice against women rather than a general challenge to society's stereotyping of women' (1971: 12). Germaine Greer, a liberationist, speaks of the necessity for women to question 'the most basic assumptions about feminine normality': a little more variation in the stereotype will not do (1970: 14). Betty Friedan believes that there is acknowledged evidence 'which throws into question the standards of feminine normality, feminine adjustment, feminine fulfilment, and feminine maturity by which women are trying to live' (1968: 31). The dichotomy between the 'reformists' who are interested in 'rights' and the 'revolutionaries' who are interested in 'liberation' is not, of course, rigid, and most women liberationists include 'reformist' proposals in their programmes. Nevertheless, the distinction is a useful one. Perhaps the notions 'instrument' and 'expression' may be relevant here: women's rightists may be concerned with overcoming 'instrumental exploitation' (involving money, jobs, consumer goods, etc.) and women's liberationists with 'expressive exploitation' (which is 'related directly to the irrational and unconscious psychological processes and motives characteristic of man's complex mental structure' [De Vos]).[11]

Social anthropologists recognize that men and women in society organize their perceptions through 'models' of varying degrees of articulation and generality. The difficulty which men (and ethnographers) encounter in identifying the models of the world which women actually use – as opposed to those which, directly or indirectly they admit to – has been raised by Edwin Ardener (1971b). He asked: 'if the models of a society made by most ethnographers tend to be derived from the male portion of that society, how does the symbolic weight of that other mass of persons – half or more of normal human populations ... express itself?' (1971b: 138). His remarks are a modern formulation of the question for which Freud said he could find no answer, despite his 'thirty years of research into the feminine soul, ... *what does a woman want?*' E. Ardener suggests that we might abstract female models of the world by a study of symbolism, since, due to the relative inarticulateness of women, they are less ready to speak, and ethnographers are less attuned to hear them.[12]

It seems to me that the women's liberation movements can best be understood as attempts 'to speak': their volubility is, indeed, a marked feature. Yet women, it seems, encounter many difficulties in doing so, for 'this world, always belonging to men, still retains the form they have given it' (de Beauvoir 1953: 641), and, 'one of the results of the sexual role-playing which both Freud and society as a whole encouraged, is' (according to Figes 1970: 141)[13] 'that most women, even if asked, would no longer really know what they wanted'. 'Women', writes Firestone

> have no means of coming to an understanding of what their experience *is*, or even that it is different from male experience. The tool for representing, for objectifying one's experience in order to deal with it, culture, is so saturated with male bias that women almost never have a chance to see themselves culturally through their own eyes. So that

finally, signals from their direct experience that conflict with the prevailing (male) culture are denied and repressed (1972: 149).

Women, then, are searching for new models of themselves and the world around them. All women, and all men, belong to many different sets, for each of which we may expect there to be different models. Tiger notes that 'being human is more persuasively characteristic of a human male than being male' (1971: 56) and similarly 'being a male is part of being a person' (p. xiv). This could be rephrased: the set 'person' (and the set 'human') includes the set 'male'. In such a scheme, we might presume that it also includes the set 'female'. Ardener in his 1969 paper on Bakweri models of men and women states:

> The objective basis of the symbolic distinctions between nature and society, which Lévi-Strauss recently prematurely retreated from, is a result of the problem of accommodating the two logical sets which classify human beings by different bodily structures: 'male'/'female'; with the two other sets: 'human'/'nonhuman'. It is men who usually come to face this problem, and because their model for *mankind* is based on that for *man*, their opposites, *woman* and *non-mankind* (the wild), tend to be ambiguously placed. Hence in Douglas's terms (1966), come their sacred and polluting aspects.

'Women' he continues, and he is thinking primarily of Bakweri women, 'accept the implied symbolic content, by equating *womankind* with the men's wild' (published 1971b: 154). While it might be true that Bakweri like other women are often prepared to play men's games, as we have seen they sometimes, like the proverbial worms, turn. We also find, implicit in recent writings of the women's liberation movement, the very complaint that while 'male' may indeed be ascribed to the set 'human', the set 'female' does not have an equal place in it.[14] Firestone explicitly states that: 'Women, biologically distinguished from men, are culturally distinguished from "human"' (1972: 192). Her answer is 'not just the elimination of male *privilege* but of the sex *distinction* itself: genital differences between human beings would no longer matter culturally' (ibid: 19).

Thus among the models being sought are many in which the criterion of sex is apparently to be regarded as not of diacritical importance, a position which may appear to point to statements that there is no difference at all between men and women. Yet in fact the differences are rarely if ever denied; indeed, the opposite is usually true: they are stressed. '[T]here will always be certain differences between man and woman', writes de Beauvoir, 'her eroticism, and therefore her sexual world, have a special sensitivity of their own and cannot fail to engender a sensuality, a sensitivity of a special nature'

(1953: 686). Firestone, herself, states that 'men and women are tuned to a different cultural wave-length, that in fact there exists a wholly different reality for men and women' (1972: 151). Thus we find, beyond the search for new models for various sets which can include both men and women, a desire, conscious or not, to identify a specifically female model (of that 'special nature') in which the essential attributes, physical, spiritual and moral appear: a model of what we may perhaps term 'femineity'[15] of the deepest structural level and greatest degree of generality, which is quite distinct from the old, supposedly male-derived, 'femininity' with its load of associated 'secondary sexual characteristics'. Greer admits to 'relying upon a concept of woman which cannot be found to exist' (1970: 21). Firestone seeks 'an exploration of the strictly female reality', from which will be developed an 'authentic female art', a task which, she stresses, is not to be regarded as reactionary but rather as progressive. This searching for 'femineity' may possibly have a parallel in the attempts to isolate 'negritude' by some Africans. Femineity is not merely an equivalent of femininity, since it is located at a different level of abstraction and articulation.

Most men and some women find it hard to understand the appeal (not necessarily unaccompanied by criticism) which the writings of the women's liberationists have for many women (both within and without the movement) who might appear to have gained access to resources to an extent at least equal to that of their male counterparts. It is the identification of the model of 'femineity' and its relation to other models, which, I suggest, such women feel, intuitively or otherwise, to be unsatisfactory. The more sets which women consider do or should include themselves, the more critical does an acceptable model of femineity become in establishing separate sexual identity and the more critical does the question of the relevance of this identity to these other sets become.

In Cameroon, the militant techniques associated with *titi ikoli*, *ndong* and *anlu* did not originally seem to have been principally used for securing 'women's rights'. The reason for this was probably that there were other sets – e.g. bisexual kin groups – which had an interest in preserving these rights, at least to an acceptable minimum degree. A woman's access to land, to food, to clothing, to medicines, to freedom from assault, and so forth, affected her role within the groupings to which she belonged and her duties as a mother and therefore her capability of maintaining the groups. Males as well as females had an interest in her well-being, and they would intervene on her behalf in certain circumstances.[16] In Kom, in 1958 when new forces brought changes affecting women which other groupings seemed unable to control, almost it seems by an act of inspiration on the part of Mamma Neng, the processes of *anlu* were redirected to the defence of 'women's rights', but this seems to have been somewhat novel.

Insults of the type associated with *titi ikoli* (although often referring to the external organs of generation) do not seem to have been regarded as reflecting upon, or as being directly concerned with, a woman's capacity, role or 'function' as child-bearer, even though motherhood is a matter of the very greatest attention in Cameroon societies. It is interesting to note, therefore, that liberationists single out the sociological and anthropological theories of 'functionalism' for special criticism, particularly as they are applied by American educational sociologists influenced by Margaret Mead and Talcott Parsons. Functionalist description, complains Millett (1971), inevitably becomes prescriptive: 'Utility alone detains its clear and disinterested glance'. It justifies the system it perceives. Support for maintaining existing 'complementary' sex-differentiated 'roles' is derived from it. A *Times* leader writer was near the mark when he complained: 'Perhaps the real criticism of the Miss World competition should also be applied to the Women's Liberation movement: that they both exalt an essentially functionless feminism'. Possibly that is exactly what the latter wish to do. I suspect, however, that they may not agree with the *Times* that the Miss World competition is functionless: it may seem to them to reify one of those male stereotypes of women which they find so inadequate, and which may be used to exclude them from other human sets to which they feel they should have the possibility of belonging (e.g. sets defined by 'competence' perhaps, or other criteria).

Titi ikoli, then, arose in cases where neither women's rights nor their functions as mothers was the basic issue: this was of another kind. I venture to suggest that it was the dignity of a concept which they considered valuable and beautiful – the dignity of their sexual identity of the order of that which I have called 'femineity' and of which the symbol was their unique sexual anatomy. Unaware of this longstanding preoccupation among Bakweri, Greer arrives independently at a position close to theirs when she recognizes the value of such symbolism and seeks its reinstatement. 'The vagina', she complains, 'is obliterated from the imagery of femininity in the same way that signs of independence and vigour in the rest of her body are suppressed'. It may seem contradictory that women should suppose that vulgarity can be a means of enhancing dignity. It can be one when the obscenities are merely signals conveying a message which is not obscene.

Cameroon women particularly abhor the imputation that vaginas smell, an accusation which does not seem to have been common in America and England until recent years.[17] Suddenly women learn that 'there are some things even a girl's best boy friend won't tell her'. As Fiona McKenzie (1972) remarks, 'He doesn't need to. Media man does the job for him'. 'The problem of vaginal odour was invented by the toiletries industries', says Greer (1971: 28). Mary Douglas (1966: 142) has suggested that 'When male dominance is accepted as a central principal of social organisation ... beliefs in sex pollution are not likely to be highly developed'.[18] It is tempting to follow this by arguing that it was the weakening of the authority of the American male which led to the sudden discovery of the need for vaginal deodorants. But however they are explained, the reaction among women has been swift. Campaigns have been mounted against their introduction. 'As anxiety-makers, vaginal deodorants are tops: not only a fear that you may smell' writes Jane Alexander, 'but a fear that you are *sexually* offensive. They rouse terrible wrath in some people – notably sensualists and women's liberationists and people who are concerned with human dignity' (Alexander 1971: 93). The feminist magazine *Shrew* complained that 'Most women would be too embarrassed to talk about their private sexual areas to all and sundry, yet somewhere a panel of admen and probably women, must have sat round and worked out a campaign about us. The campaigns', the paper states, 'are in themselves an invasion of the special privacy of women' ('Women's secrets' yet once again!).[19]

Greer suggests that 'efforts made to eradicate all smell from the female body are part of the ... suppression of fancied animality' (1970: 38). Perhaps the accusation that women smell may seem to support the repudiation of their classification as human beings by placing them among the animals. This might account for the fact that the insult may become the concern, not merely of the victim, nor only of women who are sexually active, but of women of any age-group. It is interesting that Bakweri say that there is a special association of women with apes, in so far as women are sometimes said to be afraid that they might give birth to them, and their children are thought sometimes to be attracted away by them from human society into the wild of the bush. The word for ape should not be mentioned in their presence.[20] As a footnote, as it were, we should also note that the reaction against brassieres also appears to be the rejection of the implied accusation that women's unique anatomy is not acceptable in its natural state. 'What's wrong with being real?' says Midge Mackenzie, 'I never tell women that they should try to improve on nature'.[21]

I suggest that the Cameroon women's movements and those of women's liberation can no longer be viewed only as isolated and independent phenomena. For instance, we should consider whether, by focusing attention as Greer would wish upon the vagina, Bakweri women may be demanding respect, not merely for their sexuality in the narrowest sense, but also for a more general model of femaleness (call it 'femineity' or what you will), pride in which and acknowledgment of which is perhaps necessary for the releasing of that vigour and independence which Greer is seeking. Is this the level at which the Cameroon women and the liberationists meet? Both seem to be concerned with the 'deep structure' of human identity. 'Feminism', says Mitchell, '*is about being women*' (1971: 96). To use terminology suggested elsewhere:[22] perhaps *titi ikoli* is a programmatic statement for 'women's lib'. Few I think would doubt that 'Black is beautiful' is a symbolic statement of a programmatic type. The song '*titi ikoli* is not a thing for insults – beautiful beautiful' offers a remarkable coincidence.

The *realien* of the traditional women's militant movements in Cameroon and women's liberation in America and England are, of course, different; may not the springs of action share a common source? We have discussed the opposition of positively and negatively marked patterns of symbolic behaviour in Africa. When stating that 'In extremities of random violence or in the breaking of cultural taboos, feminists turn femininity on its head' Mitchell exemplifies this (1971: 69).[23] Greer speaks (though not approvingly) of those in the movement who 'mock' and 'taunt' men. This she may not herself do, but does not the mode by which she presents her case itself sometimes appear to be a verbal display of vulgar parts? 'The key to the strategy of liberation', she says, 'lies in exposing the situation, and the simplest way to do it is to outrage the pundits and the experts by sheer impudence of speech and gesture' (1970: 328). *Titi ikoli* indeed!

This article has attempted to do two things. First, ethnographic material from Africa has been presented which is of independent interest. Secondly, an attempt has been made to set alongside this material other data on the women's liberation movements which offers parallels. From within entirely different social contexts, women of dissimilar positions in relation to their worlds and with very different experience have produced statements and patterns of behaviour of beguiling similarity. The one element which the generators have in common apart from their humanity is their sex. If we allow ourselves to adopt, for the moment, the hypothesis that the parallels are closer than would result from chance, we are led inevitably to consider a *third* aspect: whether or not we are dealing here with phenomena of a universal kind; whether perhaps women require a model of 'femineity' of a certain nature, the maintenance of which may, in certain circumstances, seem to some to be under stress. Perhaps Germaine Greer, by an effort of the intellect, has raised to consciousness structures of thought of the set 'female' which the Bakweri (and possibly others) have intuitively perceived and expressed symbolically. The problem of whether or not the parallels which have been laid out in this article are coincidental or are a result of observational overdeterminism, or whether they represent universals of some kind, cannot yet be decided. The evidence so far does, however, draw me towards the last proposition.[24]

Notes

Reprinted, by kind permission of the Royal Anthropological Institute of Great Britain and Ireland, from *Man*, New Series, vol. 8, no 3 (September 1973), pp. 422–440. A version of this article was first read at the Institute of Social Anthropology, Oxford, on Friday 12 March 1971. The study is being further elaborated for a longer work now in preparation. [For subsequent related work by S. Ardener, see 'Nudity, Vulgarity and Protest', *New Society*, 1974; 'Arson, Nudity and Bombs among the Canadian Doukhobours: a Question of Identity', in G. Breakwell (ed.), 1983, *Threatened Identities*. Chichester and New York: Wiley, pp. 239–266; 'A Note on Gender Iconography: the Vagina', in P. Caplan (ed.), 1987. *The Cultural Construction of Sexuality*. London: Tavistock, pp. 113–142. Research in this field by various authors since this 1973 publication includes work by Susan Diduk and Paul Nkwi, to name but two.]

1. Bonjongo Civil Cause Book 2/1956 (164/56).
2. Bonjongo Civil Cause Book 2/1956 (135/56).
3. Lisoka Civil Cause Book 1/1957 (112/56).
4. Muea Civil Cause Book 1956 (17/56).
5. This extract and others which follow have been taken from a very interesting unpublished paper on *anlu* by F. Nkwain (1963) written for an informal seminar Edwin and I convened in Buea, Cameroon. Estimates of the number of women involved are his own. Another account of these events is given in Ritzenthaler 1960.
6. See Ritzenthaler 1960: 152.
7. Personal communication: 'The use of sexual gestures in disputes' (1972).
8. An illustration of Kikuyu women performing a vulgar dance may be found in Wellard [n.d.].
9. For a discussion of 'meeting' and 'greeting' behaviour in animals and man see, for example, Callan 1970: ch. 7.
10. Possibly the use of terms for sexual organs as expletives primarily symbolizes the power to control the part referred to and is at some level a

threat to do so. Thus the uttering of the term for female genitals might represent the threat of rape. Support for this may be suggested by the rarity in England, outside the middle class, of this use of the term for penis, and the presence of the term for testicles, which possibly represents the threat of castration (perhaps a relatively weak threat since men are more easily able to defend themselves). Of course, even if such primary referents applied, they might not necessarily be in the awareness of those using the terms: speakers might only associate their use with robustness or aggressiveness of a general kind. We should not in any case overlook the 'social content' of rape: perhaps the component 'assertion of dominance' greatly outweighs that of 'sex'.

11. G. de Vos, 'Conflict, Dominance and Exploitation in Human Systems of Social Segregation', quoted in Tiger 1971: 77.

12. Edwin Ardener's comment that even female ethnographers have faced difficulties in gathering and presenting effectively data on women's models of the world is borne out, not only by an examination of work done in past decades, but by looking at a recent attempt to present a female view of Hagen life by Marilyn Strathern. In her interesting book *Women in Between* (1972) she finds it necessary to write at the beginning of the crucial chapter on 'Pollution and poison': 'It is with male dogma that I have to deal in the main, for men ... are the more articulate and coherent in their statements. Women do not make contrary assertions with the same apparent cogency; they half, although only half, agree with what men say' (1972: 159). Ioan Lewis has argued in a number of publications (e.g. in *Ecstatic Religion*, 1971) that the relative inarticulateness of women is part of the reason why women so frequently speak in tongues and get possessed.

13. In answer to Freud's question, which she quotes.

14. Hence, I suggest, the extensive coverage given by writers like Millet, Greer, Figes, O'Faolain and Marines et al., to quotations from male literature which are intended to demonstrate the low esteem in which women are held by such writers. Stress is often placed on the view of women as polluting or de-civilizing influences; and complaints are often made of the dehumanization of women by their being regarded as sex 'objects'.

15. Femineity: the quality or nature of the feminine sex; womanliness; womanishness. First usage: Coleridge, 1820 (*Oxford English Dictionary*).

16. The Bakweri, for instance, have a system of double-unilineal descent (see Ardener 1956). Three different kin groups have an interest in a woman and/or her children: her patrikin, her matrikin, and later, her husband's patrikin.

17. As an example of what she ironically terms his 'neo-Freudian contribution to sexual understanding', Firestone (1972: 68) quotes the following interesting affirmation by Theodor Reik (1966): 'I believe that cleanliness has a double origin: the first in the taboos of the tribes, and the second another matter coming thousands of years later, namely in women's

awareness of their own odor, specifically the bad smells caused by the secretion of their genitals'.

18. One might perhaps rather say that sex pollution becomes a problem when there is a critical lack of fit between the male model (of, in the case of the Lele and the Hagen, supremacy over women) and a discrepant model which the actions of women force upon the attention of men. By operating according to their own distinctive models, women may seem, in this sense, to threaten to distort or pollute the male model (Douglas 1963: 113; 1966: 149, 150; Strathern 1972: ix, 150, 153).

19. Quoted in Alexander 1971: 94. Barbara Bond reported an incident among university students in Sierra Leone which might have a bearing on our discussion. It seems that female students resented publication of an article in a student journal which discussed the practice of abortion in the university. A special meeting was called and the women imposed a fine upon the men. Was this, I wonder, because they were guilty of getting their facts wrong (if so, editors beware!), or had they committed the offence of making public women's secrets? (Bond 1972, verbal communication).

20. The complex relationship between Bakweri men and women and animals has been discussed by E.W. Ardener elsewhere (1970). Bakweri men boast of the power to turn themselves into elephants. 'Some women rather half-heartedly claim the role of bush-pigs, but' states Ardener, 'like Dames in an order of chivalry or girls at Roedean, they are performing a male scenario' (1970: 155). The relationship of women to apes and water spirits (possibly originally manatees) seems to be of another, more dangerous kind.

21. Quoted in Wade 1971: 20.

22. Ardener 1971a. Cf addenda below.

23. One way the Kom *anlu* women turn 'femininity' on its head is by referring to themselves as men and by addressing men as men would women: 'Sweet girl, is there any kola nut in your bag?' (Nkwain 1963).

24. That processes of a similar nature may be found in association with other sets defined by different criteria (not necessarily biological) I hope to demonstrate in a further study now in hand.

References

Alexander, Jane. 1971. 'Down There', *New Society* 21 January 1972: 93–95.
Ardener, Edwin. 1956. *Coastal Bantu of the Cameroons*. London: International African Institute.
———. 1970. 'Witchcraft, Economics and the Continuity of Belief', in M. Douglas (ed.), *Witchcraft Confessions and Accusations*. London: Tavistock.
———. 1971a. 'The New Anthropology and its Critics', *Man* (N.S.) 6: 449–467.
———. 1971b. 'Belief and the Problem of Women', in J.S. La Fontaine (ed.), *The Interpretation of Ritual*. London: Tavistock.

Beauvoir, Simone de. 1953. *The Second Sex*. London: Cape.

Brittain, Victoria. 1971. 'A Conspiracy to Belittle Women's Liberation', *The Times* 12 January 1971: 12.

Callan, Hilary. 1970. *Ethology and Society: Towards an Anthropological View*. London: Oxford University Press.

Chilver, E.M. and P.M. Kaberry. 1967. 'The Kingdom of Kom in West Cameroon', in D. Forde and P.M. Kaberry (eds), *West African Kingdoms in the Nineteenth Century*. London: Oxford University Press.

Douglas, Mary. 1963. *The Lele of the Kasai*. London: Oxford University Press.

———. 1966. *Purity and Danger*. London: Routledge & Kegan Paul.

Evans-Pritchard, E.E. 1929. 'Some Collective Expressions of Obscenity in Africa', reprinted in *The Position of Women in Primitive Societies, and Other Essays* (1965), London: Faber & Faber.

Figes, Eva. 1970. *Patriarchal Attitudes*. London: Faber.

Firestone, S. 1972. *The Dialectic of Sex*. London: Paladin.

Friedan, Betty. 1968. *The Feminine Mystique*. London: Penguin.

Greer, Germaine. 1970. *The Female Eunuch*. London: MacGibbon & Kee.

———. 1971. 'The Smell Sell', *Sunday Times* 25 July 1971: 28.

Lambert, H.E. 1956. *Kikuyu Social and Political Institutions*. London: Oxford University Press.

Lewis, I.M. 1971. *Ecstatic Religion*. Harmondsworth: Penguin.

McKenzie, Fiona. 1972. 'A Way to Sell Cleanliness', *Oxford Review* 16 September 1972.

Millett, Kate. 1971. *Sexual Politics*. London: Hart-Davis.

Mitchell, Juliet. 1971. *Women's Estate*. Harmondsworth: Penguin

Nkwain, Francis. 1963. 'Some Reflections on the "Anlu" Organised by the Kom Women in 1958', Unpublished ms.

O'Faolain, Julia and Lauro Marines. 1973. *Not in God's Image*. London: Temple Smith.

Ritzenthaler, Robert E. 1960. '*Anlu*: a Woman's Uprising in the British Cameroons', *African Studies* 19(3): 151–156.

Strathern, Marilyn. 1972. *Women in Between*. London: Seminar Press.

Tiger, L. 1971. *Men in Groups*. London: Panther.

Wade, Valerie. 1971. 'The Women's Women', *Sunday Times Magazine* 12 September 1971: 20–23.

Wellard, James. n.d. 'Kikuyu', *Man, Myth & Magic* 4: 1561–1565.

ADDENDA

I regret that a paper by R.B. Edgerton and F.P. Conant, '*Kilipat*: The Shaming Party among the Pokot of East Africa' (*Southwestern Journal of Anthropology* [1964] 20: 404–418), escaped my attention, since it provides ethnographic data which parallels in surprising detail many elements which I have set out above. *Kilipat* is a 'weapon of considerable ferocity and effectiveness ... for the controlled expression of violence in sexual relations and the alleviation of marital antagonisms'. It is mostly associated with revenge by wives on a miscreant husband by means of ridicule and vulgarity (including exposure of their genitals, and urination and defecation on their victim). I will discuss the relevance of this paper to my own study elsewhere.

The paper submitted by Edwin Ardener at the A.S.A. Conference, 1973 ('Some outstanding questions in the analysis of events'), further explores our capacity for structuring thought. In his terms, 'femineity' would be of the order of a 'p-structure'; 'femininity' would be at the level of an 's-structure'.

Shirley G. Ardener, BSc (Econ) London, MA status Oxford, OBE, has carried out many years of fieldwork (until 1987 with her husband Edwin) in Nigeria and in Cameroon where she is still involved with the National Anglophone Archives set up by herself and Edwin, and with the Women and Gender Studies Department of Buea University. She was the Founding Director (1983–1997) of the International Gender Studies (formerly the Centre for Cross-Cultural Research on Women) at Lady Margaret Hall, Oxford. She is now a Research Associate at the IGS and at the Oxford Institute of Social and Cultural Anthropology. She has edited and contributed to several books including *Perceiving Women* (1975), *Women and Space* (1981), and *Changing Sex and Bending Gender and Swedish Ventures in Cameroon* (2002).

Chapter 5

WHO SEES THE ELEPHANT?

SEXUAL EGALITARIANISM IN SOCIAL ANTHROPOLOGY'S ROOM

Morna Finnegan

In many ways, anthropology seems a discipline terrified of its own potential. It is, for example, the only discipline in a position to make generalizations about humanity as a whole ... yet it resolutely refuses to do so.

—D. Graeber, *Fragments of an Anarchist Anthropology*

Introduction

It is 130 years since Engels (1986 [1884]) wrote *The Origin of the Family*. One of the most startling of his conclusions then was the assertion that the ownership of women by men in marriage, with the concurrent privatization of children, was an historical development and not an inevitable fact of society. Engels argued that the ascendancy of the nuclear family and private property is a relatively recent development in human history, and that the first right of ownership is of women over their fertility. Children in this scenario, borrowing from Morgan's longhouse economy, were the concern of the entire group. Since Engels wrote we have accumulated a large body of empirical data on what are now described as egalitarian societies. Yet surprisingly, given references to the centrality of female kinship and co-operative bonds, to intense sexual joking as a levelling mechanism, to the pervasive evidence of female vigilance over male hunting labour and yields, to the high social value placed upon children, and to the strong political presence of women in day-to-day organization and decision-making processes, we rarely ask how women collectively are maintaining (rather than simply benefiting from) egalitarian systems. More surprisingly, we rarely ask how children themselves might be nestled at the crux of all this co-operative activity, driving the rich domain of ritual activity from which they more than anyone benefit.

Knight's theory of the origins of symbolic culture holds that coalitions of early modern human females were able to generate the first symbolic concepts by pooling their reproductive energy and working together to ensure the survival of offspring. The model relies on a lunar framework, where female kin coalitions exert and relinquish power periodically. If we apply the structural aspect of this model to contemporary African hunter-gatherers, what do we find? Certain Central African hunter-gatherers maintain a political field based on ritual periodicity. Rooted in the tropes of sex, reproduction and desire, this system produces energy through a perpetual oscillation of power across the social landscape. Female co-operation is central to the loud corporate voice women have in these societies. As Peacock (1991) and others have shown, this is in turn linked to the high levels of communal childcare found within such groups. Why has the relationship between co-operative childcare and political power not been better explored by social anthropologists? And what are the mechanisms by which sexual egalitarianism is actually negotiated?

I use the paper by Knight and colleagues (1995) on the human symbolic revolution, in combination with recent work by Sarah Hrdy (2009) on co-operative breeding and emotional modernity, as a foundation for looking at the sexual division of labour among Central African hunter-gatherers. What I hope to bring out is the relationship between co-operative childcare, prosociality and sexual egalitarianism. Looking at women's relationship with game animals provides a lens through which to scrutinize the bigger picture. The argument I put forward, following Knight, is that the kind of prosocial power conducive to the emergence of sexual egalitarianism is driven by female co-operative strategies. As such, it differs in nature from the dominance-based power familiar to hierarchical societies. Inherently diffusive and dialogical, egalitarian power functions through a process of continual oscillation through time and space.

This kind of ambivalent power, pulling simultaneously toward autonomy and relatedness (cf Myers 1986), is, according to Hrdy's scenario, rooted in archaic evolutionary maps for sharing emotional states and empathizing with others while concurrently safeguarding the needs of subgroups. Differences between humans and other primates do not then lie in basic neural equipment, but in evolutionary ecological context. What this means is that early child development and parenting practices are critical in determining the kind of culture which later emerges. The distillation of power in the body, and the expression of it through ritual action, is inseparable from the communal parenting that distinguishes many hunter-gatherer communities.

Exploring the template of pendulum politics, together with ethnography on ritual hunting and reproduction, this chapter seeks to restore the 'complex' to 'egalitarianism' (cf Boehm 1999).

The Evolutionary Fuel of Reproductive Difference

Three decades ago when the debate about universal male dominance was at its height, Karen Endicott (1981) published a paper arguing on behalf of the existence of sexual egalitarianism. Reviewing the copious literature on dominance, and the general disciplinary scepticism about feasible alternatives, she noted that 'people who have actually lived with hunter-gatherers, and have actively looked for male bias within the society, find it far easier to accept that there can be societies where sexual egalitarianism exists than do those students of societies where men are clearly dominant' (Endicott 1981: 1). Ethnographers such as Turnbull (1961), Lee (1979), Leacock (1981), Biesele (1993) and the Endicotts (2008) have all written about the sexual egalitarianism of the people with whom they worked as a matter of fact. But in her 1981 paper Endicott also cautioned, as did Eleanor Leacock (1981) around the same time, that sexual egalitarianism would not conform to Western expectations of it. Physical differences in particular were not 'ignored or denied' (Endicott 1981: 2). Sameness, both writers emphasized, should not be confused with equality.

Hrdy (2009) has argued convincingly that the first thing to suffer where groups of males seize power from the collective is child welfare. As Callan also notes, the danger of infanticide by incoming males is widely documented for nonhuman species, and may have been an evolutionary driver in deep hominin evolution (see van Schaik and Janson 2000; Opie et al. 2013). Endicott (1981) quotes Woodburn (1980) as concluding of immediate-return hunter-gatherers that 'this system is one in which people travel light, unencumbered, as they see it, by possessions and by commitments' (1981: 3). However, in all these societies we do find the invisible, overarching commitment (literally written on the body by concepts such as *n/om* or *ekila*) to the protection of children as the nerve centre of the community. And that is what would be expected from societies in which the female procreative body has maintained a loud corporate presence. This is where Knight's (1991) theory is so compelling: Graeber (2004) comments that comparative models are essential in thinking beyond the parameters of our own cultural systems. These are not simply of documentary interest, but offer political possibilities for challenging existing models of power. Beyond ethnography, however, theories such as Knight's (1991), which attempt to reconstruct evolutionary foundations for the aggressively egalitarian behaviour of women's collectives, also have the potential to open new epistemological avenues. Barnard has recently urged social anthropologists to re-engage with the interdisciplinary study of human origins on the basis that 'it is not only ethnographic data that are relevant here, but also, and very importantly, the theoretical insights gained through the study of contemporary and recent past societies' (Barnard 2011: 17). Without insight into why people are choosing – and it is a choice – to live unencumbered by possessions or by constrictive social ties, we potentially overlook the forces driving such systems. Thus hunter-gatherer social egalitarianism has often been conceived of as an interesting exception to a general rule of hierarchy, privatization and individualism. Models such as Knight's explode that fatalist stance by arguing for a defining moment in human history where female inviolability was decisively established by coalitions of mothers supported by their kin. With complex egalitarianism no longer one possibility among many, we become a species in whose evolutionary gristle co-operative breeding is lodged, along with its corollaries – female sexual solidarity, continual infant contact, habitual sharing, motion, a healthy distrust of authority, and enshrined respect for individual autonomy.

In 'The Politics of Eros' (2013) I described a political system in which power is continually redistributed across the social landscape using a ritual dialogue premised on periodicity. At the heart of this sits the procreative body. Those themes identified by Engels as primary in the negotiation between the sexes – children, sex, desire and its uses – are central tenets in the societies referred to: the Mbuti, the Mbendjele Yaka and the BaYaka. But they are central in a positive sense. They produce energy as public magnets around which a whole range of other themes cluster. A ritual dynamic is maintained in which the collective discussion about them remains open. Why are these themes so persistent in the politics of egalitarian society? Knight and colleagues suggest that the female co-operation essential to collective childcare, the co-operation that provides women with a loud corporate voice in camp, rests on ritual vigilance. Any live system has to be recurrently performed. Keeping these issues public, where they can be debated, is crucial. There are many ways to achieve egalitarianism as Endicott (1981) stressed. There are substantial cultural differences between the Hadza, the Ju/'hoansi and the Mbendjele, all widely recognized as egalitarian in Woodburn's (1980) immediate-return sense. But if we step back and observe the kind of power that egalitarianism depends upon, regardless of the system employed to manage it, this almost without fail has a dialogical quality, moving continually across the social field. In order to remain open, it has to be subjected to a process of continual renegotiation. This model for how egalitarian power functions through the strategic opposition of one subgroup to another, the performance of conflict through dance, and the periodic ritual withdrawal of one sex from another, provides a valuable paradigm for looking at power and its uses in contemporary hunter-gatherer society.

Placing the human symbolic revolution in Darwinian context, Knight, Power and Watts write: 'If the story of human evolution is encephalisation, the materialist subtext must be how females fuelled the production of increasingly large-brained, burdensome offspring' (1995: 77). Their answer is that through a series of energetic and reproductive cycle changes, females were able to drastically increase male paternal investment. Concealment of ovulation with loss of oestrus, and continuous receptivity along with probable menstrual cycle synchrony, would have forced males toward prolonged consortships (Knight, Power and Watts 1995: 78). For the first time they would have had to invest not only in relationships with partners but crucially, with babies. The story is essentially a counter to the old 'prostitution model' derived from placing man-the-hunter centre stage in any posited evolutionary scenario. Knight and colleagues argue for a defining moment in human history when coalitions of reproductively burdened females began to unite to send mates away from base camps in order to procure meat. The ritual relationship of game blood with menstrual blood is much documented. The ethnographic literature on the requirement of hunters to return their kill to camp where it can be shared and cooked collectively, the dominance of women over cooking fire, and the symbolic connections between female blood and game blood are ubiquitous. Turnbull (1961) describes an important Mbuti ritual in which hunters explicitly attempt to steal cooking fire, and are beaten back by women (see

Power, this volume, for a full account). The insistence on routine male provisioning and paternal investment was, Knight argues, prompted by necessity, and generated a collective political statement about the inviolability of the female body. This strike moment, signalled by lunar phase-locked rituals designed to override the pair-bond and structure big-game hunting, had the practical effect of providing invaluable nutritional assistance to mothers and children. Sex-strike is in effect 'a moral strategy'.

Biological anthropologist Sarah Hrdy (2009) arrives at the same conclusion. All apes, she points out, share a capacity for Machiavellian intelligence. They are all socially astute, sharing cognitive capacities and incipient 'theory of mind'. What distinguishes humans is the need to connect and share inner states with others, to intuit intentions, communicate ideas, and be deeply affected by what others are thinking. All of this she attributes to our ancient evolutionary history of co-operative breeding. And she assembles a huge wealth of data to support her contention that these first co-operatively breeding communities were kin-based matrilineal communities where mothers had access not only to their own kin but, crucially, came to depend on assistance from others in rearing their young. The emotional sophistication that distinguishes humans could only have evolved in a context where there was a requirement to focus habitually on the thoughts and feelings of others. Since it was mothers who would have borne the brunt of growing brain size and slow-maturing offspring, it makes sense to assume they would have driven the strategic move towards communal childcare. She speculates that emotional modernity cannot have emerged concurrent with anatomically and behaviourally modern humans because in order for sophisticated language and symbolism to evolve, a foundation of 'mindreading' was required.

Hrdy's work brings out above all the contingent nature of prosocial impulses previously assumed to be an innate part of human being. She states unequivocally: 'Although highly complex co-evolutionary processes were involved in the evolution of extended lifespans, prolonged childhoods, and bigger brains ... *cooperative breeding was the pre-existing condition* that permitted the evolution of these traits in the hominin line' (Hrdy 2009: 277 emphasis mine). Social support from matrilineal kin in addition to reliable alloparental care would have pre-empted and facilitated the later development of symbolic thought and language. According to these models, Engels was right. Communal childcare is the ancient template for the human line. If in societies like the Aka, the Mbuti, the Yaka, the Nayaka or the Batek people view their world as a 'giving' place, that is because in reality it is. The philosophy is first and foremost a sensual philosophy, a thought rooted in the earliest experiences of the body in the world.

So how does co-operative childcare pan out through the division of labour among current hunter-gatherers? This is an important question because of the traditional assumption that the division of labour was something imposed on women as individuals by men as a group, when in fact the truth is more nearly the opposite. But it is also useful in understanding how the structural imperative to duality plays out within groups so that an entire symbolic field buzzes around the question of reproductive and hunting labour. Finally this area is pertinent in light of Knight's thesis about the division of time and roles to motivate hunters: the ethnography demonstrates that sexual egalitarianism is not compromised by such divisions. There clearly is a relationship between women's role as the producers of people and their ambivalent relationship with game animals and hunting technology. But if we connect biological demands to collective, cultural responses to them we can then reconceive antipathy as power.

Mbendjele communities throughout Northern Congo-Brazzaville meld together in one core polysemic concept – *ekila* – reproductive health, hunting practices and moral edicts (Lewis 2008; and see Knight and Lewis, this volume). *Ekila* refers to both women's menstrual blood and the blood of game animals, weaving successful hunting into successful childbearing, and expressing a profound taboo against the mixing of substances. Lewis (2002), in his discussion of *ekila*, stresses the complementarity integral to it: through women's ritual tracking and tying of game, they 'give' men meat. Through men's repeated contributions of sperm throughout pregnancy, they 'give' women babies. In this manner each sex contributes to the other's valued activity. This in turn echoes ethnography of Southern and East African hunter-gatherer groups, where female procreative fluids are in continual ritual conversation with male productive fluids – game blood, semen, arrow poison: 'Submission to certain observances with regard to hunting and menstruation are widespread among the Bushmen groups' (Biesele 1993: 92). Exploring the pervasive relationship between a core concatenation involving women, blood, the moon, honey, fat, game animals and male hunting success, Biesele cautions that 'the danger to hunters does not come from a condition of "uncleanness" in the woman. Rather, she is in a state of extraordinary power' (1993: 93; and see Power, this volume).

From the perspective of a heavily pregnant or lactating woman, the ideal situation is clearly one in which there is no compulsion to hunt – an activity requiring significant speed, risk-taking, travelling long distances from camp, and frequently working alone or in small units of two to three individuals. Even better if there exists a symbolic antipathy between female blood and the blood of game animals (Knight 1991). Under such circumstances, not only are women exempted from hunting, but their mates are ritually compelled to return meat to the community. Concluding a hilarious tit-for-tat sequence in which two women compete with the male trickster Kaoxa to obtain meat from him, besieging him with body parts, blood, excrement and urine, Biesele comments: 'Women are in a strong position in Ju/'hoan society. That they "like meat", for instance, is not just taken as a whim, to be gratified or not as males choose, *but as a biological and social fact with which men must creditably reckon*' (Biesele 1993: 184, emphasis mine).

When it is argued that women are 'excluded from society's most valued food-producing labour' (Brightman 1996: 688), there is a failure to factor in the copious literature describing shared access to hunters' meat, and the series of controls distancing hunters from their own kill (the 'own kill rule' in Knight's (1991) terms). However much theorists want them to, women in such communities do not *need* to hunt in order to receive meat. Here, Leacock's (1981) appeal for differentiating between equality and symmetry is useful. As for the prestige accruing to individual hunters, in immediate-return societies there is a collective ethos working against individual prestige, boasting or greater authority on the part of hunters. Conversely, and logically, there is no rule against women catching small animals, birds or rodents during foraging expeditions. Clearly some women, at some points in their reproductive cycles, are capable of hunting if they need to and if the opportunity arises. The point – a point which in order to function must be enshrined as social rule – is that they are exempted from having to do so. Were women excluded from hunting in a situation where they were also excluded from its yield, or able to scavenge only an insignificant part of this, or edged into subordinate positions by posturing hunters who used distribution to acquire power, then we might view the system as exploitative.

Antipathy as Power

There can be no doubt that there are substantive reproductive costs underlying the division of labour, as Nadine Peacock has shown. A biological anthropologist, Peacock (1991) set out to examine women's role in subsistence practices among Efe hunter-gatherers of the

Democratic Republic of Congo. Her underlying interest was in the generalized patterns that 'might be used to explain cultural features across societies' (1991: 342), and in the origins of contemporary human behaviour. She was particularly interested in the extent and origins of male dominance, as theorized by feminist anthropologists (Rosaldo and Lamphere 1974; Collier and Rosaldo 1981). Peacock's (1991) approach, however, was to examine the sexual division of labour using research methodologies (including time allocation analysis) designed to throw light on women's behaviour. While she believed that women's reproductive labour did impact on their subsistence activities, she drew an important distinction, highlighting energetic as opposed to logistic constraints. Thus, while women are in theory capable of performing high-energy, high-risk activities, even while pregnant and lactating, 'both pregnancy and lactation are extremely demanding in terms of energetic requirements ... and women may have to "choose" between the performance of energetically demanding tasks and the successful production and feeding of an infant' (Peacock 1991: 347). On a similar note, taking energetic costs as a significant determinant in co-operative behaviour, biological anthropologists Key and Aiello (1999) found that among female primates, who bear the responsibility of gestation and lactation, the energetic costs of reproduction are always high. Intrafemale co-operation is most likely to emerge where high reproductive costs are combined with dependency on a meat-based diet.

The question then shifts from whether women are able to perform the same tasks as men, to whether they choose to. Responding to the suggestion that early weaning and use of alternative caretakers is the only means by which women may make a substantial contribution to subsistence, Peacock (1991) cites !Kung mothers, whose contribution to subsistence is high, but who also keep infants and small children close, nursing frequently day and night, and not introducing weaning foods until late on (Lee 1979; Howell 1976). The crucial deciding factor appears to be whether women are able to work collectively, making use of other women's support, and engaging in labour which does not require them to leave small infants for long periods of time. Peacock's (1991) research confirmed that while women perform childcare tasks simultaneously with other subsistence activities (intensifying workloads considerably), both pregnant and lactating women do curtail strenuous work activities, cutting back on energy intensive tasks. These findings, she states, 'contradict newly emerged feminist wisdom that in its extreme portrays the subsistence work of women in foraging societies as being unaffected by pregnancy, the birth process, or childcare' (1991: 351).

Noting that activities curbed because of childcare include agricultural labour (in Lese neighbours gardens), wood and water collection, and hut-building, Peacock asks how mothers manage to take care of dependent children and meet their subsistence needs. The answer, one noted by many hunter-gatherer specialists, is co-operative mothering. Caretaking as we conceive of it requires leaving infants for extended periods of time, and is incompatible with continued breastfeeding. But Efe women nurse each others' babies while working co-operatively, and are therefore able to employ a flexible, dynamic kind of collective caretaking in which babies are passed around continually between mothers, depending on what task a particular woman is engaged in at any given moment. This is not a minor detail in contexts where continued breastfeeding and late weaning can make the difference to infant survival. The co-operation of other women, as well as older daughters, Peacock (1991) found, is in fact integral to Efe women's ability to meet their family's subsistence needs while bearing and raising children. The Efe case demonstrates that

> an intricate and varied pattern of cooperative work and mutual caretaking among women permits combinations of subsistence work and childcare that would at first glance seem unworkable. This illustrates the importance of looking at behaviour from a collectivist as well as individualist perspective; it also suggests an important lesson for scholars of human evolution, who all too often make the assumption that only cooperation between males was crucial for the structuring of early human societies. (Peacock 1991: 354)

Hewlett's (1989; Hewlett and Lamb 2007; Hewlett and Winn 2014) work on multiple caretaking and allonursing among the Aka and Efe is also revealing in showing up both the fluid nature of care in these communities and the substantial benefits for the infants of mothers living in societies where allonursing is common.

Brightman (1996) cites evidence suggesting that women's reproductive cycles – menstruation, pregnancy, birth, lactation and weaning – impinge directly upon the division of labour. Again and again a close reading of his own material reveals the reality of women's collectively made choices and strategies. But without drawing a connection between the two – physiological demands and female co-operative responses to them – he is compelled to begin and end with a culturally constituted exclusion. The central flaw in his argument is in fact this blindness to women's contractual relationships, both with other women and with husbands and male relatives. In persisting with an 'every-woman-for-herself' ethos, he misses the possibility of cultural consensus, negotiated between groups in order to elicit male provisioning, ensure sharing, and enable women to remain close to vulnerable infants. Peacock (1991) demonstrates that the subsistence and childcare work women do already exacts a high price, and requires continual intrasexual solidarity. Moreover, her work points to the value which women (and in fact everyone) in hunter-gatherer communities place on infant nurture and wellbeing. Brightman (1996) explores the subject mechanistically, as though simple logistic constraints were all that mattered. Having acknowledged the importance of fertility trends in affecting ability to hunt routinely, he then adds that these 'do not render hunting *impossible* but only limit in variable degree the percentage of workdays which individual women could allocate to it' (Brightman 1996: 698).

Theories that assert a causal connection between biology and culture, he continues, characterize women as 'sedentary rather than mobile, passive rather than aggressive, weak rather than strong, unable to reconcile maternity with a career outside the home' (1996: 704). Yet this is the last thing the models put forth by Knight, Power and Hrdy depict. Instead, we find biology fuelling powerful ritual systems which afford women a substantial cultural presence. Marian McCreedy (1994), in her examination of net-hunting ritual among the Biaka of the Central African Republic, finds women are 'the arms of the *dibouka*' (McCreedy 1994: 15). The *dibouka* refers to the throw of nets made during collective hunting expeditions, when women perform the *bobanda* ritual to ensure hunting success. Although women are not physically involved in the kill, 'if they refused to participate in the *bobanda*, it could not take place, because it is the women who are responsible for the spirit of the *bobanda*' (McCreedy 1994: 15). McCreedy uses her discussion of the *bobanda* ritual to frame Biaka ideas about the division of labour as interdependence, an expression above all of 'the work men and women do for each other' (McCreedy 1994: 20).

The *bobanda*, always called in response to a lean period when men's hunting luck is considered poor, involves mobilizing women's ritual labour – singing, dancing and conversation with game spirits – in order to restore community equilibrium. McCreedy (1994) emphasizes that it is the collective ritual energy of women that breaks the perceived impasse, symbolizing as they do vitality and movement with their large-scale singing and dancing performances, during which power is 'transferred' to a selected male *nganga* or ritual leader by beating him with leaves (1994: 31),

> Given the considerable commitment required of women to what may be
> days of hard physical and ritual activity, they demand the recognition
> of men: The men (and the entire community) are at the mercy of
> women and must convince them to perform. The women cannot be
> coerced ... and it is up to the men to convince the women that the
> situation requires their co-operation. They are called upon and formally
> recognized as the most powerful remedy to solve the problem. When
> the individual magical knowledge of the men in camp breaks down and
> fails to remedy the hunting failure, the collective energy and power of
> the women are needed. (McCreedy 1994: 33)

Likewise, Joiris (1996), in an important account of what she terms
Baka 'ritual associations', is unequivocal about women's centrality to
the hunting enterprise. Most ritual associations are in practice
multifunctional, and many are open to initiates of both sexes, but
interestingly, only the exclusively female *yeli* and *yenga poto*
associations focus primarily on large game hunting. The main initiates
or *ngonjia* are those whose responsibilities include divination,
oneiromancy (a form of divination based on the interpretation of
dreams) and organization of ceremonies. *Ngonjia* in general may be
individuals of either sex, and often spouses work together, sharing
knowledge and skills (1996: 252). Yet even where a *ngonjia* 'spirit
guardian' – usually a former elephant hunter – achieves elder status,
he is considered a camp guardian whose work is to act as peacekeeper,
and not a permanent authority of any kind (1996: 253).

Joiris (1996) points out: 'There is so much overlapping within the
ritual and political spheres that it results in a selective sharing of
responsibilities, a multiplicity of male and female actors, and an
organization that is most notable for being flexible and fluid' (1996:
254). Baka women are centrally involved in the large complex of rituals
surrounding the hunt, which are designed to locate and attract game,
designate specific hunters who will make the kill, and thank game
spirits. While ceremonies are usually performed in public prior to,
during, or following the hunt, the female *yeli* and *yenga poto* ceremonies
take place largely in private. During divination in preparation for
hunting, the *yeli ngonjia* performs a rite to establish where the game will
be found and which direction the hunter should follow (1996: 259).
Rites performed in order to attract game, says Joiris,

> are very elaborate in the *yeli* ceremony. Powerful hunting prowess is
> attributed to the 'yodel' polyphonies performed by the principal *yeli*
> initiate soloists. Some of the *yeli* songs refer to the first hunt as it is
> described in the *tibola* song fable; that story explains the origin of
> hunting power, by virtue of which *nganga* women co-operate with the
> *me* spirits to locate and call animals. (1996: 263)

This relationship – of female initiates with game spirits – is elaborated in the context of hunting, where it is overwhelmingly women who locate forest animals. It is through a privileged relationship with spirits that women participate in the hunt. These spirits, upon hearing *yeli* initiates begin to sing, start dancing out in the forest, preparing for the hunt. During this time, *yeli* initiates prepare a ritual beverage which is consumed by the whole community, in order to reinforce the ability of the song to draw game. Women also apply ritual substances to the bodies of hunters in order to 'make them invisible' and bring luck (1996: 264). Immediately prior to the hunt, the *yeli nganga* uses trance and divinatory techniques to determine the master hunter who will kill the game. During the hunt, while there are no formal rituals performed, individual *nganga* of both sexes use visionary power, communicate with spirits (made visible by consumption of ritual substances), and guide the hunting procession using divinatory rites. *Yeli* initiates, in the aftermath of the hunt, offer raw meat or cooked food as gifts to the spirits. While *yeli* is just one of many ritual associations used to assist successful hunting, it is the only one that focuses solely upon the hunt, and Joiris (1996) points out that it affords women substantial power in subsequent claims to meat.

McCreedy (1994) and Joiris's (1996) descriptions of Biaka and Baka women's song and dance performances as ritual hunting labour is relevant for the general literature on Yaka ritual and dance (Harako 1984; Bahuchet 1985; Tsuru 1998; Sawada 1990; Bundo 2001) which has tended to categorize performances by confining them to the realm of aesthetics, or by setting up a distinction between men's 'formal' spirit performances and women's 'joyful play' (Bundo 2001). Japanese ethnographers in particular have conducted meticulous empirical studies of Pygmy ritual and dance, listing even children's '*be*' or dance performances. What McCreedy (1994) and Joiris (1996) contribute is the expansive, polyphonic sociality of women's dances, which operate on several levels including as ritual interventions in the hunting enterprise. Joiris's (1996) findings are reiterated by Lewis (2002) in his discussion of Yaka women's participation in elephant hunting through the *mokondi massana* of *yele*. While in trance prior to the hunt, *yele* initiates 'tie up' the elephant's spirit, and later direct men to it: 'In effect women catch the elephant first. This accounts for this type of hunting journey being called "*mwaka ya baito*", a woman's hunting trip' (Lewis 2002: 170). Following the successful hunt, the *massana* of *Eya* is called to mark the elephant's death, during which spirits associated with it converse with women through song. For Lewis (2002), women's ritual involvement in hunting and subsequent claims to meat are part of an ongoing distribution of power represented by *massana* activities of all kinds. '*Mokondi Massana* are sophisticated, many dimensioned, aesthetic achievements ... *Massana* deliberately glorifies the forest, the gender groups, and the joy and inherent beauty of their coordination and mutual co-operation in distinctive but complimentary ways' (2002: 172).

Putting together Peacock's research into the division of labour among hunter-gatherers and the kind of co-operative work Efe women choose to do, McCreedy's (1994) analysis of Biaka women's special ritual relationship with game, and Joiris's (1996) writing on the ritual associations of *yeli* and *yenga poto*, the widespread antipathy of the female body with the flesh of game animals assumes a new significance. It is in the realm of hunting and hunted animals that equivalence is stressed. For the Mbendjele Yaka there is an explicit and obvious interplay between women's blood, voracious blood-eating forest spirits, and game animals (Lewis 2008: 307). When a hunter whose wife is pregnant kills in the forest, he must throw certain parts of the animal's intestines into the undergrowth to mollify the *edio* spirits who normally enjoy women's menstrual blood. In having 'cut her moon' (Mbendjele idiom for conception), the husband of a pregnant woman has interceded directly in this relationship, and must make some gesture towards the spirits: hence the offering of the bloody innards. 'An older man might also add the words "Take it!" or "That's yours!"' (Lewis 2002: 307). By giving up his meat the hunter bargains with the forest spirits and animals for the safe delivery of the infant.

Lewis (2008) has described how failure to respect game animals (either by going hunting while one's wife is menstruating or by laughing at a dead animal's carcass) will result either in lack of success or in direct danger to the hunter from enraged animals. The personhood afforded game animals by hunters has been noted by various ethnographers (Biesele 1993; Lewis 2002). Knight (1991) pulls together a vast array of information on blood taboos to suggest an originary rationale for all this: women's identification with game animals is in fact extremely useful in inciting hunters to return meat to camp, where it can be safely purified through cooking. In expressing a taboo, one thing is negatively connected to another. 'Negative' here is not straightforward. All hunting communities are concerned with ritual mediation of and relationship between powerful substances or entities. Brightman (1996) in his discussion of hunting taboo identifies menstruation, parturition and female sexual fluids (all bodily markers) as components in a general semantic construction of 'femaleness' with which hunting must not be mixed. 'Femaleness and hunting are thus represented in foragers' ideologies as existing in a condition of metaphysical antipathy that threatens the hunting enterprise' (Brightman 1996: 706). This is correct. But how we choose to read that antipathy means everything. According to the data provided above, we need to explore those ways in which women are involved with hunting without threatening its success. While it is true that great pains are taken by hunter-gatherers to prevent metaphysically charged substances – such as menstrual blood and the blood of animals – from merging, to the extent that hunters whose wives are menstruating may not participate in the hunt, this is conceived of as one of the most powerful, if not the most powerful, of relationships in the cosmological and religious sphere. The concept of *ekila* as elaborated by Lewis (2008) demonstrates this.

There is a logic woven into antipathy in these contexts. Women are not physically debarred from hunting with no other comment made. Their absence signifies power. Knight (1991), Knight, Power and Watts (1995), McCreedy (1994), Power (1993), and Power and Watts (1999) contend that it is in this very move – away from the bodies of game animals – that women collectively become sacred. This is illustrated by the fact that in times of hunting crisis, they alone can use their ritual presence to intervene (McCreedy 1994), and by the fact that they generally are believed to maintain a privileged conversation with large game that both attracts and (the point seized upon by most Western theorists), if not correctly managed, repels animals and the spirits integral to their capture. The hidden elephant, which it takes women's ritual work to reveal, could be viewed as an appropriate metaphor for the sexual egalitarianism lurking in anthropology's intellectual room. If egalitarianism were to be acknowledged as an evolutionary fact, where would that lead us as a discipline (and as a society)? The indisputable reality that humans are co-operative childcarers, together with the rich symbolic field opened around the reproductive body in those contexts described here, indicates the most basic materialist rationale possible: that of survival. There is nothing stronger than the will to stay alive, except perhaps the will to keep one's child alive. And some might argue that we are in desperate need, as a species, of potential alternatives to the kinds of power arrangement that have led us to where we now are.

Wengrow and Graeber (2015), discussing the longstanding dichotomy between egalitarianism and hierarchy, have chosen to focus on seasonal variations in political modes among Upper Palaeolithic European hunter-gatherers, where they argue that societies fluctuated periodically between hierarchical and egalitarian social arrangements. They have therefore little to say about African hunter-gatherers or sexual politics. In the political networks described here, by contrast, hierarchy is absorbed into egalitarianism, disposing of the categorical line between 'simple' egalitarianism and 'complex' hierarchy. Instead, under the one rubric of complex egalitarianism (with 'complex' no longer pertaining to states, armies or monuments, but relational and socio-political complexity) we are able to recognize virtual networks of increase and contraction, or harmony and entropy: inter-relational fields of skill and power which seem to stump social anthropology's thinking on sex and the body. This is because we are not in fact talking about cognitively rooted networks. While Wengrow and Graeber make good use of the principles of flux and oscillation in questioning models which effectively freeze societies into monotypes – egalitarian or hierarchical – I contend that strategic reversal of authority is not confined to 'societies with marked seasonal variations' (Wengrow and Graeber 2015: 605) because there are other potential clocks for organizing and subverting power. The work of Knight and colleagues for example, demonstrates the ubiquity of lunar templates in scheduling activity in African hunter-gatherer society. Further to that, it would seem that in societies such as the Mbendjele the clock (or pendulum) is kept ticking continually on a microcosmic level, where dynamic duality has been drawn right down into the body using music, dance and corporeal concepts such as *ekila*. Individuals raised in these societies are masters in the art of flux, and of political shapeshifting. There are many terms we could use to describe the eternal process of juggling and funnelling power, but 'simple' is not one of them.

Complex Egalitarianism

In the story assembled by Knight, Power and Watts (1995), female blood is first used to signal a relationship between animals and women – meat and sex – important to women in their collective capacity as mothers. Knight (1991) insists that it is impossible to theorize the cross-cultural relationship between women and game animals without a prior understanding of the constraints placed upon women by reproductive demands, and their collective response to these. Peacock's (1991) findings support that. And the ethnographic examples I have cited here on women's ritual relationship with game animals confirm it. The intense signalling power of female blood represents the first taboo: the moment it is pooled and pluralized, culture commences. Against the assumption that expressed power – the power to be – is the only power, rests the power of withdrawal, the power not to be, the power of strike. And this is the other, missing half of the circle. Communities whose core mnemonic devices hinge on menstrual blood, and who highlight and positively value sexual, bodily difference are communities to whom the full power range is still accessible. Labour roles and constraints in such societies focus explicitly on the power of menstrual blood, gestation, sex, the bodies of game animals, the blood of game animals, and the relationship between women and meat. 'Work' is something done for the opposite sex. Rival (1997), Gow (1989), Overing (2003), Bodenhorn (1990), McCreedy (1994), Biesele (1993) and Lewis (2002) all make reference to this as an explicit conviction among the egalitarian peoples with whom they work. It runs through the realms of hunting, childbirth, ritual hunting, childbirth rites, and general sociality: productive action is what one does willingly as part of a flow of complimentary effort between the sexes.

Gow's (1989) analysis of this is particularly useful in clarifying the trajectory from subsistence to symbolism. He notes: 'The unmarried adult does not produce, or produces very little and sporadically, *because he or she has no one for whom to produce*' (Gow 1989: 572, emphasis mine). Echoing Biesele's (1993) use of the Ju/'hoan adage 'women like meat', Gow (1989) reiterates that people's desire is what binds them. These are not 'abstracted desires that can be satisfied in a variety of different ways', but desires which 'link people inevitably to certain other people' (Gow 1989: 568). Desire, hunger and sharing are what animate the lines running between women and men, sex and meat. Like Lewis (2002), Gow (1989) double-frames the biocultural flow of items and substances between women and men, giving the impression of a relational toing and froing. Women produce manioc beer; men distribute it. Men produce meat; women distribute it. Women secure meat; men produce it. Men secure babies; women produce them. Thus 'productive labour is gender-identified ... But at the level of circulation the gender identity of a product is transformed' (Gow 1989: 571). The construction of the person as a producer in the subsistence economy is systematically connected to sexual desire, in a persistent 'metaphoric relation between food items and sexual substances' (1989: 574).

Gow (1989), in common with Central African writers (Devische 1993; Ichikawa 1987; Lewis 2002; 2008), describes a system in which corporeal processes are already part of a general social concern, and questions why this is the case. His answer, resonating strongly with Knight's (1991) assertions, is that the power of corporeal idioms derives from 'the importance of the sexual, productive and consuming body and its pleasures in the structuring of the subsistence economy ... *The body and its desires lies at the heart of the economy, serving as a point of attachment for social concerns*' (Gow 1989: 580, emphasis mine). Amazonian societies do not operate around the creation of subjects who 'own' particular goods (proprietorship), nor around the gift exchange idioms familiar to bridewealth societies, but rather 'through the relations established between people by means of their different bodies and corporeal desires' (ibid.: 580). It is in the relational, dialogical space between 'different bodies and corporeal desires' that sociality, and hence society, is made. Women's ritual relationship with game animals and meat is inseparable from the politics of mothering in such communities, and from men's corresponding ritual involvement in female fertility.

The lunar clock suggested by Knight is important, because it suggests a continual motion as society undergoes a fission/fusion process swinging back and forth between sexual solidarity and marital solidarity, between segregation and release. The public aspect of Mbendjele ritual entails a definite ritual confusion of quotidian relationships. As Knight, Power and Watts state: 'the first symbolic construct [is] women's assertion of their ritual inviolability' (1995: 85), with dance and bodypainting constituting the first symbolism. That first symbolic construct opens up into a rich cultural weave through which both time and power become dialogical in nature. The use of sexually graphic and abusive language is another loosener of normative relations and obligations. But evidence suggests that among contemporary forest hunter-gatherers, we can draw this down to an even tighter level, where power is a diffuse element in continual circulation, left simmering in the recesses of women's collective song and dance (see Finnegan 2015). The origins model I have discussed here is theoretically and ethnographically relevant because it illuminates these two distinct categories of time, two distinct concentrations of power – social and sexual, or domestic and ritual – between which society swings perpetually.

Knight's theory is compelling because it offers a detailed paradigm for another kind of power. Clastres (1977) claimed that society was acting all the time against the spectre of the state. I would go further. Society here is using the spectre of the state, using the potential for collapse, using concentrations of power and conflict on the most primal level – that of the body – and using a sophisticated dialogue with raw force in order to churn up the political landscape and keep the argument live. Real prosocial power then is at root ambivalent. It is characterized by its dialogical quality. It shuttles back and forth continually between groups and poles using an entropic loss and gain of energy a kind of controlled withering and flourishing. The range of technologies employed by the Mbendjele to achieve this include vocal polyphony, highly skilled dance choreographies, the myriad methods and effects of communal parenting, and an entire cosmology held in the polysemic concept of *ekila*.

Sex-strike is, as Knight and colleagues (1995) insist, a moral strategy. It generates the 'morally authoritative intangibles' (1995: 92) central to the symbolic domain, where blood is linked to a whole repertoire of other phenomena including dance, fertility, the spirits and hunting. Woodburn, identifying what differentiates egalitarian societies from others, notes that: 'These societies systematically eliminate distinctions – *other than those between the sexes* – of wealth, of power and of status' (Woodburn 1982: 434, emphasis mine). We can now see that far from being concerned to eliminate distinctions between the sexes (as though this were something they have failed to achieve yet) these societies are elaborating on such distinctions, in a power dialogic designed to thrive on difference. The temporal aspect of the model, and the predictions it generates for a certain kind of political system which waxes and wanes across the social landscape, are what matter here. This is why I believe dance is such a vital aspect of Mbendjele social life. Not only are the motifs embedded in the spectacle of dance crucial, but on a phenomenal level dance represents the freedom of movement of the collective and the subversive quality immanent in egalitarian power. This is why the spirits dance, and love to dance: they, like the Khoisan trickster as described by Guenther (1999), are depositories for the complex chains of symbols that represent the moral energy of the collective.

What happens, Hrdy (2009) asks, when people begin to move away from this sensual culture, this open and giving system? We know that towards the end of the Pleistocene human communities began to undergo a profound change not only in structure and size but in nature. As people settled, building permanent dwellings with fences and walls, storing food rather than sharing it, privatizing children as individual possessions through which hereditary lines could safely run, you could say that we began to turn from prosocial animals to antisocial ones. Crucially, 'child survival became increasingly decoupled from the need to be in constant physical contact with another person, or surrounded by responsive, protective caretakers' (Hrdy 2009: 286). Children could now survive without contact, and without the kind of nurture their brains and bodies had evolved to expect. Property, higher population density, and social stratification transformed the nature of social groups, turning the intersubjective focus from relational to defensive. The deep need for social support in raising our young endures, yet 'for the first time in human history, exceedingly high rates of child survival coincide with sobering statistics about the emotional wellbeing of children' (2009: 289). Hrdy ends her book on a grave note, pointing out that the result of new parenting models which set out to detach children from their carers early on, prioritizing the needs of adults as workers instead, is leading to a generalized phenomenon of 'disorganized attachment' (Hrdy 2009). Children are losing emotional capacities refined over a long period of evolutionary history. Such children, no longer permitted to attach securely as infants, grow into adolescents who 'have difficulty interpreting the needs of others, are significantly more aggressive towards peers, and are prone to behaviour disorders' (2009: 289).

The model developed by Knight, Power and Watts has two levels of significance. There are the scientific repercussions, the archaeological and ethnographic data they bring in support of their thesis, and their own stated readiness to be tested on it. But there is another level – the broader moral and political repercussions of this model for contemporary anthropology. Why are social anthropologists not paying more attention to origins scenarios such as this? Implicit in the lack of interest of many (though not by any means all) social anthropologists in our common evolutionary heritage is the assumption that male political alliance is the obvious foundation for society. Even the most radical thinkers – Rousseau, Kropotkin – never got close to the possibility that human nature might have been formed in a whole other kind of evolutionary milieu, one in which coalitions of mothers and allomothers take centre stage. From 'man the hunter', or 'man the warrior', then, we come around not to some female equivalent, but to the figure of the child which culture evolved to protect.

References

Bahuchet, S. 1985. *Les Pygmées Aka et la Forêt Centrafricaine.* Paris: SELAF.
Barnard, A. 2011. *Social Anthropology and Human Origins.* Cambridge: Cambridge University Press.
Biesele, M. 1993. *Women Like Meat.* Bloomington: Indiana University Press.
Brightman, R. 1996. 'The Sexual Division of Foraging Labour: Biology, Taboo, and Gender Politics', *Comparative Studies in Society and History* 38: 687–729.

Bodenhorn, B. 1990. 'I'm Not the Great Hunter, My Wife Is', *Inuit Studies* 14: 55–74.

Boehm, C. 1999. *Hierarchy in the Forest: the Evolution of Egalitarian Behavior*. Cambridge, MA: Harvard University Press.

Bundo, D. 2001. 'Social Relationship Embodied in Singing and Dancing Performances Among the Baka', *African Study Monographs* Suppl. 26: 85–101.

Clastres, P. 1977. *Society Against the State*. Oxford: Blackwell.

Collier, J. and M. Rosaldo. 1981. 'Politics and Gender in Simple Societies', in S. Ortner and H. Whitehead (eds), *Sexual Meanings: The Cultural Construction of Gender and Sexuality*. Cambridge: Cambridge University Press, pp. 279–325.

Devische, R. 1993. *Weaving the Threads of Life*. Chicago and London: University of Chicago Press.

Endicott, K. 1981. 'The Conditions of Egalitarian Male/Female Relationships in Foraging Societies', *Canberra Anthropology* 4: 1–10.

Endicott, K.M. and K.L. Endicott. 2008. *The Headman Was a Woman. The Gender Egalitarian Batek of Malaysia*. Long Grove, IL: Waveland Press.

Engels, F. 1986 [1884]. *The Origin of the Family, Private Property and the State*. Harmondsworth: Penguin Books.

Finnegan, M. 2013. 'The Politics of Eros: Ritual Dialogue and Egalitarianism in Three Central African Hunter-gatherer Societies', *Journal of the Royal Anthropological Institute* 19: 697–715.

———. 2015. 'Dance, Play, Laugh: What Capitalism Can't Do', *Hunter-Gatherer Research* 1: 85–105.

Gow, P. 1989. 'The Perverse Child: Desire in a Native Amazonian Subsistence Economy', *Man*, New Series, 24(4): 567–582.

Graeber, D. 2004. *Fragments of an Anarchist Anthropology*. Chicago: Prickly Paradigm Press.

Guenther, M. 1999. *Tricksters and Trancers*. Bloomington: Indiana University Press.

Harako, R. 1984. 'Religious World of the Mbuti Pygmies' (in Japanese), in J. Itani and T. Yoneyama (eds), *Studies on African Cultures*. Kyoto: Academia Shuppankai, pp.137–164.

Hewlett, B. 1989. 'Multiple Caretaking Among African Pygmies', *American Anthropologist* N.S. 91: 186–191.

——— and M. Lamb. 2007. 'Integrating Evolution, Culture and Developmental Psychology', in H. Keller (ed.), *Between Biology and Culture: Perspectives on Ontogenetic Development*. Cambridge: Cambridge University Press, pp. 241–270.

——— and S. Winn. 2014. 'Allomaternal Nursing in Humans', *Current Anthropology* 55: 200–209.

Howell, N. 1976. 'The Population of the Dobe Area !Kung', in R. Lee and I. DeVore (eds), *Kalahari Hunter-Gatherers*. Cambridge, MA and London: Harvard University Press, pp. 137–151.

Hrdy, S. 2009. *Mothers and Others*. Cambridge, MA: Harvard University Press.

Ichikawa, M. 1987. 'Food Restrictions of the Mbuti Pygmies', *African Study Monographs* Supplementary Issue No. 6.

Joiris, D.V. 1996. 'A Comparative Approach to Hunting Rituals Among Baka Pygmies', in S. Kent (ed.), *Cultural Diversity Among Twentieth Century Foragers: An African Perspective*. Cambridge: Cambridge University Press, pp. 245–275.

Key, C. and L. Aiello. 1999. 'The Evolution of Social Organisation', in R. Dunbar, C. Knight and C. Power (eds), *The Evolution of Culture*. Edinburgh: Edinburgh University Press, pp. 15–33.

Knight, C. 1991. *Blood Relations*. New Haven and London: Yale University Press.

———, C. Power and I. Watts. 1995. 'The Human Symbolic Revolution: A Darwinian Account', *Cambridge Archaeological Journal* 5: 75–114.

Leacock, E. 1981. *Myths of Male Dominance*. New York and London: Monthly Review Press.

Lee, R. 1979. *The !Kung San: Men, Women, and Work in a Foraging Society*. Cambridge: Cambridge University Press.

Lewis, J. 2002. 'Forest Hunter-Gatherers and Their World', PhD dissertation. London: University of London.

———. 2008. '*Ekila*: Blood, Bodies, and Egalitarian Societies', *Journal of the Royal Anthropological Institute* 14: 297–315.

McCreedy, M. 1994. 'The Arms of the Dibouka', in E. Burch and L. Ellanna (eds), *Key Issues in Hunter-Gatherer Research*. Oxford: Berg, pp. 15–34.

Myers, F. 1986. *Pintupi Country, Pintupi Self*. California: University of California Press.

Opie, C. et al. 2013. 'Male Infanticide Leads to Social Monogamy in Primates', *Proceedings of the National Academy of Sciences* 110(33): 13328–32. doi: 10.1073/pnas.1307903110.

Overing, J. 2003 'In Praise of the Everyday: Trust and the Art of Social Living in an Amazonian Community'. *Ethos* 68(3):293–316.

Peacock, N. 1991. 'Rethinking the Sexual Division of Labour', in M. Leonardo (ed.), *Gender at the Crossroads of Knowledge: Feminist Anthropology in the Postmodern Era*. Berkeley, CA: University of California Press, pp. 339–361.

Power, C. 1993. 'The Woman With the Zebra's Penis', MA Dissertation. London: University of London.

——— and I. Watts. 1999. 'First Gender, Wrong Sex', in H. Moore, T. Sanders and B. Kaare (eds), *Those Who Play With Fire*. London: Athlone Press, pp. 101–132.

Rival, L. 1997. 'Androgynous Parents and Guest Children: The Huaorani Couvade', *Journal of The Royal Anthropological Institute* 4: 619–642.

Rosaldo, M. Z. and L. Lamphere (eds). 1974. *Woman, Culture and Society*. Stanford, CA: Stanford University Press.

Rousseau, J.-J. 1973 [1755]. *The Social Contract and Discourses*. London: Dent.

Sawada, M. 1990. 'Two Patterns of Chorus Among the Efe Forest Hunter-Gatherers in Northeastern Zaire – Why Do They Love to Sing?' *African Study Monographs* 10(4): 159–195.

Tsuru, D. 1998. 'Diversity of Ritual Spirit Performances Among the Baka Pygmies in Southeastern Cameroon', *African Study Monographs* Suppl. 25: 47–84.

Turnbull, C. 1961. *The Forest People.* London: Chatto & Windus.

Van Schaik, C.P. and C.H. Janson (eds). 2000. *Infanticide by Males and its Implications.* Cambridge: Cambridge University Press.

Wengrow, D. and D. Graeber. 2015. 'Farewell to the "Childhood of Man": Ritual, Seasonality, and the Origins of Inequality', *Journal of the Royal Anthropological Institute* 21: 597–619.

Woodburn, J. 1980. 'Hunters and Gatherers Today and Reconstruction of the Past', in E. Gellner (ed.), *Soviet and Western Anthropology.* London: Duckworth, pp. 95–117.

———. 1982. 'Social Dimensions of Death in Four African Hunting and Gathering Societies', in M. Bloch and J. Parry (eds.), *Death and the Regeneration of Life.* Cambridge: Cambridge University Press, pp. 187–210.

Morna Finnegan received her PhD from Edinburgh University in 2010. She has since published several papers in journals including the *Journal of the Royal Anthropological Institute* and *Hunter Gatherer Research*. Her contribution as co-editor on the present volume is her first editing experience. She is currently combining motherhood with work on a monograph based on her doctoral thesis, which will focus on reproductive politics among egalitarian hunter-gatherers.

Chapter 6

FROM METAPHOR TO SYMBOLS AND GRAMMAR

THE CUMULATIVE CULTURAL EVOLUTION OF LANGUAGE

Andrew D.M. Smith and Stefan Hoefler

Introduction

Human language is unique among the communication systems that evolution has brought about in its use of symbols and complex grammatical structures. While some view human language as a specific biological adaptation, others consider it the product of more general cognitive and cultural processes. In either case, one needs to account for the transition from a prelinguistic stage, where humans (or their ancestors) did not possess language, to a stage where language, as we know it today, had emerged. To this aim, researchers frequently postulate an intermediate stage during which a so-called protolanguage (Bickerton 1990) was in place. There has been significant and at times vehement debate over both the nature of protolanguage and how it developed into modern language (see, e.g., Arbib and Bickerton 2008) with opposing camps characterizing it either as containing word-like units which were composed into sentences (Bickerton 2003; Tallerman 2007) or as containing sentence-like units which were split into words (Wray 2000; Arbib 2005). There is nevertheless broad agreement that protolanguage was symbolic but had no syntactic structures or grammatical machinery. This means that the evolution of language is almost always thought of in terms of two distinct aspects with different evolutionary origins: the emergence of symbolic communication into protolanguage, and then the development of grammatical structure and the consequent emergence of language itself. As Michael Tomasello puts it: '[l]anguage is a complex outcome of human cognitive and social processes taking place in evolutionary, historical and ontogenetic time. And different aspects of language – for example, symbols and grammar – may have involved different processes and different evolutionary times' (Tomasello 2003: 109). In the present chapter, we challenge this conception: we suggest that there is in fact a common explanation for both aspects of language, i.e. that the emergence of symbolism and the emergence of grammatical structures are both products of the same cognitive and cultural mechanisms, and moreover that these mechanisms have been at the foundation of all human communication from its prelinguistic beginnings to the present day. We argue that the capacity for figurative use witnessed in the creation of novel metaphors plays a crucial part in this process, which underpins a cultural origin for language from these fundamental cognitive properties.

The chapter is organized as follows. We first introduce the ratchet model of cultural evolution, which explains how complex cultural artefacts can emerge as accumulations of innovations that are maintained through faithful social transmission. We then explain how the ostensive-inferential nature of linguistic communication, the ad-hoc creation of metaphors, and their subsequent conventionalization can lead to just such an accumulation of innovations in language. Finally, we detail how the cognitive and cultural mechanisms underlying this phenomenon can account for the emergence of both symbols and grammar.

The Ratchet Model of Cultural Evolution

Although evidence of cultural traditions and social learning can be found in many animals, it is clear that human culture is unprecedented in terms of its flexibility, diversity and complexity. These characteristics of human culture have been shown to arise as a result of cumulative cultural evolution (Boyd and Richerson 1996; Tomasello 1999; Dean et al. 2013), in which multiple incremental cultural innovations made by different people can accumulate over time and spread through a community. Tomasello, Kruger, and Ratner (1993) famously described cumulative cultural evolution in terms of a ratchet effect, which is made possible by a combination of accurate social learning and innovative modification: creative innovations are maintained within a population through their faithful transmission, and their cultural entrenchment provides a new platform for future innovations to build on, so that new learners are provided with a shortcut to the results obtained by their predecessors rather than having to 'reinvent the wheel'. Each application of this innovation-entrenchment cycle serves to ratchet up the complexity of the cultural artefact, allowing the development of accumulated traditions which are too complex to have been invented by a single individual (Tomasello 1999; Caldwell and Millen 2008a). A general ratchet model of cumulative cultural evolution relies on three crucial components, namely the artefact which evolves, and the processes which make its cumulative cultural evolution possible, viz. transmission and innovation:

1. In a ratchet model of cultural evolution, artefacts are considered not just to be actual physical objects such as axes, but rather the more general skills and behaviours which allow individuals to make and use them. An innovation to an artefact occurs whenever behaviours are modified, and this is often characterized in terms of adaptation to the wider environment (Tomasello 1999): whenever an individual is confronted with a novel situation which is not congruent with their existing behaviours, they modify these behaviours in response. In principle, innovation of cultural artefacts is potentially ubiquitous, because they are effectively always used in new contexts, which are at least minimally different from previous experiences.

2. Transmission, of course, is the process through which an artefact is passed between individuals; this process is necessarily approximate, because there is no direct link between different individuals' representations of the behaviour, and transmission must be mediated by some kind of public expression of the behaviour. This can clearly be seen in the case of language, which exists in two distinct guises: (i) as persistent, internal linguistic representations stored in an individual's mind, and (ii) as ephemeral, external linguistic usage in communicative situations. Language continually oscillates between these two manifestations, with each begetting and being begotten by the other: speakers use their internal linguistic representations to express utterances, and utterances are the raw data from which internal representations are abstracted through learning (Hurford 2002). Such oscillation between the private and public spheres is characteristic of the

social transmission of cultural artefacts more generally: one individual uses their internal representation of the artefact to execute a public performance of it, and another individual uses their observations of the public performance to infer an internal representation.

3. The oscillation model of cultural transmission provides two opportunities for the innovation required for the cultural evolution of language to take place: either in the comprehension of a novel internal representation in the light of a given utterance, or in the production of a novel external utterance based on a given internal representation. In comprehension-based approaches (Burling 2005; Smith 2006), innovation occurs through misinterpretation during the inference of meaning for an utterance: because there is a mismatch between the world knowledge of speaker and hearer (Kuteva 2001), the meaning inferred by the hearer may differ slightly from that intended by the speaker, and so the utterance is associated with a novel meaning; it has effectively been reinterpreted by the hearer. In production-based approaches, on the other hand, language use is itself innovative: when producing an utterance, the speaker invites the hearer to interpret it creatively, with a meaning which differs from its conventional meaning (Traugott and Dasher 2005). In Hoefler and Smith (2009), we have shown that both types of innovations rely on exactly the same underlying cognitive mechanisms, and each can be considered a special case of the other, but an account which places innovation in the production process and maintains fidelity in transmission comes closest to the general ratchet model (Tomasello, Kruger and Ratner 1993).

In addition to the many natural examples of cumulative culture in humans, not least in the incremental progress of science and technology, there is much evidence from controlled experimental studies exploring the transmission of different kinds of behaviours and knowledge along chains or within groups of participants (Mesoudi and Whiten 2008). Caldwell and Millen (2008b), for instance, used microsocieties (i.e., small groups of experimental participants) organized into transmission chains of overlapping generations to show the emergence of cumulative culture in tasks like constructing a tower from sticks and modelling clay, or building a paper aeroplane from a sheet of paper. They found not only measurable improvements in objective performance (tower height, distance plane travelled) over generations, but also evidence of accumulated traits, with designs within chains being rated more similar than those across chains.

Experiments using artificial languages in similar microsocieties have also shown the emergence of linguistic structure under the interaction of competing pressures for both expressivity and learnability (Kirby, Cornish and Smith 2008; Kirby et al. 2015) and the emergence of regularity from unpredictable variation (Smith and Wonnacott 2010).

Accumulated culture is common in humans, yet very rare or non-existent in other animals (Boyd and Richerson 1996; Caldwell and Millen 2008a); although social learning is relatively common in nonhumans, and animals have been seen to create distinct local behavioural traditions, such as potato-washing behaviour in Japanese macaques (Kawai 1965), there is little evidence that such innovations accumulate across generations or that they amount to more than a single individual could invent for themself (Dean et al. 2013). This has led to much discussion over the cognitive mechanisms which are required for the emergence of cumulative culture, with the most important mechanism being high-fidelity transmission: Lewis and Laland (2012), for instance, have demonstrated, using a mathematical model, how the existence of the ratchet effect requires transmission fidelity above a certain threshold. In humans, high-fidelity transmission is itself underpinned by sociocognitive capabilities such as imitative learning and active teaching, both of which are extremely rare in nonhumans (Dean et al. 2013), and both of which require individuals to take the perspective of another person and recognize each other as intentional beings (Tomasello 1999). This last capacity has also been identified as the key prerequisite for human ostensive-inferential communication, which leads us to the question of how the ratchet effect applies to that particular domain.

The Ratchet Effect in Linguistic Communication

Having introduced the general ratchet model of cumulative cultural evolution, we now investigate how this model applies in the particular case of language, first exploring the workings of the 'linguistic artefact' through ostension and inference. Then, we see how linguistic innovations emerge through metaphor, and how they are socially transmitted and spread through a community by a process of conventionalization.

Ostension and Inference

The function of language is communication, and it is in understanding how linguistic communication works that we can understand what is necessary for language to emerge. A common way to understand communication is in terms of the transfer of information from one individual's brain to another's; in the absence of telepathy, of course, direct inter-brain transfer is not possible, so we use the intermediate step of a code, in which the information to be communicated is translated into an associated signal that can actually be conveyed to the intended recipient, and thence decoded back into the desired meaning. In order for this system to work, the interlocutors clearly need to share the same code, in which every signal fully and unambiguously specifies a distinct meaning.

From an evolutionary point of view, however, this so-called code model of communication is extremely problematic, because a code cannot easily change while still remaining viable; every innovation in a code needs to be matched by a corresponding innovation in everyone else's code, and could occur only extremely rarely at best (Smith 2008). Even worse, codes are by definition made up of symbolic associations between forms and meanings, and cannot therefore help us to explain the evolution of symbolism itself. In the next section we will show that rather than being a prerequisite for communication, symbolism is actually an emergent property of accumulated communicative interactions. Fundamentally, though, the code model is unsatisfactory because communication is not simply a process of encoding and decoding, but rather depends profoundly on inviting and making inferences from context (Grice 1957, 1975).

Human linguistic and non-linguistic communication is best characterized instead by the complementary processes of ostension and inference, respectively the production and interpretation of evidence for the speaker's informative and communicative intentions (Sperber and Wilson 1995). In this ostensive-inferential model of communication, the speaker considers not just which message to communicate, but how any signals they produce might help the hearer to retrieve the intended message. The cognitive requirements for this kind of communication are very different from working with a code: it operates through metapsychological reasoning about an interlocutor's thoughts and knowledge and recursive mindreading (Scott-Phillips 2015: 63–75), as it is based on the notion of common ground, i.e. the mutual knowledge that interlocutors assume they share with each other (Clark 1996). Much work has been done on trying to tease out the various aspects of common ground, but a number of its widely recognized facets include: the shared recognition of each other as potential communicative partners; recognition of each other's communicative intentions and an understanding of the goal of the communicative episode (Grice 1975; Tomasello et al. 2005); an understanding of what is relevant in the current interaction (Sperber and Wilson 1995); and knowledge of existing shared conventions, including linguistic knowledge.

Ostensive-inferential communication is therefore achieved through two interdependent acts: the speaker carries out an ostensive act, whose deliberate and atypical nature marks it out as potentially relevant, thereby expressing their communicative intention and inviting the hearer to construct an appropriate meaning; the hearer is prompted by the ostensive act to infer a relevant meaning for the ostensive act, using the context in which the act occurs and their shared common ground to do so. Importantly, and in contrast to the algorithmic mappings which underpin the code model, the inferential construction of meaning is an inherently approximate and uncertain process (Hurford 2007: 21; Smith and Hoefler 2015: 125), which depends on the interlocutors' individual cognitive representations of the world and of their existing cultural conventions. Linguistic communication is therefore just a particular type of ostensive-inferential communication, one whose immense power comes through the provision of expressive and precise cues, which guide the interpretation and construction of meaning.

Metaphorical Innovation

The linguistic artefact can therefore be considered as a set of conventional associations between form and meaning. Our next crucial step is to explain how an ostensive-inferential communication system can support innovation. Although many computational models of language evolution use a process of random invention to introduce new linguistic material (see e.g. Hurford 2002), because their primary focus is the effect of imperfect cultural transmission on linguistic structure, random linguistic innovation is in fact extremely rare in actual language use (Trask 2000: 369). By contrast, the most productive and widespread type of linguistic innovation is metaphor (Deutscher 2005: 118), which is the key to ostensive-inferential innovation.

Metaphor is the creative use of an existing linguistic form to express a meaning similar to, but not identical to, its conventional, 'literal' meaning (Kövecses 2002). If we think of this in terms of transfer, as the Greek etymology of the word suggests, then the form might be considered to move from its conventional meaning to the new meaning, or from its source meaning to a target meaning (Lakoff and Johnson 1980). Traditionally, metaphor has thus been viewed as exaggerated, embellished and exotic language, which can be contrasted with, and distinguished from, the lucidity, precision and truth of literal, everyday, language. On this view, literal language, such as the sentence 'John is greedy', expresses its meaning directly, while a comparable sentence 'John is a pig' can express the same meaning metaphorically, and can be translated into the 'true' meaning due to the fact that greediness is one of the qualities we conventionally associate with pigs.

Insights from cognitive linguistics focusing on actual language use, however (e.g. Lakoff and Johnson 1980; Gibbs 1994), have pointed out a number of serious problems with this traditional view. Figurative language is not a rare and exotic deviation from the norm, but is remarkable chiefly for its ubiquity in everyday language (Deutscher 2005). Much of our everyday way of talking about common events makes use of pervasive metaphors like motion and location to describe abstract entities which cannot be located or move anywhere, e.g. 'the unemployment figures are *going* down', 'the opposition is *in* a state of shock after their election defeat' (Evans and Green 2006). Furthermore, there are countless examples where translations of metaphorical meanings into literal meaning does not happen, and indeed appears impossible. Abstract concepts like TIME cannot be represented except in terms of concepts like SPACE or MOTION (Evans 2004), e.g. 'he has a great future *in front of* him', 'the summer is *flying by*'. In fact, we systematically conceptualize fundamental experiential concepts such as ANGER in metaphorical terms, for instance by representing it as HOT FLUID IN A CONTAINER, with the intensity of anger being expressed through metaphors of increasing pressure and the production of steam, e.g. 'my anger kept building up inside me', 'I was fuming' and 'he was bursting with anger' (Kövecses 2002: 96–97). Some generic conceptual metaphors, particularly those which derive from human physiology like the representation of ANGER as a PRESSURIZED CONTAINER, are extremely widespread cross-linguistically and perhaps even universal, while their elaboration into specific metaphors is dependent on the cultural context and physical environment in which the language is spoken (Kövecses 2005).

The creativity found in metaphors clearly poses a severe problem for explanations of language which rely on the code model of communication, because using a form creatively is pointless in that it defeats the object of having a code. The certain result of the non-conventional use of a coded signal is communication failure, because the hearer will inevitably decode the literal meaning. We can perhaps envisage metacommunicative additions to a code (such as emoticons) to signal to the hearer that certain items are to be interpreted non-literally, but these only fix us in a catch–22 situation: they are no help unless they specify how the non-literal part of the message is to be decoded, and if they do specify how it is to be decoded, then they are not necessary. As metaphors are both constructed and interpreted through the drawing of analogies between source and target meanings, it is thus important to emphasize that interpreting signals as having non-literal meanings is only possible at all in a communication system in which meaning is not decoded, but inferred through the interpretation of evidence provided for that purpose, as discussed above.

In order to infer an appropriate meaning for a metaphor, we need to focus on what is relevant in the communicative context: the metaphor 'John is a pig' mentioned above does not necessarily have to be interpreted as 'John is greedy', but could mean he is messy, fat, rude, has behaved badly, or countless other possibilities, depending on the interlocutors' knowledge about John and which of the characteristics conventionally associated with pigs are most relevant and are therefore most likely to be being alluded to (Smith and Hoefler 2015). We can see therefore that metaphors routinely overspecify the meaning they are being used as cues for: their successful interpretation requires the hearer to disregard large parts of their conventional meaning (features such as the facts that pigs make a distinctive noise, have a curly tail and trotters, and are a common source of meat) due to their lack of relevance. Other parts of the meaning may not be represented by the form at all, but are inferred from shared common ground and context (perhaps, for instance, the person referred to as John), so the form also underspecifies the inferred meaning. Indeed, in ostensive-inferential communication generally, the cues provided by the speaker exhibit what has been dubbed pragmatic plasticity: they both over- and underspecify their intended contextually relevant meanings at the same time (Hoefler 2008, 2009).

The traditional sharp distinction between literal and metaphorical use can therefore be seen as fallacious, and the two are better conceptualized as a continuum (Langacker 1987; Sperber and Wilson 1995), with figurativeness being a matter of degree, and its extent corresponding to some measure of the difference between the form's conventional meaning and the meaning actually inferred in context:

the greater this distance, the more strikingly figurative the usage appears. Metaphor is a basic, universal cognitive process, both enabled by ostensive-inferential communication, and in fact an inexorable result of the inherent imprecision and indeterminacy of a communicative system based on the provision and interpretation of evidence, where a piece of evidence is inevitably interpreted differently by different people, with different memories, interests and concerns, in different contexts.

Conventionalization

Metaphor creation is an ephemeral, ad hoc process of innovation, but successful metaphors can be shared between interlocutors, and ultimately throughout a whole community, through a process of conventionalization, which is rooted in general learning. At its most general, learning describes a cognitive change that comes about through experience and memorization: through doing something or observing someone else doing something, and remembering the event. When an individual is involved in a successful communicative event, for instance, they may remember that a particular form was successfully used to prompt for the inference of a particular meaning.

Such memorization of communicative experience has two important consequences. Firstly, it strengthens the interlocutors' cognitive association between the form and the meaning. If the form-meaning association is repeatedly used in similar circumstances, memorization can lead to the entrenchment or habitualization of the association, which becomes a psychological unit in its own right (Langacker 1987); the more frequently the association is used, the more entrenched it becomes (Barlow and Kemmer 2000; Bybee 2007). Importantly, once the association has reached a certain level of entrenchment, the meaning can be inferred automatically simply from the production of the form, without the need for the potentially complex inferential reasoning which was required in the first place, and it can thus become independent of the context in which the association was first created. Secondly, the memorization of communicative experience establishes further common ground knowledge between the interlocutors, which can be used in future communicative situations as part of the background knowledge against which new ostensive acts are interpreted. This not only allows the metaphor to be more easily interpreted in subsequent communicative episodes, but may eventually allow it to be invoked directly, independently of the context in which it was originally created

(Kuteva 2001; Traugott and Dasher 2005) as a convention in its own right. A similar process can also be seen in a series of graphical communication experiments derived from the game 'Pictionary' (Garrod et al. 2007; Fay, Garrod and Roberts 2008; Fay et al. 2010; Garrod et al. 2010; Caldwell and Smith 2012), in which participants must communicate concepts to their partners through drawings. Initially, the drawings must be contextually motivated in order to be communicatively successful, but over repeated use they become part of the participants' common ground, and the relevant meanings can be identified simply from their shared history of use. Importantly, the drawings become more abstract and simplified over time to reflect this developing common ground: they need only resemble a previous drawing of the form rather than the concept itself (Garrod et al. 2007).

The two processes of entrenchment and common ground creation therefore reinforce each other, resulting in the conventionalization of originally ad hoc form-meaning associations. Conventionalization itself is a matter of degree, depending on both use and coverage within a community: a form-meaning association becomes increasingly conventionalized as it is used more frequently in communication and as it is encountered by more individuals who remember it. This observation is at the heart of cognitive and usage-based approaches to language (Barlow and Kemmer 2000; Croft 2000; Croft and Cruse 2004), which argue that it is through conventionalization that linguistic structure emerges.

Through this process of innovation and conventionalization, language users are able to express meanings which were previously inexpressible; existing associations are effectively used as stepping stones from which to reach new meanings through metaphor, and, once conventionalized, these metaphors can serve as the basis for further innovation to open up further meanings. The repeated application of these processes of innovation and memorization is, of course, the ratchet effect we discussed earlier, and so we can see how the ostensive-inferential nature of communication allows the cumulative conventionalization of innovative metaphors, and thus enables the creation of an increasingly expressive and complex system of linguistic representation.

The Emergence of Symbols

The examples we have given in the previous section consider the conventionalization of metaphors in terms of a creative linguistic phenomenon, but in this section we will show that the underlying cognitive and cultural processes of innovation and conventionalization actually predate language and indeed underpin the emergence and complexification of symbols more generally. Symbols are usually differentiated from other signs through the arbitrary and habitual nature of the association between form and meaning (de Saussure 1916). Arbitrariness, moreover, is often regarded as one of the most important 'design features' of language (Hockett 1960). Icons, on the other hand, are signs where the relationship between form and meaning is motivated and based on some kind of perceptual similarity (Keller 1998). Motivated icons can commonly be found in public places like airports and tourist attractions, where they are used to represent passport control, food, bookshops, car rental services and the like, precisely because using language is unreliable where there is likely to be a considerable proportion of people who do not have the shared common ground to understand the particular linguistic conventions of the country.

Motivatedness and, conversely, arbitrariness, are a matter of degree, however, rather than all-or-nothing measurements, and our account of the evolution of symbolic representations is one of gradual emergence rather than sudden appearance. Symbols did not materialize from a void, but rather non-arbitrary, motivated, iconic associations first emerged, and these iconic associations then became arbitrary. Both these steps are made possible by ostensive-inferential communication and the memorization of communicative experiences.

Icons

The simplest and most trivial form of ostensive-inferential communication involves the provision of direct evidence, where the speaker produces an ostensive stimulus which is itself the relevant communicative meaning inferred by the hearer; the display of an object, for instance, draws the attention of the hearer to that object. It is not even always necessary for the hearer to recognize the communicative intent of the speaker in order to extract the meaning; the mere observation of an ostensive act which provides direct evidence is enough for the meaning to be acquired.

More frequently, however, the stimulus is not the meaning itself, but rather shares some salient perceptual properties with it, and these properties make up the evidence on the basis of which the meaning can be reconstructed. Anyone who has found themselves needing to obtain some information in a foreign country whose language they cannot speak will be familiar with this kind of basic ostensive-inferential communication: we use gestures and vocalizations to make some kind of ostensive stimulus which resembles, in as conspicuous a way as possible, the meaning we are trying to convey. These gestures and sounds do not themselves constitute the meaning of the communication, but our interlocutor can nevertheless recognize our communicative intent from their ostensive nature, and can infer an informative meaning which resembles some perceptual feature from them, thereby maximizing their relevance in the context in which the communicative act takes place. A particular gesture or sound can of course be interpreted differently depending on the context: using our hands to mimic a sphere might yield an apple or an orange in a greengrocer's, or directions to a football stadium on the day of a match.

An icon is therefore an ostensive stimulus used with pragmatic plasticity, or metaphorically: parts of it are mutually recognized as irrelevant and ignored, while other aspects resemble part of the intended meaning and so serve as a cue to help the hearer identify it; this meaning may then be enhanced using information from the common ground (Hoefler 2008; Smith and Hoefler 2015). This is a presymbolic, prelinguistic use of ostensive-inferential communication. It is also iconic, as the form is still directly perceptually associated with, and so similar to, its meaning. This iconic association may of course be remembered, and potentially re-used successfully in the future, especially if the resemblance between form and meaning is particularly striking and therefore easily recognized.

This account of the development of icons therefore shows that ostensive-inferential communication predates, and indeed does not require, the existence of symbols. Once the cognitive capabilities of social intelligence and co-operation underpinning ostensive-inferential communication had evolved, icons would have automatically emerged from simple gestures and vocalizations, through their conspicuous resemblance in some respect to the meanings they were being used to represent.

Symbols

The key difference between icons and symbols is in the arbitrary nature of the form-meaning association, and therefore the key process which needs to be explained is how a non-arbitrary association can become arbitrary. There are two ways in which this can take place: either the form changes so that it is no longer similar to the meaning, or the meaning changes so that it is no longer similar to the form (or

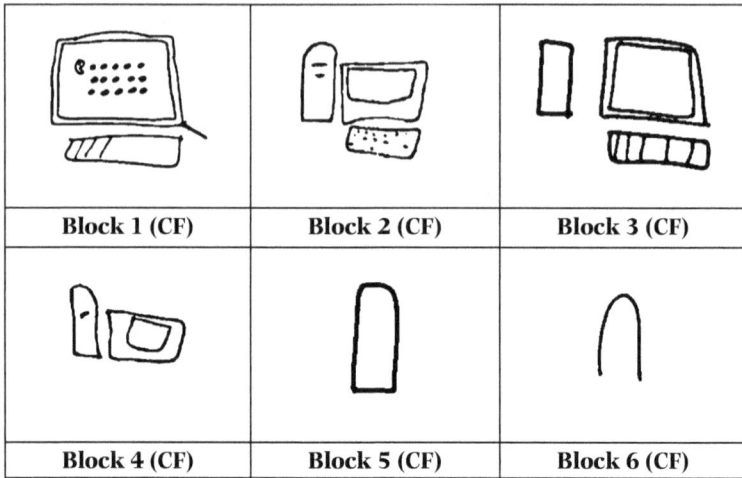

Block 1 (CF)	Block 2 (CF)	Block 3 (CF)
Block 4 (CF)	Block 5 (CF)	Block 6 (CF)

Figure 6.1: Drawings representing 'computer monitor' become increasingly arbitrary over repeated interactions. Figure from Garrod et al. 2007, published with permission from John Wiley and sons.

both change). Both types of arbitrarization are made possible by ostensive-inferential communication, metaphorical innovation and conventionalization.

The emergence of shared symbols from icons through the first process of form change can be seen very clearly in the ostensive-inferential 'Pictionary' experiments described in the previous section. In these experiments, participants were given a set of pre-specified, fixed meanings that they had to repeatedly convey to the other participants by means of drawing. The individual meanings thus had to be drawn (ostension) in a way that would allow for them to be identified, i.e. distinguished from the other meanings (inference). The key result, observed under many different conditions, is unambiguous: at the start of the experiment the drawings are contextually motivated icons which resemble the meanings they are meant to represent, but over repeated interactions there is a 'drift to the arbitrary' (Tomasello 2008: 220) as the drawings become increasingly conventionalized, simplified, schematic and arbitrary. Effectively, 'there is a shift of the locus of information from the sign itself to the communicators' representations of the sign's usage' (Garrod et al. 2007: 965). Interaction between interlocutors and the memorization of usage are critical to this process: a successful communicative episode fixes the drawing-object association in both individuals' memories. Over repeated use, the association becomes increasingly entrenched and conventionalized, so that progressively less information is required in the drawing for the meaning to be recovered, and the form can therefore become increasingly simple and less similar to its meaning without any loss of communicative success, as seen in the changing representations of COMPUTER MONITOR in Fig. 1. Eventually, the form can no longer be identified by a naïve observer who has no memory of its previous usage, and so has become a symbol (Caldwell and Smith 2012). Without interaction in the experiments, however, conventionalization does not occur, and indeed the forms often, by contrast, become increasingly complex and retain their iconicity (Garrod et al. 2007; Fay et al. 2010; Tan and Fay 2011). When the pre-existing meanings are conceptually related to each other in a structured manner, then the emerging forms tend to match this underlying structure, thereby becoming not only symbolic but also systematic and compositional (Theisen, Oberlander and Kirby 2010).

The Pictionary experiments show how the development of shared common ground in the context of ostensive-inferential communication allows innovation to spread and become conventionalized within a community. These experiments are artificially constrained so that the meanings remain invariant, which means that all the innovation has to take place in the form used to represent them; in actual language use, of course, the creative use of an existing form to represent a novel meaning, as described in the previous section, is much more prolific. This second route for icons to turn into symbols, therefore, is through metaphorical use of the existing iconic form to represent a different, but related, concept. It is not hard to imagine examples such as an iconic form of the sun being used to represent related abstract concepts like HEAT or DAY, and indeed parallels to this can be found in many natural languages which use the same word for such concepts (e.g. Hungarian *nap* means both SUN and DAY).

Both routes from icons to symbols, though, are enabled by the ostensive-inferential nature of human communication. Repeated communicative interaction leads to the simplification of forms, because a rich history of shared common ground allows their meanings to be inferentially recovered from minimal evidence, even though the particular simplified form may never have been used before. Likewise, an innovative, metaphorical use of an existing form to represent a novel meaning can succeed when the communicative context makes clear that the conventional meaning is not relevant and must be abandoned.

Ascertaining whether a linguistic sign is an icon or a symbol is not a truly objective process, however, as it depends on how obvious the connection between form and meaning is seen to be, which itself depends on the general knowledge which allows an evaluation of the extent to which the form accurately represents the meaning. Knowledge of the history of a form-meaning association can make it seem less arbitrary, as we saw in the Pictionary experiments, and so to a large extent, symbolism is in the eye of the beholder. We would argue, indeed, that the arbitrariness of an association can only properly be judged as such from a synchronic perspective; diachronically, almost all can theoretically be traced back to their non-arbitrary origins, with only a very few exceptions where new words have been deliberately invented (Trask 2000).

The repeated use of any new association leads to further entrenchment and conventionalization; once the new association is part of common ground, it can serve as the basis for more creativity and innovation. The cumulative iteration of this process leads, through the ratchet effect described above, to increases in the complexity of the communicable meaning space, with previously inexpressible meanings being reached gradually via a sequence of new associations used as stepping stones (Hoefler 2008, 2009). This leads us, therefore, to the conclusion that the very same processes of ostensive-inferential communication led not only to the original emergence of symbols from their iconic origin, but also to the expansion of the communication system towards the level of expressivity we see in human language.

The Emergence of Grammar

Research in cognitive linguistics (see, e.g., Evans and Green 2006) suggests that language can be described exhaustively as a set of form-meaning associations, i.e. that grammatical constructions are form-meaning associations just like lexical items; this is the so-called symbolic thesis. Traditional generative theories of grammar (Chomsky 1981; Chomsky and Lasnik 1993), in contrast, divide our knowledge of language into two distinct elements: a lexicon, or set of words which connect forms with meanings; and a computational system of rules which operate on abstract lexical units to generate the grammatical sentences of a language (Chomsky 1965; Pinker 1999). One fundamental distinction between the elements is that all arbitrary idiosyncrasies which link forms and meanings reside in the lexicon, while the general grammatical rules provide a systematic (and putatively comprehensive) explanation of how words are combined into valid utterances. However, idioms such as *kick the bucket* or *all of a sudden* pose a problem to this traditional characterization of grammar, because their meanings are neither predictable from the meanings of their parts nor derivable from general syntactic patterns (Fillmore, Kay and O'Connor 1988; Goldberg 1995). The association between form and meaning in such constructions is arbitrary, yet they appear to be made up of familiar word-like parts. Other constructions are more schematic, with parts of the construction fixed and parts somewhat flexible (Kay and Fillmore 1999), such as the constructions *the* X-*er, the* Y-*er* (e.g., 'the more, the merrier' or 'the bigger they come, the harder they fall') and *what's* X *doing* Y? (e.g., 'what's Jane doing making that face?' or 'what's this fly doing in my soup?'). Such constructions cannot be explained in general terms, but only as individual items on their own terms, with their own specific grammatical and semantic idiosyncrasies, and with meanings that are not solely derivable from their component parts.

It is this observation that has led cognitive linguists to the symbolic thesis, i.e. to the conclusion that all linguistic units have meaning, that the basic unit of language is the association of a form with a meaning, and that linguistic knowledge is thus more profitably viewed as a single, structured, redundant inventory of more or less conventionalized form-meaning associations (Langacker 1987; Croft and Cruse 2004; Evans and Green 2006; Hoffmann and Trousdale 2013). Under the symbolic thesis, the differences between lexical and grammatical units are qualitative rather than essential: lexical items and grammatical constructions form a continuum of form-meaning associations with different degrees of complexity, productivity and schematicity (Gisborne and Patten 2011). On this continuum, one finds prototypical lexical items with an atomic arbitrary form expressing a concrete, basic-level meaning (e.g. *cat* denoting CAT) as well as prototypical grammatical items expressing functional meanings (e.g. PAST, NEGATIVE) and consisting of schematic forms (e.g., the passive construction X *be* V-*ed by* Y denoting that some X is affected by an action V carried out by an agent Y).

The emergence of grammar can then be characterized as the emergence of schematic forms (so-called syntacticization) and the emergence of functional meanings (so-called grammaticalization); both processes have been documented extensively in the literature (Heine, Claudi and Hünnemeyer 1991; Hopper and Traugott 1993), which broadly describe the loss of an item's independence of use coupled with an increasingly functional meaning (Givón 1979). We now argue that if grammatical constructions are form-meaning associations just like lexical items are too, then the most parsimonious explanation for these two processes is one that appeals to the same cognitive and cultural mechanisms that have been used to explain the emergence of those other form-meaning associations. In what follows, we therefore detail how the same mechanisms that are responsible for the emergence of symbols (ostensive-inferential communication, metaphor, conventionalization) can also account for the emergence of grammar, i.e. of schematic forms and functional meanings.

Schematic Forms

Schematic forms originally emerge when, in an act of ostensive-inferential communication, multiple forms are concatenated, i.e. uttered one after the other to convey some compositional meaning, for example 'man stink' or 'food good'. There is immediately a potential for internal schematic analysis of such a concatenation of signals, because the inevitable linear order of the signals can itself be used to identify parts of the inferred meaning. If concatenation is used repeatedly to convey the same meaning, it can itself become conventionalized as the signal associated with that meaning. Hurford (2012), indeed, argues that the first syntactic construction is likely to have emerged in this way, from the expression of 'proto-sentences' containing two distinct items and an invited inference that their order signifies the fundamental communicatively functional distinction between the topic of the communicative episode (the thing the speaker is drawing attention to) and a comment about it. The topic is something already in the interlocutors' shared common ground, while the comment is new information about the topic, the imparting of which to the hearer is effectively the objective of the communicative episode. Over repeated use, this communicative distinction will mean that the distribution of items appearing in each slot in the construction will not be uniform, but rather that the topic slot will mostly be filled by forms referring to stable objects, and the comment slot will, conversely, mostly be filled by forms referring to actions or changing states. Eventually, the conventionalization of such frequency-driven patterns then leads to the familiar subject/predicate structures that pervade human language (Hoefler 2009: 110–112; Hurford 2012; Smith and Hoefler 2015).

The syntacticization of discourse in this way is not restricted to the original emergence of language, however, but can be found wherever recurrent patterns in form and meaning are remembered and generalized into schemas (Givón 1979). Waltereit (2011) shows, for instance, how speakers choose to order their discourse in particular ways for rhetorical purposes, and the coincidental ordering properties of their usage are conventionalized and co-opted for specific grammatical purposes like discourse markers or modal particles. New simple schematic conventions can be used as stepping stones from which more complex and more expressive syntactic patterns emerge: in this way the repeated innovation and conventionalization of usage leads inexorably to the cumulative development of linguistic structure.

Functional Meanings

Functional meanings are those which provide information about grammatical concepts like tense, aspect, modality, case and agreement. Words expressing functional meanings develop historically through grammaticalization from words which originally expressed concrete meanings. Many of these developments are extremely common and occur independently in unrelated languages across the world, such as the development of prepositions from forms originally referring to body parts, or the development of tense markers from common verbs like *go*, *want* and *have* (Heine and Kuteva 2002). The relative location of certain body parts, for instance, allows them to act as a metaphor to denote deictic location, so words meaning HEAD come to specify UP, those meaning FEET come to mean DOWN, and those meaning BELLY or HEART come to mean INSIDE, among many other examples. The human body is a particularly good metaphor for denoting spatial relations, because it is fundamental to human embodied understanding of the world (Lakoff and Johnson 1980), and is therefore almost certain to be part of the interlocutors' shared common ground.

Functional meanings thus emerge from innovative inferences invited by the speaker and established by the hearer (Hoefler and Smith 2009; Smith and Hoefler 2015). As before, a particular form is used in a context which is incompatible with its existing conventional concrete meaning: this meaning – or at least some of its aspects – must be temporarily disregarded, so that a new more relevant functional meaning can be inferred by using the conventional meaning in a metaphorical way. This functional meaning may eventually, if used frequently enough, itself become conventionalized, so that it no longer needs the context to be retrieved. The form thus becomes part of two competing 'layered' conventions which are both subject to further entrenchment through use: one expressing a concrete meaning, the other a functional meaning (Traugott and Dasher 2005; Nicolle 2011).

Example 1 illustrates this process with one of the most frequently analysed cases of grammaticalization, namely the historic development of the English construction *be going to* from denoting the concrete concept of MOTION to expressing the more abstract concept of INTENTION and finally serving as a marker for the grammatical concept of FUTURITY.

(1) a. I am going to play football.
    b. I am going to stay at home.
    c. It is going to rain tomorrow.

Example 1 demonstrates that *be going to* is currently used in at least three different constructions in English, which have both different meanings and different syntactic properties. 1(a) can, in modern English, be interpreted as any of the three historical meanings: 'I am moving somewhere to play football'; 'I intend to play football'; 'in the future, I will play football'. In 1(b), however, the motion interpretation is ruled out due to the semantic clash between 'go' and 'stay', while in 1(c) only the futurity reading is possible. The meaning changes are also accompanied by considerable expansion of the subjects and main verbs which can be used with the construction, and this provides evidence of the actualization of the meaning change (Trask 1996). In the original construction, for instance, *be going to* required an animate subject and a verb describing actual motion, but its transformation into a purely grammatical tense marker means it can now be used without restriction, with any main verb and any subject, even the dummy subject 'it' shown in 1(c).

The historical development of *be going to*, and equivalent occurrences in many other languages (Heine and Kuteva 2002) happen primarily because the various meanings are closely connected to each other: a particular usage may invite several interpretations, of which the existing conventional meaning may not be the most relevant. MOTION, for instance, is strongly associated with INTENTION (Bybee, Perkins and Pagliuca 1994: 268), because humans are intentional beings who decide where to move themselves, and so in a context where MOTION must be disregarded, INTENTION is likely to be considered very relevant; likewise, INTENTION can give rise to FUTURITY, because things we intend to happen can only take place in the future, so when both MOTION and INTENTION are irrelevant, the existing form provides good evidence for the more abstract FUTURITY to be inferred. From this perspective, the process of meaning change is exactly the same as that involved in metaphor, with established forms used to express abstract meanings, albeit that in grammaticalization these new meanings are specifically related to increasingly grammatical functions.

Examples of content words changing into function words abound across the world's languages, but the reverse process is far less likely (although not impossible, see, e.g., Norde 2009), and so grammaticalization is often considered to be overwhelmingly unidirectional (Haspelmath 2004). This unidirectionality emerges due to the imbalanced nature of the associations between the various meanings, and particularly the likelihood that a word with one meaning could successfully be used as evidence for the inference of another within the dyadic communicative situation (Heine, Claudi and Hünnemeyer 1991; Traugott and Dasher 2005). Firstly, words with concrete meanings are pressed into service to represent more abstract meanings precisely because the abstract meanings cannot easily be represented, while the converse is not true. Secondly, the underlying associations which allow the necessary innovative meaning inferences are themselves not generally reversible: although our intentions can only be realized in the future, for example, things that happen in the future are not all necessarily intended; the use of a form representing INTENTION is therefore potentially good evidence to infer FUTURITY, but not vice versa.

We have discussed here just one specific example of how grammatical structure is created in language to explain the general cognitive and cultural mechanisms at work. Hurford (2012) provides a detailed account setting out how grammaticalization can proceed from the original emergent topic/comment structure described above to basic syntactic categories and the development of subjects and predicates, and thence to more specific word classes. Heine and Kuteva (2002) have similarly collated numerous attested instances of grammaticalization and produced a detailed 'evolutionary network' (Heine and Kuteva 2007: 111) which links clusters of grammatical categories into developmental layers of evolutionary history, and demonstrates the ultimate origin of all syntactic categories in nouns and verbs, showing for instance how nouns can become adverbs which become demonstratives which become pronouns which become agreement markers. Crucially, the cognitive and cultural mechanisms underlying these processes are the very same mechanisms that also account for the emergence of symbols: ostensive-inferential communication, the metaphorical use of an extant convention and its subsequent conventionalization.

Conclusion

The evolution of language is usually considered in terms of two distinct evolutionary puzzles: the emergence of symbolic communication; and the development of grammatical structure. In this chapter, we have shown that a common solution to both issues can be found in the cognitive capacities which underpin cumulative cultural evolution and ostensive-inferential communication, namely the recognition of common ground, the recognition of communicative relevance, and the memorization of shared experience. Common ground provides the basis for successful ostensive-inferential communication by delivering a backdrop against which cues can be used and interpreted creatively, and especially metaphorically, depending on the context. The memorization of such innovative form-meaning associations, and their entrenchment through repeated use, leads to the establishment of further common ground. The repeated application of innovation and their conventionalization is an example of the ratchet effect of cumulative cultural evolution, allowing the expression of previously inexpressible meanings by using existing associations as stepping stones to reach new meaning areas. In this way, arbitrary symbols arose from originally non-arbitrary iconic associations through the establishment of rich common ground allowing for gradual simplifications of form and gradual shifts in meaning. Similarly, schematic forms emerged where concatenation was interpreted as a communicative cue and was conventionalized in association with the meaning it helped to convey; metaphorical use in context would also allow for the shift of concrete meanings towards ever more functional meanings. On the basis of this unified account, we suggest that the assumption of different origins for symbolism and grammar is unwarranted: they both emerge from the general processes of ostensive-inferential communication and cumulative cultural evolution.

References

Arbib, M.A. 2005. 'From Monkey-like Action Recognition to Human Language: an Evolutionary Framework for Neurolinguistics', *Behavioral and Brain Sciences* 28(2): 105–124.

———— and D. Bickerton (eds). 2008. *The Emergence of Protolanguage: Holophrasis vs Compositionality*. Amsterdam: John Benjamins.

Barlow, M. and S. Kemmer. 2000. *Usage-based Models of Language*. Chicago: University of Chicago Press.

Bickerton, D. 1990. *Language and Species*. Chicago: University of Chicago Press.

———. 2003. 'Symbol and Structure: A Comprehensive Framework for Language Evolution', in M. Christiansen and S. Kirby (eds), *Language Evolution*. Oxford: Oxford University Press, pp. 77–93.

Boyd, R. and P.J. Richerson. 1996. 'Why Culture is Common but Cultural Evolution is Rare', *Proceedings of the British Academy* 88: 73–93.

Burling, R. 2005. *The Talking Ape: How Language Evolved*. Oxford: Oxford University Press.

Bybee, J.L. 2007. *Frequency of Use and the Organization of Language*. Oxford: Oxford University Press.

———, R. Perkins, and W. Pagliuca. 1994. *The Evolution of Grammar: Tense, Aspect and Modality in the Languages of the World*. Chicago: University of Chicago Press.

Caldwell, C.A. and A.E. Millen 2008a. 'Studying Cumulative Cultural Evolution in the Laboratory', *Philosophical Transactions of the Royal Society of London, series B – Biological Sciences* 363: 3529–3539.

———. 2008b. 'Experimental Models for Testing Hypotheses about Cumulative Cultural Evolution', *Evolution and Human Behavior* 29: 165–171.

Caldwell, C.A. and K. Smith 2012. 'Cultural Evolution and Perpetuation of Arbitrary Communicative Conventions in Experimental Microsocieties', *PLoS one* 7(8): e43807.

Chomsky, N. 1965. *Aspects of the Theory of Syntax*. Cambridge, MA: MIT Press.

———. 1981. 'Principles and Parameters in Syntactic Theory', in N. Hornstein and D. Lightfoot (eds), *Explanation in Linguistics: The Logical Problem of Language Acquisition*. London: Longman, pp. 32–75.

——— and H. Lasnik. 1993. 'The Theory of Principles and Parameters', in J. Jacobs, A. von Stechow, W. Sternefeld and T. Vennenmann (eds), *Syntax: an International Handbook of Contemporary Research*. Berlin: Walter de Gruyter, pp. 506–569.

Clark, H.H. 1996. *Using Language*. Cambridge: Cambridge University Press.

Croft, W. 2000. *Explaining Language Change: an Evolutionary Approach*. Singapore: Longman.

——— and A.D. Cruse. 2004. *Cognitive Linguistics*. Cambridge: Cambridge University Press.

de Saussure, F. 1916. *Cours de Linguistique Générale*. Paris: Payot.

Dean, L.G. et al. 2013. 'Human Cumulative Culture: a Comparative Perspective', *Biological Reviews* 89(2): 284–301.

Deutscher, G. 2005. *The Unfolding of Language: an Evolutionary Tour of Mankind's Greatest Invention*. New York: Metropolitan Books.

Evans, V. 2004. *The Structure of Time: Language, Meaning and Temporal Cognition*. Amsterdam: John Benjamins.

————— and M. Green. 2006. *Cognitive Linguistics: an Introduction*. Edinburgh: Edinburgh University Press.

Fay, N., S. Garrod and L. Roberts. 2008. 'The Fitness and Functionality of Culturally Evolved Communication Systems', *Philosophical Transactions of the Royal Society of London, series B – Biological Sciences* 363: 3553–3561.

Fay, N. et al. 2010. 'The Interactive Evolution of Human Communication Systems', *Cognitive Science* 34(3): 351–386.

Fillmore, C., P. Kay and M.K. O'Connor. 1988. 'Regularity and Idiomaticity: the Case of Let Alone', *Language* 64(3): 501–538.

Garrod, S. et al. 2007. 'Foundations of Representations: Where Might Graphical Symbol Systems Come From?', *Cognitive Science* 31(6): 961–987.

————. 2010. 'Can Iterated Learning Explain the Emergence of Graphical Symbols?', *Interaction Studies* 11(1): 33–50.

Gibbs, R.W. 1994. *The Poetics of Mind*. Cambridge: Cambridge University Press.

Gisborne, N. and A. Patten. 2011. 'Construction Grammar and Grammaticalization', in H. Narrog and B. Heine (eds), *The Oxford Handbook of Grammaticalization*. Oxford: Oxford University Press, pp. 92–104.

Givón, T. 1979. *On Understanding Grammar*. New York: Academic Press.

Goldberg, A.E. 1995. *Constructions: a Construction Grammar Approach to Argument Structure*. Chicago: University of Chicago Press.

Grice, H.P. 1957. 'Meaning', *Philosophical Review* 66: 377–388.

————. 1975. 'Logic and Conversation', in P. Cole and J.L. Morgan (eds), *Syntax and Semantics*, Vol. 3. New York: Academic Press, pp. 41–58.

Haspelmath, M. 2004. 'On Directionality in Language Change with Particular Reference to Grammaticalization', in O. Fischer, M. Norde and H. Perridon (eds), *Up and Down the Cline: the Nature of Grammaticalization*. Amsterdam: John Benjamins, pp. 17–44.

Heine, B., U. Claudi and F. Hünnemeyer. 1991. *Grammaticalization: A Conceptual Framework*. Chicago: University of Chicago Press.

Heine, B. and T. Kuteva. 2002. *World Lexicon of Grammaticalization*. Cambridge: Cambridge University Press.

————. 2007. *The Genesis of Grammar: a Reconstruction. Studies in the Evolution of Language*. Oxford: Oxford University Press.

Hockett, C.F. 1960. 'The Origin of Speech', *Scientific American* 203: 88–96.

Hoefler, S. 2008. 'Pragmatic Plasticity: a Pivotal Design Feature?', in A.D.M. Smith, K. Smith and R. Ferrer i Cancho (eds), *The Evolution of Language (EVOLANG 7)*. Singapore: World Scientific pp. 439–440.

————. 2009. 'Modelling the Role of Pragmatic Plasticity in the Evolution of Linguistic Communication', PhD dissertation. Edinburgh: University of Edinburgh.

Hoefler, S. and A.D.M. Smith. 2009. 'The Pre-linguistic Basis of Grammaticalisation: a Unified Approach to Metaphor and Reanalysis', *Studies in Language* 33(4): 886–909.

Hoffmann, T. and G. Trousdale. 2013. *The Oxford Handbook of Construction Grammar*. Oxford: Oxford University Press.

Hopper, P.J. and E.C. Traugott. 1993. *Grammaticalization*. Cambridge: Cambridge University Press.

Hurford, J.R. 2002. 'Expression/induction Models of Language Evolution: Dimensions and Issues', in E. Briscoe (ed.), *Linguistic Evolution Through Language Acquisition: Formal and Computational Models*. Cambridge: Cambridge University Press, pp. 301–344.

———. 2007. *The Origins of Meaning: Language in the Light of Evolution*. Oxford: Oxford University Press.

———. 2012. *The Origins of Grammar: Language in the Light of Evolution*. Oxford: Oxford University Press.

Kawai, M. 1965. 'Newly-acquired Pre-cultural Behaviour of the Natural Troop of Japanese Macaques on Koshima Islet', *Primates* 6: 1–30.

Kay, P. and C. Fillmore.1999. 'Grammatical Constructions and Linguistic Generalizations: the What's X doing Y construction', *Language* 75: 1–34.

Keller, R. 1998. *A Theory of Linguistic Signs*. Oxford: Oxford University Press.

Kirby, S., H. Cornish and K. Smith 2008. 'Cumulative Cultural Evolution in the Lab: an Experimental Approach to the Origins of Structure in Human Language', *Proceedings of the National Academy of Sciences* 105(31): 10681–10686.

Kirby, S., et al. 2015. 'Compression and Communication in the Cultural Evolution of Linguistic Structure', *Cognition* 141: 87–102.

Kövecses, Z. 2002. *Metaphor: a Practical Introduction*. Oxford: Oxford University Press.

———. 2005. *Metaphor in Culture: Universality and Variation*. Cambridge: Cambridge University Press.

Kuteva, T. 2001. *Auxiliation: an Enquiry into the Nature of Grammaticalization*. Oxford: Oxford University Press.

Lakoff, G. and M. Johnson. 1980. *Metaphors We Live By*. Chicago: University of Chicago Press.

Langacker, R.W. 1987. *Foundations of Cognitive Grammar: Theoretical Prerequisites*, Vol. I. Stanford, CA: Stanford University Press.

Lewis, H.M. and K.N. Laland. 2012. 'Transmission Fidelity is the Key to the Build-up of Cumulative Culture', *Philosophical Transactions of the Royal Society of London, series B – Biological Sciences* 367: 2171–2180.

Mesoudi, A. and A. Whiten. 2008. 'The Multiple Roles of Cultural Transmission Experiments in Understanding Human Cultural Evolution', *Philosophical Transactions of the Royal Society of London, series B – Biological Sciences* 363: 3489–3501.

Nicolle, S. 2011. 'Pragmatic Aspects of Grammaticalization', in H. Narrog and B. Heine (eds), *The Oxford Handbook of Grammaticalization*. Oxford: Oxford University Press, pp. 401–412.

Norde, M. 2009. *Degrammaticalization.* Oxford: Oxford University Press.

Pinker, S. 1999. *Words and Rules.* London: Weidenfeld & Nicolson.

Scott-Phillips, T. 2015. *Speaking Our Minds: Why Human Communication is Different, and How Language Evolved to Make it Special.* London: Palgrave MacMillan.

Smith, A.D.M. 2006. 'Semantic Reconstructibility and the Complexification of Language', in A. Cangelosi, A.D.M. Smith and K. Smith (eds), *The Evolution of Language,* Singapore: World Scientific, pp. 307–314.

———. 2008. 'Protolanguage Reconstructed', *Interaction Studies* 9(1): 100–116.

——— and S. Hoefler. 2015. 'The Pivotal Role of Metaphor in the Evolution of Human Language', in J.E. Díaz Vera (ed.), *Metaphor and Metonymy across Time and Cultures.* Berlin: Mouton de Gruyter, pp. 123–139.

Smith, K. and E. Wonnacott. 2010. 'Eliminating Unpredictable Variation through Iterated Learning', *Cognition* 116: 444–449.

Sperber, D. and D. Wilson. 1995. *Relevance: Communication and Cognition.* Oxford: Blackwell.

Tallerman, M. 2007. 'Did our Ancestors Speak a Holistic Protolanguage?', *Lingua* 117(3): 579–604.

Tan, R. and N. Fay. 2011. 'Cultural Transmission in the Laboratory: Agent Interaction Improves the Intergenerational Transfer of Information', *Evolution and Human Behavior* 32(6): 399–406.

Theisen, C., J. Oberlander and S. Kirby. 2010. 'Systematicity and Arbitrariness in Novel Communication Systems', *Interaction Studies* 11(1): 14–32.

Tomasello, M. 1999. *The Cultural Origins of Human Cognition.* Harvard: Harvard University Press.

———. 2003. 'On the Different Origins of Symbols and Grammar', in M. Christiansen and S. Kirby (eds), *Language Evolution.* Oxford: Oxford University Press, pp. 94–110

———. 2008. *Origins of Human Communication.* Harvard: MIT Press.

——— et al. 2005. 'Understanding and Sharing Intentions: The Origins of Cultural Cognition', *Behavioral and Brain Sciences* 28: 675–735.

———, A.C. Kruger and H. Ratner. 1993. 'Cultural Learning', *Behavioral and Brain Sciences* 16: 495–552.

Trask, R.L. 1996. *Historical Linguistics.* London: Arnold.

———. 2000. *The Dictionary of Historical and Comparative Linguistics.* Edinburgh: Edinburgh University Press.

Traugott, E.C. and R.B. Dasher. 2005. *Regularity in Semantic Change.* Cambridge: Cambridge University Press.

Waltereit, R. 2011. 'Grammaticalization and Discourse', in H. Narrog and B. Heine (eds), *The Oxford Handbook of Grammaticalization.* Oxford: Oxford University Press, pp. 413–423.

Wray, A. 2000. 'Holistic Utterances in Protolanguage', in C. Knight, M. Studdert-Kennedy and J. R. Hurford (eds), *The Evolutionary Emergence of Language: Social Function and the Origins of Linguistic Form.* Cambridge: Cambridge University Press, pp. 285–302.

Andrew D.M. Smith is Lecturer in Language Studies in the School of Arts and Humanities at the University of Stirling. He received his PhD in Linguistics from the University of Edinburgh. His main research interests are in evolutionary and cognitive linguistics, focusing in particular on grammaticalization, the inferential socio-cultural and cognitive bases of communication, metaphor, cultural evolution and word learning mechanisms. His most recent book is the edited collection *New Directions in Grammaticalization Research* (2015, with Graeme Trousdale and Richard Waltereit).

Stefan Hoefler is a research fellow at the University of Zurich. He holds a MA in English Linguistics and Literature and Computational Linguistics from that same university, and a PhD in Linguistics from the University of Edinburgh. A substantial part of his research has been concerned with exploring the role of pragmatic plasticity in the cultural evolution of language. Recently, he has focused on studying the connections between language and law, the linguistic conventions that have emerged in the legal domain, and the ways in which these conventions facilitate or obstruct comprehensibility.

Chapter 7

RECONSTRUCTING A SOURCE COSMOLOGY FOR AFRICAN HUNTER-GATHERERS

Camilla Power

In this chapter I explore the possibility of reconstructing a source cosmology for African hunter-gatherers. Given what we now know about the deep history and relationships among populations including Bushman groups, Western and Eastern Central African forest hunters and East African groups such as the Hadza, what are the implications for a comparative project on magico-religious beliefs? The idea that these groups are remnants of a formerly widespread proto-Khoisan-Pygmy aboriginal population, argued in respect of the Bushmen by Tobias (1964), has been challenged (e.g. Morris 2003; Schepartz 1988). But population genetics currently validates two key points:

(i)   these populations all share ancestry with distinctive deep-time phylogenetic clades;
(ii) the time-depth of separation among the populations reaches back into the Middle Stone Age (MSA) to dates equal to or greater than the movement of modern humans outside Africa, that is in the order of 50–100,000 years ago.

African forager populations (Khoisan, Western and Eastern Pygmies, and Hadza) conserve the most ancient human lineages with the highest phylogenetic diversity. We can use these ancient haplotypes to trace population dispersals from southern across to East Africa, during

Marine Isotope Stage (MIS) 5 – the penultimate interglacial – from 128,000 years ago (Rito et al. 2013). This is associated with 'the beginning of the megadroughts in central Africa, also the time at which *Homo sapiens* becomes much more visible in the archaeological record' (2013: 12, and see Fig. 5).

While all populations show some admixture, African hunter-gatherers are differentiated between themselves and in comparison to other African populations (Henn et al. 2011). This suggests they represent geographically distinct populations isolated over tens of thousands of years. Khoisan, Hadza, Sandawe and Pygmy populations could indeed be remnants of a historically more widespread population of hunter-gatherers (Tishkoff et al. 2009). Kalahari Khoisan groups show a deep-time (30,000 years) separation corresponding to a NW/ SE geographic divide (Pickrell et al. 2012). Pickrell and colleagues also substantiate shared Khoisan genetic sequences in Hadza (and Sandawe) East African click-speaking forager groups. According to Rito and colleagues (2013: 5), this 'ancient link in genomic data between Khoesan populations and East African populations' could be a trace of the ancient migration, whereas the spread of click consonant languages was probably much more recent. Previously a time-depth of 15,000 years was suggested for Sandawe/Hadza separation, and in the order of 35–55,000 years separation for Hadza from Bushman lineages (Tishkoff et al. 2007). Western vs. Eastern Pygmy groups show separation at a time-depth of over 20,000 years (coinciding with the Late Glacial Maximum), while divergence between Bushman and Biaka (Western) Pygmy – populations with significant shared genetic material – could date back 100,000 years (Chen et al. 2000).

In terms of shared cultural roots, what is the implication of the ancient shared ancestry, with deep-time subsequent separation of populations? Each of these African hunter-gatherer populations bears a cultural heritage independent of the others over long time periods. If significant commonalities between magico-religious traditions were demonstrated, these could be of considerable antiquity, tracing back to source cosmologies contemporary with the emergence of modern human symbolic behaviour. The most conservative aspects of cultural continuity, which potentially include archaic structures of ritual and cosmology, could therefore stem from the Middle Stone Age.

From this perspective, a comparative ethnography of African hunter-gatherer ritual and myth could illuminate the archaeological record of early symbolism. In recent decades, with few exceptions, social anthropologists have abandoned grand unifying theory in the style of Claude Lévi-Strauss or Luc de Heusch. In his exhaustive analysis of Central Bantu epic cycles, *The Drunken King*, de Heusch considers reconstituting earliest Bantu mythic complexes, by analogy with linguistic reconstruction: 'structuralist method ... enables us to take a basic and decisive operation, that of laying bare the outlines of one of the great semiological complexes derived from this lost mythic kernel' (1982: 2). Does our picture of hunter-gatherer deep history in Africa permit recovery of 'lost mythic kernels' of African (and therefore modern human) cosmology? Can we pursue a kind of cultural cladistics, identifying shared derived characteristics likely to have belonged to ancestor populations? At the very least, can we constrain possible models for the emergence of symbolism by attention to such ethnographic detail?

A Hypothetical Baseline?

Someone who has stepped in this direction is the musicologist Victor Grauer (2011). Aware of the recent population genetics findings, he starts by observing the close affinities of Pygmy and Bushman music, with their highly characteristic interlocking hocketing polyphonic singing styles. These appear to be shared cultural traits, despite the long-term effective separation of these populations.

Grauer goes on to examine other traits found specifically among Bushman and Eastern and Western Pygmy groups to build a picture of a 'Hypothetical baseline culture' (HBC) for the source populations of present-day African hunter-gatherers. He describes his 'triangulation' method as follows:

> Any distinctive tradition, in the form of a value system, belief system, performance practice, behavior pattern, artifact or attribute, not likely to be the result of outside influence, found among at least three different groups representing each of the three populations with the deepest genetic clades, i.e., Eastern Pygmies, Western Pygmies and Bushmen (EP, WP, Bu), may be regarded as a potential survival from an older tradition traceable to the historical 'moment' of earliest divergence, and thus ascribable to HBC. (2011: 44)

Such shared traditions, he argues, are unlikely to have arisen from convergence in a similar environment, or through mutual influence given such long-term separation.

Table 7.1 summarizes Grauer's list of traits proposed for the baseline culture, triangulating from Bushman groups and Western and Eastern Pygmy groups (2011: 57). Clearly almost all these traits can also be found among the Hadza as immediate-return hunter-

Table 7.1: Grauer's list of traits of a 'Hypothetical baseline culture' of ancestral African hunter-gatherers, compared with the Hadza.

HBC trait?	Hadza
Pygmy/Bushman vocal style	Distinctive polyphony
Subsistence: hunting, gathering, honey	Yes
Social organization: nomadic small bands	Yes
Kinship? Language? Location?	
Economics: communal	Yes
Politics: acephalous	Yes
Physical: short stature	Yes
Beehive huts	Yes
Weapons: spears, bows, arrows? poison?	Yes
Tools: stone, bone, wood	Yes
Ritual/religion: proto-shamanistic, healing, trance, initiation, funerary; healing techniques	Yes
Body decoration: body paint, scarification	Yes
Egalitarianism: levelling, sharing of resources	Yes
Gender: relative equality	Yes
Cooperation, non-aggression, conflict avoidance	Yes

gatherers (Woodburn 1982a). I intend to bring the Hadza into this comparison to add force to Grauer's triangulation method.

While Grauer provides a reasonable starting point, with several valid observations, some major aspects (kinship, language, geographic location and environment) remain unresolved. Here, I aim to expand on the brief remarks Grauer offers concerning religion or cosmology. First, though, I propose a significant addition to his list, which bears on economic transaction in marriage and residence patterns. The default among African foraging groups is bride-service, initially matrilocal (e.g. W. Pygmy Yaka, Lewis 2002: 74, 127; Ju/'hoansi, Lee 1979: 240–242; Marshall 1959: 352; 1976: 169; Hadza, Woodburn 1968: 108). It is standard for a son-in-law to live for several years with his wife and her parents; a woman's first and perhaps second child is likely to be born where her mother is. Work in population genetics is now showing a distinct matrilocal bias, evident in the localization of mother-to-daughter mtDNA lineages compared to father-to-son Y-lineages. This is the diametric opposite of the finding in neighbouring

Bantu farming and pastoralist populations, and it involves long timescales (Verdu et al. 2013 for Central African Pygmies; Schlebusch 2010 for Khoisan). A similar tendency for female relatives to stay together is found in Hadza longitudinal residence data (see Blurton Jones, Hawkes and O'Connell 2005: 229–231; Woodburn 1968; Wood and Marlowe 2011).

A Lunar Template

Turning now to cosmology, one core feature shared among these groups can be suggested immediately. The moon, as it oscillates between phases, figures prominently. Lunar cosmology is widespread in Khoisan traditions (Hahn 1881; Schapera 1930; Barnard 1988; Guenther 1999; Watts 2005). A story found among almost all Khoisan groups, the *Moon and Hare*, relates the origins of death (Barnard 1992: 83; Guenther 1999); among widespread Bushman groups, the waning moon is linked to spirits of the dead, the new moon to new life (Watts 2005; Barnard 1992: 56; Guenther 1999: 65; Hewitt 1986: 42). Such potent entities as Trickster and Eland are identifiably lunar – they grow large, fade away, come back alive (Power and Watts 1997). Moon phases – notably the appearance of new moon – schedule menarcheal ritual and prayers for hunting luck, and have the power of cooling arrow poison. While the new/waxing moon is associated with hunger and hunting, the fat full moon signifies repletion and feasting (Watts 2005). As Diä!kwain told Lucy Lloyd, 'Our mothers spoke, they said: "Wait, we must watch because this moon it is a thing like this. We must see if our men will not get a tortoise. For it is a thing that knows the time at which we shall get food."' (Digital Bleek and Lloyd BC 151 A2 1 65: 5209–11). The time of hunger may be linked among the !Xũ to menarche at dark moon when camp fires are extinguished (Watts this volume, citing Viegas Guerreiro), a motif echoed in several 'anti-cooking' narratives among southern Bushman groups.

    While the Hadza lack such riches of lore about the moon, their primary ritual *Epeme* can only be danced at night when no moon is in the sky (Woodburn 1982b). For them, the 'moon is brother to all women' (*seeta atits'i yayeta akwitibe wa inaeta*). This compares to Nharo Bushman lore: 'he doesn't like the boys, just the girls' (Guenther 1989). For the Western Pygmy BaYaka, 'women's biggest husband is the moon' (Lewis 2008: 299). When the *Malobe* ritual is called on a night of no-moon, it leads to a special intense and aesthetic experience (Lewis 2002: 150–151). Just as in *Epeme*, camp fires are extinguished so the singing group, largely women, sit in complete moonless dark; they may hold 'mystical conversations' with the moon; their singing lures luminescent forest spirits to dance around them (which, as at *Epeme*, are secretly engendered by male initiates). For the BayAka of the Central African Republic, this ceremony is *Boyobi*, noted by Sarno as 'probably one of their oldest forms of music' (2012: 14).

Schebesta's (1950) review of religious beliefs among different Eastern Pygmy groups makes recurrent mention of the moon as prominent in Pygmy myth and 'in close communion with God' though apparently not 'greater or mightier' than God. One notable structural story from the Efe and Mbuti is the tale of Matu, aged mother of Tore, who is master of game and lord of the dead; using liana swings, Tore is 'the one who swings to and fro over the abyss'. Matu sleeps by his fire, but one day an Efe ancestor steals the fire and flees. Waking cold, Matu calls to Tore to swing out after the culprit, who is captured, and the fire is restored. A second Efe brother tries to get the fire, but is caught again by Tore's swing. The third, disguised as a magical bird, flies down on the unguarded fire. Matu wakes with a startled scream again, but this time Tore can't swing far enough to stop the thief. He calls the man his brother, of the same mother, saying if only he had asked he would have given him the fire. When Tore returns to camp, the old mother is dead and cold. Now Tore curses the people with the punishment of death. The tale explains the origin of both death and fire, while Tore is the name of Efe men's secret society. Matu, her name connoting menstrual blood, is the dying moon, mother of the dead and the game (Schebesta 1950: 28–29, 36, 52, 188; see also Zuesse 1979: 21–22).

Turnbull (1959: 55–56) provides an Mbuti variant in the story of a 'crippled and diseased' Pygmy girl, abandoned alone in a camp. She cannot walk, only drag herself, but a bird (*fifi*) calls and shows her a rattan vine swing onto which she climbs. Three times, while she swings back and forth, she is assailed by a MuBira villager, each one coming with a weapon to kill her; each time the weapon attacks the attacker, so they stream with blood and die. Because 'she has the evil eye', the villagers come in a gang to dispatch her, or 'she will surely kill us all', but they find instead the *fifi* bird, swinging back and forth on the vine. The structural identity of these stories is clear. A disabled girl or an old woman is left alone in camp three times, and assailed by a murderer or thief. Each time a swing is used to evade death, or steal the fire. Both tales involve a magical bird. Both reveal oscillation between fire/no fire or a motif of reversal of weapons which draws blood. The swing motif here can be compared to that of the final myth quoted in *the Naked Man* (Lévi-Strauss 1981: 600, M810), the Ojibwa story called *the Two Moons*.

Schebesta experienced some confusion in sorting out the various names and manifestations of God, known in Bantu style as Mungu, who turns into a snake and a rainbow when climbing to the sky (also the Moon and lightning, who fight over the woman Otu). Equally bewildering were the different named ancestor and culture heroes, the agents and creators in Ituri stories (e.g Tore, Epilipili, Baatsi, Mbali). Of these too, there was some uncertainty as to whether they were deities or mere spirits, while the latter included an array of variegated ghosts, shades, imps and forest spirits (*keti, lodi, mbefe, balimo*). This cosmology has the same kind of fluidity as the ambiguous Bushman collection of 'gods'. As discussed by Barnard (1988), the general observable structure is of a great, high or sky god, an associated lesser deity and various spirits of the dead.

In her discussion of the ambiguity of Bushman high god/lesser god, creator and trickster figures, Biesele (1993: 180) prefers to separate out the trickster incarnations of story from the lesser or creator god. Guenther (1999: 96–125), by contrast, plays on the contradictory, fluid and ontologically ambiguous character of the trickster, arguing that this multifarious creature is the same entity under different names and guises. Keeney (2007: 85) suggests that the different words for the 'name of God' arise through names of names – respect words uttered when direct utterance would risk 'too much evocative power'. Here, we could consider whether the vagueness, ambiguity and incoherence so often commented on in Bushman religion can be seen as characteristic of all these forager cosmologies. Typical Bushmen sky god/lesser god or trickster pairings include for the /Xam *!Khwa* and /*Kaggen*; for Ju/'hoansi *Gao!na* and *G//aoan*, or at Nyae Nyae specifically Sky God *!Xon!a'an*, Trickster /*Xuri Kxaosi*, and ancestral spirits *g//auansi*, similarly Nharo //*Gãuwa* and //*gauwasi*. Among the Western Pygmy Yaka groups the sky god may be personified as *Komba*, but ritual practice focuses on the control of forest spirits, *mokondi* – spirits which have an aspect of trickery and danger until brought under the control of initiate groups (men's, women's or children's). For the Mbuti, the central ceremonial is named with the general word for spirit, *Molimo*. For the Hadza, although the sky god *Haine* exists in stories of creation, the key ritual *Epeme* refers to general spirits, more or less undifferentiated as 'ancestors' (*alungube*).

I propose that lunar time is the structuring or dialectical framework for the relationships between these various and ambiguous powers. Structuralists Lévi-Strauss (in Amerindian myth) and de Heusch (in Central Bantu myth) arrived at markedly similar outlines of an invariant syntax, revolving around certain 'hard' relations of identity and opposition and persisting through all ideological manipulation (see de Heusch 1982: 133–134). For example:

celestial fire vs. cooking fire
noise vs. cooking
blood vs. fire
incest vs. marriage
sky vs. earth
bitter moon vs. honey moon

Lévi-Strauss was ambiguous as to what such structures represented, by the end of *Mythologiques* seeing these as emergent properties of the human mind in its tendency to classify and create logical relations devoid of specific content. De Heusch recognized in the logical transformations of Lunda, Luba and Kuba royal epic cycles an ideological function of validation of the divine kingship, but saw that these rested on 'anthropo-cosmogonic discourse ... manifestly antecedent' to such historic development. Following structuralist method, but locating it within his evolutionary model of a Palaeolithic or Middle Stone Age 'sex-strike', Chris Knight generated a 'time-resistant syntax' (Knight, Power and Watts 1995: 91; see also Power and Watts 1997: 556), as a dynamic oscillation between ritual power switched ON/OFF in relation to the waxing/waning moon. All these structuralists concur in the prominence of a lunar function in the syntax of myth, but Knight offers a material cause. Given the excellent night-vision of big cats and other predators, the impact of lunar periodicity in hominin evolutionary ecology must be of key importance for our emergence on the African savannah, stretching back millions of years before any symbolic culture. The moon and its phases have critical material effects on prey-predator interactions – a Ju/'hoan metaphor for a lion is 'moonless night' (Biesele 1993: 24). But the focus here is on the last hundred thousand years of onset of symbolic culture. That lunar framework provides the matrix within which the earliest cosmological structures were embedded. Recurrent among these African hunting cultures are links between the phase of dark moon, menstruation, hunger and extinction of cooking fire.

Healing Dances

As Grauer notes, all these hunter-gatherer populations engage in healing or medicine dances. These may lead to ecstatic experiences, as healers summon or come into contact with spirits, more or less nebulous 'ancestors' rather than personified or named figures. Such rituals rest on polyphonic singing performance. In most traditions both genders participate, although certain rituals may be single sex, but the collective of women as singers are generally major contributors. The classic example is the community healing dance of the Ju/'hoansi (Katz 1982; Keeney 2007), representing a more widespread Bushman tradition (Guenther 1999; Lewis-Williams 1981). Katz and colleagues stress the synergic communal effort allied to individual painful experience of summoning *n/om* (energy or potency) to enter *!aia.* (transcendent or enhanced awareness). Keeney avoids reference to 'trance states', highlighting instead the dynamic, transformative aspects of shamanic bodily and emotional arousal, becoming interconnected through all senses. Chris Low (this volume) emphasizes the role of sensory stimuli, especially smell, and mechanisms of stress applied to the body of a dancer.

Lewis (2002: 150) compares the 'trance-like' experiences of Yaka *mokondi massana* especially where performances last for hours or even days (e.g. *Ejengi* who must dance for three days). He describes euphoria, a 'dreamy, heightened experience and appreciation of sound and movement' charging people with irrepressible energy to sing and dance. *Mokondi massana* are aesthetic, atmospheric, multimedia sensory creations for bringing joy to the community; even where male initiates are the spirit-controllers (as in *Ejengi*), women's mood, energy and performance are vital for luring and seducing the capricious spirits. For the Mbuti, *Molimo*, most famously described by Turnbull (1960a), is created and performed by male initiates, as they summon the 'great animal of the forest' through light and sound effects in the darkness, using a bamboo trumpet or even a drainpipe. When singing the great *Molimo* songs, says Turnbull, 'the pygmy is quite plainly in another world, staring into the fire or up at the tree-tops ... communing with a power which he believes to exist in the forest' (1960a: 319). One of those songs says: 'the forest is good; there is darkness in the forest (so) darkness is good'. Even though women and girls should retire to their huts during *Molimo*, Turnbull (1960a: 323–329) has left the vivid account of two episodes where young girls, led by an entranced old lady, effectively took over the ceremony with their singing of the *Molimo* songs, learned during *Elima* initiation. Among the Hadza, the dark moon ceremony *Epeme* is again supposedly male-governed, yet there can be no performance without enough women prepared to sing through the cold night. It is when women are moved to euphoric collective dancing, swirling close around but not touching the single male spirit dancer, that participants approach enchantment beneath the stars. *Epeme* is both a general community medicine dance for well-being, and forthcoming success in the hunt, as well as a context for healing techniques to be applied to sick individuals (Peterson 2013: 162; Power 2015; Skaanes 2015; Woodburn 1982b).

Return to First Creation: Initiation and Gender Polarity

The remarkable ethnography of the Keeneys (2007, 2013a, 2013b) working with Nyae Nyae Ju/'hoan healers has revealed the frame of healing as seeking re-entry to First Creation – original time 'before time and place' when nothing was named or fixed in form, everything kept changing, there was no death or sickness, and people had 'eland heads'. Trickster, inhabiting the western sky (as the new moon and spirits of the dead), is gatekeeper of this inchoate world in perpetual flux, 'central denizen of the First Order of existence' (Guenther 1999: 96). Puberty rites, storytelling and healing dances all serve in the 'hunt' for *n/om* (Keeney and Keeney 2013a: 13). The first (and second and third) appearance of a girl's menstrual blood is interpreted as 'an opening to First Creation'; she now exists inside First Creation, constantly changing her form, and this fills her with strong *n/om*. The powerful charge of her presence in First Creation requires careful ritual precaution to ensure nobody is left behind (2013a: 8). All the community need to move through the door with her. To do this, they dance naked, as in First Creation no one wore clothes; they dance as eland, since the ancestors had eland heads. The girl now can change form to become an old woman, a man, boy, animal or hybrid; so, too, can all those inside the dance (2013a: 9). To make everyone 'more like the girl', an elder *n/om kxao* makes small cuts in each person's ear so they bleed. This results in 'blood dropping to the ground and deepening their entry and identity with the girl' (2013a: 9). The great danger is that the girl can become a strong male hunter while a man becomes an eland and she can then hunt and kill him. (For the Ju/'hoansi, no man would hunt while his wife was menstruating, for fear of becoming hunted himself.) So long as everybody bleeds together, they are all changing together and this effects the 'border crossing' into First Creation. A boy's initiation, connected to 'first kill', will have the same structure: he is made to bleed with cuts to the forehead; everyone must bleed so they have no fear of his strong *n/om* and changing (2013b: 74).

For the other African hunter-gatherer populations, we can find significant evidence in initiation rituals of re-enactments of original scenarios, which could be understood as versions of first creation.

These also involve aspects of gender reversal. Notably, the male initiation societies of Hadza *Epeme* (Power 2015; Power and Watts 1997; see also Woodburn 1964), Mbuti *Molimo* (Turnbull 1960a: 338) and the Yaka *Ejengi* (Lewis 2002: 175–177) all recount 'matriarchy myths' of the original ownership of women. In the ritual practice of these societies, and particularly in the corresponding female initiation groups, we find re-enactment of women's primacy, entailing mutability of gender and/or species. The Hadza girls' initiation, *Maitoko*, involves a group of girls, young women and adult women, and turns on the story of the origins of *Epeme*, 'The woman with the zebra's penis', Mambedako or Epemako. This hunter heroine used to hunt male zebra and tie their penises onto her belt, commanding the men to bring *epeme* meat to her great pot. From this she would feed her 'wives' – a name used to refer to the girls at *Maitoko* (Mouriki and Power 2005). Eventually men overthrew her wicked rule and seized *epeme* meat and the dance for themselves. During three days of *Maitoko*, girls chase men and boys out of camp, acting and dressing as hunters, while male hunters are disarmed. These girls have endured a collective cutting (which may involve genital cutting or stomach incisions); because they are bleeding together and running together, the whole community is carried back to the original scene of Mambedako. The drama culminates in a contest between boys and girls scrambling to take possession of a pot full of delicious food – Mambedako's pot (Power 2015; see also Peterson 2013: 148).

For the Mbuti *Molimo*, as mentioned above, *Elima* girls intervened during the ceremony witnessed by Turnbull, under the tutelage of an old woman who 'tied up' the hunters with the twine used for hunting nets. Only once 'paid' would she free them, and then the girls commenced dancing and singing *Molimo* songs, processing behind the old lady who had received a trophy from the men made of the hunting twine (Turnbull 1960a: 323–324). A few days later, the same old lady danced ecstatically to challenge the men's possession of the *Molimo* fire, dramatizing the story of the origin of fire (cf Matu, above). During the *Elima* initiation that followed, the girls were every bit as ruthless and relentless as Hadza girls are during *Maitoko*, in hunting down young men, chasing and whipping them with sticks. These two rituals bear a striking similarity. The *Elima* girls in Turnbull's account also caused trouble with the Bantu villagers by adopting *Nkumbi* male initiation dress, paint and masks as their preferred latest fashion (1960b: 186–187).

Mbendjele *Ejengi* initiation similarly culminates in a drama re-creating the origins story. Each gender group has its own version of how at first the two sexes existed separately; either men found women (men's story) or women found men (women's story). Both agree that women held *Ejengi* in the beginning and that girl babies fell out of the male spirit's raffia skirts; men meanwhile had to use hard *mapombe* fruit to copulate with to get boys. The men 'hunted' the women as if encircling wild pigs, but they used weapons of honey parcels, sweetening them up so much that the men could soon throw away their *mapombe*. The men say they took *Ejengi* (which takes the form of an ejaculating penis) off the women by force to make sure women had to come to them for babies. By contrast, women say 'we gave it away to the men', with the implication they kept even better things for themselves (Lewis 2002: 177). During *Ejengi* initiation, the men's group attacks the women's with *mapombe* fruit, which scatters them, since they believe they will die if any should hit them. Shortly after, initiates come charging out at the women, driving them into their huts with sticks. While there are several aspects of co-operation and collusion by the women in giving up their sons to *Ejengi*, the message enforcing respect for men's ownership is driven home forcefully (Lewis 2002: 182–183). As *Ejengi* holds dangers for women, so too does women's *Ngoku* for men. Then men must retire. Women can smile at the tale of men's taking of *Ejengi* since they kept the two most powerful *mokondi*, *Ngoku* and *Yele*: 'We'll never give them to men!' (2002: 191). As the women dominate the camp space during *Ngoku*, their songs and dances are full of sexual taunting to the men; their chant 'We the Yaka, we the Yaka, twice the intelligence!' implicitly refers to the mythic past when women owned all the *mokondi* and got babies from *Ejengi*, with no help from men (Lewis 2002: 194). In one hilarious dance, older women reverse gender, mimicking men trying to have sex with younger initiates.

Finnegan (2013, and this volume) has written eloquently on the pendulum of power, now with one gender, who guard their boundary with secrets, now with the other group, each one contesting the space and time in a to-and-fro periodic motion. This structure of gender polarity and contest is strongly shared by these African hunter-gatherer groups. We can compare directly the dynamic between the secret societies of men and women (from West to East) *Ejengi/Ngoku* (Yaka); *Molimo/Elima* (Mbuti); *Epeme/Maitoko* (Hadza). We can further compare the equivalence of the Ju/'hoan shamanic re-entry with the menarcheal girl in the Eland dance opening the door to First Creation. While elder male healers and grandfathers may be involved as eland dancers (e.g. among Ju/'hoansi or Nharo), it is also possible in the Kalahari for women alone to hold the horns in the Eland dance, as witnessed by Valiente-Noailles with the 'Kua' (G/wi or G//ana) (1993). There women dance around the menstrual seclusion hut using the horns to keep men at a respectful distance. The picture of disarmed or immobilized hunters on the receiving end of sticks wielded by women appears similar to the context of the *Maitoko* girls or *Elima*.

Animal de Passage

Lewis-Williams' original conception in *Believing and Seeing* of a shared structure governing Bushman female and male initiation and the healing rituals is surely validated by the Keeneys' ethnography. He drew together the nineteeth-century /Xam southern Cape Bushman ethnography of the Bleek and Lloyd collection with Kalahari fieldwork on contemporary Ju/'hoansi to illuminate rock art across southern Africa. Subsequently, an emphasis on healing experience as the primary 'symbolic work' (Lewis-Williams 1982; Lewis-Williams and Dowson 1989) led to a bandwagon effect of all enigmatic images being ascribed to trance, with less attention paid to initiation contexts. Some scholars, notably Anne Solomon (1992), continued to point to stories of initiation as providing significant insight into interpretations of rock art. The narratives concerning First Creation of the Nyae Nyae elder /Kunta Boo, a main informant for both Biesele and the Keeneys, give us a clearer perspective on this debate. Any attempt to counterpose healing and initiation misses a fundamental aspect of Bushman representation of supernatural potency. Whether belonging to a healer or a menarcheal girl, a first-kill hunter or a storyteller, it is the same potency, fuelling re-entry into First Creation when people had 'eland heads'. Lewis-Williams evocatively described the Eland Bull as the '*animal de passage*' of Bushman initiation (1981: 72). Healers and initiates identify powerfully with the eland as it fattens, is shot with a poisoned arrow, dies, is consumed or fades away. As she shape-shifts, the Ju/'hoan maiden has both 'shot an eland' and is herself the fattening eland bull. In First Creation, the eland-headed people had hooves that made the sound of clapping – sounds invoked in the initiation and healing dances – and these became the first *n/om kxaosi* (Keeney and Keeney 2013a: 2). In fact, rather than the hooves, it is the knees of mature, heavy eland bulls that emit a castanet-like clicking sound (Bro-Jørgensen and Dabelsteen 2008).

   This characteristic is apparently referred to in the sounds and rhythms not only of Ju/'hoan healing and Eland dances, but also in Hadza *Epeme*. There is significant similarity of belief concerning eland among the Hadza. The sound of ankle bells on the right foot of the *epeme* dancer brought down in a ponderous stamping rhythm mimics the eland (Skaanes 2015, this volume). This remarkable trait also permits mature eland bulls to be tracked and hunted on dark nights with no moon – that is, at the time of *Epeme* (James Woodburn, pers. comm. 2015). The ideal *epeme* animal, the eland offers a motif of reversal. Nocturnal hunting is usually only possible towards full moon – except in the unique case of the eland. Lewis-Williams learned from the Ju/'hoansi that among antelopes, females always had more fat – except in the unique case of the eland (1981: 72). For both Ju/'hoansi and the Hadza, eland fat with its ambiguous gendering is critical for the initiation of boys and girls. With the Hadza, it is held in decorated gourd containers that may be used at *Epeme*. Similarly to the Bushmen (e.g. Marshall 1957), the Hadza hold beliefs of eland body fluids affecting the weather, and of their fatness changing in respect of the animal's sex and of the phase of the moon (Mouriki and Power 2005).

Clearly eland – not a forest antelope – is not going to figure in Pygmy cosmology. We could however consider the chain of symbols concatenated around eland, as identified by Sigrid Schmidt (1979: 219–220): 'trickster/ moon/ lightning/ rain/ fertility/ ... horns'. The burning of eland horns was used by a Ju/'hoan hunter to manipulate the weather-affecting forces of *n!ow* (Marshall 1957). Biesele relates a tale of the trickster G!ara calling down the lightning with eland horns to lay low his antagonists, the lions (1993: 103–115). Thomas (2006: 38–39) observes that antelopes like eland will watch the sky for lightning, since wildfires will burn off dry grass and produce new growth. Human hunters would have learned to exploit this, deliberately burning off grass to attract game.

We might predict similar aspects of cosmology among Pygmy groups, for instance with antelope such as bongo (with 'huge and dangerous *ekila*' for Mbendjele, see below) and in the connection of horns, lightning and hunting magic. Turnbull (1988: 90–91) describes the Mbuti use of *anjo*, a hunting medicine regarded as anti-social since it brought about an excess of good luck at others' expense. It comprised: 'various parts of an antelope, particularly the heart and eye. The charred flesh is mixed with spittle and ground to a paste, then put in an inverted antelope horn and stuck in the ground near the family fire' (1988: 90). Schebesta (1950: 108ff.) tells of a BaMbuti idea of the lightning as a 'he-goat that descends from heaven to earth with a terrific noise', while the Efe have a celestial 'goat' sent to earth by God, 'all the game of the forest being goats of the deity'. For Ituri groups, powerful hunting magic is ascribed to pipes and whistles carved from the wood of trees struck by lightning, or one 'on which the horns of an antelope have been sharpened'.

Other species strongly associated with a lightning-like movement between sky and earth are 'snakes' of varying descriptions, including Rainbow snakes (Low 2012; Sullivan and Low 2014; and see Watts, this volume, for eland and snake connections).

Rules of Respect of Game

Bushman tricksters recurrently act as guardians of the game, especially the eland (e.g. /Kaggen and Cagn, known as the Mantis among southern Bushmen groups). The trickster might take the form of a louse or insect to intervene and spoil hunting outcomes (e.g. //Gãuwa, Nharo); among the Hei//om, //Gamab would shoot a hunter with death arrows for abusing an animal (Guenther 1999: 111–112). The trickster is prayed to for release of the game when the people go hungry (Marshall 1962: 247).

For Western Pygmy Yaka groups, the creator god Komba insists that 'animals must not be laughed at' (Lewis 2002: 121). To do so would ruin one's *ekila* (see below). Among Eastern Pygmy groups, Schebesta recounts the game being guarded in caves and waterfalls by the Rainbow, allied to thunder and lightning (and the Moon), for the distant high god (1950: 16–20, 31, 41–42, 59–66, 203–212). In such awful places, *Molimo* trumpets can be secreted from the uninitiated. A hunter will only make a kill if Tore walks ahead of him, leaving signs. Then, when he has succeeded, he should leave a thanks-offering to the Master of the Game or to the hungry spirits under his tutelage, the *Lodi*. Storms are viewed as punishments of transgressions on the hunt or within the band. When lightning strikes, Mbuti may offer not only prayers but also their own blood to repair such wrongs (see Zuesse 1979: 28, 38n.30 for discussion). Hunting pipes and whistles can be used to avert the terrible dangers of storms, transforming violent noise and confusion (*akami*) into the quiet and calm of a camp in harmony (*ekimi*).

Hadza society is fundamentally structured through the respect rules of *Epeme*, referring to certain fatty parts of large game animals, as well as to the spirits who guard against any violation of *epeme* rules. The origins myth of Mambedako concerns the original distribution of *epeme* meat (to Mambedako's pot) and how it was violently claimed by the men. Now initiated men interpret the will of the ancestors, policing any violations on the part of women or children coming near the *epeme* initiates' feast, which would result in dire consequences for their health and punishment of the women of a camp. At the feast, the mythical ancestress lights the sacred fire, and cooks the meat, which the ancestors come to eat – but the secret of the initiates is the trick played by the men on the women, that they in fact do the eating (Mouriki and Power 2005; Woodburn 1964). The Hadza also attach similar beliefs to the mantis as are found in relation to Bushman trickster figures. If found in the bush, a mantis is regarded as uncanny, a bad omen, but it cannot be harmed or it would go badly for the hunt. Associated with the dead and with the Pleiades, known as 'children of the Moon', the mantis features in *Epeme* songs (Mouriki and Watts 2015).

The Ideology of Blood

Parallel to the trickster role as guardian and creator of the great game antelopes is the trickster's jealous guardianship of maidens at first menstruation. The counterpart to /Kaggen among the /Xam, the male Rain, Rain bull or snake !Khwa would be roused to wrath by any failure in the menarcheal observances (Hewitt 1986: 284–285). /Xam informants stressed 'the odour of the girl' as what attracted !Khwa. The maiden could only come in very guarded contact with water, but had to paint the young men of the band with haematite stripes 'like a zebra' to protect them from !Khwa's lightning (cf the lightning as guardian of game among Eastern Pygmy groups, see above). Violations caused the utmost social calamity: culture itself unravelled, skin bags reverting to 'raw' form as game animals, while the girl and her kin were transformed into frogs, the 'Rain's creatures' (Hewitt 1986: 77–79). This can be compared with the threat of the Ju/'hoan girl's strong *n/om* if she alone re-enters First Creation.

This is a particular example of a basic principle found in all these hunter-gatherer groups. Everywhere we find mystical intertwining of production (hunting) with reproduction (menstruation, pregnancy and childbirth). This amounts to an 'ideology of blood': two forms – menstrual blood on the one hand and the blood of game on the other – must never be allowed to mix (Testart 1986; and see Knight 1991: 396–398). As in the stories of !Khwa, the idiom is one of smell arousing anger. So game animals would be able to smell whether a hunter had sex with his wife and, offended, will flee. Worse still, they would be able to smell that he had sex when she was menstruating; this would provoke the animal to attack, turning the hunter into the hunted (see e.g. Biesele 1993: 92–93 for Ju/'hoan; Lewis 2008: 299

for Mbendjele; Schebesta 1950 for Mbuti elephant hunts; Woodburn 1982b: 188 for Hadza).

While animals may be jealous and insist on being wooed by hunters, in apparent opposition to women, girls at first menstruation are also hunters who shoot animals. In Ju/'hoan idiom 'she has shot an eland' (Lewis-Williams 1981; Keeney and Keeney 2013a: 9) while she is also an eland in the constant shape-shifting of First Creation. The Hadza have exactly the same idea: 'she has shot her first zebra!' (Woodburn pers. comm. 1993), placing the girl into the role of Mambedako which she plays during the collective ritual of *Maitoko*. The Hadza and Ju/'hoansi also share the same idea that the reason a man cannot hunt while his wife is menstruating is that his arrow poison will cool and be destroyed. When the *Maitoko* girls are running, after undergoing collective forms of bloodshed, this blood is clearly treated as if it were menstrual, since hunters cannot carry bows – their arrow poison would be destroyed. For the /Xam, it is the moon's water, like honey, which cools the poison of the arrow and allows the game to revive and escape (Hewitt 1986: 79). A Hadza man whose wife is pregnant cannot walk on the tracks of wounded game, or it will revive, nor should he mock or laugh at a dead but not yet dismembered carcass of game, or the unborn baby would be born with the same defects (Woodburn 1982b: 188). We can propose a fundamental structure of equivalences shared by these bow-and-poisoned arrow hunters: a menstrual woman is as a hunter who has shot game; while a woman who gives birth is as a hunter who kills game.

In this volume, Finnegan recounts examples of ritual hunting labour performed by women's collectives in Western Pygmy groups, including *Bobanda*, in response to lean hunting among the Biaka; in the Baka *Yeli*, women locate large game through special polyphonic performances; and in the closely related *Yele* of the Mbendjele, the women's trance before the hunt 'ties up' the elephant's spirit so that hunters can be sent to find it, this being a 'woman's hunting trip'. These contexts show how the opposition between women's body and blood and those of game animals transforms into a powerfully attractive equivalence.

The most elaborate example of hunter-gatherer 'magical' interrelation of production and reproduction is *ekila*, documented in detail by Jerome Lewis among the Yaka Mbendjele (2002: 103–123; 2008; and see Knight and Lewis, this volume). Lewis notes that numerous linguistically diverse Western Pygmy groups have *ekila* practices, while Eastern Pygmy groups like Mbuti and Efe share the concepts and practices under different names (2008: 297, 313, n.1,2;

and see Ichikawa 1987: 102). This implies that the complex is of considerable antiquity. *Ekila* invokes a polysemic cluster revolving around 'menstruation, blood, taboo, a hunter's meat, good hunting luck, the power of animals to harm humans, and particular dangers to human reproduction, production, health and sanity' (Knight and Lewis, this volume). The core metaphorical equivalences of *ekila* equate men killing animals and women birthing children; the spearing of animals and the penetration of women's bodies in intercourse; menstrual blood and the blood of the hunt.

Differing experience of *ekila* by sex (and to some extent age) is the basic organizer of gender roles and relations. A senior hunter informed Lewis (2008: 298) that 'his *ekila* was big, very big' since he slept alone on a mat without his wife. To mix *ekila* with lots of people causes a hunter's luck to be ruined, creates problems for a woman in childbirth and affects her infant's health. 'Women have *ekila* too', the informant continues, 'A woman's *ekila* is with the moon. When a woman is e*kila* [menstruating] her husband takes her smell. So he doesn't go hunting or walking in the forest with friends. Animals flee when they smell a woman's *mobeku* (ritual danger). The animals smell her on him'.

Structures Shared beyond Hunter-gatherers

Shared structures found among African hunting populations separated over long periods of time are likely to be ancient, and may provide evidence about early symbolic cosmologies of modern humans dating back to the Middle Stone Age. Structures identified here as potentially archaic can also be identified in African cultures where hunting no longer predominates, whether they be farmers or pastoralists. It is beyond the scope of this chapter to extend comparisons to Bantu, Nilotic and other language groups. But a few points can be made as to how this affects my argument.

In terms of politics, economics and subsistence technologies, hunter-gatherers clearly offer the greatest continuity to Middle Stone Age populations. By examining hunter-gatherer ritual, myth, taboos and beliefs, we can gain insight into extremely conservative and stable symbolic complexes. It is not surprising if those complexes will be retained in derivative forms in the cultures of groups who are no longer nomadic hunter-gatherers. Historic material change in subsistence is likely to affect the ways these ideologies are manipulated and transformed, yet the core ingredients of ritual power are unlikely to alter.

An example is found in de Heusch's analysis of the Central Bantu myths of kingship, which as he noted entailed 'anthropo-cosmogonic discourse' much older than divine kings. Specifically, he equated Rainbow Snake entities to menstrual (and incestuous) ritual queens as signifiers of permanence threatening the periodicity of the wet/dry seasons. We can expect a switch of emphasis from lunar to seasonal cycles while still correlating with archaic waxing/waning metaphors. Menstruation becomes opposed to rain and fertility, identified with sterility. This can be understood in terms of a shift of gender politics in relation to new, more permanent forms of marriage by bride-price (as against hunter-gatherer bride-service). For hunters, menstruation belongs to categories of transformative potency like *ekila* and *n/om*, while for farmers and cattle people, it becomes a source of pollution and ill-omen. Its power and centrality to ritual remains.

Conclusion

While this is a preliminary and cursory attempt at comparative ethnography, a few conclusions can be drawn about the source African cosmology:

a) It was lunar and 'menstrual' in that ritual and practice around menstruation manifestly affected relationships between women, men and the animals they hunted. Processes of production and reproduction were intertwined and showed this metaphoric equivalence: to menstruate is to shoot a poisoned arrow; to give birth is to kill large game. This conforms to the lunar/menstrual character of the invariant syntax of myth described by Lévi-Strauss, de Heusch and Knight.

b) Healing and spirit dances involved polyphonic singing performance (largely of female choruses), leading to euphoric or 'trance' experiences through rhythmic repetition of sound and movement invoking nebulous spirits of the dead or the forest.

c) The potency of shamans/spirit dancers and menstrual maidens was one and the same power capable of carrying the community into 'first creation'. Gendered initiation groups re-presented origins scenarios through the reversal of sexual attributes and/or species mutability. These motifs of reversal coincided with the switch of lunar phases, and oscillation between taboo and relaxation of taboo. A dynamic of reverse-dominance allowed each gender group – but especially women – to assert egalitarian relations and mutual interdependency.

d) Large horned antelope, like eland, supplied metaphors of transformation in initiation and healing dances, again predicated on the waxing and waning of the moon. The guardians and creators of these *animals de passage* impose respect rules for all game. These were effective supernatural sanctions governing the proper sharing of flesh (human and animal).

There appear to be genuine and non-trivial shared structures of ritual and belief among African hunter-gatherers that are likely to be very archaic. Those structures can be regarded as data that constrain possible models of human symbolic origins. Any model for the symbolic cultural origins of modern humans should not only address evidence in the archaeological record, but also pay attention to structures of a possible source cosmology of equivalent antiquity.

References

Barnard A. 1988. 'Structure and Fluidity in Khoisan Religious Ideas', *Journal of Religion in Africa* 18: 216–236.

———. 1992. *Hunters and Herders of Southern Africa*. Cambridge: Cambridge University Press.

Biesele, M. 1993. *Women Like Meat. The Folklore and Foraging Ideology of the Kalahari Ju/'hoan*. Johannesburg and Indiana: Witwatersrand University.

Blurton Jones, N., K. Hawkes and J.F. O'Connell. 2005. 'Older Hadza Men and Women as Helpers: Residence Data', in B.S. Hewlett and M.E. Lamb (eds), *Hunter-gatherer Childhoods*. New Brunswick, NJ: Aldine Transaction, pp. 214–236.

Bro-Jørgensen, J. and T. Dabelsteen. 2008. 'Knee-clicks and Visual Traits Indicate Fighting Ability in Eland Antelopes: Multiple Messages and Back-up Signals', *BMC Biology* 6:47. doi:10.1186/1741-7007-6-47.

Chen, Y.-S. et al. 2000. 'Mitochondrial DNA Variation in the South African Kung and Khwe – and their Genetic Relationships to Other African Populations', *American Journal of Human Genetics* 66: 1362–83.

de Heusch, L. 1982. *The Drunken King, or the Origins of the State*. Bloomington: Indiana University Press.

Digital Bleek and Lloyd. http://lloydbleekcollection.cs.uct.ac.za/index.html (retrieved 4 February 2015).

Finnegan, M. 2013. 'The Politics of Eros', *Journal of the Royal Anthropological Institute (N.S.)* 19: 697–715.

Grauer, V. 2011. *Sounding the Depths. Tradition and the Voices of History*. Pittsburgh: Create Space. http://soundingthedepths.blogspot.co.uk/ (retrieved 1 February 2015).

Guenther, M. 1989. *Bushman Folktales: Oral Traditions of the Nharo of Botswana and the /Xam of the Eastern Cape*. Stuttgart: Franz Steiner Verlag Wiesbaden.

———. 1999. *Tricksters and Trancers*. Bloomington: Indiana University Press.

Hahn, T. 1881. *Tsuni//goam: the Supreme Being of the Khoikhoi.* London: Trubner and Co.

Henn, B.M. et al. 2011. 'Hunter-gatherer Genomic Diversity Suggests a Southern African Origin for Modern Humans', *Proceedings of the National Academy of Sciences,* USA 108: 5154–62. doi:10.1073/pnas.1017511108. PubMed: 21383195.

Hewitt, R.L. 1986. *Structure, Meaning and Ritual in the Narratives of the Southern San.* Hamburg: Helmut Buske Verlag (Quellen zur Khoisan-Forschung 2).

Ichikawa, M. 1987. 'Food Restrictions of the Mbuti Pygmies, Eastern Zaire', *African Study Monographs.* Supplementary Issue 6: 97–121.

Katz, R. 1982. *Boiling Energy. Community Healing among the Kalahari Kung.* Cambridge, MA: Harvard University Press.

Keeney, B. 2007. 'Batesonian Epistemology, Bushman n/om kxaosi, and Rock Art', *Kybernetes* 36: 884–904.

Keeney, H. and B. Keeney. 2013a. 'N/om, Change, and Social Work: A Recursive Frame Analysis of the Transformative Rituals of the Ju/'hoan Bushmen', *The Qualitative Report* 2013 18, Article 9: 1–18, http://www.nova.edu/ssss/QR/QR18/keeney9.pdf

Keeney, B. and H. Keeney. 2013b. 'Reentry into First Creation: A Contextual Frame for the Ju/'hoan Bushman Performance of Puberty Rites, Storytelling and Healing Dance', *Journal of Anthropological Research* 69: 65–86.

Knight, C. 1991. *Blood Relations: Menstruation and the Origins of Culture.* New Haven and London: Yale University Press.

———, C. Power and I. Watts. 1995. 'The Human Symbolic Revolution. A Darwinian Account', *Cambridge Journal of Archaeology* 5: 75–114.

Lee, R.B. 1979. *The !Kung San. Men, Women and Work in a Foraging Society.* Cambridge: Cambridge University Press.

Lévi-Strauss, C. 1981. *The Naked Man. Introduction to a Science of Mythology,* vol.4. London: Cape.

Lewis, J. 2002. 'Forest Hunter-gatherers and their World', PhD dissertation. London: University of London.

———. 2008. '*Ekila*: Blood, Bodies, and Egalitarian Societies', *Journal of the Royal Anthropological Institute (N. S.)* 14: 297–315.

Lewis-Williams, J.D. 1981. *Believing and Seeing. Symbolic Meanings in Southern San Rock Paintings.* London: Academic Press.

———. 1982. 'The Social and Economic Context of Southern San Rock Art', *Current Anthropology* 23: 429–449.

——— and T.A. Dowson. 1989. *Images of Power: Understanding Bushman Rock Art.* Johannesburg: Southern Book Publishers.

Low, C. 2012. 'KhoeSan Shamanistic Relationships with Snakes and Rain', *Journal of Namibian Studies* 12: 71–96.

Marshall, L. 1957. 'N!ow', *Africa* 27: 232–240.

———. 1959. 'Marriage among !Kung Bushmen', *Africa* 29: 335–365.

———. 1962. '!Kung Bushman religious beliefs', *Africa* 32: 221–252.

———. 1976. *The !Kung of Nyae Nyae.* Cambridge, MA: Harvard University Press.

Morris, A.G. 2003. 'The Myth of the East African "Bushmen"', *The South African Archaeological Bulletin* 178: 85–90. doi: 10.2307/3889305

Mouriki, E. and C. Power. 2005. 'The Importance of the Moon in Hunter-gatherer Ritual: the Case of the Hadzabe', Theoretical Archaeology Group Conference, Sheffield, December 2005.

Mouriki, E. and I. Watts 2015. 'Striking Similarities in KhoeSan and Hadza Mythology: Some Preliminary Remarks', Conference of Hunting and Gathering Societies 11, Wien, September 2015.

Peterson, D. 2013. *Hadzabe. By the Light of a Million Fires* (with R. Baalow and J. Cox). Dar es Salaam: Mkuki na Nyota.

Pickrell, J.K. et al. 2012. 'The Genetic Prehistory of Southern Africa', *Nature Communications* 3: 1143. doi: 10.1038/ncomms2140. PubMed: 23072811.

Power, C. 2015. 'Hadza Gender Rituals – *Epeme* and *Maitoko* – Considered as Counterparts', *Hunter Gatherer Research* 1: 333–358. doi:10.3828/hgr.2015.18.

——— and I. Watts 1997. 'The Woman with the Zebra's Penis. Gender, Mutability and Performance', *Journal of the Royal Anthropological Institute* (N. S.) 3: 537–560.

Rito, T. et al. 2013. 'The First Modern Human Dispersals across Africa', *PLoS ONE* 8(11): e80031. doi:10.1371/journal.pone.0080031.

Sarno, L. 2012. 'Recording Sounds of Music and Community in the Rainforest, Interview with Noel Lobley', *Radical Anthropology* 6: 5–16.

Schapera, I. 1930. *The Khoisan Peoples of South Africa: Bushmen and Hottentots.* London: George Routledge and Sons.

Schebesta, P. 1950. *Die Bambuti-Pygmäen vom Ituri, Ergebnisse Zweier Forschungsreisen zu de Zentralafrikanischen Pygmäen Bd. II, Teil III Die Religion,* Mémoires, Institut Royal Colonial Belge, Section des Sciences Morales et Politiques, Coll.-in-4°, IV. Brussels: Georges van Campenhout, 1938–50.

Schepartz, L.A. 1988. 'Who Were the Later Pleistocene Eastern Africans?', *African Archaeological Review* 6: 57–72.

Schlebusch, C.M. 2010. 'Genetic Variation in Khoisan-Speaking Populations from Southern Africa', PhD dissertation. Johannesburg: University of Witwatersrand.

Schmidt, S. 1979 'The Rain Bull of the South African Bushmen', *African Studies* 38: 201–224.

Skaanes, T. 2015. 'Notes on Hadza Cosmology: *Epeme*, Objects and Rituals', *Hunter Gatherer Research* 1: 247–267.

Solomon, A. 1992. 'Gender, Representation and Power in San Ethnography and Rock Art', *Journal of Anthropological Archaeology* 11: 291–329.

Sullivan, S. and C. Low. 2014. 'Shades of the Rainbow Serpent? A KhoeSan Animal between Myth and Landscape in Southern Africa – Ethnographic

Contextualisations of Rock Art Representations', *Arts* 3: 215–244. doi:10.3390/arts3020215.

Testart, A. 1986. *Essai sur les Fondements de la Division Sexuelle du Travail chez les Chasseurs-cueilleurs*. Paris: Editions de l'Ecole des Hautes Etudes des Sciences Sociales.

Thomas, E.M. 2006. *The Old Way. A Story of the First People*. New York: Sarah Crichton Books.

Tishkoff, S.A. et al. 2007. 'History of Click-speaking Populations of Africa Inferred from mtDNA and Y Chromosome Genetic Variation', *Molecular Biology and Evolution* 24: 2180–95.

———. 2009. 'The Genetic Structure and History of Africans and African Americans', *Science* 324: 1035–44. doi:10.1126/science.1172257. PubMed: 19407144.

Tobias, P.V. 1964. 'Bushman Hunter-gatherers: a Study in Human Ecology', in D.H.S. Davis (ed.) Ecological Studies in Southern Africa. The Hague: Junk, pp. 67–86.

Turnbull, C. 1959. 'Legends of the BaMbuti', *Journal of the Royal Anthropological Institute* 89: 45–50.

———. 1960a. 'The *Molimo*: A Men's Religious Association among the Ituri BaMbuti'. *Zaire* 14: 307–340.

———. 1960b. 'The *Elima*: a Premarital Festival among the BaMbuti Pygmies'. *Zaire* 14: 175–192.

———. 1988 [1961]. *The Forest People*. London: Triad/Paladin.

Valiente-Noailles, C. 1993. *The Kua*. Rotterdam and Brookfield: A.A. Balkema.

Verdu, P. et al. 2013. 'Sociocultural Behavior, Sex-biased Admixture and Effective Population Sizes in Central African Pygmies and non-Pygmies', *Molecular Biology and Evolution*, first published online on 7 January 2013. doi:10.1093/molbev/mss328.

Watts, I. 2005. 'Time, too, Grows on the Moon', in W. James and D. Mills (eds), *The Qualities of Time: Anthropological Approaches*. Oxford and New York: Berg, pp. 95–118.

Wood, B.M. and F.W. Marlowe. 2011. 'Dynamics of Postmarital Residence among the Hadza', *Human Nature* 22: 128–138.

Woodburn, J. 1964. 'The Social Organization of the Hadza of North Tanganyika', PhD dissertation. Cambridge: University of Cambridge.

———. 1968. 'Stability and Flexibility in Hadza Residential Groups', in R.B. Lee and I. DeVore (eds), *Man the Hunter*. Chicago: Aldine, pp. 103–110.

———. 1982a. 'Egalitarian Societies', *Man* (N.S.) 17: 431–451.

———. 1982b. 'Social Dimensions of Death in Four African Hunting and Gathering Societies', in M. Bloch and J. Parry (eds), *Death and the Regeneration of Life* Cambridge: University Press, pp. 187–210.

Zuesse, E. 1979. *Ritual Cosmos*. Athens: Ohio University Press.

Camilla Power is Senior Lecturer in Anthropology at the University of East London. Her research focus is the evolutionary emergence of symbolic culture, with cross-disciplinary perspectives from biological and social anthropology. Fieldwork with the Hadza in Tanzania has explored gender ritual and women's culture. She has previously co-edited *The Evolution of Culture* (1999, with Robin Dunbar and Chris Knight), and published numerous articles.

Chapter 8

SOUNDS IN THE NIGHT

RITUAL BELLS, THERIANTHROPES AND ELAND RELATIONS AMONG THE HADZA

Thea Skaanes

The darkness endures half of the time when one is situated close to the equator. The sun sets before 7 pm and twelve hours later it sweeps the darkness away as it nears the horizon, spreading light and heat as it travels upwards in the sky. The following night before 7 pm the cool darkness yet again finds its way and people find their comfortable places to rest. Being in a Hadza camp, the rhythm of the shifting day and night is an ordering principle that plays on the chords of difference; structures that are followed habitually in the daytime are reversed during the night. The nights have other sounds than the days; the frogs' mellow, polyphonic choir from the swamp takes over from the insistent rays of sound coming from cicadas during the day. The fires are lit around camp as the children carry burning firewood from one fire to start another. Men and women find each other again after a day spent apart and the voices are softer and breathier as the conversations arise from around the huts and gradually ebb away as mouths are fed and sleepiness flows in. The night's breezes and comfortable temperature make a break from the gendered daytime structure in which women together dig for tubers, pick berries, get firewood or water while men set out more independently for honey, go hunting or circle around the women at a distance as guardians in case of peril. The night re-establishes the family unit; night rituals extend the family with visits from the dead and therianthropes – human-animal hybrid beings.

The Hadza camp I am describing is situated at the bottom of the Kideru Hills in the Great Rift Valley of Northern Tanzania. The camp is placed at the foot of the mountains so that people could outrun wandering elephants in the steep terrain; nearby streams run down the mountain to the Yaeda swamp. A large baobab tree provides an ample supply of baobab fruit and the swamp's fertile soil quickly brings seeds disseminated by animals to sprout, supplying leguminous plants as well as gourds and edible flowers from the gourd family (*cucurbitaceæ*) to the community.

The wider area is semi-arid and strenuous to live in: during the rainy season water pours down from the surrounding mountains flooding the rivers, streams and the swamp; the dry season demonstrates dramatic fluctuations of water levels, turning the main parts of the nearby soda Lake Eyasi into a salty desert reflecting the scorching sun. The contrast between the fertile green environment after the rainy season and the windy, dry, inhospitable heat at the peak of the dry season is stunning.

This chapter addresses inter-species spiritual connections among Hadza hunter-gatherers by tracing symbolic referents of material objects used in ritual. In pointing to some aspects of the *epeme* night dance and eland hunts, we learn of the cosmological bond the Hadza share with the eland.[1] A comparative approach to hunting rituals drawn from interviews by the /Xam of the Cape in 1870s, the !Kung in the 1970s and the Hadza of today suggests traces of shared cosmological perceptions not previously acknowledged. The correlations indicate a regionally shared hunter-gatherer cosmology comprising ontological fluidity, species ambiguities and therianthropic transformation (Guenther 2015).

The Hadza have been regarded by different scholars as present-day exemplars of an archaic way of life – a living laboratory that enables empirical insights about the general human condition (Hawkes, O'Connell and Blurton Jones 1997; Marlowe et al. 2011; Hill et al. 2014). As such they have been the subject of studies of archaic man (cf Kohl-Larsen 1958); moreover, this group is reportedly supposed to lack religious beliefs (Peoples and Marlowe 2013; Woodburn 1982a). However, new research reveals considerable cosmological depth; what is more, the contours of these beliefs share remarkable resemblances to other known hunting and gathering belief systems.

The Hadza

The Hadza are semi-nomadic hunter-gatherers. A census conducted by Brian Wood in the spring of 2012 showed the total population to be relatively small, at around 1200 individuals (Pontzer et al. 2015). Despite this small population, the Hadza display remarkable cultural and linguistic resilience, still speaking Hadsane, a linguistic isolate (Sands 1998), as their primary language. There is a strong movement towards more sedentary lifestyles, primarily due to other ethnic groups settling in the area as a result of a general shortage of land, necessitating strategies for the Hadza to keep their attractive land. Although some Hadza have taken up wage labour, and a few are attending formal education in urban settings, the livelihood of approximately 300 Hadza is sustained primarily by hunting and gathering in the bush areas south and west of Lake Eyasi (Marlowe 2010: 38).

This livelihood is sustained through daily trips in the mountains and into the bush. A division of labour sharply divides the sexes. Men hunt with bow and carefully fletched arrows, some arrows being poisonous, some with metal heads, and some all-wooden arrows with sharpened points. Hunting is mostly done by men tracking game alone, but also in groups hiding in ambush at waterholes, usually on moonlight nights. Women provide the main staple foods of the camp by digging for tubers and roots with a wooden digging stick. Berries and fruits are eaten instantly, and only in some cases is a surplus of tubers, meat, honey and fruit carried back to the camp. The remarkable immediate-return system of labour, thoroughly described by James Woodburn (Woodburn 1979, 1982b, 1998), permeates the practices around provisioning and consumption.

The particular camp I am describing here consists of an old couple, the old woman's brother, a handful of their adult children and these adults' wives, husbands, and young children. I spent hours listening to the sounds of the night when I would put my one-year old daughter to sleep in the tent. The coughs coming from the grandmother's brother, short cries from tired children, a quarrel underway, men gathering around a larger fire, telling stories of how they would move and track down the prey chosen for tomorrow, snoring, and occasional laughs. But some nights every month the sounds would be different. Then I would find myself with other women singing and clapping vigorously, and we would hear the rhythmic ringing of bells tied around the ankle of a dancer stamping the ground for maximum effect. The sounds of the ritual *epeme* night dance would fill the air and change the constellations of people present at the camp.

The *Epeme* Night Dance

The *epeme* night dance is a dance for the unity, balance and restoration of the significant family ties of the people within the camp and it is performed to strengthen the cohesion of the camp in general (Woodburn 1982a: 190). In principle it is danced every month when the darkness is perforated only by the stars, sheltered from the light of the moon, which must be beneath the horizon. Not to perform the *epeme* night dance is considered dangerous (Woodburn 1982a: 190). Generally, the dance is performed at monthly intervals, when the conditions are right as aforementioned, but also after successful hunting of large game. The initiation of young men to *epeme* likewise happens after a successful hunt. This means male initiation (*maito*) is instigated by an *epeme* dance. The connection between *epeme* and prey animals is central. This was made clear to me when I asked three senior Hadza *epeme* men what *epeme* was. While I imagined the word would be infinitely polysemic and far-reaching, they answered simply: 'meat' – *manako. Epeme* is meat. The main explanation I received when asking how to understand this was that without the hunted animals there would be no *epeme*. If there would be no hunting of the large prey animals, no new members could be initiated into *epeme* and the *epeme* collective would not be reproduced, but die out. I shall explore further the implications of this carnal theme of meat, prey and hunting below.

The ritual setting is characterized by a gender divide with men and women separated by a physical barrier such as a large hut, or a cliff (Marlowe 2010). The divider should prevent people from seeing from one side to the other, but people should still be able to hear one another. The *epeme* men place themselves on one side and the women and small children on the other side of the divider.[2] This way, there are two entrances to a common dance clearing, one for the women and one for the men.

The group of initiated men, simply called *epeme* like the dance ritual, perform solo dances first in their own name, subsequently in the names of family members. The *epeme* dancer has the capacity to incarnate other family members' spirits during the ritual. The dancer's ontological identity is strikingly ambiguous in this state: he is both himself and the other beings he incarnates in an ontological entanglement (Guenther 2015; Viveiros de Castro 1998; Willerslev 2007). Initially, the dancer whistles to communicate for whom he dances and the spirit of the person then enters the dancer through his head.[3] As dancers they are the centre of attention in the ritual while the women sing, clap and dance first at the periphery, close to their entrance point, before moving gradually further inwards into the dance clearing. As a collective, the women respond to each dancer as he enters the dance clearing.

Sometimes the *epeme* dancer encounters a person seeking to be healed crouched under a rug as he enters the dance clearing. This person can be anyone among the participants – there are no onlookers. He or she is divested of any gender identity, remaining simply a person seeking the assistance of the *epeme* and the spirit-beings they incarnate in the dance. The *epeme* dancer will aid the person by blowing *kelaguko*, the healing *epeme* power substance, onto the person.

On one occasion during a dance an hour into the ritual, the dance was interrupted with a message conveyed by the *epeme* collective from the forebears or ancestors to the person who had been crouching under the rug earlier in the dance. The message was soothing and comforting: 'Everything is going to be fine! Don't worry, this will be solved!' And the women sighed in relief and cheered for this good news.

Hearing but not seeing the *epeme* ritual is an important characteristic of the ritual; this division of the senses is emphatically marked. A strong convention prohibits capturing the ritual visually through video, photographs or even through one's own eyes, which is why all fires are extinguished and no light is to be shed during the ritual. The reason the night dance is performed under moonless skies is exactly because the light from the moon would make the ritual a visual performance, a spectacle, a show, and that is to be avoided at all costs. Just before the moon rises over the horizon shining its pale light, the dance is rapidly dissolved. However, another sense is given primacy in the ritual: sound.

The individual *epeme* dancer whistles[4] before dancing; the initial whistles will summon the forebears to the dance, making it a meeting between the living and the dead, and between humans and nonhumans, which I discuss further below. The dancer wears bells tied on to one leg that are rhythmic when danced with; the women clap while vigorously and powerfully singing their multivocal and polyphonic songs; the sounds of the ritual clearly overpower the visual dimness in the dark.

The ritual demands special objects to be effective. The bells worn by the dancer mimic the sound of an animal presence, that of the eland. This presence, evoked through the ringing bells, underlines the special relationship of the Hadza with the eland. The sound of the eland walking is a distinct clicking sound. In fact, the sound comes from the eland's knees, made by the tendon. It vibrates as it slips over the carpal bone in the knee; easily heard from a distance, the sound is a signal indicating the size of a mature eland bull to competitors.[5] I will expand on the significance of the eland in order to broaden the perspective to a potential comparative analysis with cosmology of Southern African hunter-gatherer traditions.

Dancing Therianthropes

The dancer in the *epeme* night dance is transformed in performance, turning into another being while dancing. This transformation is enabled by a wide range of essentials: the darkness, the whistles, the sounds, the women's clapping and singing. In addition, mediating objects enable the man to dance in the name of a woman; the power substance *kelaguko* is used as a healing power during the dance; and ritual paraphernalia are worn or carried by the dancer.

A Hadza camp is materially dependent upon having an ostrich headdress in order to perform this important ritual.[6] The bells are equally essential, and there are examples of bells being carried from camp to camp just so that the *epeme* night dance can be performed. The bells, like the headdress, have to be traded, but they are more enduring and more easily obtained from close neighbouring groups and local markets.

So, what or who exactly is the other being that the dancer, through the *epeme* dance, transforms into? Notable metamorphosis between animal and human is taking place during the *epeme* night dance as the dancer manipulates his physical appearance, wearing the headdress, a cloak, and the bells.[7] The transformation, however, is beyond just appearance; the dancer himself transforms and becomes 'another' – an ambivalent figure both in terms of spirit (see Skaanes 2015) but also in terms of species (Guenther 2015).

From different accounts of hunting peoples, there appears to be a high degree of flexibility and adaptability in regards to human-animal relations. Mathias Guenther reports on hunting and gathering people from the Kalahari that '[they] seem untroubled mentally and emotionally by such cosmological and logical incongruities as humans merging identities with the animals of myth and veld' (1999: 227). I find this to be the case among the Hadza as well. Let us focus this investigation on one of the ritual objects used by the dancer which are part of turning the dancer into a dancing therianthrope, a cross-species between animal and human being: the high-sounding bells that are given such primacy in the dance.

The bells are presently made of iron, but before iron bells were available, other materials would most probably have been used.[8] It is not the material of the bell, rather it is the sound that is central. The iron is hammered flat and then bent into an oval shape encapsulating a small iron ball. The oval capsule is spacious and open, leaving a gap for the sound to diffuse clearly and intensely from the bell. The bells are laced onto a leather strap by a thin leather strip in order to be able to fasten it around an ankle or around the leg below the knee. In the *epeme* ritual the dancer ties the bells on the right leg. The sound of the bells fills the air during the dance, and it is often the first sound after the whistled communication (Meyer 2008) to indicate that the dancer is entering the dance clearing. The dance is performed with one leg held high and stamped into the ground for maximum bell-sound in order to mimic the clicking sound of the eland.

Figure 8.1: Bells and other *epeme* objects are stored inside the hut. Photo: courtesy of Derrick Butler.

Accounts of elands as central to cosmology and as dancing healers are found among southern African Khoisan groups. In the South African, Namibian and Botswana material the eland has a special place in mythology (cf Vinnicombe 1972; Lewis-Williams 1981; Power and Watts 1997; Guenther 1999). Keeney and Keeney (2013) record from healers' narratives how the eland is one form assumed by the shape-shifting ancestors of primordial times known by the Ju/'hoan of Botswana and Namibia as the First Creation, and in this shape they became the first dancing healers:

> In the First Creation (≠Ain≠aing≠ani), the original ancestors kept changing into different animals. Among these creatures were the eland-headed people who had hooves that made clapping sounds. They became the first dancing n/om-kxaosi or traditional doctors. None of the various kinds of animal-headed people ever became sick or died in First Creation. (Keeney and Keeney 2013: 70)

We find in this quote a reference to shape-shifting therianthropes, hybrid animal-human beings, exemplified by the eland-headed people walking with clicking sound. These were the first dancers, equivalent to *epeme* in the Hadza context of the dancing forebears and healers.[9] In Hadza myths, the description of the ancestors corresponds with these therianthropes, with animal heads and human bodies (cf Power and Watts 1997; Power 2015; and Skaanes forthcoming).

The Primacy of Eland

What are the wider implications of the above? We have the darkness, the ritual, the bells and the reference to an animal. There is nothing new in mimicking animals during a ritual, as this is reported in many other rituals among other groups, and bells are often used in rituals that take place with the cover of the night. What is new, you may ask, in my analysis?

The Hadza's special relation to the eland might be ancient but it has yet to be described in published material. We have numerous accounts of eland ritual, symbolism and myths from Khoisan groups in Southern Africa as aforementioned, but not from the Hadza. Comparing Hadza and Khoisan groups in Southern Africa is not a novel thought. Linguists have examined the relationship between the Hadza and Khoisan groups to discover whether Hadsane would indeed be an isolate or related to other click-languages in East and Southern Africa (Sands 1998; Güldemann and Vossen 2000). Geneticists have studied the groups in order to establish any genetic linkage of populations (Tishkoff et al. 2007; see Power this volume). Anthropologically, we find the primary correlations of shared hunting cultures and technology, e.g. individual hunters tracking prey using the same technology of poisoned arrows possibly dating back before 30,000 years ago (d'Errico et al. 2012). Ontological schemas pervading cosmology seem to be another sphere of cultural resilience and comparing ethnographies across time and space we also find symbolic, ontological and cosmological correlations shared between the groups. Let us turn to such ethnographic accounts.

The eland is the most pristine animal for ritual action among the Hadza. In addition to the night dancer's imitation of the sound of the eland, we find a number of other rituals where the eland is an integral part: the eland fat is poured into special gourds and reserved for ritual action and it is smeared on the *naricanda* stick when a baby girl is named (Woodburn 1970; Skaanes 2015). The finest animal to be initiated by is the eland, and when a man wants to marry he will confirm the marriage by providing an eland to the woman's parents. Hence, the eland is closely linked to ritual action and also supplies rich quantities of the cherished and ritually potent fatty meat.

In an interview, conducted primarily in Swahili, with two *epeme* men ('I' and 'Q') on the special rites connected to an eland hunt, the special spirit bond between Hadza and eland was indicated:

> I: If I would go on hunt and I had shot an eland, I could not come back to camp and say that I shot an eland. I would say I had shot a lion, *seseme*, or bells, *!'iŋgiribi*, because when the eland walks, it makes the sound of the bells. To say the eland's name, *komat*, is really bad. These are the two names used for the eland. Now if I shot it and it died right away or if I would come back to tell the older men I could not say *komat* during the night. If you say the name of the eland the older men would be very angry: 'Why are you saying the name of this animal!? This name is big! Why are you saying this name?!' and they could hit you. You have to say bells or lion. When you say it is bells or a lion, people know it is an eland and they will keep quiet. It is bad to utter the name of the eland because the poison is tiring the eland and it walks in the bush there. If you say the name it will gain strength and it will overpower the poison. Because so many times the eland has come from the Hadza spirits.
>
> ...
>
> T: The eland is very special –
> I: Very, very special! Ohohoh, I cannot even say its name. You know and if I shoot an eland with a poisonous arrow the poison enters and the shaft of the arrow falls to the ground. I cannot pick the shaft up, like I would do with any other animal. I have to go and look without picking it up, to see if there is blood and if it has been a good

shot. OK, [stating it has been a good shot] and I leave. Because the older men will ask: 'So you shot this bell?', 'Yes', 'Did you bring the shaft from the arrow?' I say: 'No, no, I watched it lying there'. 'Right, that is good. Leave it there'. The older men they will take it. If you pick the shaft up from where it is they will hit you. 'You are a complete moron! Go away with that shaft. I don't want anything to do with you! Go track the eland yourself! You are fucking around!' Yes, the older men will go on like this … So it is important to know how it is. If you did it right, then the next morning the older men will come slowly to see where the shaft fell from the arrow when it hit the eland. They say: 'Hubue!' – they make this sound. 'Hubue!' This is to say: 'Die! Now it's time to die!', they say this when they see that the shot was a nice shot. And then the older men take the shaft.

…

They do not speak, only by whispers. They get up and walk, walk and walk. The eland was tired because of the poison that was killing it. It stood still to rest. Where the eland rested the old men will rest and smoke. Twice. And walk again. Three times. The older men will say: 'Now, it will die'. They get up and they will see it. They say: 'Hubue!' this is a sound for any animal, but it is important for the eland. Three times. One man will see the eland and say to the others to go back to the shade to sit there. They will sit there. The one will take off his shoes – it is a strong animal the eland in Hadza stories! All right, the man goes to cut off the ears of the eland and bury them in the soil, then he cuts the animal's legs off. He will then bring the legs to the people waiting in the shade. They make a fire and eat the legs. The eland will swell up like a football. When they have eaten the legs the man will choose two other men to accompany him to the eland, without shoes, to butcher the eland and they see all the oil. Even though they are very excited they do not talk! If they talk the fat will disappear.

Q: And they cannot pass the head.

I: And to pass around the eland's head when it lies like it is sleeping like that is absolutely bad. They go around to butcher the meat of the eland, and when all has been cut they will call for the others waiting there to come to get pieces of meat. They will never go around the head of the eland resting there while cutting. Because if they pass around the head they get huge problems. Without doubt! They will be sick when they return to camp, and they will not be able to even consider eating the meat of the eland. Not any meat of the eland and it will be like that for a long time. Because the eland is from the Hadza spirits.

T: When you describe this, I am thinking about a dead person. Because the head of the deceased is the place where the spirit enters –

I: Yes, and to go around the head is bad. Yes, eland is like that. It is important because the eland is the sound/voice of the Hadza spirits.

…

T: So it is like a person, you cannot go around the head?

I: Yes, you cannot. Because if you go around the head you will get dreams of the dead man. And the eland is like the dead man. It is very important, that animal, for the Hadza. When the eland is shot, we will initiate three boys for *maito*, because it is a powerful animal and it has a lot of fat. Yes, it is a big story, we will not finish it now.

Q: The eland is a spirit from the Hadza spirits since ancient times.

I: The story is much richer than this, Thea, I will tell you more later. [Pauses] You know the first time a young man sees a dead eland he must take the heart of the eland and cut it to take the blood from inside the heart and paint himself here [indicates above the bridge of the nose between the eyes, on the atlas vertebra, in the cavity between the clavicles]. That is very good, now they can eat it without any problems. They will not be haunted in their dreams by the eland. If they don't do that they will cry out in their dreams and people will ask 'Why?', but it is from the spirits there. The eland comes from them. The eland is so powerful. There is no other animal like the eland.

Q: The eland is like a man of other people for Hadza.

T: It is like another person, or?

I: Yes. It is very important; it is a Hadza spirit. Now, you know the big story of the eland.

(Interview excerpt)

This is a central interview that elicits a number of significant relations to the eland. In this interview the eland is described as a Hadza spirit. The careful bodily manoeuvres around a dead person, human or nonhuman, prevent the dangers of being in friction with the dead person's spirit as it travels to and from the head of the deceased (Skaanes 2015). The young man's inability to eat the eland meat the first time he encounters the dead eland, if the heart has not been cut open to access the blood inside and to ritually transmute the blood to a substance of protective power for the young man, was uttered in a way that hinted at the same disgust as one imagines would surface if one were to be served human flesh. These ritual precautions form remarkable gestures that demonstrate the uniqueness of the eland to the Hadza and the shared spiritual capacities between them. If the body is not conducted carefully around the dead eland or a dead person and if the right rituals have not been performed, the person will suffer from agonizing dreams and distaste for the precious eland meat.

I will now turn to a comparison with the central significance of the eland in southern African Bushman cosmology. In South African rock art depictions found in the Drakensberg, the eland accounted for a striking 43 per cent of the paintings (Barnard 2010). Patricia Vinnicombe's analysis of the rock art depictions further established the symbolic preoccupation of the historical Bushmen of the area:

Another way Vinnicombe's book was influential was in its use of statistical analysis. It may seem obvious today, but the Bushman painters of the past were not merely recording what they saw. Otherwise, they would have been painting small antelope in proliferation, or lots of ordinary activities like food gathering, fire tending and so on. What is actually depicted in rock art to a much greater extent is the symbolically and ritually important eland, as well as ritual activity itself.

...

It was among the first publications to argue that Bushmen do not particularly paint what they eat, and it did so with spectacular illustrations, supportive statistics and sound reasoning. (Barnard 2010: 663)

If we compare the stories of the rituals around eland hunting provided by David Lewis-Williams and Megan Biesele (1978) with the story told in the interview above we find salient similarities. Lewis-Williams and Biesele compared !Kung material from Botswana that they had gathered themselves in 1975 with the historical accounts of the now extinct /Xam of South Africa gathered by Wilhelm Bleek and Lucy Lloyd from around 1870 on the one hand (cf Bleek 1932; Bleek and Lloyd 1870–1880) and the Lesotho stories provided by James Orpen in 1873 on the other (Orpen 1874).

Lewis-Williams and Biesele (1978) write:

The first stage of both the regular and the first-kill ritual is initiated when an arrow is shot at the eland. The !Kung arrows, like those formerly used by the southern San ... are constructed in a link-shaft principle: the poisoned point remains embedded in the animal while the reed shaft falls to the ground. The hunter advances to find the shaft and examines it to see how it has broken and whether there is blood on it. He is thus able to estimate the extent of the wound. A !Kung boy who concludes from the evidence of the shaft that he has shot his first eland does not touch the shaft as he examines it: he turns it over with the point of his bow.

...

If the boy is alone, he leaves the shaft where it has fallen. He returns to the spot on the next day with the older men who then pick up the shaft and place it in the boy's quiver. If the boy were to touch the shaft, the informants explained, the eland would not die. The /Xam hunter also avoided touching the arrow. ... [An informant told: '] The man who has shot the eland really goes off on his einen [own], and some other old man carries the quiver which contains the offending arrow'.

The hunter's return to the camp is another crucial point in the ritual. A !Kung boy who believes he has shot his first eland remains in the veld until late afternoon. During this period he lights a fire and, taking the ash, makes a circle in his forehead and a line down his nose; this represents the tuft of coarse red hair on the eland's forehead and is a visual representation of the bond which now exists between him and the wounded animal. When he enters the camp, he does not speak: the people see the mark on his forehead and know that he has shot an eland. The children are told to be quiet, because if they make a noise the eland will hear them and run far from the camp: 'the eland is a thing which has n/um, therefore if there is loud speech it will die far from the camp, especially if the children toss up dust'. ... Among the /Xam the hunter also avoided the women and stood silently on the edge of the camp until an old man, realizing that something important had happened, asked him if he had shot an eland. He replied evasively that a thorn had pricked his foot. ... 'The game knows the things we do when we are in our home ... The game is on the hunting ground, it seems to know what we are doing there'. ... In the morning the tracking of the wounded eland commences. The !Kung hunters loosen their bow strings and set out to pick up the eland's spoor. As eland sweat and the foam which comes from the mouth of a pursued eland are considered by the !Kung to possess powerful n/um, certain precautions have to be taken. The spoor must be followed obliquely ... Among the /Xam the hunter who had shot the eland did not take part in the tracking; he directed the others to the spot where the animal was shot so that they could pick up the spoor. ...

Another critical stage is reached when the eland is finally found dead. The !Kung boy who shot the eland does not approach the animal directly ... No hunter, whether young or old, may approach the dead animal with a torn loin cloth or with flaps hanging down from his loin cloth; these loose parts are tucked between the buttocks. If this were not done, the informants explained, the eland would be thin and lean and the fat would 'fall to pieces' like the leather loin cloth. Precautions regarding the eland's fat were also observed in the south. The man who had shot the eland did not approach the animal until the heart had been cut out. In the published account the text is incomplete, as the word /kɔːʃde has not been translated; as we have seen, this word is translated elsewhere as 'magic power'. The translation should, therefore, read, 'When they have cut it to pieces and cut out the heart, then he joins the men who are cutting up, after the heart is out because they are afraid that it is a thing which has magic power'. (D.F. Bleek 1932: 237) (Lewis-Williams and Biesele 1978: 124, 125–126, 127)

As we see there are salient coincidences in the accounts acquired from /Xam, !Kung, and my interviews with Hadza *epeme* men, from the 1870s, 1975 and 2013 respectively. Traversing the time and space divides we find narratives that correspond in great detail.

- We find the features of ontological entanglement (Viveiros de Castro 1998) between the hunter and the eland. Both share 'spirit' or '*n/um*' and despite the different carnal forms of the two the hunter is connected in an ontological sense to the eland as the eland is affected by the hunter's actions, words and sentiments;

- The hunter faces an own-kill taboo (Knight 1991). This is not directly in the sense that he is not to eat his own kill; however, we find it in the sense that after having shot the eland, he will have to bodily and verbally act in a deprecating way in relation to his deed. He will create and maintain distance to the eland, e.g. not touching the arrow, not pursuing the eland spoor himself, not exclaiming aloud 'I shot an eland';
- The necessity to proceed correctly performing the ritual obliquely. The mention of the heart's 'magic' or ritually potent capacity; the blood, ashes and eland fat as efficacious substances; and the dependence on the elders or the *epeme* to mediate the dangerous situation of hunting an animal that you share spirit with.

What we gain from bringing in the comparative material provided by Lewis-Williams and Biesele is a series of questions with which to supplement the Hadza material. This could point to omissions in my own material, as well as promise interesting perspectives if one were to consider the Hadza cosmological schema, eland relations and hunting rites when reviewing the extinct /Xam's accounts and rituals provided by Bleek and Lloyd, Orpen and the rock art interpretations. One of the interesting findings in this comparative work is that we see salient correlations between cosmologies of distinct groups (*pace* linguistic and genetic research findings) possibly rooting the eland in one of the oldest cosmological narratives that we know of.

Concluding Remarks

In this paper I have not tied the knot; I have not formed the narratively complacent structure of the closed circle. Instead, I have moved straight as an arrow,[10] departing from one point and not to return (cf Wasaki 1970). In this approach, the narrative pierces through a wealth of material following one trajectory and moving onwards. In this chapter I have investigated a ritual object worn during the *epeme* night dance. The methodology has been moving through the material portal of an object in order to trace just some of the references it connotes. The choice fell on one ritual object among others and in the responses to the inquiries, paths opened to be followed.

We began the investigation with the *epeme* night dance ritual. The night's darkness shields the ritual from being transparent and visually accessible. However, if the dance is not supposed to be a spectacle for the eye, the *epeme* dance is still very sensuous as an intimate, transformative and audible act with the rhythmic bells forming a lead for the women's singing and clapping. The bells mimicry of the eland indicated the potency of having an animal, here specifically eland, evoked or present during the *epeme* night dances.

Elaborate accounts of the animal aspect during dances are also found in relation to rituals performed in the Kalahari as described by Mathias Guenther:

> Being the Significant Others they are in Bushman cosmology – beings who are close to humans physically and mystically despite their otherness, beings talked about frequently, literally or metaphorically, prosaically or poetically, in everyday parlance or oral literature, beings represented through art, ritual, dance, and mimicry – it is perhaps not surprising that some humans should have the ability to assume animals' identities. The eland dance ... may be so intense and self-absorbing a ceremony that one wonders if the performer may not, at certain moments, actually feel as though he or she has transcended his or her species boundary and assumed the identity of the animal that lends its name and symbolic substance to the dance. (Guenther 1999: 79–80)

This excerpt applies as aptly to Hadza as it does to the Kalahari hunter-gatherers. The ritual dance enables an *epeme* man to transform into something else. He becomes a being that stands on the threshold between the dead and the living; during the ritual he is the medium of communication between forebears and living people, connecting primordial times with the present (Keeney and Keeney 2013). The dancer has the potency of carrying both male and female spirit; and, the dancer conflates the composite hybrid expressions and species incarnated into this therianthropic form.

The eland, as we have seen, is both in Hadza and in accounts from Southern Africa a specifically ritualized animal. I received affirmative answers to a question I asked several times to make sure that I did not misinterpret a metaphor or ambiguous wordings: do eland and Hadza share spirit? Having this confirmed on various occasions a principle is secured. Whether hunting an eland entails killing and eating an ancestor spirit or whether it is killing and eating a shared spiritual force, the hunted eland is still 'like a person'. Eating the powerful *epeme* meat of the animal with whom you share spirit entails a sense of eating your own flesh.

Guenther eloquently describes this poetic and mystical relationship between animal and human as an intersection characterized as paradoxical and irreducible, the literal and prosaic aspects coinciding with metaphoric and ambiguous playfulness of the imaginary. There is a thin, breathing membrane between the spheres of tangible and the intangible and between human and animals.

The *epeme* dancer transcends species boundaries as a hybrid, neither human nor animal, or both animal and human, a highly ambiguous figure of great power during the night dance under the moonless sky. Through the bells, *!'iŋgiribi*, that are both a euphemism, mimicry, and the very presencing feature of the eland, the dancer engages in a ritual that bends time. Ritual provides a technology for bending time that galvanizes the 'symbolic substance' and mythic narratives about standing on the threshold between the living and the dead, between species and between self and other. This position allows the hybrid dancing being to connect to the time before the origin of humans; to connect to the time of potential, power and hybridity, and to fuel the present with these powers for a strong future.

Acknowledgments

A shorter version of this paper was presented at CHaGS11, 11 September 2015 in Vienna. I would like to thank the editors for inviting me to submit that paper to this volume. It was a bold decision to include a new contribution at that time; and I am grateful that they chose to do so. A warm appreciation is due to Alan Barnard and Camilla Power for reviewing the chapter. I also want to thank my supervisor Rane Willerslev and friend and colleague Sasha Rubel for reading and commenting on the paper. Thank you all for your valuable input. And lastly, I would like to thank James Woodburn for his call for sensibility at CHaGS11. These matters are delicate and it could be harmful to rush to the field and ask people about these findings at large. Sharing of this knowledge should be deliberated on and only disclosed after careful consideration of whether this information is suited for the person in question, since sharing with those individuals who are not considered ready to receive this esoteric knowledge would be destructive to the delicate webs which make up the fabric of ritual culture among the Hadza.

Notes

1. The common eland (*Taurotragus oryx*) is the second largest antelope in the world, slightly smaller than the giant eland.
2. Note that we have a large group that would not be accommodated in this setting: all the boys who are no longer small children, the young men, and the men who have not been initiated into *epeme*, e.g. the womanly *mambu*, or men who are not considered to possess the right characteristics for *epeme* (Skaanes 2015). People who are not accommodated in the ritual must avoid it; to simply not attend is not enough, rather the whole ritual should be actively avoided, for instance, by running into the bush. So even though it is a ritual for the cohesion of the camp, we also find a strong segregation aspect played out.
3. When dancing in female family members' names, the dance will be mediated by material objects. This aspect deserves far more space than is available here, and has been described more elaborately elsewhere (Skaanes 2015).
4. James Woodburn describes the audible aspect of the dance as follows: 'After every individual dances a dialogue is held between the *epeme* dancer, who uses a special ritual whistling language used only in this context, and the women who call their affectionate greetings using the kinship term applicable to the "person" for whom that particular dance has been held' (Woodburn 1982a: 190). Whistles are used to create a language conveying messages and the ones who can decode it understand the message. I am not able to distinguish, let alone understand, the whistles used in the ritual and the whistles during daytime, e.g. calling to the honeyguide bird, or the practical whistles communicating findings over distance. There is a marked distinction between using whistles in the ritual that differentiate them from the ordinary whistles during daytime (Meyer 2008). Whistles in the dark are purely for ritual purposes; a careless whistle during night time will summon the dead spirits from Sanzako, Dundubi or Anao and without the protective measures of the ritual the whistler will face the danger of going mad.
5. Studied by zoologists, the correspondence between sound and the possible size of the eland shows the potential that sound signals have in non-vocal animal communication: 'The discovery that knee-clicks in eland honestly indicate body size reveals an unusual potential for non-vocal acoustic communication in mammals' (Bro-Jørgensen and Dabelsteen 2008).
6. The headdress is extremely powerful and difficult to obtain as ostrich feathers would normally be bought from Maasai, as there are virtually no ostriches left in the Yaeda Valley and surrounding areas. Not having the ostrich headdress can cause a long pause in the *epeme* dance rituals.
7. The symbolic connotations of the different paraphernalia and how they are invested with power is treated in more detail in my PhD dissertation (Skaanes forthcoming).

8. The same material flexibility is found in relation to glass beads that are used both mundanely and ritually, e.g. in the *maito* or *maitoko* initiation rituals. Glass beads are, like iron, a recent development in Hadza material culture; however, prior to glass beads different materials were used: flower-petals would be pasted onto the face and body as adornment, ash-paint used in the rituals, and small yellow flowers could be fastened to the ear as pretty, high-contrast ornaments. Likewise, sandals that are currently made of reused tyre-rubber or other materials figure in ritual actions, e.g. taking them off before addressing the god, putting them to face the fireplace as a precaution for other animals not being able to track a hunted animal left in the bush. These were previously made of leather (dry season) or baobab bark (rainy season) prior to the current material; in this way, the material of the objects does not seem to be indicative of the ritual's origin.

9. In the Hadza myth of Mambeta, the ancestor spirits were also described as dancing the *epeme* and having heads of different animals (Skaanes forthcoming). However, in this myth we find the story of Mambeta as the first *epeme* and the women to be the *epeme* dancers under the harsh reign of Mambeta (cf Power and Watts 1997; Power 2015; Skaanes forthcoming).

10. This formulation stems from encouraging interlocutors and friends in the field where I was urged to 'go straight as an arrow', not to linger, not to regress, not to go back, but to pursue the next step of inquiry keeping the insights gained in mind.

References

Barnard, A. 2010. Book review: Patricia Vinnicombe *People of the Eland: Rock Paintings of the Drakensberg Bushmen as a Reflection of their Life and Thought*; and Benjamin Smith (ed.), *The Eland's People: New Perspectives in the Rock Art of the Maloti-Drakensberg Bushmen. Essays in Memory of Patricia Vinnicombe, Africa* 80: 663–664. 10.3366/afr.2010.0407.

Bleek, D. 1932. 'Customs and Beliefs of the /Xam Bushmen. Part III: Game Animals', *Bantu Studies* 6: 233–249. doi: 10.1080/02561751.1932.9676285.

Bleek, W. and L. Lloyd. 1870–1880. Bleek and Lloyd notebooks. *The Digital Bleek and Lloyd.* http://lloydbleekcollection.cs.uct.ac.za/index.html.

Bro-Jørgensen, J. and T. Dabelsteen. 2008. 'Knee-clicks and Visual Traits Indicate Fighting Ability in Eland Antelopes: Multiple Messages and Back-up Signals', *BMC Biology* 6: 47. doi:10.1186/1741-7007-6-47. Online at: http://www.biomedcentral.com/1741-7007/6/47.

D'Errico, F. et al. 2012. 'Early Evidence of San Material Culture Represented by Organic Artifacts from Border Cave, South Africa', *Proceedings of the*

National Academy of Sciences (USA) 109: 13214–13219. doi: 10.1073/pnas.1204213109.

Guenther, M. 1999. *Tricksters and Trancers: Bushman Religion and Society*. Bloomington: Indiana University Press.

———. 2015. '"Therefore their Parts Resemble Humans, for They Feel that They are People". Ontological Flux in San Myth, Cosmology and Belief', *Hunter Gatherer Research* 1(3): 277–315. doi:10.3828/hgr.2015.16.

Güldemann, T. and R. Vossen. 2000. 'Khoisan', in B. Heine and D. Nurse (eds), *African Languages*. Cambridge: Cambridge University Press, pp. 99–122.

Hawkes, K., J.F. O'Connell and N. Blurton Jones. 1997. 'Hadza Women's Time Allocation, Offspring Provisioning, and the Evolution of Long Postmenopausal Life Spans', *Current Anthropology* 38: 551–577.

Hill, K.R. et al. 2014. 'Hunter-Gatherer Inter-Band Interaction Rates: Implications for Cumulative Culture', *PLoS ONE 9(7):* e102806. doi:10.1371/journal.pone.0102806.

Keeney, H. and B. Keeney. 2013. 'Reentry into First Creation. A Contextual Frame for the Ju/'hoan Bushman Performance of Puberty Rites, Storytelling, and Healing Dance', *Journal of Anthropological Research* 69: 65–86.

Knight, C. 1991. *Blood Relations. Menstruation and the Origins of Culture*. New Haven and London: Yale University Press.

Kohl-Larsen, L. 1958. *Wildbeuter in Ostafrika: Die Tindiga – ein Jäger- und Sammlervolk*. Berlin: Dietrich Reimer Verlag.

Lewis-Williams, J.D. 1981. *Believing and Seeing*. London: Academic Press.

——— and M. Biesele. 1978. 'Eland Hunting Rituals among Northern and Southern San Groups: Striking Similarities', *Africa* 48: 117–134.

Marlowe, F. 2010. *The Hadza Hunter-gatherers of Tanzania*. Berkeley, CA and London: University of California Press.

Marlowe, F. et al. 2011. 'The "Spiteful" Origins of Human Cooperation', *Proceedings of the Royal Society, B.* 278: 2159–2164. doi: 10.1098/rspb.2010.2342.

Meyer, J. 2008. 'Typology and Acoustic Strategies of Whistled Languages: Phonetic Comparison and Perceptual Cues of Whistled Vowels', *Journal of the International Phonetic Association* 38: 69–94.

Orpen, J. 1874. 'A Glimpse into the Mythology of the Maluti Bushmen', *Cape Monthly Magazine* 9: 1–13.

Peoples, H.C. and F.W. Marlowe. 2013 'Big Gods: Religion in the Beginning', *Paper presented at the Tenth Conference on Hunting and Gathering Societies (CHaGS 10)*. Liverpool University, June 2013.

Pontzer, H. et al. 2015. 'Energy Expenditure and Activity among Hadza Hunter-Gatherers', *American Journal of Human Biology* 27(5): 628–637. doi: 10.1002/ajhb.22711.

Power, C. 2015. 'Hadza Gender Rituals – *Epeme* and *Maitoko* – Considered as Counterparts', *Hunter Gatherer Research* 1: 333–358. doi:10.3828/hgr.2015.18.

————— and I. Watts. 1997. 'The Woman with the Zebra's Penis. Gender, Mutability and Performance', *Journal of the Royal Anthropological Institute* (N. S.) 3: 537–560.

Sands, B. 1998. 'The Linguistic Relationship between Hadza and Khoisan', in M. Schladt (ed.), *Language, Identity, and Conceptualization*, vol. 15, Quellen zur Khoisan Forschung. Cologne: Rudiger koppe.

Skaanes, T. 2015. 'Notes on Hadza Cosmology: *Epeme*, Objects and Rituals', *Hunter Gatherer Research* 1(2): 247–267. doi: 10.3828/hgr.2015.13.

————— (forthcoming). 'Cosmology Matters', PhD Dissertation. Aarhus University.

Tishkoff, S.A. et al. 2007. 'History of Click-Speaking Populations of Africa Inferred from mtDNA and Y Chromosome Genetic Variation', *Molecular Biology and Evolution* 24: 2180–2195. doi: 10.1093/molbev/msm155.

Vinnicombe, P. 1972. 'Myth, Motive, and Selection in Southern African Rock Art', *Africa* 42: 192–204.

Viveiros de Castro, E.B. 1998. 'Cosmological Deixis and Amerindian Perspectivism', *Journal of the Royal Anthropological Institute* 4: 469–488.

Wasaki, Y. 1970. 'On the Tribes of Mangola Village', *Kyoto University African Studies* 5: 47–80.

Willerslev, R. 2007. *Soul Hunters: Hunting, Animism, and Personhood among the Siberian Yukaghirs.* Berkeley, CA: University of California Press.

Woodburn, J. 1970. *Hunters and Gatherers. The Material Culture of the Nomadic Hadza.* London: The British Museum.

—————. 1979. 'Minimal Politics: The Political Organization of the Hadza of North Tanzania', in W. Shack and P. Cohen (eds), *Politics in Leadership. A Comparative Perspective.* Oxford: Clarendon Press, pp. 244–266.

—————. 1982a. 'Social Dimensions of Death in Four African Hunting and Gathering Societies', in M. Bloch and J. Parry (eds), *Death and the Regeneration of Life.* Cambridge: Cambridge University Press, pp. 187–210.

—————. 1982b. 'Egalitarian Societies', *Man* (N. S.) 17: 431–451.

—————. 1998. 'Sharing is Not a Form of Exchange: an Analysis of Property-sharing in Immediate-return Hunter-gatherer Societies', in C. Hann (ed.), *Property Relations: Renewing the Anthropological Tradition.* Cambridge: Cambridge University Press, pp. 48–63.

Thea Skaanes has been curator of the ethnographic UNESCO Collections at Moesgaard Museum, Denmark, since 2008. She is currently finalizing her doctoral thesis at Aarhus University. Her PhD research has been on cosmology, rituals and *epeme* among the hunter-gatherer Hadza of Northern Tanzania. Besides fieldwork among the Hadza, she has examined different ethnographic museum collections on Hadza material culture and established a Hadza collection for Moesgaard Museum.

Chapter 9

HUMAN PHYSIOLOGY, SAN SHAMANIC HEALING AND THE 'COGNITIVE REVOLUTION'

Chris Low

Introduction

Thirty years ago scholars introduced the idea of a 35,000 year-old 'Human Revolution' (Stringer 2011: 116). The idea refers to the onset of human modernity indicated by a wide range of changes in the European archaeological record, from the appearance of art, complex burials and body decorations to long-distance trade and demographic change. In the 'revolution' model these phenomena were linked to the sudden emergence in anatomically modern humans of new cognitive capacities including symbolic thought. For many scholars this arrival of symbolism further indicated the arrival of syntactical language (Henshilwood and Dubreuil 2009: 44).

Since the introduction of the 'revolution' idea, new findings in Africa have emerged, including ochre use, geometric engravings and bead use. These findings underpin the now overwhelming agreement of scholars that humans capable of symbolic thought and language emerged in Africa and not Europe, at a minimum date of 75,000 to 100,000 years ago (d'Errico and Vanhaeren 2009), which is far earlier than the date proposed in the original 'revolution' model.

Less certain is whether human species earlier than *Homo sapiens* might also have had similar cognitive abilities, have been thinking symbolically and used language (Stringer 2011: 124). Zilhão (2011), for instance, proposes that symbolic thinking and language appeared not with *H. sapiens*, some 150,000 to 200,000 years ago, but far earlier, possibly with *Homo heidelbergensis*, 500,000 years ago. In McBrearty's and Brooks' (2000) view, the notion of a revolution both downplays the richness of the African Middle Stone Age and introduces an inappropriate separation of humans from the rest of the biological world.

In the following I draw on my background in southern African San anthropology and my professional background in osteopathy, to explore certain ideas of a cognitive revolution that sit uneasily with what the San say and do. Although some have questioned the value of turning to recent hunter-gatherers to inform the past, arguments for the validity of this approach, based on continuities of subsistence strategy and biology, are now well established and convincing (Barnard 2011; Bloch 2012; Dubois 1976; Waldron 2009; Lewis-Williams and Dowson 2000).

Using the San to inform interpretation of our African origins has a long and chequered history but the increasing recognition of archaeological and genetic relationships between the San and key sites associated with modern humans, including Blombos cave and even perhaps the 'snake rock' of Botswana's Tsodilo hills (see Watts, this volume, Fig. 10.1), brings new and special ammunition to claims of their relevance (Stringer 2011: 134).

A striking feature of human origins accounts is how often the use of shell beads is read as a hallmark of the arrival of symbolic abilities, on the basis that body adornment among recent hunter-gatherers is all about attention to personal identity and conveying meaning across groups (Botha and Knight 2009; Henshilwood and d'Errico 2011; d'Errico and Vanhaeren 2009: 35; McBrearty and Brooks 2000: 521). Alternatively, as Henshilwood and Dubreuil (2009: 56–57) observe, if body adornments are not thought to have been playing a symbolic role, they are attributed with having 'only' had an aesthetic or decorative function.

Despite claims that these assumptions are based on recent hunter-gatherer use of body adornments, these ideas do not fit well with, at least, why the San wear body adornments or, in a related sense, use perfume or rub fat and colourful substances on themselves.

I suggest that it is not enough to present San and other hunter-gatherer ideas of representation and re-representation without taking into account their fundamental ontology, or understandings of how one thing is, or is not, connected to another. Moreover, it is not enough to treat aesthetic or decorative use of adornments as if these are familiar and straightforward explanations in themselves. In San contexts, meaningful things in the world are not disconnected from their source in the sort of abstract sense that symbolic body adornment implies. If San use of body adornment can tell us anything about past hunter-gatherers, it is that issues of identity and using adornments to change relationships with themselves and others is far more rooted in a sensuous engagement in the natural world than archaeologists acknowledge in their interpretations of symbolism.

This problem links to my wider concern with cognitive or symbolic revolution models, which is the implication that human beings are essentially different from other animals because our brains work symbolically. If we consider how the San and other hunter-gatherers work in nature, this suggests that human specialness is one kind of animal consciousness and that we must be careful to contextualize symbolic thinking within our wider human and animal ways of making sense of the world.

Biologists have long recognized the essential biological similarity of humans to other mammals and recent evidence finds this even in the subtle structural origins of our brain (Charvet and Striedter 2011). Furthermore, scholars recognize culture and even ritual in the animal kingdom (Winkelman 2010: 263). As we learn more about ourselves and our natural world, from the distinctly non-rational nature of our decision-making processes (Kahneman 2011) to the transglobal communication abilities of whales and problem-solving capacity of crows with their tiny brains, it is increasingly clear that, although we are undeniably unique, so too are all animals (cf Foley 1987).

So, if we are essentially animal and not super-animal, the question remains, what do we make of the evidence for a cognitive revolution? I believe this evidence does not represent the start of humanity's estrangement from nature, as revolution models imply, but it does represent an unusual absorption with our feelings and impulses and our particular type of sensory engagement with the world as human hunters and foragers.

Fossil cranial evidence indicates that the brain of *H. sapiens* did not change significantly on the outside over the time period when the human revolution was thought to have occurred. On this basis some scholars have argued that the changes in the brain that underpin the appearance of new behaviours must have been inside the brain and too anatomically subtle to be detectable in cranial evidence. From the numerous arguments proposed, those that emphasize a new role for endorphins and dopamine (Prince 1982; Previc 2009) are particularly relevant to my findings among the San, and Winkelman's (2010) related argument for the shamanic origins of the cognitive revolution is especially relevant. I suspect there is a significant link between shaking in San dancing and dopamine (Low 2015). Winkelman also makes a link between dopamine and shamanism and, furthermore, places the topic in the context of human origins.

Winkelman builds on Mithen's thesis that early *H. sapiens* had modules for social, technical and natural history intelligences and through a new integrative functioning in the brain (the revolution), thinking progressed from protosymbolic to fully symbolic and abstract thought (Mithen 1996: 154; and see Ellen, this volume). Mithen pins the new integration of the brain on the arrival of language. By contrast, Winkelman pins cognitive change on the emergence and proliferation of shamanic dancing.

Winkelman's thesis is based on the 'false stress hypothesis', in which shamanic dances are contexts where shamans induce stressful scenarios and then work with the physiological responses that follow. Winkelman highlights a key role for endorphins and dopamine in shamanic rituals, in feelings of ecstasy, flying and benevolence, to feelings of disassociation. He argues that early shamanic rituals held largely social benefits for communities and hence became positively selected for in evolution and this propagated a new kind of symbolic thinking.

Winkelman's linking of false stress to shamanic dancing fits exceptionally well with my independent attempts to understand ecstatic shaking in San dancing. What I find difficult in Winkelman's argument is that, despite his phenomenologically informed discussion of the neurochemical, social and evolutionary basis of ritual (Winkelman 2010: 231–266), he downplays the essential role of feelings in making and working with knowledge, and he does so because his cognitive evolutionary model separates feelings from thought. For Winkelman (2010: 262), 'our knowledge of the external world is limited to the representations produced within our brains'. I suggest that his account of how a cognitive revolution 'rewires' poorly related modules of the brain fails to capture the intrinsic role of the body and feelings in making and using knowledge. His cognitive model thereby supports the idea of a new and exceptional kind of human intelligence. It pushes us out of the animal kingdom and opens the path for the subjugation of nature and Cartesian separation from nature, with all the moral and environmental implications this holds.

Alternatively, the new hunter-gatherer behaviours suggested by the archaeological evidence of the human revolution seem to me to represent outputs of a fluid intelligence, not tightly pinned to language, that is developing in contexts of human hunting and foraging skills, an increasing absorption with feelings and increasing attention being paid to the knowledge and changes that feelings bring.

It is only in recent years that feelings and the internal processes of what people do and say have become a legitimate field of anthropological enquiry. Bloch (2012: 150) attributes this position to the blinkered cultural dominance of the Boasian intellectual legacy. But, despite Bloch supporting work that examines how we learn, store and use information, he also criticizes much anthropology that seeks to address these issues through 'practice' and embodiment theory because, as he rightly observes, all too often discussion of 'habitus' and embodiment remains remarkably vague and empty. As a solution Bloch advocates that anthropologists build their theories on firm neuroscientific foundations (Bloch 2012: 146–151). It is notable, however, that despite Bloch's call to, literally, flesh out embodiment theory, his biological emphasis remains on what happens in the brain. At the same time he gives little reference to an actual neurological model that supports the sort of embodied theory he is describing.

In the following I begin by presenting details of a relatively new model of cognition, grounded cognition theory, that seems best placed to capture the sort of mind-body relationship that anthropological embodiment theories require. I then go on to consider San healing dances and body adornment, in terms of how the San, like other hunter-gatherers, are highly attuned to their external environment and their internal feelings.

Working with San ethnography highlights a key role for feelings in the making and using of knowledge. What the San experience as hunter-gatherers is, not surprisingly, essential to how they heal, wear body adornments and to everything else they do and think. My aim is to locate a San perspective within a wider account of what makes us human, which pulls together scientific, osteopathic and anthropological insights of who we all are, as more or less recent hunter-gatherers. I emphasize that much of what we do, even at the highest levels of performance, is not necessarily related to 'symbolic' thinking – whatever that is – but comes from sensuous, yet nonetheless concrete, ways of working in the world.

My argument supports an origins theory that recognizes the extraordinary skills of early human species for survival. I believe that something special did happen in our evolution that pushed us down a distinctive trajectory but, rather than think of this in terms of the arrival of something new, an abstract symbolic mental capacity, we might better understand who we are by recognizing this as a shift in our sensuous orientation in the world.

I am not arguing that abstract symbols as found in language and wider representation do not exist, but that even our predilection for abstraction and coding speaks of an absorption with meaning and metaphor, and feeling our way towards hidden realities. Far from this self-absorption elevating us from the animal world, it confirms that we belong – a position that brings its own responsibilities. From the San perspective, what seems crucial is that paying close attention to their senses teaches them that nothing can exist unconnected to anything else or exist without being in relationship. The way in which those relationships are recognized and worked with is essentially sensuous, even at the heart of their cognitive processes, which are, of course, fundamentally identical to all of ours.

In his comparison of ancient Greek and Chinese medicine, Kuriyama (2002) argues that different ways of sensing the world generate different types of knowledge. This suggests that careful thinking is required with models of cognitive revolution that link symbolisms to a 'release from proximity' (Stringer 2011: 116; Gamble 1998).

A particular problem I see for theories of a Middle Stone Age symbolic revolution is that the core of being a hunter-gatherer lies in working with signs of things that are not there. Far from a release from proximity coming at a late stage in human evolution, it was surely inherent in the first moment hominins followed their feelings towards resources they could not directly perceive and the first time they observed their own footprints. Over time, visually following footprints and other clues towards resources became our animal speciality. This special animal skill unfolded as something inherently metaphorical, mimetic, empathetic and empirically rooted.

Hunting revolves around that fundamental metaphorical difference, prey or not prey, and an animal track brings a new dimension to this – the animal is there and not there in a similar but far more poignant and critical manner than any Tylorian dream vision or vaguer feeling. Spoor can tell you real things about the animal at the end of the tracks – is it big, female, pregnant, hungry or afraid? But the animal is not there. The animal is in a different space and time – how long ago, how far? And where is the injured animal? How long to travel there? To follow the saliva, the urine, the smell, drops of blood, the noise, the broken grass, the dislodged stone? How long will my spear shot take to kill that animal, the strong male one I have seen many times?

It may therefore be that the significant changes that lie behind the emergence of modern society lie not in the arrival of symbolism, which seems intrinsically bound up in hunter-gatherer experience and ideas of relationship, but in a new type of symbolism, related to new modes of perception. I do not see this as a cognitive shift from proto-metaphor and symbols to 'real' metaphor and symbols as some scholars have proposed (Stringer 2011: 210–211; Winkelman 2010: 98–99). This seems to me a confusing movement from one kind of 'same but different' metaphorical and symbolic knowledge of the world to another, which ultimately wants to say one kind of metaphor is more real, from our Western academic perspective, than another. What changes is the link between how the world is experienced, how those feelings are worked with and how the world is, literally, made sense of. Reading animal tracks entails interpreting the world, from weather to stratigraphy and ethology (Liebenberg 1990). When did it last rain? How much wind has there been? What is the soil type? Was the animal going to a regular midday shady spot? Where is the food the animal will eat? Is that food there at this time of year? But despite all this, if you ask a San person how they track, they will tell you they just follow the tracks – that is unless you push them towards thinking about something the performance of which they do not normally think about. For San trackers the vast majority of their analysis is felt and unspoken. Yet, at the same time many hunters go out in small groups and a lively discussion ensues when tracks and signs become unclear.

It could be argued that tracking does not deal in symbols but in signs, but teasing out the difference and implications of this distinction is far from easy. The measure of a good tracker lies in what sort of phenomena they can bring into the equation, from footprints to tiny smelly animal secretions on grass stalks to memories of recent weather patterns. I suspect most San do not ask why a sign is a sign of something, they just know that it goes together with what they are interested in. Tracking, then, at least deals in levels of abstraction and conceptions of time, so these aspects of symbolism should not be seen as something exclusive to symbolism. And, if the arbitrary nature of a symbol is what defines it, then how does this differ from something that just tells you about something else and this information is remembered and shared? Trackers have to learn what signs mean just as much as we all have to learn what symbols mean. The point seems to be that different sorts of relationships are learnt in different ways and some are more obvious or important than others.

In terms of scholars who argue for a progression from proto-symbolism to true symbolism, it is also worth recognizing that a sign is a 'there' or 'not there' phenomenon; there are not degrees of signs, although there may be degrees of uncertainty as to whether the sign is a sign. As a symbol is also a thing of a known relationship, surely a symbol is also, therefore, either a thing that is known or it is something not perceived at all.

With these various themes in mind, from body adornment to tracking skills, the 'Human Revolution' seems less a movement towards the symbolic and away from the animal world of emotion and sensitivity, and more a movement into a particular kind of sensitivity, perhaps even what amounts to an addiction to physiological reward mechanisms tied to an insatiable curiosity.

Much of the archaeological evidence at the heart of the cognitive revolution, from red ochre to glittering haematite, flourishing art practices, making music or even making nets, seems as much about sensual engagement as intellectual engagement. While intention and preparation are part of creativity, the other part is following urges to pick something up and hold it, rub it, draw with it and discover what comes out. In the case of the earliest rock art, the artists of Chauvet and other sites were surely following urges and exploring their sensory, imaginative, remembered and creative world, as much as deliberately covering surfaces with symbolic meaning. Even for the most technical of modern artists the process of art is one rooted in feelings of discovery and reward and carried out with a less than conscious, highly skilled, flow of performance. It is the physiological role of this performance and feelings that I now wish to focus on and track down.

Cognitive Theory and Being 'In the Mood'

It is not surprising that there is a close connection between archaeological models of a cognitive revolution and theories of brain function that have been in circulation over recent and not so recent decades. It is also not surprising that, given the difficulties of interdisciplinarity, there have been recent changes in neuroscience that have not filtered through evenly to archaeology and anthropology. In the following I outline a theory of brain function, called 'grounded cognition theory', that seems to capture the sort of embodied neuroscience that Bloch is calling for. Grounded cognition theory also provides a neuroscientific model for human origins accounts that emphasize long-term gradual change, rather than a 'eureka'-like moment. The theory also avoids the estrangement from nature that is inherent in accounts of a cognitive revolution that depend upon a movement from isolated brain modules to fully integrated modules, or a movement from animal-like awareness to human, fully symbolic and abstract thought.

In recent years the psychologists Barsalou and Kiefer have emerged as leading proponents of grounded cognition theory. Barsalou and Kiefer propose that the human cognitive system is not comprised of concepts as amodal mental entities or sensory information transformed into a common abstract representational format. Instead, the conceptual system is grounded in a) sensory modalities; b) the body and action; c) the physical environment; and d) the social environment (Kiefer and Barsalou 2013: 381–389). This multi-component grounding of cognition involves a central role for the body and senses in how we think.

In contrast to classic theories in which the brain captures representations of modal states, in grounded cognition models, the brain directly captures states of relevant modal systems. These become 'integrated over time using associative mechanisms'. 'As internal states of emotion, interoception and mentalizing occur, attentional and associative mechanisms integrate them into conceptual structures' (Kiefer and Barsalou 2013: 385). The heart of grounded cognition lies in recognizing that the sensory and motor systems play a fundamental role in learning and knowing as well as doing. Concepts are held not in abstraction but in bodily states. Bodily states, including 'facial expressions and postures, causally affect cognition' and 'cognition in turn affects bodily states' (Kiefer and Barsalou 2013: 381). In grounded cognition different combinations of modal information, including emotions, change the way information is perceived. In other words, how you feel and perceive alters what you learn. Furthermore, to perform action requires processing and enacting previous modal sensory-motor states: thus skilled making and doing depends not just on muscle memory but on 'getting in the mood'.

Grounded cognition gives a cognitive basis to kinaesthetic and theoretical accounts of body-based, and emotion-related, cognition (Downey 2002; Daniel 2005). Furthermore, it gives a neurological basis to recent work by Gieser, an anthropologist who builds on Ingold (2000) and Milton (2002) to highlight the role of emotion and empathy in perception, knowledge-making and performance. Gieser (2008) suggests that mimesis is more than just replication of actions but involves a situated taking on of the mood of the person undertaking a task, as represented in their body use and mental disposition. In this way mimesis is a learning process that carries information and culture. Gieser observes: 'we develop a feeling for which movements bring us closer to success and which do not' (Gieser 2008: 307). This reminds me of the remarkably stylized way in which San hunters crouch down and hold their head and bow at an angle as they draw

Figure 9.1: Three San hunters. Note the way they tilt their heads and lean into the bow. San hunters all over the Kalahari adopt very similar positions when using their bows.

Figure 9.1a: Ju/'hoan San hunter, Nyae Nyae 2014. Photo courtesy of Ben Cole.

Figure 9.1b: Ju/'hoan San hunter, 'Hereroland' 1987. Photo courtesy of Paul Weinberg; **Figure 9.1c**: 'Kneeling man with bow', early 1900s San. Reproduced with kind permission from UCT Libraries: Special Collections, BC 151 The Bleek Collection, album J2.1.

the string, poised to release the arrow, or equally of the particular way San healers peer into the body to check that the potency inside is lying in the right manner.

In the photographs above we see three San from different San groups in different places at different times. Despite these differences it is hard to miss the remarkable similarity in the way they hold themselves in relation to the bow and arrow. What these pictures do not represent are San who have been formally instructed in bow use. For these San being a good hunter is about their posture, their mood and 'doing things nicely' (Low 2014: 357). This phrase is a translation offered by San translators working across San languages and dialects when explaining the processes behind many skilled San practices or endeavours. It reminds us that wearing body adornments as decoration is related to aesthetics and that aesthetics in turn relates to working with the world in ways that bring the results you desire and value.

'Doing things nicely' means bringing to bear the body positions and mind states that make things work, like looking calmly for the right woods and then making fire. It entails applying yourself to critical tasks with absolute relaxed commitment; or moving in a particular way when hunting a particular animal; raising the bow, tilting your head, as you have seen the successful hunters work. One San hunter described how deciding where to sleep in the bush boiled down to 'what feels right'. Understanding the implications in such phrases adds the sort of details Bloch requires for his fleshing out of what embodiment means. Knowledge is stored, worked with and communicated in the performance.

San Healing Dances and the 'False Stress' Hypothesis

My kinaesthetic engagement with San dancers has led me to three conclusions. Firstly, San healers are highly skilled at inducing not only specific physical responses in themselves and others but specific sorts of feelings that go with these experiences. Secondly, replicating stress and inducing physiological stress responses seems to lie behind the shaking that healers utilize and the feelings that result. Thirdly, in the healing dance San healers work with the same habits of 'listening' that they use as part of their hunting and foraging lives.

San healing dances focus on shaking (Keeney 2007), set within wider contexts of extreme psychosomatic stimulation. Healers typically dance for hours at night around a fire, to the polyphonic yodel-like singing of a group of San women. The singing is hypnotically regular but interspersed by voices that suddenly drop in and out, pulling attention away from the hypnotic train. The shamans' dancing involves a highly rhythmic shuffle, punctuated by short sharp stamps on the ground, the shocking thud of which resonates through the dancer. The rhythm of the thud is exaggerated by the noise of moth cocoon rattles strapped to their ankles. While shuffling and stomping, healers set their legs and torsos into patterns of incessant shaking with their hands trembling. The shaking and dancing warms up their abdomen and wakes up their internal healing potency.

The process of becoming a healer integrates the imaginative and cosmological world of the San with stylized ways of moving, thinking and performing like other healers. Set within San knowledge, folklore and ontology, the feelings that healers encourage in themselves and one another are interpreted as divine healing potency that 'wakes up' in their bodies. This potency is called *n/om* among the Ju/'hoansi and is known by other names among other groups. When a healer's potency is fully boiled healers typically experience an orgasmic-like explosion in their heads and often fall over. Helpers then massage them back to their feet, at which point they start to heal those gathered at the dance. Healers do this by placing their hands, or another part of their body, on a person, and putting in invisible arrows (thorns) of healing potency and pulling out sickness. Sickness is conceived or physically manifested in different ways, from invisible arrows to small stones. Healers throw the removed sickness away from the gathering, into the darkness.

The San healing dance is an egalitarian performance in which potency is shared and healers are 'opened'. A dance can involve all manner of procedures that shock the body and mind into a hyperexcitable and vulnerable state, such as fragrant plants being rubbed on the body or set alight and wafted under the nose, or a healer being swatted with animal tails, poked, rubbed and chopped in small 'karate'-like hand movements, threatened with burning stumps searing the torso, or having healers surprise you with a sharp breath blow in your ears or vigorous rubbing of their sweat over your face and body.

In the dance precise parts of a healer's body are stimulated. Much of a healer's intent is to encourage the body to shake by remapping and hyperstimulating muscle and nerve relationships. In a number of dances it became clear to me that my intense shaking was reminding my body of fear but then, as the dance progressed, the fear gave way to strong feelings of power and empathy. These cycles fit firmly within the false stress hypothesis developed by Winkelman, alongside wider interpretations of ecstatic dancing (Low 2015; Fuller 2008: 118).

As the false stress hypothesis proposes, the San healing dance replicates and works with physiological mechanisms associated with hunter-gatherer lifestyles. It does this in two key ways. Firstly, there is fear and shock which links to anxiety states and enhanced excitability and pattern-seeking behaviour. Secondly, there are the feelings of euphoria, empathy, disassociation and entry into imaginative realms and altered states of consciousness. These feelings are akin to, and overlap with, ideas found all over the world of welcoming in the spirit or love of god (Keeney 2003). The potency that healers work with are the feelings and changes in interoception and body function they induce by pushing the body towards exhaustion, at which point the protective and recuperative task-solving mechanisms kick in. The potency they circulate, the invisible arrows they fire and the sickness they remove, are all known because they are experienced.

The two poles of San dancing, fear and empathic euphoria, relate to hyperstimulation of the sympathetic nervous system leading to hyperstimulation of the parasympathetic nervous system. By stimulating the body in ways that simulate stress responses, shamans experience 'false' or learned stress that results in sweating, heat, increased heart rate and breathing, disorientation, hypervigilance and hypersensitivity alongside hallucinations and physical collapse. The overload induces a range of physiological mechanisms that favour goal-oriented success, including pain blocking, and feelings of renewed vigour, exhilaration and euphoria. (Winkelman 2010: 259).

The key to the false stress hypothesis is the limbic system that consists of the hypothalamus, amygdala, hippocampus and limbic cortex. The limbic system regulates the autonomic nervous system and endocrine function. It is principally concerned with self-preservation and species preservation and is intimately connected to emotional stimuli (Swenson 2006). Sapolsky (2004: 336) recognizes 'the cornerstones of psychological stress' as lack of control and predictability that turns on the sympathetic nervous system, stimulates the release of glucocorticoids and mobilizes dopamine. Drawing on Previc (2009), Winkelman singles out dopamine as key to understanding shamanism and shifts of consciousness (Winkelman 2010: 27–28).

The dopamine/serotonin balance seems to hold the key to the progressions from fear to empathy and ecstasy that San and other shamanic dancers cycle through. Excess dopamine from disinhibition of the serotonin-dampening mechanism encourages altered states of consciousness and profound feelings of detachment. Although details remain unclear, dopamine action also seems to release endogenous opioids, norepinephrine and oxytocin, which have a painkilling effect and affect levels of emotional arousal, social empathy and social warmth. The opioids, which include endorphins, are released in response to extreme physical activity, such as a prolonged healing dance or running in a San hunt. Dopamine is released most when cycles of anticipation build up but the reward is not guaranteed and the situation is novel, unsure and 'edgy', just as in a hunt and a healing dance (Winkelman 2010: 27–29; Sapolsky 2004: 340).

The shaking that San healers encourage develops as a form of tremor that seems to relate to stress tremor and manifests as induced clonus – rhythmic involuntary muscular contractions and relaxations. Alongside inducing tremor, healers encourage spasmodic contractions of the abdomen. This results in abdominal pain and brings changes in respiration which are again associated with stress.

The false stress scenario relates strongly to fear. Key components of fear concern how we learn, the role emotion plays in this and the increased perceptivity and sensitivity that accompanies it. These phenomena are all thought to relate to the amygdala. The amygdala is associated with vigilance, anxiety and emotion. If the amygdala responds to a stimulus, the event becomes an aspect of memory and conditioned learning which in turn determines motor or performative response when the stimulus is encountered in the future (Davis and Whalen 2001). Sapolsky additionally observes that if an initial stimulus is accompanied by a further stimulus, that further stimulus can also trigger 'conditioned' fear (Sapolsky 2004: 320).

With the role of the amygdala in mind, the training of a San dancer becomes a process of learning conditioned fear, and entering 'into the mood' of the dance constitutes inducing a learnt anxiety that leads to a conditioned autonomic response. Moreover, given that stress and glucocorticoids make amygdala synapses more excitable and the neurons grow more connections, it also becomes apparent why experienced healers can trigger their healing states with less and less need to dance and less use of elaborate triggers than those needed by novice healers.

The function of the amygdala reveals the interwoven nature of fear and vigilance. As in dopamine activity, the amygdala becomes especially activated in conditions of uncertainty and ambiguity, such as those achieved in San dances and wider hunter-gatherer life. And in ways that relate both to hunting and healing, the amygdala seems especially involved in hypervigilance. In Western contexts hypervigilance may be interpreted as an anxiety disorder (Davis and Whalen 2001: 27).

An increased startle response is a biomedical sign of anxiety disorders that is linked to the amygdala (Sapolsky 2004: 323). The San place a strong emphasis on shock as a way of boiling healing potency. Shock also underpins San explanations of how potency and sickness are moved in and out of the body by healers, and how sickness enters the body from the environment, such as the penetrating shock of a snake encounter. San dance is therefore a way of working with awareness, shock and the startle response.

A further striking feature of San dances is the emphasis placed on smell, not just as a way of opening the body and awakening memories in the body, mind and emotions, but as a tool for detecting sickness. The mammalian limbic system is closely connected to the olfactory system and the human amygdala plays an important role in processing aversive olfactory stimuli and the transduction of neural signals from smells into emotional responses (Zald and Pardo 1997). The San have learnt how to work with increasing olfactory sensitivity, such that this key survival sense has becomes a diagnostic tool. But more than this, certain San groups not only smell sickness in people, they sniff sickness out of them.

The way the healing dance is described by the San reveals traits common to us all, of using the familiar to explain the unfamiliar. Accordingly, when a healer points and fires 'potency' and induces a shock reaction in another healer the mechanism is thought of as a familiar arrow. Similarly, sharp pains in the body are described using ideas of arrows, thorns or nails; healing potency 'boils' like steam; and healers 'ripen' like fruit. These are metaphors based on experience (Lakoff and Johnson 1980; and see Smith and Hoefler, this volume) that hold relational realities for the San.

Habits of Listening

Lewis observes that hunter-gatherer Mbendjele forest dwelling Pygmies cultivate their listening skills and attentiveness (Lewis 2009: 239). Like the San, these Pygmies live in environments where they have to be resourceful and alert. They operate in a constant subconscious state of attentiveness through which they process the opportunities, dangers and trajectories of their environment. Similar dispositions of attentiveness are frequently recorded in hunter-gatherer ethnography (Berman 2000: 8). Ingold (2000, building on

Gibson 1979) and Brody (1981: 43) describe this respectively as an 'education of attention' and a state of 'attentive waiting'. Elsewhere I have described this as a 'listening disposition' because it is listening with all the senses but in a habitual passive state. The body is calm but aware and poised, ready to respond.

In osteopathic college we were taught a similar listening skill that involved placing our hands on a patient and waiting for their body to 'talk to us'. We learnt to remove our attention from our hands by asking ourselves, 'what is this body trying to tell me?' I believe this question captures the unspoken disposition of many hunter-gatherers and others who are living close to critical margins. In such environments attaching meaning to things and events that outsiders might barely notice is part of their 'making sense' of the world. It is a state of mind and body that aligns with San ideas of being receptive and, in healing contexts, being open.

'Being open' is a receptive and creative condition but also one of uninhibited performance. Open performance entails absolute focus with 'an empty mind' that in popular culture is often referred to as being 'in the zone' or 'in the flow'. It is the space when anyone, from a mathematician to an extreme skier, operates without self-conscious thought. When thought cuts in, the physical performance, or 'train of thought', goes and the performance falters. Virginia Woolf links similar feelings to peak creativity when she speaks of the non-linguistic rhythm that is felt when writing, which must be caught and changed into words (Woolf 1977: 247).

Among San an opened dancer is powerful and spontaneous. A San hunter also enters a similar open zone of absolute unthinking commitment. This allows peak performance in tracking, running or firing his bow. Learning how to do this is not through formal teaching but by an apprenticeship of watching and doing. As Bloch observes, such performance requires 'fast and fluent' access to knowledge and 'the actor does not necessarily know that she knows nor what she knows, nor how she has acquired her knowledge' (Bloch 2012: 192–193).

It is this sort of high-level, unconscious performance that I suspect lies behind much of the evolutionary history of humankind. Even if we do not identify a swift revolution we still need to account for new behaviours. I question whether these represent new capacity for abstract thought and symbolism or whether we are seeing the products of metaphors based on experiential realities, 'open performance', plus creativity, plus a growing addiction to feeling.

Metaphor and Body Adornment

Winkelman suggests that it is easy to distinguish between the intentional re-enactment of mimesis and the involuntary nature of mimicry. The distinction is significant because he reads intentionality as 'a uniquely prelinguistic level of symbolization' (Winkelman 2010: 103). But how often are we clear of our intentions and should we be reading such clarity of consciousness back into the past? Moreover, where would we fit the postures of our San bowmen in this polarity?

San relationships with knowledge fit well with Gardner's (1966) conception of hunter-gatherer 'memorate' knowledge. Key characteristics of San knowledge are as follows: their oral culture permits much flexibility in people's ideas and thinking; they place great emphasis on personal experience and feelings; as they are fiercely egalitarian, their knowledge is not clearly associated with authority; they demonstrate a lack of distinction between the sacred and everyday – holding 'facts about things and facts about spirits' (Berman 2000: 233); and there is a porosity perceived between people and wider nature wherein one phenomenon or object can hold the essence of another and sometimes transform into it, such as a shaman turning into an animal.

Bloch observes that many concepts, particularly including natural kinds, are represented in the mind as 'essence'. He asserts that the nature of these essences is overwhelmingly of an unknowable *a priori* nature that is 'inaccessible to the consciousness of those whose minds operate with them' (Bloch 2012: 168). Yet we find that among the San the essence is both knowable, through experience, and worked with.

In San thinking, each aspect of the world is given its nature, or type, by god. Depending on context, this equates to giving a gift of breath, wind, smell or spirit. This essence holds the characteristics that different animal species and individual people have. In the healing dance all that a healer is, their essence, is held in their sweat. Healers smear their sweat on one another and on 'patients' to transfer their healing essence. In wider contexts the smell of people and animals holds their essence. As smells travel as 'winds', San know that the wind of certain people and animals can travel into them. Winds lodge inside them as a gift or ability, or a sickness.

The idea of essences lies behind San wearing body adornments. To wear a part of an animal is to take in, in a sense of kinship, the essence and powers or qualities of that animal. Hence strong eland antelope necklaces are given to children to wear, to make them strong. Similarly, ostrich eggshell beads are worn to bestow the qualities of the ostrich:

ostriches seldom appear sick, they sit unprotected under a relentless sun, their white eggs stand out like the sun, their necks are strong, their legs make them appear like humans at a distance, their eggs are vital water containers. All these are reasons why ostrich eggshell beads are worn. Sometimes, however, they are worn because they look nice.

In purportedly straightforward claims of beads worn as decoration, San thinking suggests we should tread carefully. If something 'looks nice', it means that it holds a power in the world, rooted in its essence and flowing potency – the power body adornment holds that makes people notice it and respond. Similarly, perfume is more than just smelly decoration, it attracts and repulses with potentially profound consequences. Life in the bush is so intimately related to the consequences of getting smells and winds right that for the San assessing these phenomena becomes 'second nature'.

Ideas of body adornment being symbolic do not represent San relationships with body adornment. San practice is better understood by notions of essence and metaphor. To the San a tiny part of an animal can hold the essence of the whole animal. Even something metaphorically related holds the essence of the 'absent' relative. The danger of thinking through symbols, at least in San contexts, lies in thinking there is no 'real' connection in a symbol. If there is no real connection then a symbol becomes more abstract, to the point where San are no longer working with realities. When working in the healing office, San are then seen, not like scientists at a job of work, but as 'others' working in rituals and rites bound up in hazy religious untruths or, at best, inaccurate 'proto-science'.

Life teaches the San what things go together. This is part of their pattern-reading proclivity that operates with imagination and without the constraints and possibilities of scientific knowledge. Hence, millipedes come out with the rain, so millipedes have a relationship with the rain. Babies born in different types of weather have a relationship with that weather. Having this relationship sets up a measure of influence and control between the two agents. Agamid lizards that look towards the rain before it comes are, accordingly, known to 'call the rain', and people who were born in storms can influence storms. In San contexts these relationships amount to metaphorical relationships that are rooted in real relational realities. San beliefs about the flowing nature of essence underpin the knowledge that one thing can be another despite external appearances. What counts is what is inside and outside, and inside there can be all sorts of different essences, from shamanic lion power to skill at dancing.

Conclusion

There are two primary problems I see with ideas of a cognitive revolution. The first is that scholars have argued for a cognitive shift based upon a new and different kind of thinking emerging. This amounts to a shift from a more basic animal-like intelligence to human capacity for abstract thought. Although only implicit, this provides an inappropriate framework for human beings stepping out of their natural home in the world.

The second and related problem with 'revolution' models is that they play down a non-linguistic way of performing and thinking that is learnt primarily through doing and remains poorly understood. I have tried to capture this through ideas of being in the flow and feelings for doing things nicely and properly and being in the right mood. Another way of understanding this is to try and think without feeling a running commentary of words inside ourselves, probably in our head and throat region. This non-linguistic, more sensuous thinking enables us to think, act and be 'in-spired', and it is this sort of thinking that I suspect underpinned the performance of early *H. sapiens* and even earlier hominins. As European cultures became increasingly literate and writing emerged, and then silent reading followed in the late Middle Ages, Western thinking has become more word-based in ways that draw our attention away from the outside natural world (Abram 2010: 179).

It is hard to deny that humankind has achieved something new on our planet, but how unnatural can this be? Few would argue that we are not natural but, as Bloch (2012: 19) observes, anthropologists are highly reluctant to talk of our animal nature because it 'threatens the very *raison d'être*' of anthropology, which assumes the uniqueness of *H. sapiens*. Abrams (2010) links writing to estrangement from sensuous language and ultimately our estrangement from the outside world, as we become increasingly self-absorbed. Looking at the San healing dance in the context of our evolution suggests similar ideas of humans becoming exceptionally absorbed with ourselves.

My linking of the San healing dance to a physiology of stress has highlighted a particular sort of relationship we humans have with our bodies that is essential to who we are and, significantly, who we are becoming. I suggest that our origins as hunter-gatherers involved surviving in contexts that were highly stressful and our success relied upon developing strong physiological coping mechanisms, including feelings of anticipation, reward, hope and euphoria. These coping mechanisms are insatiable because they are rooted in searching.

Because of our origins it is, accordingly, part of us to be absorbed in our feelings of curiosity. At the same time our particular hunting and gathering evolution has involved a special kind of intent 'listening' which is directed externally and internally. Our ancestors were particularly inclined to listen to their feelings as they tracked down and made sense of the world. As humans we are specialists at tracking down resources and working with patterns, connections, signs and metaphors.

Our human propensity to track resources down and work with our feelings makes us specialists but, far from this way of being removing us from the animal world, it asserts our belonging within the natural world. Grounded cognition theory provides a cognitive model that supports this essential sensuous entanglement in the world far better than amodal cognitive models which suggest that we can somehow work with abstract representations, removed from immediate reality.

Gieser (2008) highlights the central roles of the body, emotion and mood in learning and doing. His research indicates that doing things in the right way is as much about mental mood and performance as conscious intentionality. This broader perspective gives us the sort of physiological background that Bloch feels is missing from embodiment theory. But we can go a step further than Bloch's focus on the nervous system. The fascia is the 'soft tissue component of the connective tissue system that permeates the human body' (Schleip et al. 2012: xvii). Reflecting wider research, Van der Wal recognizes fascia as 'a body-wide mechanosensitive signalling system with an integrating function analogous to that of the nervous system' (van der Wal 2012: 81). Osteopaths have been working with fascia for decades and San for probably thousands of years. In future years I see fascia taking a place at the heart of embodiment and practice theory.

Biesele observes that the San sometimes use metaphors in their speech up to four times removed (Biesele 1993: 25). This propensity for abstraction is revealing. It reveals not only the webs of relationships perceived by the San but a need to work with the world and its relationships with care. Divinities and people have different names because some contexts need to be approached carefully, such as when a community member makes an impressive kill and must share the meat. For the San, as for us, there is no other way of working in the world than through the relationships they know. These are relationships that are experienced and they are complex relationships because the San must be sensitive to one another and their wider environment. That the San are here is testament to the efficacy of their knowledge and practice.

If we look at the past through the example of recent hunter-gatherers, the essence of being human lies in being exceptionally curious, imaginative, creative and practical. This is also our current ecological niche and we arrived here through our animal histories as hunters and foragers, as trackers driven by feelings to achieve. I once asked a San hunter what makes a good tracker. He replied: 'when you are hungry'. Perhaps we should not forget the simple realities.

Our very distant ancestors performed with an aesthetic intelligence rooted in feelings for what is right. To say that a static archaeological record, like that found in phases of the pre 'revolution' Stone Age, equates to creative and intellectual doldrums is to mistake progress for evolution, the latter being nothing more than change into which we read direction. Hunter-gatherers know you do not waste time and amplify risk by changing something unless you really have to. Perhaps the only real evolutionary direction is entropy change and our frenetic predilection for change is part of this process. Then, the problem-solving of crows is another expression of nature performing with its own entropic 'intelligence'.

Current human behavioural trends suggest that to be human is to be in a state of obsessive creativity driven by an addiction to our own goal-seeking neurotransmitter reward mechanisms. The globalizing Western capitalist model is all about more and bigger and 'better'. Our buildings, transportation, holidays and sports are ever more extreme and computer worlds ever more absorbing to the point of living in virtual realities. Perhaps the extraordinary leap in creative production evident in human evolution is humanity becoming addicted to its feelings and the promise of reward.

Acknowledgments

I gratefully acknowledge the support of the UK Arts and Humanities Research Council in the writing of this chapter (ref. AH/K005871/2) through the project Future Pasts (www.futurepasts.net).

References

Abram, D. 2010. *Becoming Animal*. New York: Vintage Books.

Barnard, A. 2011. *Social Anthropology and Human Origins*. Cambridge: Cambridge University Press.

Berman, M. 2000. *Wandering God: a Study in Nomadic Spirituality*. Albany: State University of New York Press.

Biesele, M. 1993. *Women like Meat: the Folklore and Foraging Ideology of the Kalahari Ju/'hoan*. Johannesburg: Witwatersrand University Press.

Bloch, M. 2012. *Anthropology and the Cognitive Challenge*. Cambridge: Cambridge University Press.

Botha, R. and Chris Knight (eds). 2009. *The Cradle of Language*. Oxford: Oxford University Press.

Brody, H. 1981. *Maps and Dreams*. Middlesex: Penguin Books.

Charvet, C. and G. Striedter. 2011. 'Causes and Consequences of Expanded Subventricular Zones', *European Journal of Neuroscience* 34: 988–993.

Daniel, Y. 2005. *Dancing Wisdom: Embodied Knowledge in Haitian Vodou, Cuban Yoruba, and Bahian Condomblé*. Urbana and Chicago: University of Illinois Press.

Davis, M. and P. Whalen. 2001. 'The Amygdala: Vigilance and Emotion', *Molecular Psychiatry* 6: 13–34.

d'Errico, F. and M. Vanhaeren. 2009. 'Earliest Personal Ornaments and their Significance for the Origin of Language Debate', in Rudolph Botha and Chris Knight (eds), *The Cradle of Language*. Oxford: Oxford University Press, pp. 16–40.

Downey, G. 2002. 'Listening to Capoeira: Phenomenology, Embodiment, and the Materiality of Music', *Ethnomusicology* 46: 487–509.

Dubois, R. 1976. *A God Within*. London: Abacus.

Foley, R. 1987. *Another Unique Species*. New York: Longman.

Fuller, R.C. 2008. *Spirituality in the Flesh: Bodily Sources of Religious Experience*. New York: Oxford University Press.

Gamble, C. 1998. 'Palaeolithic Society and the Release from Proximity: A Network Approach to Intimate Relations', *World Archaeology* 29(3): 426–449.

Gardner, P.M. 1966. 'Symmetric Respect and Memorate Knowledge: The Structure and Ecology of Individualistic Culture', *Southwestern Journal of Anthropology* 22(4): 389–415.

Gibson, J. 1979. *The Ecological Approach to Visual Perception*. London: Lawrence Erlbaum Associates.

Gieser, T. 2008. 'Embodiment, Emotion and Empathy: A Phenomenological Approach to Apprenticeship Learning', *Anthropological Theory* 8: 299–318.

Henshilwood, C. and B. Dubreuil. 2009. 'Reading the Artefacts: Gleaning Language Skills from the Middle Stone Age in Southern Africa', in

Rudolph Botha and Chris Knight (eds), *The Cradle of Language*. Oxford: Oxford University Press, pp. 41–60.

Ingold, T. 2000. *The Perception of the Environment: Essays on Livelihood, Dwelling and Skill*. London and New York: Routledge.

Kahneman, D. 2011. *Thinking, Fast and Slow*. New York: Farrar, Staus and Giroux.

Keeney, B. 2003. *Ropes to God: Experiencing the Bushman Spiritual Universe*. Philadelphia: Ringing Rocks Press.

———. 2007. 'Batesonian Epistemology, Bushman *N/om-Kxaosi*, and Rock Art', *Kybernetes* 36 (7/8): 884–904.

Kiefer, M. and L.W. Barsalou. 2013. 'Grounding the Human Conceptual System in Perception, Action, and Internal States', in W. Prinz, M. Beisert and A. Herwig (eds), *Action Science: Foundations of an Emerging Discipline*. Cambridge, MA: MIT, pp. 381–407.

Kuriyama, S. 2002. *The Expressiveness of the Body and the Divergence of Greek and Chinese Medicine*. Cambridge MA: Zone Books.

Lakoff, G. and M. Johnson. 1980. *Metaphors We Live By*. Chicago: University of Chicago Press.

Lewis, J. 2009. 'As well as Words: Congo Pygmy Hunting, Mimicry, and Play', in Rudolph Botha and Chris Knight (eds), *The Cradle of Language*. Oxford: Oxford University Press, pp. 236–256.

Lewis-Williams, D. and T. Dowson. 2000. *Images of Power*. Cape Town: Struik.

Liebenberg, Louis. 1990. *The Art of Tracking: The Origin of Science*. Claremont, South Africa: David Philip Publishers Ltd.

Low, C.H. 2014. 'Locating /Xam Beliefs and Practices in a Contemporary KhoeSan Context', in P. Skotnes and J. Deacon (eds), *The Courage of //Kabbo: Celebrating the 100th Anniversary of the Publication of Specimens of Bushman Folklore*. Cape Town: Juta, pp. 349–362.

———. 2015. 'The Role of the Body in Kalahari San Healing Dances', *Hunter Gatherer Research* 1: 30–60.

McBrearty, S. and A. Brooks. 2000. 'The Revolution that Wasn't: a New Interpretation of the Origin of Modern Human Behaviour', *Journal of Human Evolution* 39: 453–563.

Milton, K. 2002. *Loving Nature: Towards an Ecology of Emotion*. London: Routledge.

Mithen, S. 1996. *The Prehistory of the Mind*. London: Phoenix.

Previc, F. 2009. *The Dopaminergic Mind in Human Evolution and History*. Cambridge: Cambridge University Press.

Prince, R. 1982 'Shamans and Endorphins: Hypotheses for a Synthesis', *Ethos* 10(4): 409–423.

Sapolsky, R.M. 2004. *Why Zebra's Don't Get Ulcers*, 3rd edn. New York: St. Martin's Press.

Schleip, R. et al. (eds). 2012. *Fascia: the Tensional Network of the Human Body*. London: Churchill Livingstone.

Stringer, C. 2011. *The Origin of our Species*. London: Allen Lane.

Swenson, R.S. 2006. *Review of Clinical and Functional Neuroscience*, online version https://www.dartmouth.edu/~rswenson/NeuroSci/index.html. Accessed on 2 April 2015.

Van der Wal, J. 2012. 'Proprioception, Mechanoreception and the Anatomy of Fascia', in R. Schleip et al. (eds), *Fascia: the Tensional Network of the Human Body*. London: Churchill Livingstone, pp. 81–87.

Waldron, T. 2009. *Palaeopathology*. Cambridge: Cambridge University Press.

Winkelman, M. 2010. *Shamanism: A Biopsychosocial Paradigm of Consciousness and Healing*, 2nd edn. Oxford: Praeger.

Woolf, V. 1977. *The Letters of Virginia Woolf Volume 3: 1923–1918*, edited by N. Nicolson and J. Trautmann, 6 vols. New York: Harcourt Brace Jovanovich.

Zald, David H. and José V. Pardo. 1997. 'Emotion, Olfaction, and the Human Amygdala: Amygdala Activation during Aversive Olfactory Stimulation', *Proceedings of the National Academy of Sciences* 94: 4119–4124.

Zilhão, J. 2011. 'The Emergence of Language, Art and Symbolic Thinking', in C. Henshilwood and F. d'Errico (eds), *Homo Symbolicus: The Dawn of Language, Imagination and Spirituality*. Amsterdam: John Benjamins Publishing Company, pp. 111–133.

Chris Low is a Research Fellow at Bath Spa University, Director of Thinking Threads, a consultancy that supports the Khoekhoe and San, and is curator of !Khwa ttu San Museum, near Cape Town, South Africa. Chris retrained after a brief career as an osteopath and acupuncturist. Since 1999 he has held a series of teaching posts and research grants and undertaken extensive fieldwork on the medicine, health and environmental relationships of Khoekhoe and San of southern Africa.

Chapter 10

RAIN SERPENTS IN NORTHERN AUSTRALIA AND SOUTHERN AFRICA

A COMMON ANCESTRY?

Ian Watts

Introduction

In the late 1980s, geneticists announced that we evolved in Africa close to 200,000 years ago (200 ka), with a tentatively inferred initial migration between ~50 ka and ~100 ka. Palaeolithic archaeologists immediately recognized that these findings made the long-established consensus that there was no compelling evidence for symbolic behaviours pre-dating ~40 ka (treated as a cognitive Rubicon) look decidedly anomalous. How could the fundamental trait distinguishing our species from earlier hominins postdate our dispersal? New research in Africa was initiated, as a result of which it is now widely accepted that symbolic culture was in place by ~100 ka (d'Errico and Stringer 2011). The evidence includes habitual use of red ochre (closely associated with the dispersal), geometric engravings on ochre, beads (some with ochre residues), and (in the Levant) male burials with parts of game animals (indirectly associated with ochre). In southern Africa, the most intensively studied portion of the continent for the relevant period, it seems that ubiquitous use of red ochre can be inferred from ~170 ka, suggesting that symbolic culture correlates with our speciation (Watts 2014). Use of red and glittery pigments in southern

Africa from ~500 ka has been interpreted as the earliest evidence for collective ritual (Watts, Chazan and Wilkins 2016). At first sight, a speculative case might be made for a gradual evolution of collective ritual, out of which was forged a template of symbolic culture, at least three elements of which might be inferred by the time of dispersal beyond Africa – belief in 'other' worlds (associating the dead with game animals), cosmetic 'skin-change', and some form of 'blood' symbolism (see Knight and Lewis, this volume; Power, this volume).

For reasons concerning the history of the discipline (Knight 1991, Ch.1; Barnard 2012), social anthropologists have been slow to respond to the possible implications of our recent dispersal out of Africa. Among the first to do so was Alan Barnard, who made a case for why Bushmen, rather than Australian Aborigines, are more appropriate for thinking about early human society, identifying six areas of difference where parsimony suggested this was the case – essentially that the Australian world-view was too 'structurally evolved' (1999: 60). Within the field of belief, he considered that Australian Aborigines differed from 'all other modern hunter-gatherers ... (in) their belief in the Rainbow Serpent and the Dreaming' (ibid.). He went on to note: 'Although Rainbow Serpent-type creatures feature too in African mythology and rock art, they do not carry this symbolic weight; and that there is no African equivalent to the Dreaming' (ibid.). The Dreaming is a parallel but ontologically prior world where the distinction between animals and humans is not fixed; other Bushmen specialists do see an equivalence (Guenther 1999: 8), so Barnard's assertion is debateable. Regarding Rainbow Serpent-type creatures, a more interesting issue than their relative symbolic weight in the two regions is the implicit question about the nature of the identity, and whether this should be attributed to trivial (Mundkur 1983) or non-trivial factors (Knight 1991).

Rainbow Serpent-type creatures are representative of the wider set of dragons, serpents and rain-animals widely distributed in world mythology. The set has primarily been based on a number of recurrent themes, prominent among which have been control of water, an intimate relationship to women, transformative power (including 'death', healing and 'resurrection'), movement between 'worlds', and an antithesis to cooking and exogamous sex/marriage. They have fascinated European commentators since anthropology's emergence as a distinct discipline (e.g. Maehly 1867; Fergusson 1868; Lubbock 1870: 174–178; Wake 1873; Hahn 1881: 78–80; Elliot-Smith 1919; Radcliffe-Brown 1926, 1930; Ingersoll 1928; Propp 1958 [1928]; Hambly 1931; Baumann 1935, 1936; Segy 1954; see Knight 1991:

483 for further references). Initially, building upon an earlier, theological research agenda (Deane 1833), attention largely focused on 'serpent worship' in state societies. Even as the scope of inquiry broadened, it remained a search for fixed meanings. A notable exception was Vladimir Propp's formalist approach, which recognized that all magical tales were uniquely constrained; he concluded that Eurasian fairytales could be treated as variants of one tale only, in which a dragon kidnaps a princess. Only with the influence of structuralism in the 1970s did researchers begin to focus on the underlying logic informing such supernatural beings.

Radcliffe-Brown (1926) first noted possible parallels between Australian Rainbow Snakes and Bushman belief in snakes protecting waterholes, but without comment or citing any African literature. The issue remained dormant until a preliminary treatment by Knight (1991: 483–487), drawing on rock-art studies and limited ethnographic material (predominantly from Khoe-speaking, historically pastoralist cultures) to compare the logic of belief with that he had identified in greater detail in Australia. In the most recent and exhaustive evaluation of Khoisan Rainbow Snake-type creatures, Sullivan and Low (2014: 235) end by quoting Knight's conclusion about Australian Rainbow Snake myths. To give the full quote, 'what all these myths are referring to is not really a "thing" at all, but a cyclical logic which lies beyond and behind all the many concrete images – moon, snakes, tidal forces, waterholes, rainbows, mothers and so on – used in partial attempts to describe it' (1991: 455). Sullivan and Low's own conclusion is that the Khoisan material 'affirms in all its detail and particularity the broad contours of this "logic"' (2014: 235).

So what is this cyclical logic? Knight had proposed a model of the origin of symbolic culture in which evolving women, faced with the costs of giving birth to and rearing larger-brained, more dependent offspring, needed to secure unprecedented levels of male investment (see Finnegan, this volume). To achieve this, they had, through collective ritual action, made themselves periodically sexually unavailable, declaring themselves 'sacred' and 'taboo' until men surrendered the product of a collective hunt. This was achieved by exploiting the signalling potential of menstruation. The evolutionary logic was more precisely specified by Knight, Power and Watts (1995), identifying menstruation as a valuable cue to males of imminent fertility. The posited strategy was that the most reproductively burdened females prevented would-be philanderer males from targeting an imminently fertile menstruant at the expense of other females, forming a 'picket-line' around her, sharing the blood around or using blood substitutes to scramble the information, thereby using cultural or cosmetic means to 'synchronize' bleeding, while at the same time advertising her attractive qualities. These female cosmetic coalitions inverted standard fertility signalling, ritually pantomiming 'Wrong species, wrong sex, wrong time'. The economic logic was the imposition of a rule of distribution dissociating people from their own produce, whether the product of hunting labour (a hunter's 'own kill rule'), or reproductive labour (incest prohibitions). Synchronizing 'strike' action across communities required an environmental cue of appropriate periodicity. Collective spear-hunting of medium to large game – liable to take several days and nights – needed to optimize available natural light, making the days and nights immediately before full moon ideal, implying that the 'strike' began at dark moon. The cyclical logic is the movement from blood-defined kinship solidarity to 'honeymoon', from temporary death (to marital relations) to resurrection, from ritual power 'on' to ritual power 'off'. If lack of meat motivates the sex strike, it should also be a cooking strike, and if women's blood marks them as periodically taboo, then killed and bloody game animals should also be taboo, until they are surrendered and the blood removed through cooking. Treating metaphor as the underlying principle of symbolic culture (Knight and Lewis, this volume), the fundamental metaphor is that women's blood be equated with that of game animals. What kind of phenomena might be suitable for elaborating the logic informing this metaphor? Anything that could represent periodicity, movement between worlds, association with wetness, ambiguous sex, minimal morphological differentiation, skin-change, and transformative powers (e.g. death dealing) would be appropriate. Rainbows meet some of these requirements, and for a tropically evolved species, pythons would also be particularly good to think with (cf Lévi-Strauss 1966).

In this chapter, I compare aspects of Yurlunggur (the Yolngu Rainbow Snake of Arnhem Land, northern Australia) and !Khwa (the Rain Bull of the /Xam Bushmen in the Upper Karoo, South Africa). Following Knight, I focus on the relationship of these supernatural beings to menstrual blood, hoping to show how this throws their logic and structural role into sharpest relief.

Background

The study of Rainbow Snakes in Australia can be divided into two main phases: an initial period identifying and describing the phenomena in the late 1920s; and structuralist influenced work in the 1970s and early 1980s (e.g. Hiatt 1975; Buchler and Maddock 1978; Knight 1983). Some Aboriginal cultures permitted relating the mythological entity to ritual practice (e.g. Warner 1958 [1937]). The second phase recognized the Rainbow Snake as perhaps the ultimate symbolic representation of paradox and transformation.

The Yolngu live in northeast Arnhem Land, in the Australian tropics. Seasonal flooding and a difficult landscape made the area unattractive to Europeans, allowing the Yolngu to keep their culture relatively intact well into the twentieth century. The myth of how, as a result of the actions of the two Wawilak Sisters, Yurlunggur created the present world is the most extensively recorded and thoroughly analysed of Australian Rainbow Snake myths (e.g. Warner 1958; Berndt 1951; Lévi-Strauss 1966; Knight 1983, 1987, see p. 242 for citations of other versions), allowing me to present an abridged version here.

A history of research on Khoisan Rainbow Serpent-type creatures in southern Africa is beyond the scope of this paper (see Schmidt 1979, 1998; Morris 2002; Sullivan and Low 2014). Suffice it to say that they have been indigenously described as 'Watersnakes', 'Great Snakes', eland-bulls, 'Rain Bulls', and indeterminate large quadrupeds. Such creatures are considered to lie at the heart of 'a dynamic assemblage of *extant* cognitive associations between snakes, rain, environmental/landscape dynamics, water, fertility, blood, fat, transformation, dance and healing' (Sullivan and Low 2014: 218, emphasis in original).

The /Xam were Bushmen of the Upper Karoo, the interior, semi-arid region south of the Orange River. Because they were killed or brutally assimilated into the colonial frontier economy of the late eighteenth and first half of the nineteenth centuries, virtually everything we know about them is through the remarkable linguistic endeavours of Wilhelm Bleek and his sister-in-law Lucy Lloyd in the 1870s, and the equally remarkable co-operation of a succession of /Xam prisoners released into their custody, several of whom stayed well beyond their prison terms. This vast corpus of material (Skotnes 2007) included information on ritual and an extensive body of mythology. The myths can be supplemented by Gideon Retief von Wielligh's Afrikaans narratives, recorded from /Xam farm workers in the 1880s (von Wielligh 1919), while Ansie Hoff's salvage anthropology among contemporary descendants of the /Xam provides valuable fragmentary details concerning ritual and belief (Hoff 1997, 2007).

Linguistically, the /Xam belonged to the southern group of three Khoisan language families (Barnard 1992). There is considerable overlap in beliefs between historically pastoralist Khoe-speaking cultures and historically hunter-gatherer (Bushmen) Khoe and San speakers (ibid.). Bushman religion is best characterized in terms of fluidity and ambiguity, both within and between linguistic groups, but menarcheal ritual and healing dances are remarkably uniform in their performative structure and associated beliefs (ibid.; Guenther 1999). Both are means of entering into what the Ju/'hoan call First Creation, where the distinction between animals and people is not fixed (Keeney and Keeney 2013; see Guenther 1986 for similar Nharo conceptions).

The Wawilak Sisters

This summary is largely taken from Warner (1958):

> Two Dreamtime sisters of the Dua moiety, the elder carrying a baby boy, the younger pregnant, are crossing the land. They carry stone-tipped spears, bush-cotton and hawk's down. During their travels, they kill iguana, opossum and bandicoot, giving them the names they bear today, saying that they will become *maraiin* (sacred), in the meantime putting them in their dilly bags. The younger sister gives birth during their travels. They intend to circumcise the boys. They meet classificatory brothers and have sex with them. They finally arrive at the big waterhole near the coast, Mirrimina ('snake swallows') or Ditjerima ('menstruation blood'). The older sister tries to cook the animals they've caught, but each time one is placed on the fire, it comes back to life and jumps into the waterhole. A drop of her menstrual blood falls into the water (in another version, this 'pollution' is ascribed to the younger sister and occurs before the animals are placed on the fire [Chaseling 1957: 141–142]). Lying at the bottom of the waterhole, Yurlunggur, also of the Dua moiety, smells the blood, and rises to the surface, drawing the water level up with 'him' or 'her' (the seasonal flooding that's such a determinant factor to life in Arnhem Land). He spits water into the air, to become a small, black cloud. The sisters, alarmed by the growing cloud that came from nowhere, start to sing and dance, performing increasingly sacred songs; in some versions, the younger sister starts to bleed. It is at this point that Yurlunggur entrances them, licks them, bites their noses to make them bleed, swallows them alive and rises up into the sky, where he is joined by other snakes (all Dua moiety, each speaking a different language). Regretting their different tongues, Yurlunggur calls upon them to sing out together, making an

unprecedented noise and creating a common ceremony. Confronted over his incestuous cannibalism, he regurgitates the sisters and their children onto an anthill, to dry. They are revived by Yurlunggur's trumpet and the biting ants. The swallowing and regurgitation are repeated (only the sisters are regurgitated again, it being legitimate to consume flesh of the opposite moiety – the sons), Yurlunggur finally returning the sisters to Wawilak country.

Meanwhile, two Wawilak men saw the lightning and heard the thunder accompanying all this commotion and tracked the sisters to Mirrimina, where they find their blood and scoop it up, gather hawk's down and bush cotton, and fall asleep. The sisters appear in their dreams and recount everything that happened, instructing them in the songs and how to perform male circumcision ceremonies. They sang Yurlunggur and Muit (another name for Yurlunggur, with a proposed Kareira root meaning: 'blood & red & multi-coloured & iridescent', von Brandenstein 1982: 58). 'You must dance all the things we saw and named on our journey, and which ran away into the well'.

The myth of the Wawilak Sisters is re-enacted in various male initiation rituals, notably the interclan Djungguan ritual, when boys are circumcised. The day before, initiated men are blown over by the Yurlunggur trumpet, and produce arm blood to hold the hawk's down and bush-cotton on the dancers' bodies and the Muit emblems. That night, the neophytes are shown the snake for the first time, two padded poles 'with the rock pythons painted in blood on white surfaces gleaming in the light of the many fires' (Warner 1958: 304). The men say they stole this power from women. As an informant told Warner:

> The cycle of the seasons with the growth and decay of plants, copulation, birth and death of animals as well as men, is all the fault of those two Wawilak Sisters. If they hadn't done wrong in their own country and copulated with Dua Wongar men and then come down to the Liaalaomir country and menstruated and made that snake wild, this cycle would never have occurred. (Warner 1958: 385)

Aspects of Bushman Cosmology

Before turning to Bushman myths bearing on Rainbow Serpent-type creatures, comment is needed on the connection between eland and snakes, and on the place of menarche in Bushman cosmology.

Eland and Snakes

The eland, the largest and fattest of African antelope, has been described as the Bushman *'animal de passage'* (Lewis-Williams 1981:

72). The connection with snakes has largely been etically derived (Vinnicombe 1976; Lewis-Williams 1981), drawing primarily on rock art (e.g. antelope-headed snakes) and interpretation of the testimony of Qing, a Bushman of the Maloti Mountains (Lesotho), to Joseph Orpen in 1873 (Orpen 1874; McGranaghan, Challis and Lewis-Williams 2013). When apparently explaining a painted scene in one of the rock shelters they had visited (but see Challis, Hollman and McGranaghan 2013), Qing referred to a large quadruped being charmed out of the water by Bushmen as a 'snake'. Explicit emic support consisted of little more than two ethnohistorical accounts of Sotho and Nama (Khoe pastoralist) beliefs that a snake resided in the red forelock of the eland (Arbousset and Daumas 1846: 46; Hahn 1881: 81). A third nineteenth-century account, previously unremarked, suggests that the belief extended further east, to the Swazi and/or Zulu (Montague 1894: 66).[1] Vinnicombe (1976: 233) implied that this was also a Bushman belief, something only recently confirmed by Low among the Hai//om (2008: 240). Low adds an insight that helps to explain the association: 'Tixai ≠Gkao, a Ju/'hoan Bushman, described to me that the Eland and the Python are the same: "the eland gets that fat from the python into him. It just comes with the wind"' (2008: 240–241). Low interprets this as implying an ontological primacy of the python over the eland (2012: 89). Python fat, in addition to being symbolically potent (see Sullivan and Low 2014 in relation to healers), is physiologically so (Riquelme et al. 2011).

Similarly, the eland's red forelock is particularly appropriate for symbolizing eland potency: bulls rub their forelocks in their own urine, and forelock size provides a reliable agonistic signal in inter-male competition (Bro-Jørgenson and Dabelsteen 2008). The forelock is thought to provide the model for the red pigment motif painted on the brow of the Ju/'hoan menarcheal girl (Keeney and Keeney 2013: 73), and again at marriage (Marshall 1959: 356–359); a boy paints the same pattern on himself using ash when he has shot his first eland (Lewis-Williams and Biesele 1978: 125). A later, collective part of this initiation ritual involves lighting a medicine fire by the forelock, so that in future encounters the boy's face will be brilliant, causing the eland's face to split (Lewis-Williams 1981: 70). The Ju/'hoan term for brilliance in this context (//hára) is identical or very similar to the /Xam term for glittery specularite (ibid.: 60). Given the linguistic distance between the two cultures, this suggests an ancient ritual substrate and associated constructs informing etymology (Biesele, pers. comm. July 2013). Moreover, for Bushmen of the Maloti Mountains, Lewis-Williams has proposed an etymological link

between another term for specular-haematite (qhang qhang) and the
trickster, Qhang (Cagn, /Kaggen) (Lewis-Williams and Pearce 2004:
106). Like the snake in the forelock, /Kaggen also sits between the
horns of the eland, protecting his favourite animal from hunters
(Wessels 2009: 101). /Kaggen and !Khwa appear radically different,
but here their attributes seem to merge.[2] I suggest that the eland's red
forelock was the original form of the brilliant blaze, light, glistening
stone or diamond on the brow of the Watersnake or Rain Bull (von
Wielligh 1919: 75; Laidler 1928; van Vreeden 1955; Carstens 1975;
Hoff 1997; Schmidt 1998). In any event, the forelock is a symbolic
nexus, bringing together the potency of eland and snakes, adolescent
male and female initiates, redness and brilliance, !Khwa and /Kaggen.

Bushman Menarcheal Ritual

A Ju/'hoan circumlocution for first menstruation is 'She has shot an
eland' (Lewis-Williams 1981: 51; see Knight and Lewis, this volume);
the Eland Bull dance is one of the most widespread features of
Bushman menarcheal ritual. At the first sign of blood, the girl is
sequestered by older female kin and all the women of the band
pantomime eland courtship behaviour.[3] She is paradoxically identified
with the eland bull and as a hunter, an epitome of 'wrong species,
wrong sex, wrong time' (Power and Watts 1997; see Knight and
Lewis, this volume). Her food is restricted, but she bestows the benefit
of 'fatness'; she must be kept away from water, but she controls water.
After the girl's emergence from seclusion, timed in relation to the
moon, ritual acts performed often included a reintroduction to water
(Fourie 1927: 58; Guerreiro 1968: 227–278; Hewitt 1986; Hoff
1997; Le Roux and White 2004: 101), or she might be taken to run
through a symbolic shower of rain (Silberbauer 1963: 22).[4] Where
reintroduced to a water source, this may be personified as a Rain Bull
or a Watersnake (Hoff 1997; for more detailed accounts from extant
or historically Khoe-speaking cultures, see Schmidt 1998: 272 with
refs.; Hoff 1995; Waldman 2003: 665).[5] She is believed to help to
ensure fertilizing, soft 'female' rain, and success in forthcoming hunts.
In this last capacity, both the overall ritual and specific acts upon her
emergence (Power and Watts 1997 with refs) can be seen as a
Bushman counterpart to Pygmy women's 'ritual hunting labour'
(Finnegan, this volume).

The /Xam guardian of menstrual observances was !Khwa, the
Rain Bull or Rain Animal, who sometimes appeared as a bull eland.
!Khwa was also the term for water, rain and – in at least one instance

– menstrual blood (Hewitt 1986: 40, 284). !Khwa dwells in waterholes and controls lightning, thunder, whirlwinds and rain. He is strongly attracted by the scent of the girl, which is given as an explanation for her seclusion and the extensive use of *buchu*, an aromatic bush, which paradoxically both arouses and pacifies !Khwa and is used to raise and calm energy or potency as required in context (Sullivan and Low 2014: 223). *Buchu* may mask the smell of the blood, but by association it may also be indexical of blood. The menstrual hut was referred to as the 'house of trembling', which has been connected with the somatic experience of trance, the potency in both contexts being essentially identical (Lewis-Williams 1981; Keeney and Keeney 2013; see also Low, this volume). Upon her emergence, the new maiden sprinkled *buchu* and red ochre on the waterhole in current use, reintroducing herself to !Khwa (Hewitt 1986).

The Bushman Myths

The Smell of the Girl's Blood Conjures !Khwa

The following /Xam tales of girls at menarche can be compared with the Australian material:

> The Rain formerly courted a young woman, while the young woman was in her hut because she was still 'ill' (on account of her blood, either post-partum or menstrual). The Rain scented her and went forth on account of it; as the Rain came forth, it became misty. He trotted up to her hut and courted the young woman on account of her scent. ... And she lay, smelling the Rain's scent, and the place was fragrant. She rode away on the Rain Bull, but rather than be taken down into the waterhole, she put him to sleep with *buchu* so she could return to her child and kin. (Paraphrased from Bleek and Lloyd 1911: 192–198, parentheses added)

> A menarcheal girl, who had not yet been reintroduced to the water, and still had the smell of *buchu* on her, went into the veld to dig for bulbs, against her mother's advice. She saw a 'little waft of mist' but ignored it; next time she looked up, it had become a great cloud directly overhead, covering the whole sky, 'like a beast of prey'. She dropped her bag and ran for home, but too late: the lightning cleaved the ground and 'the earth ascended with the maiden; it became a whirlwind'. The maiden's mother, seeing this from the camp, spoke: 'You see the earth rising over there? It rises from the place where !Khwa struck. [untranslated line] It rises over there; it is the earth. The maiden truly became dust, while she felt that she was a snake. Whirling, she ascended'. And the sorcerers sang: '!Khwa is now the one who takes her away, she becomes a snake'. Lucy Lloyd noted that the narrator,

Dia!kwain, said that this was 'A large snake, whose name was feared', as portrayed in a rock-art copy sent by George Stow to Wilhelm Bleek. The snake was known as //*kheten* (//*xeiten*) or !*nuin*.[6] (Paraphrased from Lewis-Williams 2000: 273–276)

The preliminary manifestation of !Khwa as a small, but rapidly growing cloud, is strikingly similar to the preliminary manifestation of Yurlunggur; but it is the operational identity that is significant. In both cases, the girl's blood conjures this 'snake' from the water and is responsible for her either being swallowed by – or morphing into – a snake. This is the only point in the Bleek and Lloyd narratives where either !Khwa or the menarcheal girl is identified with a snake, but it is an identity confirmed by von Wielligh (1919: 59–66, 95–100) and by /Xam descendants (Hoff 1997).

In recounting this story (heard from his mother), Dia!kwain commented: 'when she is a maiden, she has the rain's magic power' (Lewis-Williams 2000: 273). She is responsible for the redness of the rain, a deep structure in Khoisan cosmology (Power and Watts 1997: 546 with refs). Paradoxically, the ontological transformation of the new maiden, her entry into First Creation, and her ability to take the whole community with her (Guenther 1999: 176; Keeney and Keeney 2013), occurs irrespective of whether she complies with or breaches correct behaviour; only the positive or negative valence of transformation changes. It is this same potency that some men (and fewer women) might train for years to harness, as rain shamans, game-shamans or healers (Lewis-Williams 1981; Hoff 2007). Although this could be acquired naturally (Low, this volume), it is the new maiden's as of right, accorded by a culturally constructed 'nature'. The !Kung and the /Xam regarded a new maiden to be 'the source of *n/om* (or /*k'ode*), the healing potency normally associated with the male trance healers' (Guenther 1999: 175, citing Lewis-Williams 1981: 51–52). This challenges the use of Bushman ethnography to support the thesis that early religion was shamanistic (Lewis-Williams 2010).

Anti-cooking

In the Wawilak Sisters' story, the fact that the animals come alive upon being placed in the fire can be ascribed to the sisters' bloody state, and to the fact that the sisters had declared that the animals would become sacred totems, of the same flesh (moiety) as themselves. The following is another /Xam myth about a new maiden:

A girl is in her seclusion hut; she peeps out to make sure nobody is about, and goes down to the waterhole. Sitting on the bank, she splashes the water: 'Ripples, twirl the water'. A 'waterchild' (resembling a calf) sprang out; she nabbed it, banged it on the head, flung it over her shoulder, and jogged back to camp. There she hastily made a fire, cut up the 'waterchild', roasted it, and ate it all. She then burnt the bones to ashes, tidied up the fire, swept away her footprints, and returned to the 'house of trembling'. This is repeated over several days. On the fifth day, the waterchild did not come out easily; it was a male, horned rain child. When she had cut it up and placed it on the fire, the fire hissed and spluttered, water came out of the ground, extinguishing the fire, as it felt that !Khwa was angry with the girl. A cold whirlwind whisked her up and dropped her into the waterhole as a frog. The same happened to her kin out on the veld, while organic cultural artifacts reverted to their original, natural state. (Paraphrased from Bleek and Lloyd 1911: 197–205; Hewitt 1986: 80–85)

A second anti-cooking narrative is the only !Khwa story in the Bleek and Lloyd collection not concerned with menarcheal observances:

A man out hunting mistook a manifestation of !Khwa for an eland and shot it. Later, following the spoor with companions, they found the eland and set about butchering it and cooking the meat. To their consternation the meat kept disappearing from the fire. They and their temporary shelter were surrounded by water; they were turned into frogs and hopped away. (Paraphrased from Lewis-Williams 2000: 222–223)

There is no obvious reason to take misidentification as the true cause of the misfortune; it seems more likely that !Khwa was angered by the attempt to cook eland meat on the hunting ground, rather than being surrendered as the ideal form of bride-service (Lewis-Williams 1981: 70); such men were called 'decayed arm' (ibid.: 63).[7]

Returning to menarcheal observances, among all Bushmen groups the girl is placed under strict dietary restrictions; among the /Xam, her immediate kin also ate less (Hewitt 1986: 280–281). Viegas Guerreiro (1968: 221) was told that the !Xû of southern Angola extinguished all cooking fires at the onset of a girl's first menstruation. Anti-cooking also figured prominently in one of Qing's narratives:

A young woman arouses the jealousy of the young men in her community by taking up with a mature bachelor, Qwanciqutshaa, the son of Cagn (/Kaggen), previously spurned by all women – including herself. The young men applied snake fat to the meat the old man was roasting. As he tried to eat the meat it repeatedly fell out of his mouth and he bled profusely from the nose.[8] He threw his possessions into the sky and himself into the river, transforming into a snake. (Paraphrased from Orpen 1874: 6–7)

An important theme in the full narrative is that Qwanciqutshaa, in human or snake form, stands in antithesis to marriage.

Periodicity

The following plot outline is taken from von Wielligh's recording of a /Xam myth about the creation of the moon:

> /Kaggen made for himself a pair of shoes. But the right shoe chafed his foot, so he instructed his daughter, the Hammerkop, to soften it by throwing it into the waterhole. At the bottom of the waterhole, the Watersnake was enraged by the polluting shoe and causes the water to freeze. When the Hammerkop retrieved the shoe, it came out with a piece of ice attached. In turn angered, /Kaggen threw the ice-bound shoe into the sky, where it became the moon. Ever since, people had light at night, enabling them to hunt porcupines and to wait for game at waterholes.[9] The jealous Sun shot the shining ice with hot arrows, causing it to melt and Moon to die. The people were distraught. The Watersnake intervened, creating a fountain on the moon so it would be reborn. (Paraphrased from von Wielligh 1919: 95–100, translated by Jeanine van Niekerk)

Whatever else the shoe may signify (see Vinnicombe 1975: 386), it is necessarily dirty, and in this sense polluting. The fact that it chafed /Kaggen's foot suggests it may have been bloodied. Other versions specify that the shoe was red owing to the dust of the Karoo (Bleek 1924: 5). Blood would probably have been emically inferred – another of the Hammerkop's roles was to inform the Watersnake if 'young maids' polluted the fountain in any way (von Wielligh 1919: 110). The interaction of blood, or the smell of blood, and the Watersnake is ultimately responsible for lunar periodicity, just as it is responsible for seasonal periodicity in Arnhem Land.

This story relates to a larger myth concerning /Kaggen's creation of the eland from his son-in-law's shoe, where the conflict between kin and affines substitutes for the theme of pollution (Lewis-Williams 1997). This also concludes with the creation of the moon, but the reason for the creation is not addressed by Lewis-Williams. According to Knight's template, the conflict is cyclically created and resolved through lunar periodicity. Throughout the waxing moon, 'affines' are an out-group to be exploited by uterine kin; at full moon they temporarily conjoin.

The 'Snake' as New Maiden

Among more northerly groups of Bushmen, equivalents to !Khwa – in terms of punishing breaches of menstrual observances – receive less elaboration in mythology, but may take the form of 'underground snakes' (Silberbauer 1965: 83; Valiente-Noailles 1993: 95).[10] In Ju/'hoan creation mythology, the archetypal 'new maiden' is G!kon//'amdima or Python Girl,[11] shimmering, sparkling like the sun, gliding like a grand person, having plenty of fat (Biesele 1993: 134, 148).

> G!kon//'amdima is already married and pregnant. Tricked by Jackal, her younger sister, to climb onto the branch of a berry-tree overhanging the waterhole, she falls into the deep well. Her seclusion at the bottom of the well becomes a birth seclusion. The negatively coded aspects of menarcheal seclusion are ludically transferred to Jackal (see Guenther 1999), who deceitfully assumes G!kon//'amdima's place as Kori Bustard's wife. Meanwhile, various animals try to rescue Python Girl; only the giraffe, with his long legs, succeeds. She re-emerges with her newborn (implying that post-partum blood is in the waterhole). In most versions, she emerges as beautiful as ever, but in Richard Lee's version, her father, the Elephant is heartbroken that 'she no longer sparkles as before' and declares that henceforth, the animals will be animals. (Paraphrased from Biesele 1993: 124–133, 137–138)

The male initiatory counterpart to the well of creation is the branding fire of creation, where animals are given their distinctive markings, henceforth remaining as animals. This is where G!kon//'amdima acquired her beautiful shining stripes (1993: 121). Both myths are interpreted by Biesele as a fall from grace, when attributes become fixed (1993: 138).

Synchronous Bleeding

We saw that the myth of the Wawilak Sisters underwrites Yolngu male initiation, where men bleed together (as initiated men in the preparation of ritual paraphernalia and as novitiates undergoing circumcision when they are introduced to Yurlunggur). The template for men's synchronous bleeding was the blood of that Wawilak sister entering the well and arousing Yurlunggur, and then both sisters bleeding prior to being swallowed, through synchronized menstruation brought on by dancing the most sacred dances (Knight 1983), and/or by being bitten on the nose by Yurlunggur. We have also seen how the blood of the new maiden in southern Africa arouses the Rain Animal/ Watersnake.

According to /Kunta Boo (the principal informant about healing for Biesele and the Keeneys), on the occasion of a Ju/'hoan girl's first menstruation, 'everyone must bleed in order to be assured full entry into First Creation' (Keeney and Keeney 2013: 73). This is achieved by making cuts on the ears of everyone present, with drops of blood falling to the ground. First Creation is characterized by a constant morphing of identities between animals and people, with no illness or death. The act of naming (or painting) the animals, establishing constant forms, is – according to the Keeneys – 'The Great Turning' or 'Second Creation' (Keeney and Keeney 2013: 67). The price of establishing permanent forms was sickness and death.

It is perhaps not surprising that a male healer should emphasize his role (making the cuts) in bringing about synchronized bloodflow to help ensure safe movement to First Creation. It might appear that such a detail is without parallel in wider Bushman menarcheal ritual. But, symbolically, it compares with the /Xam maiden giving her blessings to the whole community upon her transformation, distributing red ochre to the women of the band, and painting 'zebra' stripes with ochre on the legs of young men to protect them from !Khwa while out hunting, and sprinkling ochre on the current water-source to appease !Khwa (Hewitt 1986).

Discussion

We have here a set of highly suggestive cross-cultural symbolic similarities, all unfolding from a brute fact of nature, that women periodically bleed:

1) A girl menstruates for first time, conjuring a symbolic construct of supreme potency;
2) This construct is not something outside of herself, but her own ontological transformation into an animal (snake or eland), acquiring male attributes (having them from the outset in the Australian case);
3) Transformation to the 'wet';
4) She takes her kin, particularly female kin, with her, with suggestive and sometimes explicit indications of synchronous bleeding (see also Knight, Power and Watts 1995: 92 with refs)
5) In this 'other' world, mundane activities like cooking or mundane states (being 'married') are negated (the snake's antithetical relation to marriage was scarcely touched on here, but see Carstens 1975, Knight 1991);
6) Periodicity is thereby established (whether seasonal or lunar) and the 'right' way of doing things.

These correspondences certainly accord with the cyclical logic outlined by Knight. There is, however, a striking difference between the two sets of data. The myth of the Wawilak Sisters sanctions the ritual practice of senior male relatives grabbing hold of boys, establishing an ingroup/outgroup boundary between initiated and non-initiated, and subjecting a collective of novitiates to an artificial second birth that involves inverting their ontological status, with men admitting that they stole the language of this ritual power from women. The /Xam myths sanction the ritual practice of senior female relatives grabbing hold of a girl at menarche, establishing an ingroup/ outgroup boundary between uterine kin and men as 'husbands', and inverting her (and their own) ontological status. The similarities suggest a common origin or process, but the opposite outcomes in terms of gender hierarchy and ritual power would seem to call for a historical explanation.

What is going on here? The fundamental narrative is about women, and how they are simultaneously biologically and symbolically constituted. Becoming a woman is mythologically constructed as the ultimate empowering experience, such that other culturally constructed transformations – becoming an initiated man in Australia, becoming an initiated hunter in southern Africa, and apparently becoming a healer – are modelled on the process. Rainbow Serpent-type creatures provide an appropriate vehicle and logic for this narrative.

In the introduction it was suggested, on archaeological grounds alone, that as some modern humans left Africa, they took with them a template of symbolic culture, which included belief in 'other' worlds (associating the dead with game animals), ritual practice of cosmetic 'skin-change' and an associated ideology of 'blood'. A more precise delineation of such a template, derived from Knight's model, was then summarized. Knight had initially tested his model against the Yolngu myth of the Wawilak Sisters and their relation to Yurlunggur. Barnard had proposed that such supernatural creatures presented an area of difference between Bushman and Australian Aboriginal beliefs, but the difference identified was quantitative rather than qualitative, begging the question why there should be any similarity. Through a preliminary examination of the nature of the similarities, informed by Knight's model, I hope to have shown how and why they are similar. We may conjecture that something like a Rainbow Serpent-type creature was also part of the symbolic template of early *Homo sapiens*, an elaboration of the logic informing the world's first metaphor – equating women's blood with the blood of game animals.

Rhino Cave is a narrow fissure in the Tsodilo Hills of Botswana. In 2011, archaeologists reported findings which suggest that supernatural snakes might extend back in the order of 60,000 to 100,000 years (Coulson, Staurset and Walker 2011). The site is difficult of access and hidden from general view; its most striking feature is an almost freestanding rock that resembles the head and forebody of a giant snake emerging from the back of the fissure.

The resemblance is naturally enhanced by a crack resembling a mouth and a depression resembling an eye, and artificially enhanced by ground cupules covering the entire 'body', like scales. A spalled fragment from the cupuled surface and grinding stones with width dimensions similar to the cupules were recovered from Middle Stone Age (MSA) deposits below the 'snake'. These deposits, also containing abundant stone points and a ground piece of specularite (a glittery form of haematite), could not be directly dated, but the points resembled those from dated contexts in neighbouring and regional sites. The focus of the report was on how the points, in their sheer quantity, exotic procurement, selection of bright colours, and deliberate burning without use, provided compelling evidence for complex ritualized behaviour.

Figure 10.1: Rhino Cave, Botswana. Carved rock panel on the south wall in afternoon light. Photo courtesy of Sheila Coulson, Dept of Archaeology, Oslo.

Archaeologists would wish for more secure evidence linking this apparent zoomorph to the MSA and for absolute dating estimates. A cautious attitude is certainly required; the 'snake' may prove to be much younger. But, in view of the evidence marshalled here, I would argue there are strong theoretical and empirical grounds for anticipating that the temporal association will prove valid.

Notes

1. Montague claimed to have seen 'a small green snake which sometimes takes up his residence there (in the forelock of an eland bull)' (parentheses added). This directly follows his reporting a 'Caffre' (probably Swazi or Zulu) belief concerning a 'maggot' in the brain of wildebeest. Montague possibly took the snake/forelock association from Arbousset (changing the colour from yellow to green), but I found nothing else to suggest he plagiarized the extensive southern African travel literature.

2. A deep, if masked, relationship between /Kaggen and !Khwa would be consistent with a wider pattern, where Bushman tricksters, in their ritual personae, oversee adolescent initiation (e.g. Guenther 1986); tricksters may assume the persona of the great watersnake (e.g. Valiente-Noailles 1993: 196–197).

3. In drier regions, gemsbok may replace eland (Heinz 1994). The fact that the girl is identified with both fatness and rain accounts for why one of the menarcheal dances performed among the G/wi and //Gana is named after and mimics the nuptial flight of a species of termite. These also epitomize fatness and their nuptial flights occur at the start of the rains (see Mguni 2006: 62, citing Nonaka 1996: 31).

4. For lunar scheduling, see Watts 2005: 100–101, see also Imamura 2001: 130.

5. The widespread (but not ubiquitous) reintroduction to water is a feature missing from Guenther's characterization of the ritual (1999: 167). It was present among the Nharo, Guenther's own study group, the girl slapping the water with a branch (Le Roux and White 2004: 101), consistent with hints of a former belief in the Rain Bull (D. Bleek, A3.11, pp. 27–28; A3.18, p. 422 rev.) and possibly the Watersnake (A3.20, p. 592).

6. //xeiten or //kheten, a supernatural snake associated with rain and whirlwinds, is comparable to Khoe *Keinaus* or *Kaindaus* (Morris 2002; Low 2012), and an aspect of the G/wi and //Gana trickster !*Koanxa* (Valiente-Noailles 1993: 196–197).

7. This term of abuse for selfish – not to say 'incestuous' – behaviour by hunters (see Knight 1991: 88–121) suggests a link between the fate of these men and the fate of men (including /Kaggen) out on the hunting ground tricked into massaging the neck of the menorrhagic tortoise (grandmother or older sister to the males); their arms decayed (see Watts

2005: 101 with refs). Tortoises were also one of the Rain's creatures (Hewitt 1986), and among the Griqua (of Khoe descent), who share very similar beliefs and practices with the /Xam, they provide a metaphor for vaginas (Waldman 2003: 665).

8. Bleeding from the nose is one of the key motifs associated with entering into trance (Lewis-Williams 1981). This is also the state in which the Wawilak sisters were swallowed by Yurlunggur.

9. Ambush hunting by waterholes at night, restricted to dry-season nights leading up to full moon, was one of the most productive forms of Bushman hunting (Watts 2005: 105 and note 27 with refs). In the MSA it would have played a critical role, as one of the few techniques where hunters could get close enough to use a spear with much chance of success. In southern Africa, eland are the only herbivores to regularly use waterholes at night (Hayward and Hayward 2012: 120); they dominate the large mammal assemblages of many MSA sites (Faith 2008; Weaver, Steele and Klein 2011).

10. See also Hoernlé (1987: 130) for a similar Nama belief. Conversely, among the Ju/'hoan, correct observance on the part of the girl was believed to protect the band from snakes (Lewis-Williams 1981: 52). Given the habitual use of metaphor, circumlocution and respect words for animals of exceptional potency (Biesele 1993), I suggest that the Ju/'hoan explanation for why the new maiden hits the young hunters with an ochre-covered wand – to protect them while out hunting from being pricked by a stick (Lewis-Williams 1981: 77) – is a metaphor for being bitten by a snake, as in G/wi and //Gana belief. Similarly, the /Xam new maiden painted haematite stripes on the young hunters to protect them from !Khwa's lightning while out on the veld. Damara and Hai//om equate lightning strikes with the bite of a snake (Low 2008).

11. G!kon//'amdima has multiple identities (Biesele 1993: 22, 147–150, 207). The first syllable of her name is the word for termites; Biesele was told this was not significant (1993: 148), but see note 3.

References

Arbousset, T. and F. Daumas. 1846. *Narrative of an Exploratory Tour to the Northeast of the Colony of the Cape of Good Hope*. Cape Town: Robertson.

Barnard, A. 1992. *Hunters and Herders of Southern Africa: A Comparative Ethnography of the Khoisan Peoples*. Cambridge: Cambridge University Press.

———. 1999. 'Modern Hunter-gatherers and Early Symbolic Culture', in R. Dunbar, C. Knight and C. Power (eds), *The Evolution of Culture: an Interdisciplinary View*. Edinburgh: Edinburgh University Press, pp. 50–68.

————. 2012. *Genesis of Symbolic Thought*. Cambridge: Cambridge University Press.

Baumann, H. 1935. *Lunda. Bei Bauern und Jägern in inner-Angolan*. Berlin: Würfel Verlag.

————. 1936. *Schöpfung und Urzeit des Menschen im Mythus der afrikanischer Volker*. Berlin: Dietrich Reimer Verlag.

Berndt, R. 1951. *Kunapipi: A Study of an Australian Aboriginal Religious Cult*. Melbourne: FW Cheshire Ltd.

Biesele, M. 1993. *Women Like Meat. The Folklore and Foraging Ideology of the Kalahari Ju/'hoan*. Johannesburg and Indiana: Witwatersrand University Press.

Bleek, D. 1924. *The Mantis and his Friends*. Cape Town: Maskew Miller.

————. unpublished notebooks. 'The digital Bleek and Lloyd', updated at http://lloydbleekcollection.cs.uct.ac.za/.

Bleek, W. and L. Lloyd. 1911. *Specimens of Bushman Folklore*. London: Allen.

Bro-Jørgenson, J. and T. Dabelsteen. 2008. 'Knee-clicks and Visual Traits Indicate Fighting Ability in Eland Antelopes: Multiple Messages and Back-up Signals', *BMC Biology* 6:47. doi:10.1186/1741-7007-6-47.

Buchler, I.R. and K. Maddock (eds). 1978. *The Rainbow Serpent*. The Hague: Mouton.

Carstens, P. 1975. 'Some Implications of Change in Khoikhoi Supernatural Beliefs', in M.G. Whisson and M. West (eds), *Religion and Social Change in Southern Africa*. Cape Town: David Philip, pp. 78–95.

Challis, S., J. Hollmann and M. McGranaghan. 2013. '"Rain snakes" on the Senqu River: New Light on Qing's Commentary on San Rock Art from Sehonghong, Lesotho', *Azania: Archaeological Research in Africa* 48: 331–354.

Chaseling, W.S. 1957. *Yulengor, Nomads of Arnhem Land*. London: Epworth.

Coulson, S., S. Staurset and N. Walker. 2011. 'Ritualized Behavior in the Middle Stone Age: Evidence from Rhino Cave, Tsodilo Hills, Botswana', *PaleoAnthropology* 2011: 18–61.

Deane, J.B. 1833. *The Worship of the Serpent Traced throughout the World: Attesting the Temptation and Fall of Man by the Instrumentality of the Serpent Temptor*. London: J.G. & F. Rivington.

d'Errico, F. and C. Stringer. 2011. 'Evolution, Revolution or Saltation Scenario for the Emergence of Modern Culture', *Philosophical Transactions of the Royal Society, Series B*. 366: 1060–1069.

Elliot-Smith, G. 1919. *The Evolution of the Dragon*. Manchester: The University Press.

Faith, J. 2008. 'Eland, Buffalo, and Wild Pigs: Were Middle Stone Age Humans Ineffective Hunters?', *Journal of Human Evolution* 55: 24–36.

Fergusson, J. 1868. *Tree and Serpent Worship, or Illustrations of Mythology and Art in India*. London: W. Allen.

Fourie, L. 1927. 'Preliminary Notes on Certain Customs of the Hei//om Bushmen', *Journal of the South West African Scientific Society* 1: 49–63.

Guenther, M. 1986. *The Nharo Bushmen of Botswana: Tradition and Change.* Quellen zur Khosan-Forschung 3. Hamburg: Helmut Buske Verlag.

——. 1999. *Tricksters and Trancers.* Bloomington: Indiana University Press.

Guerreiro, M.V. 1968. *Bochimanes !khu de Angola; Estudo Ethnografico.* Lisbon: Instituto de Investigacao Cientifica de Angola, Hunta de Investigacoes do Ultramar.

Hahn, T. 1881. *Tsuni!-Goam. The Supreme Being of the Khoi-Khoi.* London: Trübner.

Hambly, W. 1931. *Serpent Worship in Africa.* Chicago: Field Museum of Natural History, Publication 289.

Hayward, M. and M. Hayward. 2012. 'Waterhole Use by African Fauna', *South African Journal of Wildlife Research* 42: 117–127.

Heinz, H. 1994 [1966]. *The Social Organization of the !Kõ Bushmen.* Quellen zur Khoisan-Forschung 10. Cologne: Rüdiger Köppe.

Hewitt, R.L. 1986 [1976]. *Structure, Meaning and Ritual in the Narratives of the Southern San.* Quellen zur Khoisan-Forschung 2. Hamburg: Helmut Buske.

Hiatt, L.R. 1975. 'Swallowing and Regurgitation in Australian Myth and Rite', in L. Hiatt (ed.), *Australian Aboriginal Mythology.* Canberra: Australian Institute of Aboriginal Studies, pp. 143–162.

Hoernlé, W. 1987. *Trails in the Thirstland: the Anthropological Field Diaries of Winifred Hoernlé,* ed. P. Carstens, G. Klinghardt and M. West. Cape Town: Centre for African Studies, University of Cape Town (Communications no. 14).

Hoff, A. 1995. 'Puberteitsrite van 'n Khoekhomeisie', *South African Journal of Ethnology* 18(1): 29–41.

——. 1997. 'The Water Snake of the Khoekhoen and /Xam', *South African Archaeological Bulletin* 52: 21–37.

——. 2007. *Medicine Experts of the /Xam.* Quellen zur Khoisan-Forschung 19. Cologne: Rüdiger Köppe.

Imamura, K. 2001. 'Water in the Desert: Rituals and Vital Power among the Central Kalahari Hunter-gatherers', *African Studies Monographs (Supplementary Issue)* 27: 125–163.

Ingersoll, E. 1928. *Dragons and Dragon Lore.* New York: Payson & Clarke.

Keeney, B. and H. Keeney. 2013. 'Reentry into First Creation: A Contextual Frame for the Ju/'hoan Bushman Performance of Puberty Rites, Storytelling and Healing Dance', *Journal of Anthropological Research* 69: 65–86.

Knight, C. 1983. 'Levi-Strauss and the Dragon: Mythologiques Reconsidered in the Light of an Australian Aboriginal Myth', *Man* (N.S.) 18: 21–50.

——. 1987. 'Menstruation and the Origins of Culture: A Reconsideration of Lévi-Strauss's Work on Symbolism and Myth', PhD dissertation. London: University of London.

——. 1991. *Blood Relations: Menstruation and the Origins of Culture.* New Haven and London: Yale University Press.

————, C. Power and I. Watts. 1995. 'The Human Symbolic Revolution. A Darwinian Account', *Cambridge Archaeological Journal* 5: 75–114.

Laidler, P. 1928. 'The Magic Medicine of the Hottentots', *South African Journal of Science* 25: 433–444.

Le Roux, W. and A. White (eds). 2004. *Voices of the San*. Cape Town: Kwela Books.

Lévi-Strauss, C. 1966. *The Savage Mind*. London: Weidenfeld & Nicholson.

Lewis-Williams, D. 1981. *Believing and Seeing. Symbolic Meanings in Southern San Rock Paintings*. London: Academic Press.

————. 1997. 'The Mantis, the Eland and the Meercats: Conflict and Mediation in a Nineteenth-century San Myth', in P. McAllister (ed.), *Culture and the Commonplace*. Johannesburg: Witwatersrand University Press, pp. 195–216.

————. 2000. *Stories that Float from Afar*. Cape Town: David Phillip.

————. 2010. *Conceiving God: the Cognitive Origin and Evolution of Religion*. London: Thames and Hudson.

———— and M. Biesele. 1978. 'Eland Hunting Rituals among the Northern and Southern San groups: Striking Similarities', *Africa* 48: 117–134.

———— and D. Pearce. 2004. *San Spirituality: Roots, Expression and Social Consequences*. Cape Town: Double Storey.

Low, C. 2008. 'Working with Potency: the Role of Weather in KhoeSan Healing', in C. Barboza and V. Jankovic (eds), *Weather, Local Knowledge and Everyday Life: Issues in Integrated Climate Studies*. Rio de Janeiro: MAST, pp. 235–244.

————. 2012. 'KhoeSan Shamanistic Relationships with Snakes and Rain', *Journal of Namibian Studies* 12: 71–96.

Lubbock, J. 1870. *The Origin of Civilization and the Primitive Condition of Man*. London: Longmans.

Maehly, J. 1867. *Die Schlange im Mythus und Cultus der classischen Völker*. Basel: von C. Schultze.

Marshall, L. 1959. 'Marriage among !Kung Bushmen', *Africa* 29: 335–365.

McGranaghan, M., S. Challis and D. Lewis-Williams. 2013. 'Joseph Millerd Orpen's "A Glimpse into the Mythology of the Maluti Bushmen": a Contextual Introduction and Republished Text', *Southern African Humanities* 25: 137–166.

Mguni, S. 2006. 'Iconography of Termites' Nests and Termites: Symbolic Nuances of Formlings in Southern African Rock Art', *Cambridge Archaeological Journal* 16(1): 53–71.

Montague, C. 1894. *Tales of a Nomad: or, Sport and Strife*. London: Longmans, Green & Company.

Morris, D. 2002. 'Driekopseiland and "the Rain's Magic Power": History and Landscape in a New Interpretation of a Northern Cape Rock Engraving Site', MA dissertation. Cape Town: University of Western Cape.

Mundkur, B. 1983. *The Cult of the Serpent: An Interdisciplinary Survey of its Manifestations and Origins*. New York: State University of New York Press.

Nonaka, K. 1996. 'Ethnoentomology of the Central Kalahari San', *African Study Monographs, Supplement* 22: 29–46.

Orpen, J. 1874. 'A Glimpse into the Mythology of the Maluti Bushmen', *Cape Monthly Magazine* 9: 1–13.

Power, C. and I. Watts. 1997. 'The Woman with the Zebra's Penis: Gender, Mutability and Performance', *Journal of the Royal Anthropological Institute* 3: 537–560.

Propp, V. 1958 [1928]. *Morphology of the Folk Tale*. Trans. Laurence Scott. Austin: University of Texas Press.

Radcliffe-Brown, A.R. 1926. 'The Rainbow-Serpent Myth of Australia', *Journal of the Royal Anthropological Institute* 56: 19–25.

———. 1930. The Rainbow-Serpent Myth in South-east Australia', *Oceania* 1(3): 342–347.

Riquelme, C. et al. 2011. 'Fatty Acids Identified in the Burmese Python Promote Beneficial Cardiac Growth', *Science* 334: 528–531.

Schmidt, S. 1979. 'The Rain Bull of the South African Bushmen', *African Studies* 38: 201–224.

———. 1998. 'Mythical Snakes in Namibia', in A. Bank (ed.), *Proceedings of the Khoisan Identities and Cultural Heritage Conference*. Cape Town: Infosource, pp. 269–280.

Segy, L. 1954. 'African Snake Symbolism', *Archive fur Volkerkunde* 9: 103–115.

Silberbauer, G. 1963. 'Marriage and the Girl's Puberty Ceremony of the G/wi Bushmen', *Africa* 33: 12–24.

———. 1965. *Report to the Government of Bechuanaland on the Bushman Survey*. Gaborone: Bechuanaland Government.

Skotnes, P. 2007. *Claim to the Country: The Archive of Wilhelm Bleek and Lucy Lloyd*. Athens, OH: Ohio University Press. With accompanying DVD 'The digital Bleek and Lloyd', updated at http://lloydbleekcollection.cs.uct. ac.za/.

Sullivan, S. and C. Low. 2014. 'Shades of the Rainbow Serpent? A KhoeSan Animal between Myth and Landscape in Southern Africa – Ethnographic Contextualisations of Rock Art Representations', *Arts* 3: 215–244.

Valiente-Noailles, C. 1993. *The Kua*. Rotterdam and Brookfield: A.A. Balkema.

van Vreeden, B.F. 1955. 'Die Waterslang', *Tydskrif vir volkskunde en volkstaal* 12(1): 1–10.

Vinnicombe, P. 1975. 'The Ritual Significance of Eland (*Taurotragus oryx*) in the Rock Art of Southern Africa', in E. Anati (ed.), *Les religions de la préhistoire: actes du Valcamonica symposium*. Capo di Ponte (Brescia): Centro Camuno di Studi Preistorci, pp. 379–400.

———. 1976. *The People of the Eland: Rock Paintings of the Drakensberg Bushmen*. Pietermaritzburg: University of Natal Press.

von Brandenstein, C. 1982. *Names and Substance of the Australian Subsection System*. Chicago: University of Chicago Press.

von Wielligh, G. 1919. *Boesman Stories. Deel 1, Mitologie en Legendes*. Cape Town: De Nationale Pers.

Wake, C.S. 1873. 'The Origins of Serpent-worship', *Journal of the Anthropological Institute of Great Britain and Ireland* 2: 373–390.

Waldman, L. 2003. 'Houses and the Ritual Construction of Gendered Homes in South Africa', *Journal of the Royal Anthropological Institute* 9(4): 657–679.

Warner, W.L. 1958 [1937]. *A Black Civilization: A Social Study of an Australian Tribe*. New York: Harper & Row.

Watts, I. 2005. '"Time too Grows on the Moon": Some Evidence for Knight's theory of a Human Universal', in W. James and D. Mills (eds), *The Qualities of Time: Anthropological Approaches*. Oxford and New York: Berg, pp. 95–118.

———. 2014. 'The Red Thread: Pigment Use and the Evolution of Collective Ritual', in D. Dor, C. Knight and J. Lewis (eds), *The Social Origins of Language*. Oxford: Oxford University Press, pp. 208–227.

———. M. Chazan and J. Wilkins. 2016. 'Early Evidence for Brilliant Ritualized Display: Specularite Use in the Northern Cape (South Africa) Between ~500 ka and ~300 ka', *Current Anthropology* 57(3): 287–310.

Weaver, T., T. Steele and R. Klein. 2011. 'The Abundance of Eland, Buffalo, and Wild Pigs in Middle and Later Stone Age Sites', *Journal of Human Evolution* 60: 309–314.

Wessels, M. 2009. 'Reading the Hartebeest: a Critical Reappraisal of Roger Hewitt's Interpretation of the /Xam Narratives', *Research in African Literatures* 40(2): 82–108.

Ian Watts is an independent researcher living in Athens. He has been publishing on the early record of pigment use in southern Africa for twenty years, integrating the insights gleaned into evolutionary accounts of ritual and symbolic culture. More occasionally, he has also published on aspects of African hunter-gatherer cosmology.

Chapter 11

BEDOUIN MATRILINEALITY REVISITED

Suzanne E. Joseph

Although the influence of a classical evolutionary paradigm in anthropology has waned, there has been a recent resurgence in scholarship in social anthropology on early human kinship and a questioning of the standard model of human evolution which places the patriarchal nuclear family at the centre (Knight 2008). In this chapter, I revisit proto-anthropological accounts of kinship and marriage in Arabia, not in order to use past conjectural accounts to illuminate the kinship structures of extant Bedouin peoples, but in order to reconsider those early ethnological observations in light of new insights to emerge from Bedouin ethnography and demography as well as kinship studies. Much of the discussion contained herein follows on from a previous work (see Joseph 2013: 95–116), one that readers may wish to consult for a more thorough ethnographic and comparative-historical grounding of Bekaa Bedouin kinship in particular.

Kinship and Marriage in Arabia

Theologians, historians and anthropologists have explored the topic of kinship and marriage in early Arabia in some detail. Proto-anthropologists, including John Ferguson McLennan and William Robertson Smith, expounded the view that early human societies, including those found in Arabia, were matrilineal. Archaeological evidence suggests that while tracing descent through males appears to have been the norm in pre-Islamic Arabia, there are indications of matrilineal-type descent and marriage arrangements (Hoyland 2001; Abd Al Ati 1977). Most scholars agree that it was not the coming of Islam that undermined women's freedom and status, but the accumulation of wealth, slaves and concubines via the Arab conquests that led to the devaluation, objectification and commodification of women (Ahmed 1992: 85–86). Likewise, the development of androcentric political institutions and ideas under the Abbasid dynasty ultimately meant that ethical Quranic precepts, especially teachings on equal treatment for women, were overlain by state-sanctioned Islamic legal doctrine and juridical procedures (ibid.: 88–89).

When compared to pre-Islamic Arabia, the coming of Islam is believed to have improved women's status and well-being in some respects. For example, under Islam, not only was the practice of female infanticide renounced, but women were endowed with rights of inheritance which could not be revoked by either agnates or affines (Lindholm 2008). Nevertheless, some religious restrictions on women's sexuality and marriage choices were introduced. Whereas prior to Islam, women could enter into multiple and temporary marriage alliances as well as terminate unions and change partners as they saw fit, Islamic law conferred upon men the right, in certain limited cases, to independently dissolve the marriage without arbitration or the consent of the wife (*talāq* or 'men's divorce') and outlawed polyandry and temporary unions, although the latter are still regarded as legitimate by Shi'i Muslims (Abd Al Ati 1977; Haeri 1989; Tucker 2008).

In spite of doctrinal variations within and between the four major Sunni schools of law – schools that took their final form in the tenth century – women's right to initiate *khul'* (self-redemption, divestiture or 'woman's divorce') is almost universally recognized, but it is not binding without the husband's consent and the woman is usually required to return the bride-price payment (Abd Al Ati 1977; Haeri 1989; Tucker 2008). Among Shi'i Muslim schools of law, the Zaydis constitute an exception to the dominant position on bride-price reimbursement as they do not believe that a husband is entitled to compensation by a wife who seeks *khul'* (Tucker 2008: 97). In terms of court-adjudicated divorce or annulment (*faskh* or *tafrīq*), a woman is permitted to dissolve a marriage contract without the husband's consent, provided that she has legitimate grounds for seeking dissolution and obtains a positive ruling by a judicial body. Although there is no consensus among Sunni jurists as to what constitutes a defective marriage, the following constitute some of the grounds on which a woman could obtain a judicial divorce: a woman whose husband is impotent; a woman whose marriage had been contracted on her behalf by a guardian at an earlier time and who has since reached the age of puberty; a woman suffering desertion or prolonged absence of her husband; a woman suffering mistreatment by her husband; and a woman whose husband is either physically or financially incapacitated (Abd Al Ati 1977; Tucker 2008). The advantage of judicial divorce for women is that it allows them to retain rights to the bride-price and other post-divorce compensations, as is the case for 'men's divorce' (Tucker 2008: 95). Even though 'women's divorce' may appear to be the least practicable, evidence from the time of the Prophet suggests that women who desired *khul'* for reasons of marital dissatisfaction could solicit the assistance of respected men in their community, most notably the Prophet himself, to induce the husband to terminate the marriage (ibid.: 96). Ethnographic information on twentieth-century Bedouin residing in Kuwait suggests that a woman's amourist, provided that he can convince her husband to grant the divorce, may even furnish the bride-price payment himself, effectively compensating the husband for his loss and buying back the wife's right in her person (Dickson 1983: 106).

Contemporary ethnographic accounts portray Arabico-Muslim societies as firmly agnatic in structure; that is, they are said to be organized on the basis of patrilineal descent and patrilocal residence. Indeed, it has become something of a social science truism to designate Arabico-Muslim societies as patriarchal. As Goody (1983: 27) observes, 'The Islamic world has often been looked upon as a purgatory for women, in implicit contrast to Christian Europe, a continent which some see as the particular paradise for the female sex'. However, an important distinction is frequently made between non-Bedouin and Bedouin Arab peoples, with the latter being depicted as more politically egalitarian, largely owing to their nomadic, tribal pastoral economy (Jabbur 1995). Perhaps somewhat surprisingly, while Bedouin political systems are described as egalitarian and non-hierarchical, gender and family systems are usually not. To take a well-known example from a twentieth-century ethnographic study of Awlad 'Ali Bedouin in Egypt, the gender valuation and treatment of males is described as preferential and is believed to stem from patrilineal kinship. As Abu-Lughod (1999: 122) writes, 'There is good sociological reason to prefer sons. The tribal system is organized around the principles of patrilineality and agnatic solidarity and is based on relationships between men. However important affines and cognatic kin are economically, socially and affectively, tribal segments can only grow through addition of males'.

There is a close congruence here between Bedouin and non-Bedouin Arab groups as patriarchal social structures are widely held to be the norm in urban, non-Bedouin Arab communities of the Middle East. Joseph (1993) has developed the concept of 'patriarchal connectivity' to refer to the ways in which individuals are socialized to develop relations and connections with others that ultimately facilitate male as well as gerontocratic control. Privileged actors (males and seniors) attempt to direct and control the relations of subordinates (women and juniors) largely by invoking kinship idioms, morality and the like. In as much as their efforts are successful, men and elders are able to cultivate interpersonal connections that reinforce gender and age domination. Under this model, it is recognized that Arab patriarchy takes different forms in different contexts, but the underlying social structures, including kinship structures, are thought to be patriarchal.

Whereas arguments about female subordination and patrilineal kinship structures in Arabico-Muslim societies abound, my argument, outlined below, is that Bedouin kinship has many non-agnatic features that beg for explanation and suggest a prominent role for uterine connections. Once social facts of kinship are re-examined, arguments made by proto-anthropologists that Arabs were matrilineal begin to make sense. It should be borne in mind that my main focus here is on kinship, particularly systems of descent, marriage and residence in nomadic Bedouin pastoral groups. Bedouin pastoralists share many general features – sociopolitical, economic and ecological as well as demographic – with nomadic foragers (see Joseph 2013). Aside from the converging effects of nomadism on social structure, recent research suggests that human-plant relationships may be comparable among hunters and herders (Mandaville 2011). Ethnobotanical classifications of pastoralists – both Bedouin pastoralists from eastern Arabia and non-Semitic-speaking pastoralists from East Africa – bear stronger resemblance to those of hunter-gatherers than those of small-scale agriculturalists (ibid.). Although using data on pastoral nomads to reconstruct human origins is not ideal, such material can inform research on forager systems. Ultimately, even models based on contemporary foragers must be tested against surviving Palaeolithic evidence to highlight incongruities.[1] Stiner and Kuhn (2009: 158) explain that ethnographic data should not be used to draw crude analogies between contemporary foragers and Palaeolithic foragers: 'we are not looking for matches between present and past societies, but instead are using generalized cross-cultural patterns of recent forager systems to isolate anomalies in extinct cultural systems. The anomalies must then be explained independently of these referents'.

Bedouin Matrilineality

In trying to come to terms with the unique features of human kinship or what makes human kinship human, Stone (2006: 63) writes:

> what is apparently unique to our species is the notion of descent from a common ancestor, so crucial to the formation of human descent groups and other features of human kinship systems. There is also one other important way in which human kinship is unique. Humans not only recognize kin and behave for the most part favorably toward them, they also use ideas of kinship to form bonds among persons unrelated biologically. Marriage is one way to do this, so that affines, where they are not already kin, become kin, or at least in many societies are seen as fully 'kin', as much as are those sharing biological relatedness.

Descent and marriage are key components of human kinship. Patrilineal and matrilineal descent constitute two of the four distinct descent systems identified in George Peter Murdock's ethnographic sample of human societies, the other two being bilateral and double descent. Out of a sample of 857 societies, 47 per cent are patrilineal and 14 per cent are matrilineal, with bilateral descent and double descent comprising 36 per cent and 3 per cent respectively (van den Berghe 1979: 89).

As mentioned, above, the orthodox view in anthropology is that Bedouin Arab kinship systems are unequivocally patrilineal. However, if we look more closely at how kinship is reckoned throughout the life course, we begin to notice that patrilineal kinship is not only inflected by gender, but by time, particularly life-course changes associated with marriage and reproduction. We know that in patrilineal societies both male and female children belong to the patriline; however, only men can transmit membership. This is the defining feature of unilineal descent systems: kin membership is traced through one line – either the female line or the male line. In keeping with patrilineal descent, Bedouin children belong to the same kin group as that of their socially recognized father. Under Bedouin patriliny, a woman, like her male counterpart, remains a member of her natal tribe for life. This means that a Bedouin woman's tribal affiliation does not change at marriage. She continues to be recognized as a member of her father's patriline, which in turn indicates that she is not incorporated into her husband's tribal patriline. A married Bedouin woman thus experiences a structural incompatibility vis-à-vis her children and spouse, assuming that she marries exogamously. Her children, unlike her, are fully absorbed into her husband's agnatic unit. This structural conflict is frequently presumed to be true for women in all patrilineal societies, but such is not the case. In the Kabul Province of Afghanistan where descent is patrilineal and residence is patrilocal (sometimes referred to as virilocal), a married woman changes her identity and shifts her allegiance upon joining her husband's family. She is often even given a new name to mark this life transition (Ganesh 2013).[2] Among Sunni Muslim Durrani Pashtuns who reside in the region of western Afghanistan known as Afghan Turkistan, Tapper (1991: 53) describes how a woman's agnates concede almost all 'practical rights and responsibilities towards her after her marriage to such an extent that even ideal statements about the residual rights and duties of agnates are extremely vague and contradictory'. Even the punishment for a woman accused of adultery is handled by her husband before her agnates (ibid.: 17). The only consistent right retained by a woman's kin is their right to reclaim her body for burial (ibid.: 53).

To take a more well-known example in which the structural conflict between a woman's natal kin group and her affinal kin group is resolved by loosening ties with her family of origin, consider early Roman patriliny. Under early Roman patriliny, the most common form of marriage involved a shift in a woman's kinship status upon marriage. The ancient Roman bride who entered the husband's power or *manus* had to forgo her natal kinship status and separate property (Dixon 1992). The bride was fully absorbed, both legally and ritually, into her husband's kin group at marriage. While the practice faded after the first century BC, it illustrates that Bedouin agnation is at least not of the archaic Roman or contemporary Afghan variety.

A distinctive feature of the Bedouin kinship system becomes apparent once we consider the nexus of marriage, residence and descent. What we designate as 'patrilineal' includes much that does not conform to its defining features. In addition, a society may follow a patrilineal principle when it comes to group membership, but not 'person-to-person relations' that encompass succession, ownership and inheritance (Fox 1976: 52). Patrilineal societies have been identified where women remain full members of their natal patriline for life (Stone 2006: 71), but what makes the Bedouin kinship system unique is that women are held onto so that they are not released at marriage. Women do not just retain rights and duties in their natal patriline, they are actually married into the natal patriline. Bedouin family endogamy with a marriage preference for the father's brother's son is unusual as far as the ethnographic record is concerned. While the worldwide incidence of patrilateral parallel- or patriparallel-cousin marriage (marriage between the children of brothers) is unknown, according to Murdock's (1981: 136) revised sample of

563 societies that include those most carefully and thoroughly described in the ethnographic literature, only 4 per cent of societies prefer parallel cousin marriage with a father's brother's child.

The cultural preference for patriparallel-cousin marriage[3] in the Middle East is well documented and marshalled as evidence of the primacy of patrilineal kinship bonds in Arab societies. Yet, patriparallel-cousin marriage does not simply reaffirm the importance of patrilineal kinship structures, as is frequently assumed, but signals a continuing concern over the fate of women and attentiveness to the maternal contribution to a child's kinship identity – an attentiveness that appears to be prominent among Semitic peoples. Some might see this as bilateral or cognatic kinship, but, at the very least, there appears to be a maternal bias. Lineage endogamy benefits women of the patriline who are not required to change residence at marriage. Patriparallel-cousin marriage allows Bedouin women to fully align their kin membership with that of their spouse and children. As a result, women are able to maintain natal residence and family support as well as tribal parity vis-à-vis their spouse. Marriage between the children of brothers means that, all things being equal, a woman remains near her natal family – her mother, father and brother. This distinctive feature of the Arab kinship system cannot be overstated.

The benefits of endogamy are evident in the Bedouin case as marriage within the minimal segment allows women to circumvent patrilocality. Recall that under patrilineal descent systems, women are born into the patriline, but they cannot transmit descent membership to their children. Just as patriliny 'requires husbands to let go of married sisters and monitor the fidelity of their wives', matriliny 'requires its male and female members to remain united following marriage' (Knight 2008: 73). Because authority and group identification are divvied between men and women in matrilineal descent groups, unlike patrilineal descent groups where authority and descent go through men, the structural continuity and proper functioning of such groups requires holding onto both men and women so that they do not sever ties with their group (Schneider 1962: 7–8). Strong husband-wife ties 'would spell the doom of matrilineal descent' (Stone 2006: 126). In an unusual twist, however, Bedouin men do not let go of their sisters at marriage. Marriage between the children of brothers means that a woman's bond with her husband does not come at the expense of her bond with her brother. In effect, the Bedouin have fused conjugal ties with brother-sister ties. Hence, as Murphy and Kasdan (1959: 24) cogently observed more than half a century ago, patrilineality in the conventional sense of tracing descent in the father's line to the exclusion of the mother 'cannot exist' among the Arab Bedouin precisely because patriparallel-cousin marriage results in the merging of male and female lines in the ascending grandparental generation.

Detailed demographic information on the frequency of intrafamilial marriage among Bedouin in the Middle East and North Africa is sparse; however, estimates derived from reproductive histories of 281 Bedouin women (born between 1942 and 1985) in the Bekaa Valley, Lebanon reveal that the most common forms of first-cousin marriage are patriparallel-cousin marriage (24.91 per cent) and matriparallel-cousin marriage (5.34 per cent), followed by matricross-cousin marriage (4.63 per cent) (Joseph 2013: 96). The frequency of marriages contracted between Bedouin women and their close paternal cousins (i.e. first cousins, first cousins once removed and second cousins) is approximately 32.38 per cent; the distribution breaks down as follows: father's brother's son (24.91 per cent), father's father's brother's son (3.20 per cent), father's brother's son's son (2.85 per cent) and father's father's brother's son's son (1.42 per cent). From this data, we can assert that a substantial minority of Bekaa Bedouin women are married to their close paternal cousins and, for the most part, reside in close proximity to their natal family (including their mother and brother). At the tribal level, a sizeable majority of Bedouin women married men from the same tribe, with approximately 87 per cent of ever-married women surveyed belonging to the same patriline as their spouse. Through such tribally-endogamous unions, women can avoid the discontinuities associated with patrilocality. One of the implications of the Bedouin kinship-marriage-residence pattern is that women can draw upon the support of their natal family. Residence is one of the linchpins of the entire Bedouin kinship system.

At the most elementary level, kinship can be defined as relationships between individuals and groups based on descent and marriage (Stone 2006). Residence, particularly post-marital living arrangements, is closely linked to descent and marriage practices and should be considered in tandem with them. Patrilocal residence is the normative pattern among the Bekaa Bedouin, but the term 'patrilocal' is somewhat misleading in the Bedouin context. Family endogamy creates a unique situation in which both bride and groom remain with their respective agnatic groups at marriage. A woman takes up residence with her spouse, but her natal family reside in the same general area; they are frequently her neighbours. Anthropological kinship terminology does not adequately capture this post-marital residential pattern. (Natolocal usually implies separate residence for bride and groom; for nonhuman primates, 'bisexual philopatry' is the employed designation.) The distinctiveness of the Bedouin kinship system becomes apparent once we consider residential arrangements connected with endogamous marriage.

Parkin (1997) has observed that certain social segments tend towards endogamy, including elite sections in a hierarchical society, religious communities, Indian castes and sometimes entire ethnic groups. Robertson Smith (2014 [1885]) underscored the importance of women remaining with their family of origin and rejected explanations for patriparallel-cousin marriage that centred on keeping property within the family – an explanation favoured more recently by Goody (2004). Patriparallel-cousin marriage among the Bedouin is not confined to wealthy segments of the population. Contemporary Bedouin in the Bekaa Valley note the inadequacy of patrimony to account for the practice (see Joseph 2013).

Because Robertson Smith's argument for matrilineal kinship has been oversimplified and misrepresented, it warrants re-examination. In *A History of Anthropological Thought*, E.E. Evans-Pritchard (1981) undertakes such a reappraisal, but ultimately dismisses the evidence provided by Robertson Smith to support the thesis that the Bedouin, whom Evans-Pritchard (1981: 72) refers to as 'pre-eminently patrilineal', were previously matrilineal. In reviewing the evidence put forth by Robertson Smith, Evans-Pritchard takes issue with his etymological extrapolations. For example, Evans-Pritchard rightfully questions inferring matrilineal descent from the fact that numerous tribes of Arabia use a female eponym. Such linguistic usage does not necessarily mean that the founding ancestor of the tribe was a woman and that descent was traced through women. Evans-Pritchard also correctly questions Robertson Smith's argument that the Bedouin Arab prohibition on marriage to near uterine kinswomen implies earlier matrilineal descent. The rest of Evans-Pritchard's discussion is devoted to refuting Robertson Smith's subsidiary thesis that Bedouin Arabs were historically totemic, a topic of less relevance to the current discussion.

The most puzzling feature of Evans-Pritchard's review is his failure to consider the more compelling, non-etymological evidence presented by Robertson Smith. Most notably, Evans-Pritchard does not mention practices outlined by Robertson Smith that are consistent with matrilineal descent systems, including polyandry or wife-sharing, uxorilocal marriage and the right of women in pre-Islamic Arabia to dismiss marriage partners with little fanfare – a practice that would be difficult to carry out if women did not reside with their own kin. Such oversights are especially problematic considering that Robertson Smith based his observations on reliable and canonic sources, including the Hadith collections of al-Bukhari, widely regarded as the most authentic of all Hadith collections and second only to the Quran as a source of law and authority. What troubled Evans-Pritchard (1981: 77) most about Robertson Smith's account was not his attempt to investigate earlier Bedouin culture forms or institutions, but his 'implicit acceptance of unilinear stages of social development'.

For Smith (2014 [1885]), the explanation for patriparallel-cousin marriage is linked to a previous system of matrilineal kinship. The novelty of Robertson Smith's argument lay in his contention that patriparallel-cousin marriage represents a way of fusing male and female lines after the emergence of descent through males. Robertson Smith (2014 [1885]: 60–61) argued that strict endogamy was unlikely to have been the norm either in early Islamic times or before the rise of Islam. He postulated that matrilineal kinship prevailed in pre-Islamic Arabia and was linked to marriage that was either uxorilocal (i.e. the husband(s) settled permanently with his bride's people at the time of marriage) or duolocal (i.e. the bride and groom(s) reside separately and the groom(s) periodically visits the bride at her kin's residence) and often polyandrous. Even in cases where a woman originally settled with her husband's family, he observed that, in the event of divorce, the children may choose to leave their father and return with their mother to her tribe. To support his inference that women dismiss partners with ease and reside with their own kin, Robertson Smith (2014 [1885]: 65) invoked al-Isfahani's *Kitāb al-Aghānī* (Book of Songs). To document polyandry, he referenced Strabo's *Geography* (ibid.: 133) and the Hadith collections of al-Bukhari (ibid.: 128), among others.

In accordance with Robertson Smith's observations, contemporary scholars affirm, on the basis of literary evidence,[4] that endogamous marriages were unpopular in pre-Islamic Arabia because they were believed to produce defective progeny (Abd Al Ati 1977: 130; van Gelder 2005: 11–12). Matrilineal kinship can also be gleaned from a scattering of south Arabian texts and funeral inscriptions from south and northwest Arabia (Hoyland 2001: 129–130). Research has since identified roughly fifteen different types of marriage for pre-Islamic Arabia, including wife-lending, temporary marriage, 'lovers' secret cohabitation', marriage by capture, polyandry, bride-service marriage, widow or divorcée remarriage, 'errébu' marriage (similar to little daughter-in-law marriage found in pre-modern China except that the adoptee is a son) and 'experimental cohabitation' (Abd Al Ati 1977:

101–102). Additionally, strong brother-sister bonds, one of the telltale signs of matriliny, have been discerned for the pre-Islamic era, providing further support for the matrilineality thesis. Abd Al Ati (1977: 208) observes:

> There is literary evidence that in pre-Islāmic times, brothers (a) loved their sisters and sisters' children, (b) shared their wealth with their sisters, (c) married experienced, older widows and divorced women in preference to young maidens because the former could take better care of their husbands' sisters, (d) heeded the sisters' counsel and sometimes implemented it, and protected their sisters and respected their wishes. On their part, sisters reciprocated and often favored their brothers over their husbands.

As Arabs transitioned from a matrilineal to a patrilineal kinship structure, the operability of the new system depended on recognition of descent through males as a legitimate rule. Robertson Smith deduced that the kinship bond between a mother and her children is regarded as so strong by the Arabs that in order to guarantee that children would remain faithful to their father's lineage, they merged it with the mother's line. The viability of patrilineal descent was achieved by its fusion with uterine kinship. By enjoining women to marry their father's brother's son or other close agnate, society pre-empts a split in allegiance of any future progeny. Women are kept within the family and, therefore, their children, especially their sons and future warriors, could not be drawn away from their father's descent group to join mother's kin and become potential foes. Under endogamous patriparallel-cousin marriage, there is no structural tension between a woman and her children as she belongs to the same lineage as her children and husband – a situation that strengthens the solidarity of the patriline. The bonds of descent and the bonds of marriage are united. Kinship thus continued to hinge on women and their remaining within the kin group after marriage. A new system of male kinship was created, but it was one grafted onto the old system of female kinship. As in the old system, a woman's kin continued to serve as her protectors both before and after marriage, limiting the husband's authority over his wife. As Robertson Smith (2014 [1885]: 103) put it, 'it is an old Arab sentiment, and not a Moslem one, that the women of the group are its most sacred trust, that an insult to them is the most unpardonable of insults. This feeling must have grown up under a system of female kinship'.

Women, Endogamy/Exogamy and Human Origins

While there is some ambivalence surrounding the question of women's status in matrilineal and matrilocal societies, there appears to be a general recognition that the position of women in those societies is relatively high (Lerner 1986; Hrdy 2000: 252). Anthropologists, on the other hand, generally view lineage endogamy in a negative light, with some heralding patriparallel-cousin marriage as a paradigmatic violation of the incest taboo (Tillion 1983). Tillion (1983: 18) described this form of endogamy (i.e. marriage between the children of brothers) as a 'degenerate form' linked to the 'debasement of the female condition', thus prompting her not-so-flattering characterization of the Mediterranean region as a 'republic of cousins'. It is important to keep in mind that incest and exogamy are two separate issues. Incest taboos forbid all sexual relations between certain categories of individuals defined as close kin, whereas rules of exogamy specify that one must marry outside of a kin group (van den Berghe 1979: 115). The two may often coincide, but they are not synonymous. Under Lévi-Strauss's model of reciprocal exogamy, cross-cousin marriage is exogamous and mildly incestuous as sexual relations with tertiary kin (first cousins) are permitted and sometimes preferred. A rule of exogamy is often found in conjunction with a rule that prescribes marriage to a close relative such as a cross cousin.

Lévi-Strauss (1969), following Tylor, conceived of exogamous marriage as the glue holding individuals and larger groups together. Tylor believed that endogamy leads to isolation and is the antithesis of sociality. Without exogamous marriage alliances, both theorists reasoned, human sociality would be all but impossible. For Lévi-Strauss (1969), the purpose of incest taboos is to circulate women through matrimonial exchange, giving rise to culture and allowing human beings to thrive. It follows from this model that 'women are the most precious possession' (ibid.: 62) – the objects of exchange that prop up sociopolitical alliances. To put it another way, women are seen as crucial to the constitution of society, their use as pawns a necessary sacrifice for the greater good.

Van den Berghe (1979: 123) takes a rather different view of exogamy, urging us to consider exogamy and endogamy as two sides of one coin – part of 'a system of mutually complementary rules and expectations that maintain a sufficient level of outbreeding to minimize the appearance of harmful recessive genes in homozygous form, and a sufficient level of inbreeding to retain solidarity through kin selection'. He contends that human societies have not sought to maximize outbreeding, but rather to limit it and find a compromise between inbreeding and outbreeding (ibid.). Tapper (1991) goes further and considers the possibility that ties of affinity will increase, not ameliorate, problems between opposing groups. Among Durrani Pashtuns, most marriages are bride-price marriages (ibid.: 53). Exchange marriages – estimated at 20 per cent (ibid.: 149) – are used politically to resolve quarrels, but they frequently fail to do so. Tapper (1991: 153) explains, 'The possibilities of fostering group solidarity through exchange marriages are clear. ... But, just as often, because the marriages do not necessarily coincide with changes in the control of economic and political resources, the fundamental causes of dispute remain unaltered, or even exacerbated, by the exchange marriage'. Exchange marriages (most of which are sister-exchanges) do not appear to be popular among either Durrani Pashtun women or men, albeit for different reasons. My research similarly suggests that in Bekaa Bedouin groups, where endogamy also prevails, women do not like being exchanged.

Endogamy and exogamy exist side by side as they always have in Arabia. In Bedouin communities of the Bekaa Valley, exogamy is found at different levels of human social organization, but it is not frequent at the tribal level. Exchange marriages are mostly family-exogamous marriages. An exchange marriage in the Bedouin context can be defined as a marriage whereby two men exchange wards, usually sisters, and complete the exchange without bride-price or indirect dowry payment. As a rule, the exchange of women is reciprocal and immediate, requiring no monetary compensation to either family as no side suffers reproductive loss. An exchange marriage is not regarded as autonomous, meaning that if a man divorces his spouse, his sister is required to do the same. Approximately 12 per cent of Bedouin marriages in the Bekaa Valley are exchange marriages, the vast majority of which are sister-exchange marriages.

A small subset (4 per cent) of exchange marriages are forced (*ghasb*) marriages. All forced marriages are exchange marriages but not all exchange marriages are forced. Women in forced marriages did not give their consent to be married. When confronted with forced marriages, Bekaa Bedouin women responded by eloping with a more desirable partner, appealing to tribal chiefs to intervene on their behalf so as to nullify the match, and running away and taking shelter with sympathetic kin or non-kin. Women also use spirit-possession or jinn-possession to socially challenge forced marriages. And, in one case with which I am familiar, a Bedouin women committed suicide as the ultimate act of defiance, prompting several women of her generation to elope in order to avoid a similar fate. That forced marriages should be a subset of exchange marriages is noteworthy and requires further explanation.

Forced marriages bear resemblance to what McLennan (1865) heralded as 'marriage by capture'. Ethnographers and ethnologists have paid little heed to bride capture, ceremonial, symbolic or otherwise, with the notable exception of Fox (1976: 178–179) who suggests a direct link between exchange marriage and marriage by capture:

> I do not mean here to imply that groups who exchanged women always lived in perfect amity. The opposite was usually true. Many tribes have a proverb along the lines of 'we marry our enemies' or 'we marry those we fight'. Often brides are taken from their people by a ceremonial 'capture' which has uncomfortably real overtones and sometimes ends in actual fight or at least a skirmish. (This is the custom of 'bride capture' that sparked off McLennan's interest in kinship...) Nevertheless, the fact that the capture is ceremonialized is indicative of the restraint that exogamy introduces into inter-group relations. The groups concerned may be hostile and see each other as enemies, but they are still dependent on each other for their very continuity, and hence have to come to terms, however uneasy, in order to replenish each other's stock of reproductive capacity. In animal species other than man it is precisely because the individuals or groups are in a state of permanent hostility that they have to develop ritualized means of settling disputes or risk killing off the species by internecine strife. It does not always work, of course, in either human or non-human populations, but the basic tendency is there. Many novels and plays depend for their plots on the ending of a feud by a marriage.

Fox, much like Lévi-Strauss, believes that exogamy is of fundamental importance in human societies. Fox suggests that the exchange of women may have been forced, constituting putative bride capture. While Fox argues that exogamy comes with all sorts of benefits and that those benefits outweigh the costs, he does acknowledge that the costs are far from negligible. In most societies, he believes that this tension was resolved in favour of exogamous exchange marriage. In terms of the benefits of exogamous exchange marriage, exchanging women can unite warring groups or establish political and economic alliances which are mutually advantageous to both wife-givers and wife-receivers. Exchange is linked to the logic of war and may have even grown out of war. Instead of violently exchanging blows, groups co-operate in the exchange of goods, people and information.

But the costs of exogamy still remain. If you marry your enemies, and if it is women and not men who are exchanged, then it is women who are required to leave their kin circle and settle with a foreign, distant and potentially hostile group (assuming that kin relations through marriage had not been sufficiently established). We would expect the costs for women to be high under these circumstances of male philopatry since females frequently do better reproductively when they remain with kin (Hrdy 2000: 51). One of the striking features of forced exchange marriages in Bekaa Bedouin communities is that they pit women against their brothers to the extent that third-party mediation is sometimes required to ameliorate tensions between the opposite-sex siblings (Joseph 2013). It is important to acknowledge that not all forms of bride capture are coercive. Ceremonial capture implies the bride's co-operation whereas non-consensual forms involve either coercion by male kin or a hostile party unbeknownst to the bride and her family. Bride capture occasioned by the woman's kin appears to dovetail with exchange marriage. Yet another variant of marriage by abduction can be postulated from literary evidence that dates to matrilineal, late Bronze Age, Mycenaean Greece (Hughes 2005). The mythical Helen of Sparta – the most notorious of captured brides – is carried away after being wooed by a handsome stranger (ibid.). This form of bridal abduction resembles elopement in as much as it involves the woman as willing participant.

While the relationship between exchange marriage and marriage by capture remains poorly understood, it seems unlikely that exchange marriage would be the exclusive or most sought after method for settling conflicts between rivalrous groups, given that fission and mobility provide an effective means of putting distance between oneself and one's foes. Other social and ritual mechanisms can be used to re-establish social amity and cohesion. With respect to the Bedouin, the question of how broader social allegiances are formed is addressed by Murphy and Kasdan (1959) who explained that even though patriparallel-cousin marriage promotes fissioning, larger aggregations are made possible by segmentary, genealogical tracing, which can unite all Arabs if and when necessary. This means that social unity or integration is not accomplished horizontally through marriage bonds but vertically through 'genealogical reckoning to common ancestors' (ibid.: 27).

Perhaps the most glaring problem with the exogamous reciprocal exchange model lies in its unverified claims about gender relations in early human societies. The assumption that matrimonial alliances (i.e. alliances in which women are treated like objects for exchange) are commonplace, and that women do not individually or collectively resist these exchanges, or that if they do, they are easily put down, paints a dismal picture of gender relations in early human societies and begs the question of whether women exercise meaningful control over their marital and sexual lives. It is clear that the coercion embedded in exchange is strongly contested by Bekaa Bedouin women. What is more, female autonomy is implied by high Bedouin divorce rates (for Egypt, see Abu-Lughod 1999: 149; for Saudi Arabia, see Cole 2010: 75), although divorce rates have been declining throughout Arab societies over the course of the twentieth century (Joseph 2013). While divorce rates are low in contemporary Bekaa Bedouin communities, there are no social impediments to divorcée or widow remarriage. Bedouin widows, however, generally refuse to remarry out of concern for their children's welfare, fearing that a new husband would be less devoted to children from a previous marriage (ibid.: 90–91). In Egypt, Abu-Lughod (1999: 149) reports that divorce is frequent and remarriage comes with no moral disapprobation; divorced Bedouin women receive virtually the same bride-price payments as virgin brides. Dickson (1983: 106–107), who lived with nomadic Bedouin in Kuwait between 1929 and 1936, emphasized that no stigma of any kind was attached to divorce so much so that by the time a woman reached the age of thirty, she had already had two or three husbands, with some women having been married seven or eight times. In fact, in Arabico-Muslim societies more generally, it was the Abbasid age that witnessed a shift in attitudes towards women and marriage – a shift that brought with it a newfound stigmatization to the remarriage of divorcées and widows (Ahmed 1992: 75). And yet even so, there is no simple linear decline. As Rapoport (2005) has conclusively shown, notions of female dependency, emblematic of patriarchy, are contradicted by medieval sources that point to very high levels of divorce (in the form of *khul'*) and female economic independence in medieval Mamluk society.

Evidence from contemporary Southern African !Kung (Ju/'hoansi) foragers similarly reveals that women enjoy considerable autonomy in their marital lives and can dissolve unsatisfactory marriages (Shostak 1998: 277) at any age, resulting in a high rate of divorce throughout adult life (Howell 1998: 145). Finnegan (this volume) provides further evidence of sexual egalitarianism among Central African foragers, particularly as it pertains to ritual activities and co-operative childcare. Women's ability to remain close to natal kin through endogamous marriage (observable in Bedouin communities) also prompts us to more carefully consider the interrelationship between descent, marriage and post-marital residence patterns when theorizing human origins. If early human societies were matrilineal, it seems unlikely that they practiced patrilocal residence. Only 14.5 per cent of matrilineal societies in the ethnographic record are patrilocal (van den Berghe 1979: 111). Similarly, matrilineal kinship could not coexist with a widespread practice of exchange marriage, as that would separate male and female members of the matriline and render the system unstable. It is more likely that the exchange of women is linked to the origins of the state or complex hierarchal structures, as elaborated by Lerner (1986).

In discussing the evolutionary origins of patriarchy, Smuts (1995) argues that the dispersal of females in great apes impedes their ability to create effective alliances and puts females at greater risk of male dominance, aggression, infanticide and sexual coercion. Female bonobos have found a way of sidestepping some of the ill effects of male philopatry by forming strong alliances with other females and spending a lot of time together – a practice that protects females from male aggression and sexual coercion (Silk 2001). In our own species, the majority of modern hunter-gatherers outside of Australia are mostly cognatic and Barnard (2011: 115–16) considers cognatic descent the best model for kinship at the time of early *Homo sapiens*. Even though anthropologists consider cognatic descent to be more flexible than unilineal descent, many groups with cognatic descent are believed to have a 'patrilineal bias' so that preferential treatment (e.g. residence and land rights) would be given to patrilineal descendants, sometimes to the point that differences between the two systems (i.e. cognatic and patrilineal) appear minor (Stone 2006: 173). Assumptions about 'patrilineal bias' appear untenable with respect to most hunter-gatherers. Major critiques of the patrilocal band model, or, more precisely, the 'patrilocal, territorial, exogamous band' model (Lee 1998: 75), suggest that there is a tendency towards matrilocality in hunting and gathering groups due to the prevalence of bride-service (Lee 1998; see also Marlowe 2004; Alvarez 2004).

If my reasoning heretofore is correct, then not only does the argument championed recently by Knight (2008) that early human kinship was matrilineal merit serious consideration, but the contention that the Bedouin represent an archetypal, patrilineal social system is in need of revision. It would be useful to further explore the relationship between exogamy, post-marital residence, exchange by alliance building, and marriage capture in the ethnographic record. Human beings may have a 'capacity for kinship' in the same way that they have a capacity for language (Stone 2006: 21), but the precise content of kinship, regardless of whether it entails a matrilineal, patrilineal, bilateral, or double-descent structure, should not be taken for granted. The fewer assumptions we make about kinship, and the more we subject those assumptions to careful questioning, the better.

Notes

1. One discrepancy may be the division of labour. Unlike modern and Upper Palaeolithic foragers, Middle Palaeolithic (Neanderthal) hominins may have been generalists with less gender and age-role differentiation (Stiner and Kuhn 2009).
2. It is not clear if the practice is found among all, most, or several ethnic groups (e.g. Pashtun, Hāzāra, Tājik and Uzbeks).
3. Islam neither prohibits nor enjoins cousin marriages; rather, they are categorized as 'permissible' (Abd Al Ati 1977: 136).
4. Because physical evidence of poetry in pre-Islamic Arabia consists of only two examples, scholars rely on compositions from the sixth century that began to be assembled in the eighth century (Hoyland 2001: 212). Poetry is accorded very high status in Arab society; hence, even in Islamic times there was a strong incentive towards preservation, not least because it was considered imperative for the elucidation of the Quran and the codification of Arabic grammar (ibid.).

References

Abd Al Ati, Hammudah. 1977. *The Family Structure in Islam*. Indianapolis: American Trust Publications.

Abu-Lughod, Lila. 1999. *Veiled Sentiments: Honor and Poetry in a Bedouin Society*, updated edn. Berkeley: University of California Press.

Ahmed, Leila. 1992. *Women and Gender in Islam: Historical Roots of a Modern Debate*. New Haven: Yale University Press.

Alvarez, Helen. 2004. 'Residence Groups among Hunter-gatherers: A View of the Claims and Evidence for Patrilocal Bands', in Bernard Chapais and Carol M. Berman (eds), *Kinship and Behavior in Primates*. Oxford: Oxford University Press, pp. 420–442.

Barnard, Alan. 2011. *Social Anthropology and Human Origins*. Cambridge: Cambridge University Press.

Cole, Donald P. 2010. *Bedouins of the Empty Quarter*. New Brunswick: Aldine Transaction.

Dickson, H.R.P. 1983. *The Arab of the Desert*, 3rd edn, edited and abridged by Robert Wilson and Zahra Freeth. London: George Allen & Unwin Ltd.

Dixon, Suzanne. 1992. *The Roman Family*. Baltimore, MD: Johns Hopkins University Press.

Evans-Pritchard, Edward Evan. 1981. *A History of Anthropological Thought*, edited by André Singer with an introduction by Ernest Gellner. London: Faber and Faber.

Fox, Robin. 1976. *Kinship and Marriage*. Middlesex: Penguin Books.

Ganesh, Lena. 2013. *Women's Economic Empowerment in Afghanistan 2002–2012: Situational Analysis*. UN Afghanistan Research and Evaluation Unit.

Goody, Jack. 1983. *The Development of Marriage and the Family in Europe*. Cambridge: Cambridge University Press.

———. 2004. 'The Labyrinth of Kinship'. *New Left Review* 36: 127–139.

Haeri, Shahla. 1989. *Law of Desire: Temporary Marriage in Shi'i Iran*. Syracuse, NY: Syracuse University Press.

Howell, Nancy. 1998. 'The Population of the Dobe Area !Kung', in Richard B. Lee and Irven De Vore (eds), *Kalahari Hunter-Gatherers: Studies of the !Kung San and Their Neighbors*. Cambridge: Harvard University Press, pp. 137–151.

Hoyland, Robert G. 2001. *Arabia and the Arabs*. London: Routledge.

Hrdy, Sarah Blaffer. 2000. *Mother Nature*. London: Vintage.

Hughes, Bettany. 2005. *Helen of Troy: Goddess, Princess, Whore*. New York: Alfred A. Knopf.

Jabbur, Jibrail S. 1995. *The Bedouins and the Desert: Aspects of Nomadic Life in the Arab East*, trans. Lawrence I. Conrad, edited by Suhayl J. Jabbur and Lawrence I. Conrad. Albany: State University Press of New York Press.

Joseph, Suad. 1993. 'Connectivity and Patriarchy among Urban Working-Class Arab Families in Lebanon', *Ethos* 21(4): 452–484.

Joseph, Suzanne E. 2013. *Fertile Bonds: Bedouin Class, Kinship, and Gender in the Bekaa Valley*. Gainesville, FL: University Press of Florida.

Knight, Chris. 2008. 'Early Human Kinship was Matrilineal', in N.J. Allen et al. (eds), *Early Human Kinship: From Sex to Social Reproduction*. Oxford: Blackwell Publishing Ltd., pp. 61–82.

Lee, Richard B. 1998. '!Kung Spatial Organization: An Ecological and Historical Perspective', in Richard B. Lee and Irven De Vore (eds), *Kalahari Hunter-Gatherers: Studies of the !Kung San and Their Neighbors*. Cambridge: Harvard University Press, pp. 74–97.

Lerner, Gerda. 1986. *The Creation of Patriarchy*. Oxford: Oxford University Press.

Lévi-Strauss, Claude. 1969. *The Elementary Structures of Kinship*, trans. James Harle Bell and John Richard von Sturmer, edited by Rodney Needham. Boston: Beacon Press. (Original work published in French, 1949.)

Lindholm, Charles. 2008. 'Polygyny in Islamic Law and Pukhtun Practice', *Ethnology* 47(3): 181–193.

Mandaville, James P. 2011. *Bedouin Ethnobotany: Plant Concepts and Uses in a Desert Pastoral World*. Tucson: University of Arizona Press.

Marlowe, Frank. 2004. 'Marital Residence among Foragers', *Current Anthropology* 452(45): 276–284.

McLennan, John F. 1865. *Primitive Marriage: An Inquiry into the Form of Capture in Marriage Ceremonies*. Edinburgh: Adam and Charles Black.

Murdock, George Peter. 1981. *Atlas of World Cultures*. Pittsburgh, PA: University of Pittsburgh Press.

Murphy, Robert F. and Leonard Kasdan. 1959. 'The Structure of Parallel Cousin Marriage', *American Anthropologist* 61(1): 17–29.

Parkin, Robert. 1997. *Kinship: An Introduction to the Basic Concepts*. Oxford: Blackwell Publishers.

Rapoport, Yossef. 2005. *Marriage, Money and Divorce in Medieval Islamic Society*. Cambridge: Cambridge University Press.

Robertson Smith, William. 2014 [1885]. *Kinship and Marriage in Early Arabia*, Paperback edn. Cambridge: Cambridge University Press.

Schneider, David M. 1962. 'Introduction', in David M. Schneider and Kathleen Gough (eds), *Matrilineal Kinship*. Berkley: University of California Press, pp. 1–29.

Shostak, Marjorie. 1998. 'A !Kung Woman's Memories of Childhood', in Richard B. Lee and Irven De Vore (eds), *Kalahari Hunter-Gatherers: Studies of the !Kung San and Their Neighbors*. Cambridge: Harvard University Press, pp. 246–277.

Silk, Joan B. 2001. 'Ties That Bond: The Role of Kinship in Primate Societies', in Linda Stone (ed.), *New Directions in Anthropological Kinship*. Lanham, MD: Rowman & Littlefield Publishers, pp. 71–92.

Smuts, Barbara B. 1995. 'The Evolutionary Origins of Patriarchy', *Human Nature* 6(1): 1–32.

Stiner, Mary C. and Steven L. Kuhn. 2009. 'Paleolithic Diet and the Division of Labor in Mediterranean Eurasia', in Jean-Jacques Hublin and Michael P. Richards (eds), *The Evolution of Hominin Diets: Integrating Approaches to the Study of Paleolithic Subsistence*. Dordrecht, The Netherlands: Springer, pp. 157–169.

Stone, Linda. 2006. *Kinship and Gender: An Introduction*, 3rd edn. Boulder: Westview Press.

Tapper, Nancy. 1991. *Bartered Brides: Politics, Gender, and Marriage in an Afghan Tribal Society*. Cambridge: Cambridge University Press.

Tillion, Germaine. 1983. *The Republic of Cousins: Women's Oppression in Mediterranean Society*, trans. Quintin Hoare. London: Al Saqi Books.

Tucker, Judith E. 2008. *Women, Family, and Gender in Islamic Law*. Cambridge: Cambridge University Press.

van den Berghe, Pierre L. 1979. *Human Family Systems: An Evolutionary View*. New York: Elsevier.

van Gelder, Geert Jan. 2005. *Close Relationships: Incest and Inbreeding in Classical Arabic Literature*. New York: I.B. Tauris.

Suzanne E. Joseph is Associate Professor of Anthropology in the Department of International Studies at the American University of Sharjah. She has carried out long-term fieldwork among Bedouin and peasant communities in Lebanon and Syria. Her areas of current interest are anthropological demography, kinship studies, class and gender inequality, human sociality and violence, and the consilience of the social sciences and humanities with biology. She is the author of *Fertile Bonds: Bedouin Class, Kinship and Gender in the Bekaa Valley* (2013). Her work has also appeared in journals such as *American Anthropologist* and *Current Anthropology*.

Chapter 12

'FROM LUCY TO LANGUAGE: THE ARCHAEOLOGY OF THE SOCIAL BRAIN'

AN OPEN INVITATION FOR SOCIAL ANTHROPOLOGY TO JOIN THE EVOLUTIONARY DEBATE

Wendy James

Introduction

Interest in human origins is on the rise among both academics and the general public, as evidenced by current writings in the newspapers and magazines. A recent example is the much publicized discovery of fifteen individuals of an unknown species, now named *Homo naledi*, apparently from up to three million years ago. They were found deep in a South African cave, suggesting the fascinating possibility that they were buried deliberately – though this is far from being confirmed (McKie 2015; Shreeve 2015). Like the well-known case of 'Lucy', an individual female discovered in 1974 from that broadly comparable period in eastern Ethiopia, the new find will stimulate fresh research. The big questions are obvious to all: how far are such finds part of our own heritage? Answers obviously have to take into account not only biological or archaeological evidence, but the likely presence of creative social and cultural life. Since the middle of the twentieth century, as Hilary Callan's opening chapter indicates, sustained efforts have been made to bring together the perspectives of mainstream science with those of the humanities to focus on such key questions.

A London symposium, sponsored by the Royal Society, was organized by Julian Huxley as far back as 1965, bringing together students of animal behaviour and social anthropologists. This proved a landmark, stimulating exchanges between leading scientists such as Konrad Lorenz and Nikolaas Tinbergen, along with anthropologists such as Victor Turner and Edmund Leach on the topic 'Ritualization of behaviour in animals and man' (Huxley 1966a, 1966b). It so happens that I was present at that meeting; I found it absolutely fascinating, especially all those insights into the courtship displays of the great crested grebe and the triumph ceremony of the greylag goose, but as a graduate student in social anthropology I came away feeling baffled as to how the concept of 'ritual' could properly be extended from human to animal life in this way without its meaning somehow being overstretched. Both the fascination, and the puzzle, remain with me as the volume and quality of academic work in this field has expanded beyond recognition. Direct interventions by social anthropologists have included an interdisciplinary conference on human evolution held in 1994, itself modelled on Huxley's 1965 symposium. The resulting book, *The Evolution of Culture*, edited by Robin Dunbar, Chris Knight and Camilla Power (1999), proved a real stimulus, particularly in introducing gendered perspectives into what had been an imagined world of largely male agency. In her present chapter, Hilary Callan focuses on transactions, trading zones, and sometimes confrontation between 'the (broadly) Darwinian and (broadly) superorganic approaches to the human', but points out that there have also been 'undercurrents' of a more mutually receptive kind: and as a good example, she refers to the British Academy's recent collaborative project 'From Lucy to Language'. Below, I focus on this large-scale example of interdisciplinary teamwork, the challenge it represents in relation to social anthropology, and areas in which conversations of mutual importance could be pursued.

The Lucy Challenge

The seven-year British Academy Centenary Project, 'From Lucy to Language: The Archaeology of the Social Brain' (2003–2010), turned out to be the largest body ever of co-ordinated research emerging from the UK in the field of human evolution. Directed by evolutionary psychologist Robin Dunbar, together with archaeologists Clive Gamble and John Gowlett, the Lucy programme funded a substantial number of core projects and attracted many others into its interdisciplinary framework. As understood by my generation of social anthropologists, the common approach here engages with recent major discoveries bearing on the links between the sociocultural and the physical evolution of *Homo sapiens*. The core theory shaping this work, gaining much recognition as a result, is the 'Social Brain Hypothesis', largely developed by Dunbar. This holds that the increasing size of hominin brains, specifically neocortex volumes, over the millennia is linked to the expanding size of social groups and hence to the stimulus provided by their growing communicative complexity. This itself enables what the Lucy programme often refers to as 'social bonding'. For overviews of the programme, see Dunbar's *The Human Story* (2004) and *Human Evolution* (2014a); or Gamble, Gowlett and Dunbar's *Thinking Big: How The Evolution of Social Life Shaped the Human Mind* (2014a). For detailed examples of findings from the wider Lucy project, see the two key edited volumes: Dunbar, Gamble, and Gowlett's *Social Brain: Distributed Mind* (2010), and *Lucy to Language: The Benchmark Papers* (2014).

A basic principle of the 'Lucy to Language' work is one of developmental continuity over early human history, rather than sharp breaks. Various approaches have recently called for historical continuity in the hominin-human line; see for example Finlayson (2014) who points to water in both climate and landscape as a steady, shaping influence on human evolution and migrations. Likewise, the Lucy researchers do not assume sudden revolutions, or the beginnings and endings of species or fixed stages of tool use; Clive Gamble captures this perspective in his *Origins and Revolutions* (2007). A recent paper by Gamble and his colleagues offers a nice metaphor for representing the linked continuities and overlaps of the Palaeolithic: they suggest we think here of three 'movements' of a symphony. This image 'underscores both continuity and development where themes are repeated and new elements introduced during its course as the tempo changes' (Gamble, Gowlett and Dunbar, 2014b: 24). The three 'movements' correspond roughly to the earliest emergence of the genus *Homo* (from 2.6 ma) with a community size of up to 100; and then the appearance of larger-brained hominins (from 1.5 and especially 0.6 ma) with likely community sizes of 100–120. The third 'movement' sees the beginnings of global distribution and population increase from 300 ka, during which encephalization eventually indicates community sizes of 120–150 for both Neanderthals and *Homo sapiens*. With respect to the evidence for linguistic communication, the consensus among the Lucy researchers is that its earliest emergence, perhaps following laughter, gesture, chorusing and ritual dancing, might have been around for half a million years. However, 'language as we know it' would not have been present until about 200 or even 100 ka. The 'focus' of the latest period from 60,000 years ago onwards is the global population dispersal of *Homo sapiens* from Africa. For each of these broad 'movements' in the long story of our ancestry, thoughtful details are offered for both the technology and art of material culture, along with evidence for the quality of hominin/human emotions.

I should mention right away that two of our social anthropology colleagues who have extensive knowledge of modern hunter-gatherers (Alan Barnard for southern Africa, and Bob Layton for Australia) have participated directly in some of the Lucy projects and publications. Alan Barnard has led the way in arguing the need for social anthropologists these days to engage more directly with the archaeologists and evolutionary scientists on aspects of early human history (see his books of 2011 and 2012 in particular, with a third on language, published in 2016). Again very positively, links have been developed with the Royal Anthropological Institute. A collaborative conference between the Lucy team and the RAI was held in 2005 on the topic of kinship, resulting in the edited collection *Early Human Kinship: From Sex to Social Reproduction* (Allen et al. 2008). Several themes of cross-disciplinary interest came together in this effort, some of which are further discussed below.

The Social Context of the Individual Brain

The Lucy researchers have sought to explore the reasons why, throughout the long story of human evolution, the gradient of brain capacity should parallel that of community size so closely. In complementary ways, they have pursued the primary argument that larger groups, which may well be responding to plain environmental factors (including the danger from predators), require greater and greater skills in 'social bonding'. This pressure leads ultimately to language and complex, multi-layered societies. In pursuing this theme, they relate together research findings from several different disciplines. For example, on the psychological side, the Lucy team make much of the 'Theory of Mind' whereby one creature, such as a chimpanzee, can understand the mental states or representations of another. As human children grow up, they gradually acquire further abilities, for example to guess at the opinions of A about those of B, who may assume what C's motivations are for falsely treating D as a liar... and so on. Dunbar proposes that most of us today can get up to five such 'orders of intentionality', which the audience has to manage when watching a performance of Othello, but only people like Shakespeare can demonstrate a sixth order – clearly needed for writing the drama in the first place (2004: 120, 162). This 'layered' way of presenting modern social interactions allows us to conceive of a gradual increase of their complexity over the long term. However, it is not only Shakespeare, but a good part of the audience, who need to appreciate more than a series of individual intentions. Along with the actors themselves, they need to see how these intentions fit within the unfolding storyline – the plot of the drama as a whole. Marcel Mauss, nephew and collaborator of Durkheim, conveyed in much of his writing a sense of the collective drama of human life, from Palaeolithic masquerades onwards (Mauss 2007 [1947]: 72–89; discussed in James 2014). A key quality of human social life is surely the process whereby individual intentions may interact in such a way as to lead to the collective perception of a social whole; and the imagined possibility of alternatives to this.

   In his classic work with Henri Beuchat, Mauss explored the way that the overall qualities of social life among the Eskimo swung between the winter patterns of concentration and the far flung dispersals of the summer months (1979 [1904–1905]. Taking their lead in part from his work on the Eskimo but echoing Mauss's own later reference to Palaeolithic ceremony, David Wengrow and David Graeber have drawn our attention to archaeological findings which challenge assumptions about social evolution. Across western Eurasia, once occupied by hunter-gatherers on the fringes of the last Ice Age, evidence has been found of concentrated settlements, carved stone monuments and a number of rich, elaborate individual burials. Wengrow and Graeber propose here a relationship analogous to the Eskimo case between 'seasonality and the conscious reversal of political structures' (2015: 597, 600). These peoples evidently took advantage of the seasonal aggregation of large game, creating a superabundance of wealth in specific places, attracting temporary human settlement, much festivity, and both material and cultural creativity. We should not read the situation as the beginnings of institutional hierarchy following ancient egalitarian relations. We should think of it rather as an outbreak of activity on the lines of a carnival, in contrast to the small-scale, but nevertheless recognized forms of authority and leadership exercised when the people lived as scattered nomads in harder conditions. Referring also to some classic writings of social anthropologists on the politics of tribal life – for example, Lévi-Strauss (1969 [1949]) on the Nambikwara – Wengrow and Graeber insist that from the earliest times, human communities have been able to implement regular alternations in the form of their social lives together (2015: 603–604).

Perhaps as a foil to the main themes on which the Lucy project has been focused, how might we explore the varied, perhaps seasonally variable or multiple, content of 'social bonding' in human as distinct from animal groups? The literature on hunter-gatherers worldwide, and the direct experience of fieldworkers among such groups, is obviously a crucial resource (as reflected in many of the chapters in this book). Bob Layton has written on the wider relevance of modern ethnography for evolutionary studies in general (2008a) and has written a fascinating article comparing Aboriginal and Western creationism (2008b). Understandably, a key focus has often been on ritual performance, myths and symbolism. Of course, all hunting and gathering groups – many excluded today from serious hunting anyway – have a long historical past, including aspects of environmental change and complicated relations with neighbouring groups. We know that in early times the coastal fringes of Africa and marine resources, for a start, were very important for human survival and migration. At the same time, at least in the case of north-east Africa, there is much to be found in the myths, rituals and so on of a range of communities no longer living as hunter-gatherers that resonates with recent ethnography of the rainforest hunters. Archaeologists working in the western Ethiopian borderlands have recently been studying minorities not simply as cultural remnants from great antiquity, but as people skilfully finding ways to accommodate ancestral practices and skills with ways of adapting to state expansion on the highlands (Gonzalez-Ruibal 2014).

My own original ethnographic experience was among the Uduk-speaking people of the Sudan/Ethiopian border, a Koman language group with a matrilineal system of kinship and descent (who formerly practised sister-exchange, as some other Koman groups still do). They certainly liked to think of themselves as hunter-gatherers but have been dependent on crops and domestic animals for some centuries. Nevertheless, they treasure many aspects of myth, ceremony, music and cosmology which still evoke those of the hunter-gatherer groups discussed in this volume. For example, I have collected stories about the very first women, who lived in the village but discovered men out in the forest and brought them home; myths of the great Dance at which all the animals came; stories of the evolution of humankind from antelopes; anecdotes about Rainbow Snakes; the common use of red ochre at many rites of passage – a first-time father is smeared in red ochre and dressed in women's beads when the child is brought by the mother's people to his home; stories of the moon as a male, the use of moon oil to revive the dead; and so on and on. Their music (in the 1960s anyway, and to some extent still, after decades of displacement) is largely based on percussion, on horn or bamboo flutes, and on voices (James 1979, 1988; and 2007, plus a website with audiovisual clips). I am sympathetic to Camilla Power's argument about the possible antiquity of such cultural practices, but at the same time they are rarely static and often have more complex regional histories than are yet appreciated.

Space is limited here, so I will focus on three key analytic themes which shape our approach to social relations. Our first concern is typically the interactive life within and between 'families' or households: based on a division of productive labour by gender and age, along with the regulation of mating, marriage and the upbringing of children. To varying degrees, social anthropologists have then sought to portray many collaborative activities of the human imagination, from artwork, stories, songs, dances and games through to religious performance, and to understand their contribution to what we regard these days as the architecture of 'sociality'. As my third core area of our disciplinary relevance to early human history, I believe we should highlight the political nature of community life, always subject to the way in which multiple reciprocities and competing forms of agency have acted, and are still acting, upon each other.

As anthropologists we cannot literally enter the world of early human beings. But as Collingwood famously explained, historians have to exercise their imagination in going beyond the dry evidence available, to 're-enact' the living realities of this or that past age (1946). At least we can claim the wealth of our ethnographic literature, museum collections, and more recently photographs, sound recordings and films, as inspiration for such re-enactment. In the next section, I point to ways in which the three core concerns of social anthropology just identified have already fed into the understandings, and findings, of the Lucy project and suggest where interdisciplinary conversations could be further pursued.

Taking the Conversation Forward: Kinship, Fire and Politics

'Kinship at the Core' (Strathern)

In borrowing the title of Marilyn Strathern's study of an Essex village (1981), I am reminding us all that if the phrase 'Kinship at the Core' sums up what their social world was like in the 1960s, then how much more it must have been applicable to those very early hunter-gatherers who were beginning to work out their own rules of what we might well regard as the primary 'social game'. A growing number of modern evolutionary studies do focus on childbirth, the extended periods of childcare needed as our species developed, along with the growing need for collaboration in this task. Sarah B. Hrdy has pioneered many such lines of research; an early paper with William Bennet had the intriguing title of 'Lucy's Husband: What did he Stand for?' (1981). Hrdy's mature work has become widely known, and through her work on female residential co-operation has brought a new perspective to evolutionary debates (see especially 1999, 2009). There is plenty of scope for furthering debate between the social anthropologists and evolutionary scientists about the way that interactions between infants and mothers, along with other children and adults involved in a close community, should be encompassed within the general concept of 'social bonding'. Too much of the evolutionary literature seems to assume that individuals can naturally recognize each other as kin or non-kin; but surely this has to start from what an infant learns about the world from its mother, its siblings, and other immediate caregivers. Human sociality as we should understand it includes consciously co-ordinated principles governing the way maturing individuals gradually learn to place each other in a wider context. Even before explicit language, this context must have included, firstly, the developing relation between parent/child/grandchild; and secondly, ongoing and shifting relations between males and females within any set of brothers and sisters and their various offspring. Elements of game-playing surely entered very early into the human world here, close to home, becoming more specific, and complex, as language developed. As you grow up, you learn the rules of social life, including those about breastfeeding, childcare, food-sharing, female and male work, followed by patterns of avoidance or of give-and-take in sexual relations from temporary mating up to forms of marriage.

Social anthropology has specialized in these kinds of rules and games; all living human communities have them. Most are founded on principles of some kind about 'marrying out', that is at least beyond the obvious biological connection between parent (at least mother) and child, and between brother and sister (see Allen et al. 2008). In their chapter in the present volume Chris Knight and Jerome Lewis draw our attention to a little-known early work by Durkheim on the importance of recognizing the incest taboo and clan exogamy. While anthropologists today would of course be unhappy with many parts of the argument, the key points can be seen as prefiguring the work of Lévi-Strauss; e.g. 'Thus exogamy is the binding force of the clan. This solidarity is so tight that it is, in fact, reciprocal' (Durkheim 1963 [1897]: 25). The views later developed by Lévi-Strauss (1969 [1949]) on incest-avoidance and group exogamy as the foundation of human society dominated the anthropology of kinship in the post-war decades, before fading somewhat against criticism of male bias ('men exchanging women') and the rise of a more flexible, personal and individualist approach in the late twentieth century. Lévi-Strauss himself was never drawn into the long-term evolutionary aspect of his analyses. However, the work of Robin Fox, discussed by Hilary Callan (this volume), helped to provoke fresh thinking in this area (see Fox 1967, 1975, 1980); and Bernard Chapais, whose research interests have long included both animal behaviour and social anthropology, has recently revived Lévi-Straussian insights. Chapais is rehabilitating the concept of 'deep structure' in relation to the role of kinship in early human evolution, identifying what he calls the 'exogamy configuration' as a key feature of the transition to the human (Chapais 2008: esp. Parts II and III.) He is more sympathetic than many to the need to take into account matrilineal, or at least matrifocal, aspects of kin reckoning in all circumstances, since human kinship in one way or another always has bilateral elements (Chapais 2008: ch. 19). However, Chapais does focus on the abstract principles of kinship, rather than the grounded life of males, females and children in particular places or times. Even the non-specialist can understand that with the growth of the hominin brain, childbirth is going to be increasingly difficult, and infants will need care over extended periods. The co-residential groupings of women, the need for their co-operation, and the advantage of long-lived grandmothers to help with the survival chances of the young makes sense. Whatever the precise dating of the emergence of female coalitions, along with homebases, hearths and so on, this must have been a really crucial period for the development of human sociality as we know it. For an early essay of my own referring mainly to the prevalence of matrifocality as basic to human relationships (at least in Africa), see James (1978); for a strong argument based on the primacy of matriliny in classic ethnographic literature, see Knight (2008); and compare Suzanne Joseph's chapter in the present volume.

The 'exogamy configuration' of Chapais in my view is likely in practice to have emerged, or at least been greatly strengthened, in a matrifocal setting. But it does not have to be associated with any form of unilineality. Nick Allen (2008) has developed an abstract model for 'tetradic society', representing the logically simplest form in which the principles of incest avoidance between primary kin could combine with those of recurrent reciprocity in marriage in such a way as to generate a self-sustaining structure of four sections. This pattern would result from the division of a small and fairly local society according to alternating generation moieties between which marriage is forbidden, and then the bisection of each into exogamous halves, which do intermarry. Your marital partner is of your own generation moiety but from the opposite half; your children join the generation moiety of your own parents (their grandparents). The ceremonial linking up of couples from appropriate sections might perhaps take place at seasonal festivals. It should be plain to see that although one could use the term 'pair-bonding' here, the pairs do not settle down as 'nuclear families' with the boundaries, and the closure, which this phrase suggests. Nick Allen is of the view that the tetradic pattern of double reciprocity within each marriage arrangement might have been invented as a whole, perhaps in Africa before the global exodus of *Homo sapiens* some 60,000 years ago, and persisted as a foundation for the formal moiety, generation and marriage classes we know today from parts of Asia, Australia and South America (and their echoes elsewhere).

Alternatively, as I understand it, Alan Barnard's research among the Khoisan peoples of southern Africa demonstrates that the two basic distinctions relevant to incest avoidance (between individual parents and children, and between brother and sister) are here contained within a basically egocentric network of 'universal kinship' terms, along with other informal modes of address (2008; 2011). If there were simply open networks of kinship before *Homo sapiens* left Africa, I think the argument could be made that the processes of long-term migration and repeated settlement in new lands prompted a consolidation of group categories, boundaries and reciprocal relations. The sharing of specific resources could well have led to the emergence of new forms of authority, and perhaps also the emergence of descent lines and groupings as we know them.

While the Lucy researchers are of course concerned with the ongoing reproduction of any social whole, we do need to consider as specifically as we can how far conceptual principles of reciprocity and game-like rules have helped shape the framework within which we have reproduced our own kind, through sexual/marital organization and through the successful care of children, since some early period of our evolutionary history.

Fire and its Impression on the 'Awakening Mind of Man' (Wittgenstein)

The phenomenon of fire, and the challenges it poses to both animal and human history, has been given a key place in the work of the Lucy researchers. For a very useful survey over time of the ways in which fire has played a part in the building of a 'social brain', see John Gowlett (2010). The harnessing of fire for purposes of cooking, and thus improving general nutrition and the survival chances of children, has struck a popular note (Wrangham 2009); recent updates on this theme and its early relevance can be found in a joint paper by Gowlett and Wrangham (2013). However, as Dunbar and Gowlett point out, 'fires also offer an important social focus that has largely been ignored in the discussion to date' (2014: 277). The first efforts at taking advantage of wild fire, usually caused by lightning, might have occurred as early as 2 million years ago; by 400,000 years ago there is 'unequivocal evidence for hearths in large numbers' (ibid.: 278). By this time, presumably as part of a local homebase, individuals could gather in larger numbers than previously; the core of such a community could itself have grown from earlier groups of co-resident, co-operating females, as proposed by Hrdy. From the social point of view, all in such a community could make use of the extended evening hours of light and warmth for collective socializing. This scenario provides the social anthropologists with a real opportunity to draw on their own experience from fieldwork and from the ethnographic record to find rich parallels: especially on the new opportunities for complex communication of all kinds, including gesture, music, dance, performance, drama, art and language. From the ethnography of living communities, we can gain plenty of insights into what socializing around the evening fire might have been like in early times. Polly Wiessner has recently provided detailed descriptions of fireside storytelling among the Ju/'hoansi Bushmen. Having made a substantial collection of field notes among them in north-west Botswana in 1974, on the various topics of day and night conversations, Wiessner returned several times in recent years to make digital recordings from many of the same people, and to arrange for their transcription. She gives us a rich portrait of the evening storytelling – with the warmth of the firelight, extended hours, congenial company, updates on marriage and other vital matters, gossip and laughter – providing a very good starting point for further ethnographic comparison, and a convincing evocation of the role of the communal fireside in our early history (Wiessner 2014).

Clive Gamble has himself taken the opportunity of attending a dance-gathering around the evening fire of Makuri, a Ju/'hoansi village in Namibia. 'Women sat round a fire, clapping and singing, while the men, wearing rattles on their legs and striking percussion sticks, danced around them'; a photo taken the next morning shows the scene, a modest performance space around the hearth marked out in the sand by the dancers' feet (Gamble 2012: 94–95). There would be nothing much left for the future archaeologist. But Gamble makes a bold comparison with what the archaeologist can know, or at least infer, from the site of Boxgrove in Sussex. Here, half a million years ago handaxes were being manufactured, at least one horse was butchered, and a nearby waterhole was regularly visited. This was long before our own species had arrived; the early humans here were probably *H. heidelbergensis*, ancestors to both Neanderthals and ourselves. Using what he terms 'a relational perspective between hominins, artefacts and place', Gamble nevertheless proposed that Boxgrove could be considered a 'contained performance space comparable to Makuri village' (2012: 96–99). Repeated gatherings were held there, no doubt memorable and of emotional intensity; there were sounds (such as the regular chipping of flint stones) and smells, and Gamble's perspective leads to a sense that there was probably feasting, music and dancing too (for a recent and highly authoritative overview of music and musicality in hominin/human history, see Iain Morley 2013). As yet there is no actual evidence of hearths at Boxgrove, but (quite apart from new discoveries in Africa) by 400,000 years ago they were well preserved at Beeches Pit in nearby Suffolk.

From Gamble's bold example, we in social anthropology too can find inspiration not only from our own personal field experience, but also through an informed, imaginative effort to re-enact (on Collingwoodian lines) the embodied, emotional and creative human life which must have been responsible for the archaeological remains we find today (as Gamble is encouraging us to do). We can even take heart from the philosophers. Wittgenstein once posed a relevant question: 'How could the fire or the fire's resemblance to the sun have failed to make an impression on the awakening mind of man?' (Wittgenstein 2016 [1967]: Remark No. 13). This thought was found among his fragmentary notes of the early 1930s on Frazer's *Golden Bough*. It was elaborated in later notes dealing with the social drama and symbolic ambiguity of fire ceremonies from various parts of the world, including the Beltane Fire festivals of Scotland.

What did Wittgenstein mean by an impression made on the 'awakening mind'? While this might well apply to the experience of any child, it surely evokes for us afresh today not only the psychological but also the social responses that must have accompanied the long story of our control of fire in the archaeological record. The impact of fire goes far beyond an individual mind; it affects the body too, producing fear and causing retreat (and even where not justified, can seem to threaten human death, even sacrifice). In every way, it calls out for co-ordinated action and co-operation – as in keeping children out of the way while the cooking is going on. From the point of view of the regional extension of social relations, it seems likely that the establishment of homebases with hearths and regular gatherings might be followed by patterns of coming and going between such bases, which could facilitate trade and community exchanges of various kinds. The controlled fire has long represented a focus for sociality in all its forms; as John Gowlett remarked recently, 'In a sense, fire is its own ceremony'; 'it structures things' (RAI research seminar, London, 8 October 2014). It surely helps to stimulate what has been called 'joint' or 'shared' attention. Here, we can see a real conjunction between the archaeologists' discoveries of the traces of early hearths, the biologists' identification of warmth and the comfort of companionship with a rise of endorphins to the brain, and that 'effervescence' identified by Durkheim as on the occasion of the gathering of crowds, especially on ritual occasions (Durkheim 1995). The extent to which these come together in the present adds to the strong possibility of their association in early times. But their interrelations go beyond what the Lucy researchers usually mean by 'social bonding'. In accepting Wittgenstein's insights into the potential drama of the shared fire, we can of course extend his imagery also to the 'game-like' character of life and language. The following passage discussing Wittgenstein is very helpful here:

> Our language and customs are fixed not by laws so much as by what Wittgenstein calls 'forms of life,' referring to the social contexts in which language is used. ... [This] is the reason why we all understand

each other. We do not understand each other because of a relationship between language and reality. (Sparknotes Editors 2005)

In my own work I have drawn not only on Wittgenstein's 'language-games' and 'forms of life', but have adopted his phrase 'the ceremonial animal' as a way of highlighting this vision of what certainly seems to me central in defining the essentially human (James 2003).

From Games to Politics:
Some Tensions in the Concept of 'Social Bonding'

Along with Chris Knight and others I believe it is worth returning to the concept of *Homo ludens* – 'Man the Game-Player' (Huizinga 1949 [1938]) – and asking how far human interactions as far back as we can imagine them could have arisen from a deep tendency among humans to challenge and counter-challenge. Colwyn Trevarthen has pioneered the study of musicality inherent in human communication, evident already in children; in an illustrated conference presentation he showed us how early we feel the urge to join in a rhythmic exchange – a father carries a newborn on his chest, and they exchange friendly grunts. When the father's attention is distracted, it is the newborn who prompts him to start up the 'conversation' again ('Birthlight' conference in Cambridge, May 2011). For insights into such early beginnings of rhythmic exchange in social life, see for example Panskepp and Trevarthen (2009). The father lives in a larger world, the give-and-take of which the infant has already started to pick up. Even in this vignette, as in all games, one has to begin somewhere to learn the rules governing the interactions of individuals. Even simple games also require an agreed framework of spacing and timing, perhaps a background sense of situation, to make the game possible. And perhaps here is the place of laughter. Children do this kind of thing among themselves all the time and it is arguably a model for the way that game-playing of a structured kind permeates adult family life, from productive activities to parties (in a growingly interesting literature, see for example Wyman 2014: 173–178).

Over and above the spontaneous, innovative engagements of two or three individuals, among youngsters there will always be movement towards a recognition that social consensus has to depend on rules, reciprocities, categories, conventions and notions of fairness – or shared rejection and protest against these. Behavioural studies have recently taken forward the investigation of shared attention, of the kind in which even very young children can point to objects in order to draw others' attention to them (thus provoking interaction).

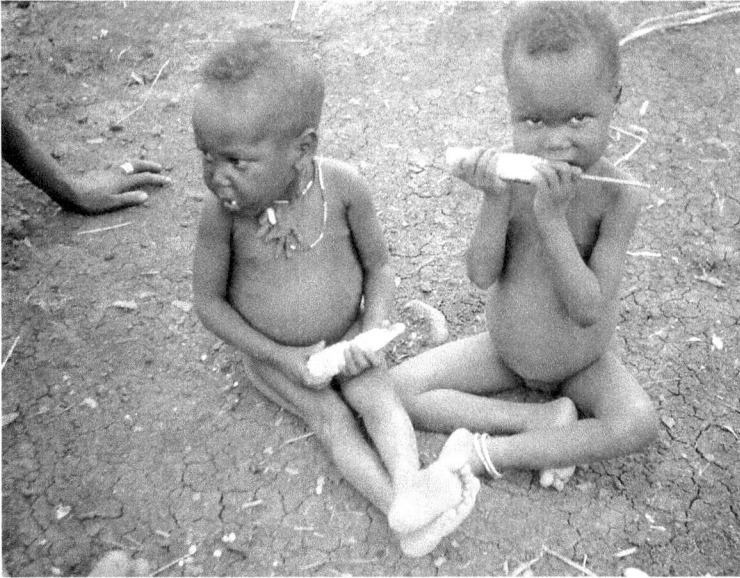

Figure 12.1: 'Hey, did you see *that?*' 'Take care! They're watching us'. Photo: Wendy James, in an Uduk village near the Sudan/Ethiopian border, 1966.

Pertinently, Michael Tomasello of the Max Planck Institute for Evolutionary Anthropology in Leipzig has asked 'Why don't apes point'? (Tomasello 2006). We are close here to current treatments of 'performance'.

A useful notion for us to develop further in this context is that of the 'arena' within which parties may compete – but always with an audience who know the rules: for example, in the case of courtship displays (Miller 1999: 71), or Shirley Ardener's focus on the political potential of women's dramatic performances based on sexual insult (republished in the present volume). Jerome Lewis has demonstrated a wonderful case of the fertile mix of women's language, play, outbursts of mimicry, theatrical sketches and music in the performances of the Congolese Mbendjele (Lewis 2009). Elsewhere too, games are competitive, sometimes collaborative, sometimes invented and spontaneous, sometimes antagonistic, often involving language or shouting, singing, play-acting, cheering, etc. This is the world evoked by Steven Mithen, in relation to the mix of social communication which may originally have produced formal language (2005).

Language, undeniably, in its emergent forms must have drawn on its predecessors, i.e. chorus-chanting, gesture, dance. All these require a person's response to the initial sounds and movements of others, and then back again, in an anticipated division of labour to make the whole meaningful. In all cases, shared spacing, timing and 'plot' underpin the encounter. Such interactivity, often competitive, is rooted more deeply than just the need for group cohesion, or the 'bonding' of larger and larger numbers. Recent ideas about the formation of human society have taken on a distinctly 'political' turn. Not everything serves the interest of all equally, even in the supposedly most egalitarian of circumstances. Chris Knight pioneered the recognition of gender politics from the earliest times, with his vision of the primal revolutionary sex-strike (1991). His and Camilla Power's most recent work develops ideas of resistance and 'counter-' or even 'reverse-dominance' as possible ways into understanding the rise of coalitions, perhaps most crucially those female coalitions devoted to sharing childcare as part of a world shared in material terms with the males who provide meat, but rich in the ritual and symbolic expression of complementary gender relations. This scenario might be a good context for the development not only of symbolic ceremony but also for deliberately discreet forms of linguistic communication – even in the sense of private, conspiratorial exchanges (for recent discussions, see Power 2014; Knight 2014).

The Lucy literature leads the social anthropologist to ponder questions of how a simple relation between language and 'social bonding' can explain very much, given the extraordinary diversity of languages in the world, and the political tensions within and between them, as far back as one can trace. It is certainly worth reflecting on the fact that in practice, language itself can obscure rational communication; it can offer privacy, even secrecy, and keep translators at bay. I remember that as children, my brother and I deliberately 'invented' a language between ourselves which our parents could not understand. Here, some of the issues have already been put up for discussion by colleagues, and it is important for us to follow through the implications in conversation with the scientists where we can (see Nettle 1999: 214–227; Barnard 2012: 83–104, esp. 97–99; 2016). From such recent work, the question does emerge as to why there is, and apparently has been since the beginning, such a diversity of languages in the world, imposing barriers to communication. Mark Pagel has reminded us that some 7000 languages are still spoken in the world today; his work with Ruth Mace has confirmed that the highest regional densities are clustered in the tropics (such as Papua New Guinea) where they are resistant to easy change. He suggests that even with the spread of writing, languages positively like to flag up their distinctiveness – for example, in relation to differences in American and British English spellings (Pagel 2014: 78). Language may also, sometimes, conceal distinctiveness in the phenomena to which it points; and this applies as much to our understandings of ourselves in relation to the world of the nonhuman creatures as to anything else.

'Mind the Gap' (Dunbar)

Robin Dunbar points out that we share a long evolutionary history with the great apes: 'Yet, it is surely obvious to everyone that we are not "just great apes"'. The crucial difference between us and the other great apes does not so much lie in anatomical or cognitive differences that have been emphasized in the past, such as bipedalism or tool-making, but, continues Dunbar, 'the real difference lies in a much more intangible set of competencies – the ability to live in the virtual world of the mind ... the world of culture' (2014b: 4). He gives storytelling and religion as archetypal examples of what this means, and points out that no other living animals have the neuronal computational power to make it possible. The social brain hypothesis, linking evidence of the growth of brain capacity to the scale and complexity of social group size, offers a framework within which we can try to place some of those more 'intangible' aspects of our evolution. Dunbar has famously proposed an overall transition from 'grooming to gossip'; but while this might stand metaphorically for what has happened over a couple or more million years, it is only since the emergence of 'language as we know it' over the last 200,000 years that we could possibly take it literally and ask what our ancestors were gossiping about, and why, and with or against whom. And in what kind of language can we ourselves try to clarify what is involved in this key transition or those which preceded it? Two examples will illustrate the problem.

'Fission and Fusion': an Example of Language on Different Levels

In their recent work, Wengrow and Graeber (2015: 600) touch on the ambiguity of the motif of 'fission and fusion', which has become a touchstone in evolutionary studies. The Lucy literature itself offers us this example of how language can shift between social anthropology and animal behaviour studies. For example, the expression 'fission/ fusion social systems' is used quite often, whether in respect of animals or early hominins (see the relevant Index references in Dunbar, Gamble, and Gowlett 2010: 522; and Dunbar, Gamble and Gowlett 2014: 498). When I first came across this usage, I assumed that the evolutionists had adopted the expression from the work of Evans-Pritchard (1940) on the cattle-herding Nuer of the upper Nile. He used it in a deeply political sense of historical feuding and potential reconciliation at different levels of the overall ideological structure of patrilineal descent lines. Emphasis is often placed on the distinct political identity of such descent groups; it is not often pointed out that although they held collective rights in the cattle herds, the cattle were actually in circulation all the time in the context of marriage settlements between lineages. All members of a patrilineage, women as well as men, had matrilateral relatives elsewhere, and such connections were often important in peace-making (Evans-Pritchard 1951; cf the Introduction by James to the paperback edition, 1990). 'Fission' and 'fusion' were not simply a description of seasonal regroupings on the ground. Adam Kuper has drawn attention to Evans-Pritchard's way of drawing various concepts from the world of physics, such as the relational qualities of social time, and space; with reference to Nuer hostilities and alliances he notes further:

> Borrowing an idiom once again from the physicists, Evans-Pritchard called this a process of 'fission and fusion'. 'Fission and fusion in political groups', he explained, are two aspects of the same segmentary principle, and the Nuer tribe and its divisions are to be understood as an equilibrium between these two contradictory, yet complementary principles. (Kuper 2015 [1973]: 57–58, quoting Evans-Pritchard 1940: 148)

Marriage ties through lineage exogamy of several kinds played an important part in the flexibility of social collaboration, since all forms of kin and family connection, including adoption, for that matter, may create ties between lineages, overlapping alliances, or even temporary friendships which can facilitate peace-making.

Could something of the character of such an overall social/cultural schema have played a part in human history from 200 ka, or even from 500 ka? Perhaps; if so, this would be very important. But the way in which today's evolutionary scientists use the expression 'fission and fusion' is not derived from Evans-Pritchard. It seems to indicate simply the regular movements of individuals gathering together and separating for pragmatic purposes of survival. 'Ultimately, however, the capacity to manage fission-fusion sociality depends on a community's ability to maintain social coherence when individuals meet each other only intermittently' (Dunbar et al. 2014: 338). This view builds on the work of animal ethologist Hans Kummer (1971), who adopted the phrase quite independently of its then existing currency in social anthropology. In a much later *Current Anthropology* debate Kummer provided one of several short 'Comments' on a collectively edited piece entitled 'Fission-Fusion Dynamics'. He explains that in his contribution he was trying

> to bridge the 40 years since my colleagues and I analysed the daily regrouping cycle of hamadryas baboons and termed it a fusion-fission society. Methods and emphases have changed since then... We were not anthropologists but ethologists relying on fine-grained observations and testing hypotheses by experiment. I welcome the comprehensive revival of the topic but also have some doubts. (Kummer 2008: 644)

This is a good example of how the slippage of words, while obviously creative, can potentially blur boundaries – a point applicable of course to Evans-Pritchard's own original borrowing from nuclear physics.

On 'Sociality': Humans vs. Spiders?

In tandem with the recent work by the Lucy researchers on early human history, there has of course been a tremendous growth in the study of the other animals. The latter studies are often amazing, and beautiful, in their revelations of the intelligence, communicative capacities and group life of other creatures. But an old problem is emerging in new forms: that is, what Hilary Callan described long ago as the 'slippage of language' between the ways in which we portray and analyse human life on the one hand, and animal life on the other (1970). I do remember a Human Science student who once emphasized to me when we were discussing pair-bonding: 'Well, but swans do get married, don't they?' I had to ask who sent out the invitations, who did the washing up afterwards, and who would be bringing up the kids later on.

The term 'sociality' has recently seen a rise in popularity, not only among social anthropologists, but to a surprising degree also among students of animal behaviour. It does seem to be a particularly slippery, if attractive, concept on which to base our conversations with the evolutionary scientists. One of the earliest examples of the use of the term occurs in Frances Hutcheson's inaugural address of 1730 as Professor of Moral Philosophy at Glasgow. Even his title in its correct translation from the Latin reads 'On the Natural Sociality [*socialitate*] of Mankind'. Distinguishing 'sociality' explicitly from that 'sociability' [*sociabilitas*] which is the 'source of nearly all our duties', he claimed that writers had not 'sufficiently addressed the general question ... of what the sociality (*socialitas*) of our nature consists in, or, finally, with what part of our nature we are rendered apt and inclined to society'. 'Society' was more than the friendliness of personal encounters, but rather to be found through the imagination of a larger world, through 'reading histories or the narratives of travellers, or even when from the stories of drama we receive a certain image of human nature, even in the remotest nations or centuries where no advantage of our own is involved' (Hutcheson 2006 [1730]; cf discussion of various other early uses in Barnard 2011: 70–71). The concept of 'sociality' as used here by Hutcheson could be said to encompass a holistic, and comparative, view of key institutions and practices of the kind covered in modern sociology and social anthropology and touched on above; it needs to be used with care in our conversations over human origins, and only with extreme care in relation to nonhuman animals. However, consider the recent spread of the term to unexpected species: 'Sociality has arisen in several different groups of spiders.... Thus spiders working together can capture larger prey than solitary individuals ... but how spiders become habituated to social living ... provides additional insight into conditions favouring the evolution of altruism' (Hui and Deacon, 2010: 181). Leaving aside the question of whether the term 'sociality' can reasonably be stretched as far as this from its human context, we have to recognize that even in the case of nonhuman primates, interactions and experiential encounters studied by the biologists are typically between conceptually separate individual agents; and often only 'of the moment' as they are observed. 'Groups' themselves tend to be understood as the sum of interactions between individuals visible in physical proximity, without a plot or storyline running through the whole, unless provided by the observer.

In Conclusion

'Religion' is one of those concepts which has resisted an easy transfer to the world of nonhuman animals – by contrast with the flexibility of 'ritual', as applied to mutually enacted performances in the animal as in the human world, and noted at the start of this chapter. It is in the area of 'Religion' that social anthropologists (among others) are likely to feel strongest reservations about the behavioural/functionalist explanations offered by the 'Lucy' approach (typically, that religion with its emotions, myths and symbols provides a large-scale form of corporate bonding). In particular, while our Lucy researchers do accept that 'beliefs' refer to an imagined world (e.g. Dunbar 2014b:

12, 14), they tend to emphasize, as explanation in itself, the warmth that can be generated by endorphins rushing to the brain in the course of collective gatherings, and thus community solidarity (the parallel with Durkheim's 'effervescence' always well taken). The immediate problem is of course that the events and experiences of religious life are more than the feeling of a moment, but are encompassed within the wider frameworks of sociality, themselves often in tension, which guide our shared lives over time – as with those seasonal outbursts of festivity among Palaeolithic hunter-gatherers of the northerly latitudes, or the lunar-phased ritual and symbolic performances of African hunter-gatherers. The advent of writing and the production of sacred texts have obviously led to the modern concept of the 'doctrinal religion', but most anthropologists would not wish to essentialize the contrast here with the religious worlds of non-literate human societies past or present.

In this chapter, I have suggested that the broad framework for human evolution provided by the 'Lucy to Language' collaborative research programme has much to stimulate social anthropologists. At the same time, I have pointed to three distinctive areas where we could engage in further discussion with the biologists and archaeologists. These include topics on which we have particularly focused in our ethnographic, comparative and analytical work on living society: the areas of 'family and kinship', of mutual creativity in linguistic and artistic production, and in the political aspect of our lives together. All three modes of social interaction are characterized by purposeful 'give-and-take' (or its refusal); that is, by game-like rules and conventions often remembered from the past but always open to revision and re-invention. Whereas a straightforward concept of 'social bonding' between smaller or larger numbers of individuals may be adequate for baboons or spiders, further refinement is required for human social life. If this can be thought about constructively in relation to the emergence of humanity, it would be a useful input into current discussions. For me, this emergence is not simply a matter of 'symbolism' or 'ritual' or shared emotion as against the pragmatic requirements of survival. It is rather a matter of growingly complex communications with those around us, drawing both on reason and on feeling which may give rise to new mutual understandings not always transparent to an observer. One marital pairing may come to be appropriately linked in mirror image with another; through conversational or musical practice between parties, new words or tunes may emerge; images of the social whole may be deliberately created and enhanced at times of seasonal or other gatherings which become highly significant festivals. Social life for us is so often a matter of joining in the game around us – and maybe competing in order to enforce, or change, the rules. It has to be more than just 'bonding'. When looking at the evidence provided by the archaeologists, biologists and psychologists for early human history, we have to ask: when did the games begin?

Acknowledgments

I am grateful both to the editors of this volume and to several other colleagues, including Robin Dunbar, Clive Gamble, John Gowlett and Colin Leakey, whose suggestions have helped me clarify the arguments of this chapter.

References

Allen, N.J. 2008. 'Tetradic Theory and the Origin of Kinship Systems', in N.J. Allen et al. (eds), *Early Human Kinship: From Sex to Social Reproduction.* Oxford and Malden, MA: Wiley/Blackwell, pp. 96–112.

Allen, N.J. et al. (eds). 2008. *Early Human Kinship: From Sex to Social Reproduction.* Oxford and Malden, MA: Wiley/Blackwell.

Barnard, A. 2008. 'The Co-Evolution of Language and Kinship', in N.J. Allen et al. (eds), *Early Human Kinship: From Sex to Social Reproduction.* Oxford and Malden, MA: Wiley/Blackwell, pp. 232–243.

———. 2011. *Social Anthropology and Human Origins.* Cambridge: Cambridge University Press.

———. 2012. *Genesis of Symbolic Thought.* Cambridge: Cambridge University Press.

———. 2016. *Language in Prehistory.* Cambridge: Cambridge University Press.

Callan, H. 1970. *Ethology and Society: Towards an Anthropological View.* Oxford: Clarendon Press.

Chapais, B. 2008. *Primeval Kinship: How Pair-bonding Gave Birth to Human Society.* Cambridge, MA: Harvard University Press.

Collingwood, R.G. 1946. *The Idea of History.* Oxford: Clarendon Press.

Dunbar, Robin. 2004. *The Human Story: A New History of Mankind's Evolution.* London: Faber & Faber.

———. 2014a. *Human Evolution: A Pelican Introduction.* London: Penguin.

———. 2014b. 'Mind the Gap: or Why Humans Aren't Just Great Apes', in R. Dunbar, C. Gamble and J. Gowlett (eds), *Lucy to Language: The Benchmark Papers.* Oxford: Oxford University Press, pp. 3–18.

Dunbar, R., C. Gamble and J. Gowlett (eds). 2010. *Social Brain, Distributed Mind.* Oxford: Oxford University Press.

———— (eds). 2014. *Lucy to Language: The Benchmark Papers*. Oxford: Oxford University Press.

Dunbar, R., and J. Gowlett, 2014. 'Fireside Chat: The Impact of Fire on Hominin Socioecology', in R. Dunbar, C. Gamble and J. Gowlett (eds), *Lucy to Language: The Benchmark Papers*. Oxford: Oxford University Press, pp. 277–296.

Dunbar, R., C. Knight and C. Power (eds). 1999. *The Evolution of Culture*. Edinburgh: Edinburgh University Press.

Dunbar, R. et al. 2014. 'The Road to Modern Humans: Time Budgets, Fission-fusion Sociality, Kinship and the Division of Labour', in R. Dunbar, C. Gamble and J. Gowlett (eds), *Lucy to Language: The Benchmark Papers*. Oxford: Oxford University Press, pp. 333–355.

Durkheim, Émile. 1963 [1897]. *Incest: The Nature and Origin of the Taboo*, trans. and introduced by E. Sagarin. Published together with A. Ellis, *The Origins and the Development of the Incest Taboo*. New York: Lyle Stuart, Inc.

————. 1995 [1912]. *The Elementary Forms of Religious Life*, trans. and with an Introduction by K.E. Fields. New York: Free Press.

Evans-Pritchard, E.E. 1940. *The Nuer: A Description of the Modes of Livelihood and Political Institutions of a Nilotic People*. Oxford: Clarendon Press.

————. 1990 [1951]. *Kinship and Marriage among the Nuer*, paperback edn with introduction by W. James. Oxford: Clarendon Press.

Finlayson, C. 2014. *The Improbable Primate: How Water shaped Human Evolution*. Oxford: Oxford University Press.

Fox, R. 1967. *Kinship and Marriage: An Anthropological Perspective*. Harmondsworth and Baltimore: Penguin Books.

————. 1975. 'Primate Kin and Human Kinship', in R. Fox (ed.), *Biosocial Anthropology*. London: Malaby, pp. 9–35.

————. 1980. *The Red Lamp of Incest*. London: Hutchinson.

Gamble, C. 2007. *Origins and Revolutions: Human Identity in Earliest Prehistory*. Cambridge: Cambridge University Press.

————. 2012. 'When the Words Dry Up: Music and Material Metaphors Half a Million Years Ago', in N. Bannan (ed), *Music, Language, and Human Evolution*. Oxford: Oxford University Press, pp. 81–106.

————, J. Gowlett and R. Dunbar. 2014a. *Thinking Big: How the Evolution of Social Life Shaped the Human Mind*. London: Thames and Hudson.

————. 2014b. 'The Social Brain and the Shape of the Palaeolithic', in R. Dunbar, C. Gamble and J. Gowlett (eds), *Lucy to Language: The Benchmark Papers*. Oxford: Oxford University Press, pp. 19–49.

Gonzalez-Ruibal, A. 2014. *An Archaeology of Resistance: Materiality and Time in an African Borderland*. Lanham, MD: Rowman and Littlefield.

Gowlett, J. 2010. 'Firing Up the Social Brain', in R. Dunbar, C. Gamble and J. Gowlett (eds), *Social Brain, Distributed Mind*. Oxford: Oxford University Press, pp. 341–366.

———— and R. Wrangham. 2013. 'Earliest Fire in Africa: Towards the Convergence of Archaeological Evidence and the Cooking Hypothesis', *Azania: Archaeological Research in Africa* 48: 5–30.

Hrdy, S.B. 1999. *Mother Nature: A History of Mothers, Infants and Natural Selection.* New York: Pantheon.

———. 2009. *Mothers and Others: The Evolutionary Origins of Mutual Understanding.* Cambridge, MA: Belknap Press.

——— and W. Bennett. 1981. 'Lucy's Husband: What did he Stand for?', *Harvard Magazine* 83, July-August: 7–9, 46.

Hui, J. and T. Deacon. 2010. 'The Evolution of Altruism via Social Addiction', in R. Dunbar, C. Gamble and J. Gowlett (eds), *Social Brain, Distributed Mind.* Oxford: Oxford University Press, pp. 177–198.

Huizinga, J. 1949 [1938]. *Homo Ludens: A Study of the Play-Element in Culture.* London: Routledge and Kegan Paul.

Hutcheson, F. 2006 [1730]. *De Naturali Hominum Socialitate. Oratio Inauguralis.* Glasgow: The University Press. Inaugural Oration included in J. Moore and M. Silverthorne (eds), *Logic, Metaphysics, and the Natural Sociability* [sic: should be 'Sociality'] *of Mankind*, trans. M. Silverthorne. Indianapolis: Liberty Fund. Available at: http://oll.libertyfund.org/?option=com_staticxt&staticfile=show.php%3Ftitle=1723&chapter=80693&layout=html&Itemid=27 (accessed 28 June 2013).

Huxley, J. (ed). 1966a. 'A Discussion on Ritualization of Behaviour in Animals and Man', *Philosophical Transactions of the Royal Society of London*, Series B: Biological Sciences 251: 249–271.

———. 1966b. 'Ritualization of Behaviour in Animals and Man', prepared as an Auxiliary Contribution for UNESCO, dated 28 February 1966. See: http://unesdoc.unesco.org/images/0015/001560/156054eb.pdf (accessed 10 August 2015).

James, W. 1978. 'Matrifocus on African Women', in S. Ardener (ed), *Defining Females: the Nature of Women in Society.* London: Croom Helm, pp. 140–162.

———. 1979. *'Kwanim Pa: The Making of the Uduk People. An Ethnographic Study of Survival in the Sudan-Ethiopian Borderlands.* Oxford: Clarendon Press.

———. 1988. *The Listening Ebony: Moral Knowledge, Religion and Power among the Uduk of Sudan.* Oxford: Clarendon Press.

———. 2003. *The Ceremonial Animal: A New Portrait of Anthropology.* Oxford: Oxford University Press.

———. 2007. *War and Survival in Sudan's Frontierlands: Voices from the Blue Nile.* Paperback edition with new Preface, 2009. Oxford: Oxford University Press. Accompanied by website with audio and video clips: www.voicesfromthebluenile.org.

———. 2014. 'Human Life as Drama: A Maussian Insight', *Journal of Classical Sociology* 14(1): 78–90.

Knight, C. 1991. *Blood Relations: Menstruation and the Origins of Culture.* New Haven and London: Yale University Press.

———. 2008. 'Early Human Kinship was Matrilineal', in N.J. Allen et al. (eds), *Early Human Kinship: From Sex to Social Reproduction.* Oxford and Malden, MA: Wiley/Blackwell, pp. 61–82.

———. 2014. 'Language and Symbolic Culture: an Outcome of Hunter-gatherer Reverse Dominance,' in D. Dor, C. Knight and J. Lewis (eds), *The Social Origins of Language*. Oxford: Oxford University Press, pp. 228–246.

Kummer, H. 1971. *Primate Societies: Group Techniques of Ecological Adaptation.* Chicago: Aldine.

———. 2008. 'Comment', in F. Aureli et al. (eds), 'Fission-Fusion Dynamics: New Research Frameworks', *Current Anthropology* 49: 627–654.

Kuper, A. 2015 [1973]. *Anthropology and Anthropologists: The British School in the Twentieth Century,* fourth edition. New York: Routledge.

Layton, R.H. 2008a. 'What Can Ethnography Tell us About Human Social Evolution?', in N.J. Allen et al. (eds), *Early Human Kinship: from Sex to Social Reproduction*. Oxford and Malden, MA: Wiley/Blackwell, pp. 113–127.

———. 2008b. 'Aboriginal versus Western Creationism', in R.A. Bentley (ed.), *The Edge of Reason? Science and Religion in Modern Society*. London: Continuum Press, pp. 31–38.

Lévi-Strauss, C. 1969 [1949]. *The Elementary Structures of Kinship*, trans. R. Needham. London: Eyre & Spottiswoode.

Lewis, J. 2009. 'As Well as Words: Congo Pygmy Hunting, Mimicry, and Play', in R. Botha and C. Knight (eds), *The Cradle of Language*. Oxford: Oxford University Press, pp. 236–256.

Mauss, M. 2007 [1947]. *Manual of Ethnography*, ed. N.J. Allen, trans. D. Lussier. Oxford and New York: Berghahn.

——— and H. Beuchat. 1979 [1904–1905]. *Seasonal Variations of the Eskimo: A Study in Social Morphology*, trans. J.J. Fox. London: Routledge & Kegan Paul. McKie, R. 2015. 'This Face tells us why we must Rethink our Views on our Ancestors', *The Observer*, 13 Sept., p.38.

Miller, G.F. 1999. 'Sexual Selection for Cultural Displays', in R. Dunbar, C. Knight and C. Power (eds), *The Evolution of Culture*. Edinburgh: Edinburgh University Press, pp. 71–91.

Mithen, S. 2005. *The Singing Neanderthals: The Origins of Music, Language, Mind and Body*. London: Weidenfeld & Nicolson.

Morley, I. 2013. *The Prehistory of Music: Human Evolution, Archaeology, and the Origins of Musicality*. Oxford: Oxford University Press.

Nettle, D. 1999. 'Language Variation and the Evolution of Societies', in R. Dunbar, C. Knight and C. Power (eds), *The Evolution of Culture*. Edinburgh: Edinburgh University Press, pp. 214–227.

Pagel, M. 2014. 'War of Words', in *The Human Story. New Scientist: The Collection*, issue 4: 77–79.

Panskepp, J. and C. Trevarthen. 2009. 'The Neuroscience of Emotion in Music', in S. Malloch and C. Trevarthen (eds), *Communicative Musicality: Exploring the Basis of Human Companionship*. Oxford: Oxford University Press, pp. 105–146.

Power, C. 2014. 'Signal Evolution and the Social Brain', in D. Dor, C. Knight and J. Lewis (eds), *The Social Origins of Language*. Oxford: Oxford University Press, pp. 47–55.

Shreeve, J. 2015. 'Mystery Man: A Trove of Fossils Found Deep in a South African Cave adds a Baffling New Branch to the Human Family Tree', *National Geographic Magazine* 228(4): 30–57.

SparkNotes Editors (2005). *SparkNote on Ludwig Wittgenstein (1889–1951)*. Available at: http://www.sparknotes.com/philosophy/wittgenstein/section3.rhtml (accessed 15 March 2015).

Strathern, M. 1981. *Kinship at the Core: An Anthropology of Elmdon, a Village in North-west Essex in the Nineteen-Sixties*. Cambridge: Cambridge University Press.

Tomasello, M. 2006. 'Why Don't Apes Point?', in N.J. Enfield and S. Levinson (eds), *Roots of Human Sociality*. Oxford and New York: Berg, pp. 506–534.

Wengrow, D. and D. Graeber. 2015. 'Farewell to the "Childhood of Man": Ritual, Seasonality, and the Origins of Inequality', *Journal of the Royal Anthropological Institute (N.S.)* 21: 597–619.

Wiessner, P. 2014. 'Embers of Society: Firelight Talk Among the Ju/'hoansi Bushmen', *Proceedings of the National Academy of Sciences* 111: 14027–14035. doi: 10.1073/pnas.1404212111.

Wittgenstein, Ludwig. 2016 [1967]. *The Mythology in our Language: Remarks on Frazer's Golden Bough*, trans. Stephan Palmié, ed. Giovanni Da Col. With a series of commentaries by anthropologists, including V. Das, D. Graeber, W. James, H. Kwon, M. Lambek, M. Puett and C. Severi. Chicago: Chicago University Press, for HAU.

Wrangham, R. 2009. *Catching Fire: How Cooking made us Human*. New York: Basic Books.

Wyman, E. 2014. 'Language and Collective Fiction: from Children's Pretence to Social Instititutions', in D. Dor, C. Knight and J. Lewis (eds), *The Social Origins of Language*. Oxford: Oxford University Press, pp. 171–183.

Wendy James, CBE, FBA, is Emeritus Professor of Social Anthropology and Fellow of St Cross College, Oxford. She has taught in various degree courses, including Human Sciences, and Archaeology and Anthropology. Her main research has been carried out in Sudan, South Sudan and Ethiopia. Her most recent books are *War and Survival in Sudan's Frontierlands: Voices from the Blue Nile* (2007/9) and *The Ceremonial Animal: A New Portrait of Anthropology* (2003), both with Oxford University Press. She served as an external member on the British Academy's Management Committee for its Centenary Project, 'From Lucy to Language: the Archaeology of the Social Brain' (2003–2010).

AFTERWORD

Alan Barnard

Our subject matter, in social anthropology, is 'humankind', and more precisely this species in the context of both its cultural diversity and its common biological foundation. It is indeed appropriate for our (sub) discipline to start thinking about such issues after so many years of neglect, particularly in the United Kingdom where social anthropology was born. Let me therefore take the opportunity to reflect on general issues, to comment on the chapters presented in this volume and to add my own views on what I have been working on in recent years. In the most recent times, this has been the origin of humankind's greatest achievement: language. But let me leave that topic aside for one moment: I will return to it later.

I am very grateful to the editors for giving the chance to add an 'Afterword'. The volume as a whole has turned out wonderfully and should provide students and professionals alike with a chance to explore new ways of thinking. By this I mean thinking in general about humanity and thinking about specific problems in the study of human origins. These are, of course, issues that social anthropology is designed to deal with, and yet so often it is left to biological anthropologists, archaeologists and evolutionary psychologists – all of whom have rather different perspectives. We can see this clearly, for example, in the British Academy's edited volume *The Speciation of Modern* Homo sapiens (Crow 2002), which has contributors from the other branches of anthropology but none from social anthropology. So let me start by having a closer look at the unique contribution that social anthropology can make to this problem.

Before *Social Anthropology and Human Origins*

Before my *Social Anthropology and Human Origins* (Barnard 2011) there was no book on the market to suggest how the two fields – social anthropology and human origins – fitted together. We all knew that they did: this had been clear some 150 years ago! Darwin, himself a Fellow of the Anthropological Institute (later the Royal Anthropological Institute), would have been astonished at the way things turned out: each sort of anthropology making its way independently of the others. The authors here continually make this point: each branch of anthropology has contributions to make, but social anthropology seems to have left the scene at about the same time that the discipline became professionalized in the United Kingdom through Malinowski, Radcliffe-Brown and their students. Interestingly, Radcliffe-Brown, who so strongly sought to build 'a natural science of society' (Radcliffe-Brown 1957), failed to pull together the social and the natural in his project. In North America, things were not that much better, and we had both the original 'four fields' model and the subsequent split of the discipline away from the early ideas of Franz Boas (see Stocking 1974).

The sequel to *Social Anthropology and Human Origins*, was called *Genesis of Symbolic Thought* (2012). It now seems such an obvious successor, in spite of the fact that I had not had it in mind until the earlier volume was almost out. It really only became a sequel once it had been written, although others had already been preparing the way, for example Wendy James's *The Ceremonial Animal* (2003), a book that pays tribute to the all-embracing nature of anthropology. The third in my own series, *Language in Prehistory* (Barnard 2016), came naturally too, but I am not sure whether my compulsion to write it came first, or whether I simply had a vision of the place of language within symbolic thought. I suspect they came almost simultaneously, rather as symbolic thought and the development of language came into being nearly at the same time. Some would indeed argue that symbolic associations (such as ochre to represent blood) preceded language, while others see the description of such things by language as necessary in a co-evolutionary sense or in actually coming first.

At any rate, that is my first set of three contributions to the field, and with the present volume it seems the notion of human origins has very rapidly come of age. Social anthropology and human origins is part of our discipline now, and the connection between the two should be taken seriously. This book is different and truly new. It is not just that there is so much to run with, but that social anthropology has until now been reluctant to do it and has a lot of catching up to do. As

I wrote in *Genesis of Symbolic Thought*, 'Symbolic thought is what makes us human' (Barnard 2012: i). There is no reason to leave all the fun to archaeologists, biological anthropologists, linguists and the like. Social anthropologists have at least as much claim to this subject matter as anyone else, and as this volume demonstrates we social anthropologists can play the game very well indeed.

In spite of Chris Knight's enormous contribution to the study of language evolution, through the many EVOLANG conferences he set up together with Jim Hurford, Chris never contributed a full volume in that field. However, his edited collections *The Cradle of Language* and *The Prehistory of Language*, both with Rudolf Botha (Botha and Knight 2009a, 2009b), set the scene for further developments in linguistic prehistory. The difference between those two volumes was that the first emphasized specifically African material, and the latter dealt with more general data. That distinction is important because, of course, Africa was the continent on which language emerged. Knowledge of that fact is actually fairly recent. It can be dated at least back to work by Luigi Cavalli-Sforza (see e.g., Cavalli-Sforza 2001), although the idea of an African origin of humanity goes back to Charles Darwin and Thomas Huxley. They were competing against nineteenth-century Asian-origin theorists like Ernst Haeckel. Through the twentieth century, many still held to the idea of an Asian origin. The exact relation between symbolic thinking and early language remains an unsolved problem. Knight would favour an emphasis on the symbolic, whereas others (particularly linguists) might give precedence to language and grammar. The chapter here by Smith and Hoefler is relevant in this context, arguing for a common source of symbols and grammar through the cognitive underpinnings of metaphor. Similar insights can be seen, for example, within the earlier volume *The Evolution of Culture* (Dunbar, Knight and Power 1999), some of whose contributors are also represented in the present volume. However, soon after that book appeared the news came that red ochre was found with clearly symbolic markings. A date of more than 70,000 years ago was given. This was followed by shells that had been strung together, then more ochre at Blombos and further sites such as Pinnacle Point. All this pointed to incontrovertible proof that humans had developed symbolic thought by 70,000 years ago and very probably rather earlier (see, e.g., Henshilwood 2009). The Middle Stone Age had been known as a separate and distinctly African phase of human evolution ever since the 1920s (see Goodwin and Van Riet Lowe 1929), but its symbolic significance was new in the late 1990s.

This very constellation of ideas is thus historically located. It has undergone multiple twists, shifts and contestations within the deeper story of anthropology as a whole. Among these are the relation of the social and the biological, the place of prehistory among the anthropological sciences, the origin and development of metaphor and language, the evolution of kinship structures and of cultural cognition, close relations with other disciplines (including genetics, sociobiology, ethnobiology, ethology and primate studies), the idea of sociality, implications for human sexuality and gender relations, the notion of a cognitive revolution, with an intense emergence of shamanism and religious belief, hunter-gatherer society as the natural condition of humanity, and symbolic uses of material culture and of animals. We also have in the present volume the essence of our discipline, which is cross-cultural comparison, and we have comparison in time: from the days of Darwin and Robertson Smith, for example, to the present, and the grand idea of deep history. That idea is present in a number of the chapters here, at least implicitly.

It is very hard to imagine what is missing from the volume. It is all here, and for me personally it feels good to be associated with this trend. I do hope though, that it is not just a trend but quite possibly marks a new configuration of anthropological ideas. It may be of interest to some that I was not in favour of simply pulling together biological anthropology, social anthropology and other 'anthropologies' when I began *Social Anthropology and Human Origins*. That would have been too easy. However, I have grown to accept the need for a more complex configuration. I do not expect social anthropologists to give up ethnography or biological anthropologists to give up biology! The point is that we should recognize our differences, while at the same time being able to comprehend each other's interests. Who knows what comes next? But that will have to wait until future debates, and I look forward to these. It is after all in our social anthropological tradition that we do not simply provide answers, but look for problems to solve. These are not an end in themselves, but a starting point for future debates. And this is a never-ending process: discovery leads to challenges, and these lead to debates. As soon as debates result in conclusions, we begin to debate again. This is the nature of our discipline.

Human Origins and Social Anthropology

The problem of human origins has in fact taxed some social anthropologists almost since the beginnings of our discipline. But most certainly, this has not been the case in recent decades! There is also to some extent a national, as well as an institutional, question: in several countries, the divisions among the anthropological sciences are fairly complex. In others, they are less so. In my own university (the University of Edinburgh), social anthropology stands alone, or rather sits along with Politics and International Relations, Social Policy, Social Work and Sociology, as well as various area studies centres, in a loosely-structured School of Social and Political Science. In other universities, the discipline of social anthropology is fully independent, or part of a larger vision of anthropology, including biological anthropology, prehistoric archaeology or material culture and (sometimes) anthropological linguistics. In other countries, particularly in the United States and Canada, it is part of a 'four-fields' constellation: social or cultural anthropology, together with physical or biological anthropology, archaeology and linguistics. Whether the practitioners of each are on good terms with the others is largely a matter of departmental politics. Certainly, in some cases over the last thirty or forty years, there have been famous splits among the four fields, and consequent separations into independent subject areas. On the other hand, smaller departments in North America are often Departments of Anthropology and Sociology, or similar.

It is no wonder then that the identity of subjects and disciplines is problematic. I would hope that this volume might help to rectify the problem, although I may not go quite as far as Adam Kuper and Jonathan Marks (2011) in suggesting that we should be going to each other's conferences. Doing that, however, might at least bring us together for discussion and debate. Like it or not, the diverse branches of a greater 'anthropology' are different subjects in many countries, and we do generally have to live within such a configuration. All I would suggest is that we talk to each other, and do understand that there is an anthropology out there that is greater than any of us can easily comprehend, or indeed bring within our specialist concerns. The biological foundations of the human condition constitute the backbone of the anthropological sciences taken as a whole, but not in the sense of the sociobiology of the 1970s. That does not mean we have to give up the 'social' in social anthropology! On the contrary, it is the social that shows that we are human, and the social dimensions of human interaction are precisely what constitutes human diversity. This human diversity, in the classic realms of economics, politics, kinship and religion, is the product of evolution. We should never forget this. That is why I now support concerted efforts to bring together the diverse branches of a larger anthropology, to the exclusion of none of them.

The Chapters

In order not to cause confusion or indeed conflict with the introduction to the present work, I will say just a few words about the chapters, taking them in alphabetical order.

Shirley Ardener's chapter, originally published as a paper in 1973, is reprinted here. This chapter offers a comparative ethnographic treatment of three groups in Cameroon: the Bakweri, Balong, and Kom. Then she compares these traditional instances of insult and militancy to other African cases and to similar forms in the British and American women's movements of that period. The opposition of respect and submission, it seems, is common both to the ethnographic cases and to Western forms of collective gender relations. The significance of this highlights the deep cultural importance of the symbolic expression of sex and of gender relations across the world. In the end, Ardener points us towards the idea of universals here, although the case is (or was in 1973) not quite conclusive.

Hilary Callan takes us back to the early stages of the interest in biosocial anthropology. This was also in 1973, but (like all the others) in a new chapter published for the first time here. In that year the Association of Social Anthropologists held its Decennial Conference on the topic 'New Directions in Social Anthropology'. The 'new direction' she takes on is that which gave rise to the volume *Biosocial Anthropology* (Fox 1975). As Callan points out, this was a time of popular interest in the 'biosocial', as exemplified within American cultural anthropology by Sahlins's (1977) *The Use and Abuse of Biology*. It was a time of academic interest in feminism, but also of a growing interest in human ethology and of resistance to the right-wing attitudes that to some commentators seemed to underlie that field. *Biosocial Anthropology* was published in the same year as E.O. Wilson's (1975) *Sociobiology: the New Synthesis*. For me, the strange thing is that social anthropology has been so slow to take on public debate on issues such as those surrounding human evolution. Perhaps, in the 1970s, the time was not right. The sociobiological world was full of public interest, and there were disagreements within the field, and possibly that is why social anthropology felt then that it had no place. To see humans as much like ants and termites would be to throw away the very nature of our discipline. Happily both biological and social anthropology have come a long way since then, and therefore the time is exactly right for a review such as Callan presents here.

Roy Ellen returns us to safer ground: the world of incised red ochre and its implications for symbolic thought. But he makes an interesting observation: whereas social anthropology looks back from the present towards the past, evolutionary biology looks towards the future from its position in the past. For me, this difference is so obvious it needs hardly any comment, but it is not an understanding that seems that apparent to some of our colleagues. Social anthropology is so used to using ethnographic analogy that it has become second-nature to us, whereas archaeologists, for example, seem endlessly to fret over their use of analogies. In a way, Ellen gets around this problem by pointing out that the world is much more complex than we give it credit for. We have to look beyond African models towards those representing the whole of humanity. He is right to point us towards the complexities of cognition and to the use of language, not to mention towards the origins of kinship and religion. However, he turns our attention, in a sense, away from these and towards a vision of natural history in the minds of early humans. If these things, natural history in the minds of early humans, are not the subject matter of social anthropology, then what are they?

Morna Finnegan takes us directly to the point. Symbolic thought, in her view, was originally the preserve of females. Yet it is dialogical: it depends on the interaction of males and females, on relations through the generations and on the development of egalitarian ideology through such sexual and generational relations. Sex, gender, power, co-operation, relations of joking and avoidance: it is all there. Finnegan's argument is based on Knight's (1991) theory of the origins of symbolic thought. I have never been a strong supporter of this view, but it does make sense in itself and of the Mbendjele ethnography that informs Finnegan's theoretical ideas. The strength of any anthropological idea has to rest on its ability to explain through the understanding of ethnography. This chapter is a splendid example of that notion.

Wendy James makes a very explicit move to bring together ideas from social anthropology and the allied subjects. Invoking fire, water and other necessities of social life, she truly makes an attempt to create a constellation of anthropological sciences. As she points out, the concept of sociality, in use at least since Frances Hutcheson's inaugural lecture (in 1730) as Professor of Moral Philosophy at Glasgow, is one element that unites both sides of the biological/social anthropology divide. But more than this, she takes us to the heart of social anthropology with her concerns with ritual and religion and kinship, not to mention language. This last element of human sociality is so fundamental that it is often overlooked. Language is also an attribute that can be used to explain an essence of human social life, for it is in language that we see the vast potential of interaction that has been with us since long before hunter-gatherers became cultivators.

Suzanne Joseph's chapter stands in partial contrast here. At first glance, its relevance is not obvious. However, closer inspection reveals really quite close connections to classical interests in the study of kinship, whose existence lies at the very foundation of anthropology (see also Layton 2006: 123–126). Joseph reawakens nineteenth-century concerns with Arabia and debates over whether patriliny or matriliny came first. With great skill, she guides us through the evidence on gender and kin relations in the Middle East and North Africa, both ancient and more recent. She returns us once again to a fundamental set of questions: what was the basis of the earliest human forms of kinship? How have kinship systems evolved and why?

Chris Knight and Jerome Lewis again take us briefly to the nineteenth century and to other fundamental problems for anthropology today. The fundaments do not change, but are part of the very fabric of anthropology itself. Like Smith and Hoefler, they see metaphor as the key, and in particular its reliance on literal falsehood. It is the logical contradiction inherent in metaphor that makes it so potent, and so useful for the explanation of things like totemism, symbolic meaning and pretty much everything that is distinctly human (see also Lewis-Williams and Pearce 2004: 81–108). They also return us to hunter-gatherer lifestyles, in central, southern and eastern Africa and Australia, and we must never forget it is among these peoples that humankind has its origins. We in the West have evolved away from such lifestyles, but beyond diversity humans are essentially just highly advanced hunter-gatherers.

Chris Low reframes the conception of another form of 'late hunter-gatherer' social life: the Upper Palaeolithic (UP). He wishes to see it not so much as a cognitive revolution, but as a set of new ways of perceiving. Much of his argument is based on Michael Winkelman's (2010) 'biopsychosocial' view of shamanism, as understood through Bushman or San ethnography. I am not so sure of the time depth here, for I tend to see the UP as a late stage of what in Africa tends to be known as the Middle Stone Age. Admittedly, the MSA (280,000 to around 50,000, or to around 25,000 years ago) lasted far longer than the UP. The UP lasted from perhaps 50,000 to around 10,000 years ago. The practice of shamanism, although it lies within this period, is so widespread that it is hard to see it as anything other than very ancient. Shamanic ritual is part of both shamanic and symbolic culture, and it is probably safe to interpret it very widely and very deeply as a marker of humankind's most spiritual essence. That said, (in Low's words) 'the dance is not a church but the doctor's office'. As good social anthropologists, we need to try to see things as our informants do: in this case, the San of southern Africa.

Camilla Power takes a different route towards the reconstruction of early cosmology. As she says, anthropology has largely abandoned the search for deep history. This is ironic, given that now through advances in genetics, not to mention a clearer idea of the predictive capacity of marine isotope stages, it should be very possible to put natural science together with archaeology and anthropology to solve such problems. In addition to the texts cited by Power, the even more expansive treatment by Michael Witzel (2012), a professor of Sanskrit at Harvard, shows equal promise. Power succeeds very well indeed in bringing together the ethnography of several hunter-gatherer groups from diverse parts of Africa. There are deep structures of belief and ritual that only a (deep) historically informed social anthropology could make sense of. Witzel does this through global comparisons of mythological systems, though without anthropological analysis.

Thea Skaanes explores the world of therianthropes and eland in the *epeme* ritual dance of the Hadza. As with several San groups, both therianthropes and eland are important in ritual activities. For me, this hints at very ancient and possibly once widespread symbolic relations between animals and people. The Hadza are of course an isolate, speaking a click language but one not traceably related to the Khoisan (Khoesan) languages of southern Africa. Among Skaanes' intriguing ethnographic findings: killing and eating an eland represents sharing a spiritual force, for the eland is like a person and spiritual kin to the Hadza. In other words, the eland is like an ancestor.

Andrew Smith and Stefan Hoefler take on a problem dear to my heart: the emergence of language and all that goes with it (metaphor, symbols and grammar). The problem is not a simple one, because the paths to its existence involve both symbolic communication and grammatical structure. The solution, according to Smith and Hoefler, is to see the problem through a ratchet effect of repeated steps in cultural evolution. In this way, grammar and symbol do not have to be separated, but evolve together within the same system. Rather than seeing metaphor as restricting meaning, they see it as enabling the next step in building new meanings. In short, what for others is so often seen as a problem has in fact a fairly simple and elegant solution. Language evolved along with what it is used for, and not as a thing completely separated from symbolic thought. Exactly which came first, and how, remains an area of contention.

Finally, Ian Watts brings us to the comparison of rain animals in southern Africa and northern Australia. This is not trivial, since it highlights the significance of these two cultural points whose divergence from the rest of humanity must lie at some 60,000 years. His conclusion is fascinating: 'the snake-like modified rock at Rhino Cave may represent the last common ancestor of [Australian] Yurlunggur and [South African] !Khwa'. Again, we are in deep history, and this deep history turns out to be decipherable. Watts puts a good case for his conjecture, and to correct Radcliffe-Brown, anthropology could do with a bit more conjecture if conjecture can reveal insights like these. The search for human origins does require the consideration of big issues, and no doubt it is time for a larger anthropology (and I include here one with archaeological insight) to take this on.

Collectively these chapters point to a refreshing future for our discipline; they suggest many ways in which there can and should be co-operation among the different anthropological sciences. That is not to say that social anthropology should give up its distinct identity. On the contrary, the subdiscipline of social anthropology is unique in its concern with the full breadth of knowledge that anthropology affords. No other subdiscipline can claim this. Social anthropologists should reclaim their role as leaders and coordinators of research into human origins. We certainly fulfilled these roles in the nineteenth century, and a return to these nineteenth-century concerns is not a return to the past. It is indeed a giant leap forward. The chapters touch on many of the concerns of social anthropology, even as narrowly defined. Trends and unifying factors include a concern with the significance of ritual and cognition, I am thinking here of Ellen, James and Low. Finnegan, Knight and Lewis, Power and Watts all make use of Knight's model of human symbolic thought. Metaphor in hunter-gatherer worldviews also features prominently in several chapters. The thing that strikes me as most interesting is that every chapter explores such concerns as this with an eye open to the bigger picture, and the debates suggested should engage not only social anthropologists but also our colleagues writing within related disciplines.

Language, For Example

Finally here, let me say something about language and how it probably came about. There are indeed many theories about this, and mine is but one. However, it is the product of a good deal of thinking and analysis, and is the result of social anthropological understanding rather than being primarily based on findings in other fields: neuroscience, evolutionary psychology, biological anthropology or whatever. My ideas are dealt with in some detail in *Language in Prehistory*, but a few words on them now seem appropriate.

In a sense, language is the essence of what it means to be human. There is nothing in primate communication (never mind in birdsong or anything else) that is remotely like language. Nevertheless, we assume great diversity in the ways sentences are constructed and used. Languages, in other words, are all the same but nevertheless differ! They probably began through some mutation, like (though not necessarily identical to) the FOXP2 mutation that is common to nearly all humans and to Neanderthals, and possibly common to other 'humans' (in this broad sense) too. Beyond mutation are several related M's: multilingualism, myth and migration. Included in myth here is also sexual selection, or the 'Scheherazade effect' (Miller 2000): narrative as an evolutionary device. The mythological Scheherazade stayed alive by never finishing her story, and prehistoric princes and princesses may have done something similar. One recent set of authors (Martin et al. 2014) might also throw in a fifth M, namely mindfulness: that thing that is lost when immediate-return hunter-gatherers make the transition to delayed-return economic systems. It is plainly obvious (at least to me) that the social norm among hunter-gatherers was multilingualism. The fictional Tarzan of the Apes is supposed to have spoken twenty-nine languages and dialects, the same number as Sir Richard Burton (Griffin 2012: 90). If that may seem preposterous, I once did meet a San man who spoke some eight languages in five different language families. This was probably not that far from the norm (in some parts of the world) for much of human prehistory.

As for migration, that is what led a group of possibly only 2000 southern or eastern African hunter-gatherers to spread ultimately across the globe to become all of us: *Homo sapiens sapiens*. This may have been after the volcanic explosion of Toba in modern Indonesia some 74,000 years ago (see Oppenheimer 2004; 2009). Toba was originally a mountain, though today it is a lake. The very idea that everyone on earth is descended from these 2000 people (or, some say as many as 10,000) is astonishing. Others, such as our Denisovan and Neanderthal ancestors, played a part too, but how many social anthropologists see this? Or see their role in the creation of language? Or indeed see the implications of a migration of an even smaller number, perhaps just 150, across the Red Sea or Gulf of Aden to Yemen, with their descendants off to India, Southeast Asia, Australia and the Americas (see e.g., Oppenheimer 2004: 155–159)? Social anthropology in general remains rather ignorant of these things, let alone reluctant to think about them or debate them. It seems strange to me that the subdiscipline that specializes in the study of the symbolic should not take an interest in pursuing such things. Not only are they interesting; they are fundamental to our connections with the disciplines that share our concern with the human species.

Language, of course, is what enables both simile and its more mystical variant, metaphor. Metaphor, symbolic thought and symbolism, gender and kinship, deep history and the tension between the social and the biological: they are all treated in one way or another within this volume. In my view, this is the stuff that social anthropology has been needing for a long time, and the present volume shows that the wider anthropology is at last coming of age. The chapters by some of the authors here, particularly the one by Smith and Hoefler, return us to this problem. Metaphor, in a sense, makes us human. It is ironic that metaphor should seem marginal, or indeed that linguistic anthropology should so rarely be taken into account within the United Kingdom. British anthropology, as much as North American, is based on learning exotic languages, understanding the idea of linguistic diversity and seeing the implications of the relation between thought and language. Language is as much a part of anthropology as the classical components: economics, politics, kinship and religion. All are necessary in a true vision of anthropology.

Economics, Politics, Kinship and Religion

In an economic sense, human social life in early times was based on what James Woodburn (1980; 1982) has called an immediate-return economic system. That is, humans evolved from an economics of immediate procurement, and towards one of what he calls delayed-return. The interesting thing is that this pre-Neolithic system has lasted at least well into the last century, if not into the present one. It is, of course, not merely Neolithic and post-Neolithic peoples who have possessed delayed-return structures, since many hunter-gatherers too have these. According to Woodburn, hunter-gatherers who store their food or otherwise 'plan ahead' in any sense are also in the delayed-return category, as indeed are Australian Aborigines because they 'farm out their women'. In other words, the men, at least, 'plan' through their concern with reproductive rights. The essence of immediate-return economics is an egalitarian principle.

This political principle is, of course, culturally defined. It also differs according to very specific cultural conventions.

Among the best known examples of exchange in hunter-gatherer societies is the Ju/'hoan practice of *xaro* or *hxaro*, known to the Naro as *//'āe*. (The spelling *hxaro* has become traditional within anthropology, although in fact there is no *h* in the word. The *x* is a voiceless velar fricative.) It is found nowhere else in the world except among Ju/'hoansi and their neighbours. According to this practice, people give non-consumable property to each other in what Lévi-Strauss might have called delayed direct exchange. Exchanges are reciprocated, but only with the delay, which could be a week or a month, and never with the same item or the same kind of item. These exchanges imply the right of an individual to use the *xaro* partner's territory to hunt and gather in (Wiessner 1982). Thus they function to redistribute property, rather as does potlatching among the First Peoples of the Northwest Coast (see Rosman and Rubel 1971). The same egalitarian principle as we find among the San is typically present in hunter-gatherer politics too. The Northwest Coast aside, this does not, of course, imply that there is only one form of egalitarianism among all hunter-gatherers. As Ellen reminds us, there is great diversity among hunter-gatherers of the world, and we cannot assume an exclusively African model for the deep past. The mechanisms for extending egalitarian principles are varied, but the idea is the same: a lack of superiority trumps the desire for greater wealth. For me, certainly, an African model is the most persuasive though for humankind as a whole (see Barnard 1999).

There is no doubt that biological and cultural evolution influenced each other, and that biological evolution did not cease when culture seemingly took over as a dominant evolutionary force. The common culture that humanity once shared was, of course, a hunter-gatherer one, although diversity extends back as far as one might expect. Hunter-gatherers do not generally accumulate wealth, but find ways to redistribute their property through social means, including both sharing and exchange. Although the details have been questioned, the idea of an 'original affluent society', made popular through the work of Marshall Sahlins (1972), was a prehistoric reality. The foraging mode of thought involved quite different sets of values from those of Western or other recent societies. The accumulation of wealth was considered antisocial, as it still is in hunter-gatherer communities such as among Kalahari San. In such communities, giving property away is idealized. Likewise, followership is, in a very real sense, favoured over leadership.

Followership shows deference to the whole community, while seeking to lead others can show self-interest.

In virtually all living hunter-gatherer kinship systems, everyone in society is classified as belonging to kin categories in relation to everyone else (Barnard 1978). In short, there is no such thing as not being 'kin': each person stands in some kind of classificatory 'kin' relationship. In fact, the very notion of 'society' entails this, and it is associated with inalienable rights of primordial possession (see Barnard 2001). Such universal systems of kin classification were probably the norm when all societies were small, and everyone knew everyone else. If Robin Dunbar's (2003) notion of a group size of around 150 is correct, this could easily be possible. This is the predicted group size for humans, based on comparisons of brain size among primates generally. Hunter-gatherers typically retain such group populations, whereas others are able to transcend this in building societies much larger in scope and with greater economic capacity.

After hunter-gatherer times came the Neolithic, a later period when humans learned to raise livestock and grow crops, especially grain. In a sense, this was a step backwards in social evolution. I am not saying that we as a species have not advanced a great deal since the Neolithic. Rather, we have lost as well as gained. Hunter-gatherers are not primitive or stupid: long ago they developed ritual and religious ideologies, mechanisms to disperse wealth as well as to accumulate it, and to overcome material shortages. Also, language, mythology and symbolic thinking had appeared long before the Neolithic. Although violence among individuals may be common, collective violence among hunter-gatherers generally is not. As the epigraph in Richard Lee's *The !Kung San* asks, 'Why should we plant, when there are so many mongongos in the world?' (Lee 1979: v). In the long run, it is agriculture that leads to collective violence more than it leads to a shortage of food.

Economics, politics, kinship and religion, then, are all interconnected (as indeed is language). Religion may seem out of place in this list, but (as Wendy James explains) it was through religious ideas that humankind developed cosmological assumptions, symbolic thought and perceptions of the world around us. It is integral to humanity and indeed to human diversity, and therefore to social anthropology's fundamental concerns. All are aspects of the order of the world, and therefore are fundamental to the 'social' things that make up social anthropology.

Conclusion

If we do not fully agree, then that is to the good. Humanity is diverse, and so too are our opinions, at least in their detail. Yet, of course, they are not mere opinions. Each of the authors here has argued a case and argued it from a vast collective knowledge of what social life is. We do not disagree, though, on the basics. In order to understand social life we must study it as well as reflect on it. In order to understand evolution, much the same is true. It is our belief that a return to evolutionary models is not only necessary for social anthropology, but also good for the idea of a true anthropology. The time is right for a reconfiguration of anthropological ideas. It is not just a matter of 'rethinking' in Leach's (1961) or Needham's (1971) sense. As the song says, those days are past now, and in the past they must remain! Rather, we are looking to build something more, with insights gained from the full gamut of anthropological ideas. We do this without prejudice for or against theoretical perspectives, but rather in an open-minded framework. I admit to being a structuralist, in the sense that I see relations between things as the key, and not things themselves. Yet that is simply my own way of looking, and it is not the only way to envisage the discipline.

This volume has brought together some of the best minds in social anthropology and allied disciplines (archaeology and linguistics, for example). It has enabled us to discuss and debate our interpretations. We hope that it serves to enlighten our colleagues, and also that it lends itself to reflection by our friends within the wider realm of anthropological sciences, including in particular our students. The future of our discipline is in their hands, and we should not be shy about speculation, about bringing together both what we know and what we wish to know. They should expect nothing less from us.

References

Barnard, A. 1978. 'Universal Systems of Kin Categorization', *African Studies* 37(1): 69–81.

———. 1999. 'Modern Hunter-gatherers and Early Symbolic Culture', in Robin Dunbar, Chris Knight and Camilla Power (eds), *The Evolution of Culture: an Interdisciplinary View*. Edinburgh: Edinburgh University Press. pp. 50–68.

———. 2001. *The Hunter-gatherer Mode of Thought*. Buenos Aires: Anales de la Academia Nacional de Ciencias de Buenos Aires (Año 2000).

————. 2011. *Social Anthropology and Human Origins*. Cambridge: Cambridge University Press.

————. 2012. *Genesis of Symbolic Thought*. Cambridge: Cambridge University Press.

————. 2016. *Language in Prehistory*. Cambridge: Cambridge University Press.

Botha, R. and C. Knight (eds). 2009a. *The Cradle of Language*. Oxford: Oxford University Press.

————. 2009b. *The Prehistory of Language*. Oxford: Oxford University Press.

Cavalli-Sforza, L. 2001. *Genes, Peoples and Languages*. London: Penguin Books.

Crow, T.J. (ed.). 2002. *The Speciation of Modern* Homo sapiens (Proceedings of the British Academy 106). Oxford: Oxford University Press for the British Academy.

Dunbar, R.I.M. 2003. 'The Social Brain: Mind, Language and Society in Evolutionary Perspective', *Annual Review of Anthropology* 32: 163–181.

————, C. Knight and C. Power (eds). 1999. *The Evolution of Culture: an Interdisciplinary View*. Edinburgh: Edinburgh University Press.

Fox, R. (ed.) 1975. *Biosocial Anthropology* (ASA Studies). London: Malaby Press.

Goodwin, A.J.H. and C. Van Riet Lowe. 1929. 'The Stone Age Cultures of South Africa', *Annals of the South African Museum* 27(7): 1–289.

Griffin, S.T. 2012. *Tarzan: the Centennial Celebration*. London: Titan Books.

Henshilwood, C. 2009. 'The Origins of Symbolism, Spirituality, and Shamans: Exploring Middle Stone Age Material Culture in South Africa', in C. Renfrew and I. Morley (eds.), *Becoming Human: Innovation and Prehistoric Material and Spiritual Culture*. Cambridge: Cambridge University Press. pp. 29–49.

James, W. 2003. *The Ceremonial Animal: a New Portrait of Anthropology*. Oxford: Oxford University Press.

Knight, C. 1991. *Blood Relations: Menstruation and the Origins of Culture*. New Haven: Yale University Press.

Kuper, A. and J. Marks. 2011. 'Anthropologist Unite!', *Nature* 470: 166–168.

Layton, R. 2006. 'What can Ethnography Tell us about Human Social Evolution?', in N.J. Allen et al. (eds), *Early Human Kinship: From Sex to Social Reproduction*. Oxford: Blackwell Publishing, pp. 113–127.

Leach, E.R. 1961. *Rethinking Anthropology* (LSE Monographs on Social Anthropology 22). London: London School of Economics.

Lee, R.B. 1979. *The !Kung San: Men, Women and Work in a Foraging Society*, Cambridge: Cambridge University Press.

Lewis-Williams, J.D. and D.G. Pearce. 2004. *San Spirituality: Roots, Expressions and Social Consequences*. Cape Town: Double Storey.

Martin, L.L. et al. 2014. 'I-D Compensation: Exploring the Relations among Mindfulness, a Close Brush with Death, and our Hunter-gatherer Heritage', in A. le C.T. Ngnoumen and E.J. Langer (eds), *The Wiley Blackwell Handbook of Mindfulness* (two volumes). Chichester: Wiley-Blackwell, pp. 290–311.

Miller, G.F. 2000. *The Mating Mind: How Sexual Choice Shaped the Evolution of Human Nature*. New York: Anchor Books.

Needham, R. (ed.). 1971. *Rethinking Kinship and Marriage* (ASA Monographs 11). London: Routledge & Keegan Paul.

Oppenheimer, S. 2004. *The Real Eve: Modern Man's Journey out of Africa*. New York: Carroll & Graf.

———. 2009. 'The Great Arc of Dispersal of Modern Humans: Africa to Australia', *Quaternary International* 201: 2–13.

Radcliffe-Brown, A.R. 1957. *A Natural Science of Society*. London: Free Press.

Rosman, A. and P.G. Rubel. 1971. *Feasting with Mine Enemy: Rank and Exchange Among Northwest Coast Societies*. New York: Columbia University Press.

Sahlins, M. 1972. *Stone Age Economics*. Chicago: Aldine.

———. 1977. *The Use and Abuse of Biology: an Anthropological Critique of Sociobiology*. Ann Arbor: University of Michigan Press.

Stocking, George W., Jr. (ed.). 1974. *A Franz Boas Reader: the Shaping of American Anthropology, 1883–1911*. Chicago: University of Chicago Press.

Wiessner, P. 1982. 'Risk, Reciprocity and Social Influences on !Kung San Economics', in E. Leacock and R. Lee (eds), *Politics and History in Band Societies*. Cambridge: Cambridge University Press, pp. 63–84.

Wilson, Edward O. 1975. *Sociobiology: The New Synthesis*. Cambridge, MA: Harvard University Press.

Winkelman, M. 2010. *Shamanism: a Biopsychosocial Paradigm of Consciousness and Healing*, second edition. Oxford: Praeger.

Witzel, E.J.M. 2012. *The Origins of the World's Mythologies*. Oxford: Oxford University Press.

Woodburn, James. 1980. 'Hunter-gatherers Today and Reconstruction of the Past', in Ernest Gellner (ed.), *Soviet and Western Anthropology*. London: Duckworth, pp. 95–117.

———. 1982. 'Egalitarian Societies', *Man* (N.S.) 17: 431–451.

Alan Barnard, now retired, was Professor of the Anthropology of Southern Africa in the University of Edinburgh, where he taught from 1978 to 2015. He has undertaken ethnographic research with hunter-gatherers in Botswana, Namibia and South Africa. He participated in the British Academy Centenary Research Project 'From Lucy to Language: The Archaeology of the Social Brain', and in 2010 he was elected a fellow of the British Academy. He also serves as an Honorary Consul of the Republic of Namibia in Scotland. His numerous publications include *Social Anthropology and Human Origins* (2011), *Genesis of Symbolic Thought* (2012) and *Language in Prehistory* (2016).

INDEX

www.ingramcontent.com/pod-product-compliance
Lightning Source LLC
Chambersburg PA
CBHW060023030426
42334CB00019B/2155